G L O B A L
ENTREPRENEURSHIP

third edition

Kendall Hunt
publishing company

Dianne H. B. Welsh
The University of
North Carolina—Greensboro

Cover image © Shutterstock.com

Photo of Dianne H.B. Welsh: © The University of North Carolina at Greensboro
Photo of Shawn M. Carraher: Courtesy of Sarah Carraher

Kendall Hunt
publishing company

Send all inquiries to:
4050 Westmark Drive
Dubuque, IA 52004-1840

Copyright © 2009, 2015, 2018 by Kendall Hunt Publishing Company

ISBN 978-1-5249-5048-4

Published in the United States of America

BRIEF CONTENTS

CONTENTS

Part Three Area Studies

PREFACE

This book focuses on what you need to know about global entrepreneurship. It explains the principles that come from entrepreneurship, international business, cross-cultural management, strategy, exporting, international education, international economics and environmental concerns, and leadership. This book summarizes what we believe are the most significant core principles that will help you to succeed as a global entrepreneur or develop your global entrepreneurship strategy. Besides the introductory chapters establishing the principles of global entrepreneurship, we also include topical specialized chapters, areas studies, and a case study on a company going international.

We live in a world with countless opportunities, and most of those opportunities are international. As electronic mediums expand, ideas that may be opportunities will multiply by the thousands. This book was developed with entrepreneurs in mind who want to identify ideas that may be opportunities beyond their borders. We believe we provide the essential background and knowledge that will give the entrepreneur the skills he or she needs to operate globally. The world economy will benefit from entrepreneurs that contribute internationally, both economically and socially.

This text presents the basic principles of global entrepreneurship and explains how to apply them. It focuses more on practical applications than on statistical surveys and empirical research. We also include examples of specific area studies that the reader may use as an example in a part of the world they would like to develop a product or service to export or import. Generally, only the essential elements of global entrepreneurship have been included. We welcome feedback on the text that was developed from the lack of accessible material available in one place and from teaching the topic for many years and compiling our own materials. We would like to thank our colleagues who contributed to this text and to the field of global entrepreneurship.

Dianne H.B. Welsh, Ph.D., Hayes Distinguished Professor of Entrepreneurship and Founding Director, Entrepreneurship Cross-Disciplinary Program, 441 Bryan School of Business & Economics, 516 Stirling Street, Greensboro, NC 27402, (336) 256-8507, dhwelsh@uncg.edu

Shawn M. Carraher, University of Texas Dallas

INTRODUCTION

This book is organized into four sections that explain global and international entrepreneurship. The first section includes the introductory chapters, which are designed to provide the reader with a broad overview of the topic and how the material can/should be used. The second section includes more specialized and focused topics on specific aspects of international and global entrepreneurship. The third section includes area studies chapters. The final section includes a case.

This book is designed so that it could be used at the undergraduate or graduate levels and should be used along with experiential exercises and written assignments. The chapters were chosen based upon a detailed study undertaken by the International Entrepreneurship Division of the US Association for Small Business & Entrepreneurship as to what educators in the areas of international and global entrepreneurship believed should be included in such a course.

In addition to studying the materials in this book, it is also recommended that students should prepare an in-depth country profile for a selected country focusing on the entrepreneurial opportunities within that country. A second recommended project is that students complete an organizational project for a client seeking to move internationally. Alternatives to this project could include supplementation with other case studies, completion of an international business plan, or an actual field project. Suggested experiential projects include an international joint venture negotiation [exercise available from CIBER of the University of Maryland], completion of a cross-cultural interview where someone from a culture different from one's own is interviewed, BaFa BaFa—a cross-cultural exercise [available from www.stsintl.com Simulation Training Systems, or even language tag in which students are asked questions in one language and must respond in a different language.

Please let us know of suggestions that you have for future editions of this book.

ABOUT THE AUTHORS

DIANNE H.B. WELSH is the Hayes Distinguished Professor of Entrepreneurship and Founding Director of the Entrepreneurship Programs at The University of North Carolina Greensboro, including the North Carolina Entrepreneurship Center and the Entrepreneurship Cross-Disciplinary Program. She has previously founded two entrepreneurship programs and centers and has held three endowed professorships. In 2015, Dianne was named the Fulbright-Hall Distinguished Chair in Entrepreneurship for Central Europe in 2015. She was honored with the Senior Teaching Award for the University of North Carolina Greensboro in 2015 and was the December Commencement Speaker. She is also a visiting professor at the renowned Aalto University International Business program as well as teaching in Poland, Slovakia, and Austria.

Dianne is a recognized scholar in the family business, international entrepreneurship, women-owned businesses and franchising, and has seven books and over 180 publications to her credit. Her research has been published in *AMJ, JIBS, ET&P, JBV, FBR, JSBM*, and *JFBS*, among other journals. She has three new books, *Creative Cross-Disciplinary Entrepreneurship*, published by Palgrave-Macmillan, *Global Entrepreneurship* (3rd edition), and *Case Studies in Global Entrepreneurship* (2nd edition forthcoming), published by Kendall Hunt. She serves on numerous journal editorial review boards and has edited several journal special issues.

She served as the 2015 Chair for the Technology and Innovation Management Division of the Academy of Management with 2,700 members. Dianne is a Fellow in the Family Firm Institute, US Association for Small Business & Entrepreneurship, and Small Business Institute. She is a Certified Family Business Counselor and holds the Senior Profession in Human Resources certification. She served as a Presidential Appointee to the US Air Force Academy and the Defense Advisory Committee for Women in the Services (DACOWITS). Dianne delivered the keynote address at the U.N.E.C.E. Conference in Azerbaijan in 2012 as well as keynote addresses in five countries. She has conducted research and visited 40 countries. She held the Fulbright-Hall Distinguished Chair for Entrepreneurship in Central Europe at WU (Vienna University of Economics and Business) in the spring of 2015. She has consulted for Fortune 50 businesses, family businesses, franchises, and high growth businesses throughout the world. She has consulted for governments on converting public sector enterprises to the private sector. She also is an expert in no-cost employee reward systems and has worked with businesses across the globe in implementing systems to improve the motivation and performance of the workforce. Dianne has assisted eight universities in implementing programs across campus in the United States and Australia.

Shawn M. Carraher received his Ph.D. in Business Administration from the University of Oklahoma. He has served as the Oxford Journal Distinguished Research Professor and Director of the Small Business Institute® and Clinical Professor in International Business at the University of Texas at Dallas as well as serving at the Undergraduate Research Director. He has served as President of the SouthWest Academy of Management, Division Chair of the Management History Division, Division Chair of the Technology & Innovation Management Division, and PDW Co-Chair and Board member for the Careers Division and the Southern Management Association. He has also served as the President of the Small Business Institute®, the Association for Small Business & Entrepreneurship, and the Association for Entrepreneurship, Family Business, & Franchising as well as an officer of six Divisions of the US Association for Small Business & Entrepreneurship.

He has published over 100 journal articles, which have been cited over 15,000 times. His most recent publications have appeared in the Journal of Applied Psychology, *Journal of International Business Studies, Journal of Occupational & Organizational Psychology, Organizational Research Methods, Decision Sciences, Educational and Psychological Measurement, Journal of Managerial Issues, Journal of Vocational Behavior, Journal of Quality Management, Journal of Applied Management and Entrepreneurship, Career Development International, Polymeric Materials: Science and Engineering, Global Business and Finance Review*, and the *Journal of Business Strategies*.

He has directed research projects in over 130 countries. His research focuses on a variety of behavioral global entrepreneurship topics in the healthcare and tourism industries, and he has worked with over 50,000 SME owners from around the world. Shawn has also worked as a consultant specializing in performance enhancement and management development. He has co-owned a family business which has been in his family since 1893. He has served as the editor of several journals including the *Journal of Management History* affiliated with Division 1 of the Academy of Management and the *Journal of Technology Management in China* affiliated with the China Association of the Management of Technology, the *Cambridge Case Studies Journal*, the *Academy of Strategic Management Journal*, the *International Journal of Family Business*, the *Global Journal of Management and Marketing*, as well as serving as the interim editor of the *Journal of Entrepreneurship Education*.

In November 2015 Shawn was named one of the top 50 Global Business Educators in the world at the Saïd Business School of the University of Oxford. While in 2016 he was named one of the top 12 [#9 based upon academic age] most impactful business professors in Switzerland and in 2017 was recognized as one of the top 30 Professors in the World by three groups in China [Four were in business]. He received the Larry R. Watts Distinguished Service Award from the Allied Academies in 2011 and has been named a Fellow of the Academy of Strategic Management, the Academy of Entrepreneurship, the Academy of Global Business Advancement, the Small Business Institute® and the Direct Selling Education Foundation. On Dec. 5, 2017, the 100-year anniversary of independence from Russia, Shawn was one of 100 recognized in Helsinki for his contributions to economic development in Scandinavia by the King of Sweden. In the last two years, he has served as the advisor of 106 students who has received grants to support their research. His students have raised over $250,000 to support their travels to present papers at Harvard, Cambridge, and Oxford Universities. They have published 31 peer-reviewed journal articles. His program of educating students with research has received an Innovative Program Award from the Small Business Institute® as well as attracting funders to his programs.

ABOUT THE CONTRIBUTORS

Ilan Alon

Dr. Ilan Alon is Professor of Strategy and International Marketing at the University of Agder, Norway, and visiting scholar at Georgetown University, USA. Prior to this, he was George D. and Harriet W. Cornell Chair of International Business and Marketing and Director of *the China and the India Centers* at Rollins College, Florida, and a visiting professor at Harvard University and Georgetown University. Dr. Alon is the author of *Global Marketing: Contemporary Theory, Practice and Cases* (Routledge, 2017).

Alon's teaching and consulting work spans the globe covering America, Europe, Asia, and the Middle East. He has taught in top business programs globally, including Shanghai JiaoTong University (China), EM Lyon (France), Ben Gurion University (Israel), Bilkent University (Turkey), and MIB (Italy), among others.

Alon research includes global franchising, political risk assessment, and the globalization of Chinese enterprises. He authored numerous peer-reviewed articles including ones appearing in *Journal of International Marketing, Harvard Business Review,* and *Corporate Governance: An International Review* and books such as *Global Marketing* (McGraw-Hill, 2012), *Global Franchising Operations Management: Cases in International and Emerging Markets Operations* (FT Press, 2012), *Franchising Globally: Innovation, Learning and Imitation* (Palgrave, 2010), *Service Franchising: A Global Perspective* (Springer, 2005), *Chinese International Investments* (Palgrave, 2013), *Chinese Entrepreneurs* (Edward Elgar, 2009), *China Rules* (Palgrave, 2009), *Globalization of Chinese Enterprises* (Palgrave, 2008), among other books.

Alon has consulted both multinational businesses and government organizations relating to marketing and international business issues. Among his clients are USAID, World Bank, Darden, Disney, illy, and Orlando International Airport.

Nadia Ballard

Nadia Ballard is currently a research manager at a global technology company. Her research, marketing, and international business expertise has helped many businesses introduce B2B products and services to domestic and international markets. During her career, Nadia has worked with diverse teams to develop strategic programs, build brands and conduct industry and competitive research. Nadia's work in market research and website design has received several international awards. She is a published author and a speaker at industry events.

Steven M. Cramer

Steven M. Cramer is the business librarian at The University of North Carolina at Greensboro, Greensboro, NC, USA (UNCG). He was awarded tenure in 2007. Steve co-teaches *MKT 426: International Marketing* and ENT 300: *Feasibility Analysis*. As a Coleman Fellow for Entrepreneurship Education, he teaches ENT/GEO/LIS 530: *Researching Opportunities in Entrepreneurship & Economic Development*.

He is the cofounder of Business Librarianship in North Carolina (BLINC), a member of ALA's BRASS, and a Carolina Consortium negotiator. Steve blogs at http://liaisonlife.wordpress.com/. Steve earned a master's degree in Library and Information Science from the University of North Carolina in Chapel Hill and a BA in Medieval and Renaissance Studies from the University of Michigan.

Madeline M. Crocitto

Madeline M. Crocitto (PhD, CUNY) is a Professor of Management at SUNY at Old Westbury. Her research on pedagogy has appeared in the *Journal of Management Education, Educator's Voice*, and *Interactive Learning Environments*. Her research interests are in the areas of careers, diversity, and people and processes, appearing in such publications as the *Journal of International Business Studies* and *Career Development International*. She has served on the Executive Boards of the Eastern Academy of Management and the Careers Division of the Academy of Management as well as editorial boards of the *Academy of Management Learning and Education* and *Career Development International* journals.

Denise M. Cumberland

An Assistant Professor in the Organizational Leadership and Learning Program at the University of Louisville, Dr. Cumberland's research focuses on entrepreneurship and global leadership. She has coauthored a book chapter on leadership in emerging markets and has published in journals such as *Human Resource Development International* and the *International Journal of Management Education*.

Li Dai

Li Dai teaches undergraduate and MBA courses in international business, strategic management, and global strategy at Loyola Marymount University, Los Angeles, CA, USA. In addition, Dai has taught extensively in the business programs at Texas A&M University and Ivey Business School, the latter ranked #1 in the world by Bloomberg Businessweek. Her studies utilizing geo-referencing methodology on firm strategy in hostile contexts are considered seminal by peers in the field of management. This research, along with her work on institutions in emerging markets, has been recognized with prestigious awards and invited for publication by Oxford University Press and featured in the highest-ranked journals in fields spanning international business, strategic management, and entrepreneurship. She is a faculty fellow of the Center for Emerging Markets at Northeastern University and serves on the Editorial Review Board of the *Journal of International Business Policy*, a flagship journal of the Academy of International Business.

Dale R. Funderburk

Dale R. Funderburk is a B.A.-holder in economics from East Texas State University. He also holds the M.S. and Ph.D. in economics from Oklahoma State University. He has over 30 years' experience in teaching at the university level. He is a professor of economics at Texas A&M University-Commerce, where he teaches graduate and undergraduate courses in the areas of macroeconomic theory and policy, money, banking and financial markets, and monetary theory. Dr. Funderburk has published articles in such journals as *The Appraisal Journal, Journal of Economics, Journal of Forensic Economics, The Real Estate Appraiser and Analyst, the National Social Science Journal, Antitrust Law and Economics Review, Trial, Advances in Global Business Research* and even *The Quarter Horse Journal.* He has presented papers and guest lectures at conferences and universities as far away as China, India, and Lebanon. In 2004 he was named the "AGBA Global Educator of the Year" by the Academy for Global Business Advancement in New Delhi, India.

Joan Gillman

As Director of Special Industry Programs, Executive Education, for the University of Wisconsin-Madison School of Business, Joan's office acted as a conduit between University resources and the business community. In this role, she hosted a daily radio show, In Business with Jody and Joan on Madison 1670 from 6 to 7 PM, focusing on local business issues for 6 years.

Joan's duties spanned executive Education from small business and entrepreneurship to teaching managers and designing executive programs. She taught in both the Small Business Development Center (Business Planning) and Executive Education for the Supervisory Management Series. She was codirector of the Agribusiness Executive Management Program that assisted farmers and agribusinesses in Wisconsin. As founder of The Family Business Center, a regional membership program which addresses the special needs of the family business dealing with succession, communication, and strategic planning issues, she successfully completed succession planning for the center. She is now Emeritus Faculty at the School of Business, the University of Wisconsin-Madison.

Gillman has two children, two grandsons, and enjoys traveling whenever possible. Her travels have been in Croatia, Macedonia, and Bulgaria for the Open Society Institute, the nonprofit foundation of George Soros, where she started centers for Entrepreneurship. She is also the second woman ever to publicly address men in Saudi Arabia. She is active in many local organizations.

Kira Henschel

With a background in international relations, geology, and an MS in engineering management, as well as more than a decade living abroad and working in the international commerce arena, Kira Henschel has supported the endeavors of entrepreneurs, as well as small and large organizations, in realizing their ambitions of becoming active international companies. In addition to serving as Honorary Commercial Attache for Wisconsin in Austria from 1985 to 1990, she held leadership roles in local, national, and international nonprofit organizations focused on business, environmental, and women's issues. She is currently Adjunct Professor at the Milwaukee School of Engineering's Rader School of Business, as well as serving as CEO/President and Editor-in-Chief of Henschel HAUS Publishing, Inc., an award-winning book publishing company headquartered in Milwaukee, WI, USA.

Frank Hoy

Frank Hoy is the Paul R. Beswick Professor of Entrepreneurship and Director of the Collaborative for Entrepreneurship and Innovation at Worcester Polytechnic Institute. Dr. Hoy earned his PhD at Texas A&M University where he developed a small business outreach program for the Texas Agricultural Extension Service. His most recent books are *Small Business Management: Launching and Growing Entrepreneurial Ventures* (18th ed. with William Petty and Leslie Palich, 2017), *The Routledge Companion to Family Business* (with Franz W. Kellermanns, 2017), and the *Handbook of Research on Franchising* (with Rozenn Perrigot and Andrew Terry, forthcoming 2018).

Alvin J. Jackson, Jr.

Alvin J. Jackson, Jr. is a graduate of Texas A&M University with a B.S. in Civil Engineering, and an MBA in Marketing and Masters of Science in Management from Commerce School of Business & Technology, and has been a marketing and sales executive for the past 10 years. His experience has included serving both private and public sectors including real estate and construction, higher education, and working for a Fortune Top 10 corporation in the telecommunications industry. Mr. Jackson works closely with local, regional, and national real estate executives and several construction, engineering, and governmental agencies to ensure the right product and lifestyle is delivered in residential, commercial, and mixed-use acquisitions. He brings marketing stewardship and an interconnection with several different governmental agencies throughout the region.

Nir Kshetri

Nir Kshetri is Professor at the University of North Carolina, Greensboro, NC, USA and a research fellow at Kobe University. He has authored seven books, one of which has been selected as an Outstanding Academic Title by *Choice Magazine*. He has published over 110 articles in various journals. Nir participated as lead discussant at the Peer-Review meeting of the UN's Information Economy Report 2013 and 2015. Nir is the winner of 2016 Bryan School Senior Research Excellence Award. He is also a two time winner of the Pacific Telecommunication Council's Meheroo Jussawalla Research Paper Prize (2010 and 2008). Nir has been quoted/interviewed and/or his work has been featured by hundreds of media outlets worldwide such as *Foreign Policy, Bloomberg TV, CBS News, Fortune, Time, Christian Science Monitor, U.S. News & World Report, New Boston Post, Observer and Salon*.

Karla Mendoza-Abarca

Karla Mendoza-Abarca is an Assistant Professor of Entrepreneurship at Worcester Polytechnic Institute, Worcester, MA. She holds an MBA in Finance and a PhD in Marketing and Entrepreneurship from Kent State University. Karla's research interests include social entrepreneurship, entrepreneurial opportunities, and entrepreneurial creativity. Her research has been published in the *Journal of Management, Journal of Business Venturing*, and *Journal of Management Inquiry*. Karla has taught courses in entrepreneurship and innovation, new venture creation, entrepreneurial marketing, and social entrepreneurship.

John A. Parnell

John A. Parnell presently is the Belk Chair in Management at the University of North Carolina at Pembroke. He is the author of over 200 basic and applied research articles, published presentations, and cases in strategic management and related areas. He earned the BSBA, MBA, and MA degrees from East Carolina University, the EdD degree from Campbell University, and the PhD degree in Strategic Management from The University of Memphis. Dr. Parnell is the author and coauthor of two current textbooks with Sage Publications, *Strategic Management: Theory and Practice*, and *Crisis Management: Leading in the New Strategy Landscape*. His current research focuses on issues related to competitive business strategies and ethics.

George M. Puia

George M. Puia, PhD holds the Dow Chemical Company Centennial Chair in Global Business at Saginaw Valley State University. He earned a PhD in Strategic Management with concentrations in international business and research methods from the University of Kansas. Dr. Puia's publications focus on contextual differences in cross-national business and entrepreneurship. Puia was named a Distinguished Fellow by the Academy for Global Business Advancement and was selected for the Oxford Journal Global Top 50 Educators Award. He actively consults entrepreneurs and SMEs on foreign market entry strategy. He serves as Associate Editor of the *Baltic Journal of Management*.

Sherry E. Sullivan

Sherry E. Sullivan (PhD, Ohio State University) researches international careers, expatriate mentoring, and networking. She is coauthor of *The Opt-Out Revolt* (Davies-Black, 2006), which introduced the Kaleidoscope Career Model. Sherry has served as Chair and Historian for the Academy of Management's Careers Division and been a member of the Executive Committee for the Academy of Management's Gender and Diversity in Organizations Division. She was named a Southern Management Association Fellow in 2006 and an Oxford Journal Distinguished Research Professor in 2016.

Barbara Weiss

Barbara Weiss is an international political economist in the field of international business who specializes in comprehensive risk and security analysis and market structure and competition. Now, a full-time researcher at the St. Petersburg Institute of International Political Economy (SPIIPE) (Florida, USA)—www.spiipe.org, Dr. Weiss began her career in industry in international trade, trade finance, and capital markets in the United States, Japan, and Canada. She has published in such areas as environmental risk mitigation, entrepreneurial risk analysis, and the relationship between risk and security, which is part of the Opportunity Risk Analysis (ORI) and Comprehensive Security research areas at SPIIPE. In the area of Market Structure and Competition, Dr. Weiss conducts industry and market structure research, as measured by firm ownership, in order identify the effect firm ownership has on market competition. Dr. Weiss has also lived in Korea and Germany.

Nicholas C. Williamson

Nicholas C. Williamson, Emeritus Professor—Marketing, and Member, Order of the Long Leaf Pine, received his AB, MBA, and PhD degrees, all from the University of North Carolina at Chapel Hill. While employed at UNC Greensboro for 34 years, both his teaching and his research specialties involved export marketing. Williamson is coauthoring with Steven Cramer an eBook entitled *Export Odyssey*, due to be released for national marketing by Kendall Hunt Publishing in 2018.

Anatoly Zhuplev

Anatoly Zhuplev is Professor of International Business at Loyola Marymount University (Los Angeles, CA, USA) since 1992. He taught in France, Germany, Poland (as Fulbright scholar), Russia, and in Boston, MA, USA. Anatoly Zhuplev has published his papers in the United States, Canada, Western Europe, and Russia. He received his PhD in Moscow, Russia in 1981.

PART ONE

Global Entrepreneurship and Global Business

George M. Puia

Dow Chemical Company Centennial Chair in Global Business, Saginaw Valley State University, Saginaw County, Michigan

Key Terms

Born global firms

Comparative entrepreneurship

Entrepreneurial capacity

GEM studies

International Entrepreneurship

Internationalization/internationalized

Liberalization/Trade liberalization

Necessity and Opportunity Entrepreneurs

Opportunity environment

Uppsala model

Learning Objectives

Upon completion of this chapter, students should be able to:

1. Define international entrepreneurship and differentiate it from domestic and global entrepreneurship
2. Describe how government policies can influence a nation's entrepreneurial capacity and the entrepreneurial opportunity environment
3. Describe the evolutionary and born global models of internationalization and how they differ from one another
4. Describe some of the ways in which differences in national culture challenge entrepreneurs
5. Understand how research projects such as Global Entrepreneurship Monitor (GEM) and the World Bank studies play an important role in improving our understanding of comparative international entrepreneurship

Introduction

After a long day at sea off the Atlantic coast, a fishing vessel landed a prized 710 lb blue-fin tuna (they can grow as large as 1,500 lbs). The fishing community in Nova Scotia has been fishing tuna from these waters for generations, dividing the catch into tuna for stores, restaurants, and food-processing plants. In the regional market, there is little production capacity for premium tuna—most locally fished tuna finds its way into cans for serving in either sandwiches or cat food.

Most boats take their catch to a local seafood processor; yet a few entrepreneurs developed a global business perspective. Using satellite phones, fishers keep track of tuna prices in world markets. Tuna is much more valuable in cities such as New York, Paris, and especially Tokyo, where it is a central ingredient in sushi and sashimi. The Nova Scotia team checked their sources and then carefully packed their catch in dry ice for an overnight flight to the Tokyo fish auction.

The Tokyo tuna auction begins well before dawn with rapid bidding similar to a stock-trading floor in the United States (though in a polite Japanese fashion). Moving from pallet to pallet, the entire auction takes less than two hours. The Tokyo Central Wholesale Seafood Market (Tsukiji) is the largest seafood market in the world, dealing with 2.3 million kilograms of seafood every day (Bestor, 2004). While local markets paid about $40–50 per pound, the Tokyo auction often pays more than double that amount. The Nova Scotia tuna reached an auction price of $117 per pound, selling for a little over $83,000. While it was a great price for their team, it was well below the record 2016 price of $265 per pound (BBC, 2016).

If the story ended here, it would be a good story about smart exporting; our global fish story does not end there. The chef who purchased this fish divided the 710-pound tuna into 2,380 servings of sushi. Because of his international reputation, the chef could sell his sushi to diners in New York and Boston in elite restaurants for about $75 a serving. After spending its life in Nova Scotia's waters, this one tuna would travel over 35,000 miles in two days to be sold as sushi for $178,500! Welcome to the world of international entrepreneurship.

Defining International Entrepreneurship

The opening story gives us a glimpse of international entrepreneurs. They compete in many of the same arenas as other businesses, but they are quick to spot unmet customer needs. When international entrepreneurs observe a need, they pull together resources, in this case a blend of very old and very new technologies, to satisfy the customer. Most of all, entrepreneurs assume the risks of starting a new venture.

International entrepreneurs share a number of characteristics with domestic entrepreneurs; they discover and evaluate opportunities, take risks, organize resources, and create new goods and services of value to customers. What makes international entrepreneurs different from their domestic counterparts is their inclination to operate on the global stage. International entrepreneurs create businesses with the intent to function across borders. To do this, international entrepreneurs must be able to identify opportunities in international contexts; they must be able to assess unique risks inherent in cross-border businesses, they evaluate opportunities with specific target countries in mind, and they marshal human and financial resources from across the globe (McDougall-Covin, Jones, & Serapio, 2014). Considering these distinctions, we define international entrepreneurship as "the discovery and evaluation of opportunities and the organization of resources to exploit opportunities across national borders to create fundamentally new goods and services."

Within this definition are several different types of entrepreneurship and entrepreneurs. One distinction is the difference between opportunity and necessity entrepreneurship. *Opportunity entrepreneurs* form news ventures because they see the opportunity for potential rewards. *Necessity entrepreneurs* create ventures for self-employment to make up for the lack of other job opportunities in their environment. There are also *family-based entrepreneurs* who create businesses with a view to employing family members and *social entrepreneurs* who create ventures with the primary goal of creating public good. Increasingly, governments look to entrepreneurs to be both a source of job creation and a force for the betterment of society (Alvarez & Barney, 2014). Entrepreneurs often utilize a *lean start-up* approach that attempts to shorten the product development stage by releasing products in iterative stages (Osterwalder & Pigneur, 2010). Each new iteration then receives customer feedback and validation (Constable & Rimalovski, 2014).

Differentiating International Entrepreneurship from International Business

There is much in common between the study of international entrepreneurship and international business. After all, both small and large businesses face similar contextual challenges as they cross borders to conduct business. Since both entrepreneurs and multinational firms share the same environments, there is obvious overlap in their interests. International business as a field tends to focus on the institutional and contextual influence on multinational corporations. International entrepreneurship differs in both scale and content. Table 1.1 compares the domains of international business and international entrepreneurship.

Table 1.1 Comparing International Entrepreneurship and International Business

	INTERNATIONAL ENTREPRENEURSHIP	INTERNATIONAL BUSINESS
Firm history	New, emerging	Established
Scope	Varies—usually, focused in early stages of business development	Comprehensive
Firm size	Small, evolving start-ups, and born global ventures	Large, multinational firms
Finance	Angel and venture capital, competitiveness, exchange rates, trade financing	International financial institutions, capital markets, macro-environmental factors, trade policies
Operations	Exporting, sourcing, market entry	Global sourcing, foreign direct investment
Intellectual Property (IP)	Intellectual property creation (patents, proprietary knowledge), IP exploitation	Technology transfer, foreign sourcing of R&D

While there is some obvious overlap between the two fields, in the past two decades, international entrepreneurship has established itself as an independent field of study; it is not a subset of international business (Coviello, McDougall, & Oviatt, 2011).

Why Study International Entrepreneurship?

We study international entrepreneurship because we understand that there is always more opportunity in the world than in any one country. As businesses increasingly rely on advanced technology and innovation in order to compete, they have discovered that crossing national boundaries opens a world of talent (Cano-Kollmann, Cantwell, Hannigan, Mudambi, & Song, 2016). Additionally, changes in technology, transportation, and trade liberalization have made international trade more accessible to smaller companies, especially new entrepreneurial firms.

A defining characteristic of our millennium is the presence of a global economy. As the opening story illustrates, in a global economy, consumers worldwide choose from a worldwide menu of goods and services. Manufacturers can purchase materials and equipment from the world's most productive and qualified suppliers. Employees can increasingly bring their knowledge to bear in new and unfamiliar countries. Technology creates new levels of information interconnectedness. Investment capital crosses national borders in record flows. Collectively, this movement of goods, labor, and capital across national borders is part of a growing trend toward globalization—the creation of an integrated interdependent world economy. Much of the growth in international business activity in the last 50 years has been the result of the globalization of the business environment.

The sheer volume of international trade is staggering. In 2015 alone, global exports totaled nearly $18.5 trillion, up 22% from 2010 (World Trade Organization, 2016). Given the size of the global economy in terms of potential customers, firms that choose to remain domestic miss great opportunities and often face increased risks. For example, a company that has achieved the enviable position of having one-third of the US consumer market for its products has only a 1.5% share of the global market.

Explosion of Growth in the Field

Just as international trade has grown, so has entrepreneurship. Over the last 10 years, new business incorporations have averaged 450,000 businesses per year in the United States alone (Baily, 2012). At any point in time, about 16% of US firms will have been in existence less than one year. These newly formed businesses are engines of local economic growth, creating the vast majority of new jobs. In the past decade, Fortune 500 companies have continued to shed jobs because of improved productivity; at the same time, small entrepreneurial firms—less than five years old—created 40 million new jobs (Case, 2013).

We refer to the fastest growing of these start-ups as high-expectation entrepreneurs, or *gazelles*. Gazelles are a small fraction of total entrepreneurs but are of great interest to national policy makers as they result in the majority of job creation.

It is well documented that small entrepreneurial firms are central to economic growth. What is less well known is that entrepreneurs are the primary source of innovation; smaller firms create 67% of all new inventions. These innovations play an integral role in the economic renewal process, creating jobs as mature industries decline, while birthing entire new industries. Entrepreneurial firms are also the major method by which the disenfranchised, minorities, and immigrants become part of the mainstream economy.

Just as the practice of entrepreneurship has grown, so has entrepreneurship as a field of study. Entrepreneurship curriculum first began to appear in the early 1970s at the University of Southern California. By the early 1980s, over 300 universities were reporting courses on entrepreneurship, and by the 1990s, that number had grown to 1,050 schools. There are now hundreds of endowed positions in entrepreneurship and an even great number of established and funded entrepreneurship centers at American universities. In addition, organizations such as the Kauffman Foundation, Entrepreneurship Division of the Academy of Management, European Council for Small Business (ECSB), and International Council of Small Business (ICSB) and its American counterpart; the United States Association for Small Business and Entrepreneurship (USASBE) helps develop a strong and rapidly emerging knowledge base for the field. In addition, organizations like NASBITE International and the Forum for International Trade Trainers (FITT) have been working to provide tools and certifications for international entrepreneurs to succeed in global markets.

Liberalization of World Markets Creates New Opportunities

In a broad sense, the global economy has existed since the early 1300s when Marco Polo and the Dutch traders fanned out to sell their goods in far-off lands. Yet, Polo faced a world where states were almost entirely independent. There were few agreements or institutions in place to integrate economic life across borders. Today, there is a high level of interconnection and integration among national economies. This new interconnected economy, facilitated by air travel, telecommunications, and computers, is one in which informed citizens, entrepreneurs, and executives track events not only in their own community or nation but worldwide (Lew, 2016). Driving the increase in world trade is the trade liberalization of national economies.

We characterize *liberalization* as the decreased role of government in the economy. *Trade liberalization* refers to policies that reduce government interventions into trade, such as the removal of tariffs of other trade barriers, the promotion of financial transparency, and the privatization of government owned industries. While these liberalization policies have an effect on domestic economic growth, they also have a substantial positive effect on trade. Simply stated, when other economic factors such as education or level of natural resources are equal, countries with liberal trade regimes experience higher levels of trade.

Trade liberalization can be a very difficult process for a country to undertake. As the World Bank noted in its annual report, "successful trade reform requires reallocating resources among economic groups, and that adjustment can be costly for some (Wolfensohn, 2000)." Despite this difficulty, dozens of governments have undertaken trade reforms.

The most common form of trade liberalization is the reduction of trade barriers like tariffs. Tariffs are a tax the host government places on imports to make them more expensive than locally produced goods. This of course favors local businesses at the expense of international entrepreneurs. Trade liberalization increases competition, improving the quality and value of goods and services in local markets while keeping consumer costs lower.

Governments often try to help their local businesses by negotiating favorable trade agreements with other countries. We commonly refer to these negotiated pacts between two countries as bilateral agreements. Negotiating bilateral agreements with 200 countries would be extraordinarily time-consuming. As a result, trading countries have chosen to enter multilateral agreements—trade agreements between large groups of countries. The largest such multilateral agreement is administered by the World Trade Organization (WTO). The WTO, established by the nations involved in a predecessor arrangement, the General Agreement on Tariffs and Trade (GATT), was created to monitor and control the international trading system. WTO members include the developed countries as well as 110 of the 152 developing countries.

Membership in the WTO requires adherence to a generally liberal set of trade arrangements that facilitate the expansion of orderly world trade. The early results have been impressive. In 1950, Great Britain and Germany had tariff rates of 23% and 26%, respectively. Now both countries hold to the WTO tariff rate of 3.9%. To put those figures in perspective, an American auto sold in the United States for $20,000 would cost an additional $780 under the current tariff. Under the 1950s tariff, the same US auto would cost an additional $4,600 in Great Britain, and an extra $5,200 in Germany. One can easily see how consumers (and therefore international entrepreneurs) can benefit from trade liberalization.

The Rise of Small-firm Supply-chain Networks

Companies produce goods and services in a value chain, a sequence of value-added steps. Consider an auto manufacturer. They would purchase raw materials, manufacture subassemblies, assemble complete cars, transport them to markets, sell, and service them. Historically, businesses conducted these steps at a single location, but not any longer. The use of intermodal transportation with giant container ships has dramatically reduced the price per unit of shipping. Similarly, voice and video over Internet Protocols like Skype, Google Hangout, and Face-Time have made international communication virtually costless. With transaction costs and trade barriers falling, firms could begin to move parts of their value chain to different locations, where entrepreneurs could offer more innovative or cost-effective solutions than local suppliers.

There are two primary methods of internationalizing a firm's inputs: global sourcing and global supply-chain management. *Global sourcing* is the process of purchasing from suppliers worldwide to provide customers with the best quality product or service at the best possible cost. One of the easiest ways to discover the breadth of global sourcing is to read the manufacturer's label on items in your own home or apartment. It may be difficult to find items manufactured in your home country. Entrepreneurial and career opportunities in global sourcing include purchasing specialists, negotiators, contract manufacturing supervisors, quality management professionals, and logistics specialists among others. Global sourcing is a critical tool for firms in developed countries as it allows them to lower the average labor cost by mixing high paying knowledge jobs in the developed economy with lower paying lower skilled jobs in the lesser developed country.

Global supply-chain management is more comprehensive than global sourcing. In global supply chain management, firms integrate their entire supply chain globally—from raw materials to finished delivered goods—to provide high levels of customer satisfaction and higher profits (see Table 1.2). Firms increasingly rely on supplier networks around the globe to improve their quality and efficiency.

Table 1.2	Moving to a Global Supply Chain	
SUPPLY CHAIN ELEMENT	**TYPICAL REGIONAL SUPPLY CHAIN**	**FUTURE GLOBAL NETWORK**
Product design	Products tailored to local and regional markets	Common standards and design principles
Procurement	Regional sourcing of materials and supplies	Global commodity sourcing
Manufacturing strategy	Plants produce to meet local requirements—capacity often duplicated across borders	Location decisions made on production and logistics costs with a view to regional and global business integration
Supply-chain planning	Inventory, forecasting, and supply controlled at the local level	Global resource planning

(Adapted from: Mainardi, CR., Salva, M., and M. Sanderson. "Label of origin: Made on earth," *Strategy & Business*, 15, 1999:42–53.)

For small entrepreneurs to succeed in a global supply chain environment, they often interconnect with dominant buyers and suppliers across the globe. They also need to cost effectively transport their goods and services to distant markets. Many international entrepreneurs find a productive niche as a member of the global supply chain of a multinational enterprise.

It is easy to take the enormous changes that have occurred in the last half of the twentieth century for granted. For example, just two generations ago in the global transportation infrastructure, commercial airfreight did not exist; firms calculated the average time to ship goods globally in weeks and months, not hours. Today, for a wide array of products from fresh flowers to electronic components, air cargo is the most reliable and cost-effective means of shipping. Many modern production management practices, including the just-in-time inventory techniques so important to multinational corporations, rely heavily on global air cargo.

Ocean shipping operations have undergone a transformation no less dramatic than that of airfreight. Ocean shipping costs have fallen by as much as 80% over the last 50 years. Supertankers holding up to 500,000 tons displacement have replaced tankers one-fifth their size *without* an increase in crew size. Similarly, containerized cargo ships are now 30 times larger than the old merchant steamers they replaced. Firms can now use advanced technology to load and unload ships with only a minimal crew, replacing expensive labor in large industrialized ports. Finally, sea freight can seamlessly integrate with domestic rail and truck transportation; firms can now ship goods as easily across the globe as they once did across town. By using intermodal transportation, a firm can load a container at their site, attach it to a semitrailer truck for shipment to a rail yard, then to a seaport, and finally by a truck to the final destination. With intermodal shipping, the cargo never leaves its container. This reduces labor costs and greatly improves shipping security.

A similar revolution has taken place in telecommunication. Because of deregulation and new technologies, telecommunication costs have become a fixed cost; users pay a fee that allows them unlimited global access. In the "old economy," it was common to attempt to keep production processes under one roof. In that setting, management could physically supervise all of the steps in the production process to ensure that they added value. New communication technologies have made it cost-efficient to separate value-adding steps of production in ways that were not previously feasible.

With new communication technologies, we feel the changes in value-chain management across a wide range of industries. For example, software entrepreneurs can logon to platforms like GITHub and bid on sections of client software projects anywhere in the world. GITHub is a platform for collaborative problem-solving that currently has over 100,000 teams working on discrete projects (Potts & Puia, 2017). In health care industries, hospitals can transmit magnetic resonance imaging (MRI) images for remote real-time diagnosis by phone or Internet. It is now possible for entrepreneurs to transfer funds internationally at nominal costs using smart phone apps. The aggregate value of these individual company transactions is staggering. Chinese companies alone exported over $2.3 trillion in total goods in 2015, up from $1.9 trillion just five years earlier (UN Comtrade, 2017). This rapid and extreme reduction of communication costs has broad implications for future international trade, particularly for the trade of services.

These dramatic improvements in information and communications technology (ICT) created new opportunities for global entrepreneurs. In New York, an Indian MBA student was using the Internet to keep in touch with friends from his home country. He learned that they were not as excited about the Spider-Man comic series as were his American friends. Sharad Devarajan understood their concerns;

Spider-Man was based on US cultural values. The fact that Spider-Man gains his power after being bitten by a high-tech spider, or that Mary Jane rejects Peter because he is a geek, are features that do not necessarily work in the rest of the world. Devarajan's answer was to create Spider-Man in India. Set in Mumbai, the Indian Spider-Man, a boy named Pavitr Prabhakar, receives his power to fight evil from an ancient yogi, wears traditional garb, leaps around rickshaws and scooters in Indian streets, and swings from monuments such as the Gateway of India and the Taj Mahal. Devarajan creates and manages each new comic in New York for production and distribution in South Asian markets (Desmaris, 2004).

The Internet has certainly been a driving force in interconnecting businesses and consumers into a global economy. Recent data shows that over 3.4 billion people use the Internet worldwide, about 40% of the world's population! The Internet has also spawned global business opportunities that were unthinkable just 20 years ago. Consider Avast; the antivirus software maker protects over 200 million computer users worldwide from its headquarters in Prague. Just 25 years old, Avast has refined the antivirus industry, offering its primary product for free worldwide. Research continues to document the explosive growth of Internet-enabled businesses (Reuber & Fischer, 2011).

The Cross-border Movement of Intellectual Property

Intellectual property—patents, trademarks, copyrights, and other proprietary processes—represents the top of the economic food chain. A heart surgeon may make thousands of dollars per hour, but he or she can only make money when they are physically working. An entrepreneur, on the other hand, can collect rent from their intellectual property. Intellectual property can move across borders without transportation costs, giving it high profit potential. By every measure, the transfer of intellectual property across borders is increasing at record rates. Each region has its own intellectual property protection regimes to align with their regional and national policies (Autio & Acs, 2010). While there are some international agreements, it is not uncommon for technology entrepreneurs to seek protection in more than one region.

Two Streams of Research

Two important streams of international entrepreneurship inform our field: internationalization and comparative entrepreneurship (Wright, 1994). *Internationalization* is the transformation of a domestic entrepreneur into one who does business in more than one country. *Comparative entrepreneurship* investigates the similarities and differences between international entrepreneurs based on their country of origin (Terjesen, Hessels, & Li, 2016). Both streams give us a greater understanding of this dynamic field. The balance of this chapter explores each of those streams to give us a better picture of international entrepreneurship.

Internationalization: Moving Ventures Across Borders

We say a firm has *internationalized* when it moves from being a domestic firm to providing goods or services overseas. Businesses measure internationalization in a number of ways. We can speak of the degree of internationalization, the breadth or scope of internationalization, and the speed with which firms move to international markets (Zahra & George, 2002). We say that an entrepreneurial firm is global if it is simultaneously operating in all the key regions of the world (no one demands a company to do business in all 190+ countries). Then the difference between an international entrepreneur and global one is largely an issue of scope. In some cases, firms are global because they provide essentially the same product or service worldwide. They are global by virtue of the global universality of their goods; we use products such as oil, metal fasteners, and tires the same way in every country. Other industries feel consumer pressure to adapt their product or service to meet local conditions. Companies that produce processed foods, advertising, certain items of clothing, and types of entertainment are among businesses that feel a constant pressure toward local adaptation to each market. The more extensive the need for adaptation, the greater the time required to adapt to local conditions.

Discovery of International Opportunities

One of the distinguishing characteristics of entrepreneurs is their ability to recognize opportunities. The great management writer Peter Drucker once lamented that managers of large corporations were so focused on threats that they never properly understood opportunities, while businesses could only grow by exploiting opportunities (Drucker, 1974). In practice, opportunity finding takes two forms, reactive and proactive. International opportunities confront *reactive* entrepreneurs in ways that force them to respond (Foley, 2013). For example, a firm may have a prospective international customer who discovers the company on the Internet. An existing customer may open an overseas operation and require service overseas. A guest to a trade show may ask to represent the firm in their country.

What the aforementioned three examples have in common is that they represent *reactive* international entrepreneurship. There is little planning or strategy involved. The major problem with a reactive approach is that the entrepreneur may miss better opportunities by focusing on immediate ones. A proactive strategy, one where the entrepreneur plans their international activity in advance, is far more likely to achieve success. In a proactive strategy, the firm identifies a set of selection and criteria and reviews all possible export markets for the best fit with their criteria. As a result, they are more likely to select markets with growth potential that match the depth, breadth, and market familiarity of the company's leadership team (Jones & Casulli, 2014).

Internationalization Models

Internationalization occurs when a domestic firm begins to sell or operate across national borders. It can also describe the activities a company undertakes to expand its limited international activities to more countries. With internationalization, the entrepreneur confronts new business practices, laws, regulations, and cultures. A firm can internationalize without operating offshore; many international firms are importers—firms that acquire their products or services abroad. More often, internationalization describes a company's first attempts at exporting or licensing. We will now explore two major models that attempt to describe how firms internationalize.

The Uppsala Model

The Uppsala model is named after the Swedish University where researchers Johansen and Vahlne developed a process theory of internationalization. In their model, businesses evolve from a domestic to an international firm in a series of discrete steps over time (Johanson & Vahlne, 1977). Firms tend to expand domestically first, followed by incremental international expansions. It is essentially a "learning-curve" model as the manager or entrepreneur develops extensive new experiential knowledge, and then they are able to make new international commitments. The acquisition of new knowledge helps the entrepreneur discover new opportunities abroad.

Researchers developed the Uppsala model before the current wave of globalization. At that time, countries varied more greatly in the extent to which their own internal markets were internationalized. While the Uppsala model predicted an evolutionary approach to internationalization, it recognized that some entrepreneurs were "early starters" in internationalizing their business. These entrepreneurs made their decision to move more quickly, independent of whether the market they wished to serve was more or less internationalized.

As markets evolved, they became more global; the Internet, CNN, Facebook, Twitter, and other global media helped consumers in developing markets discover that there were better goods and services available than their local market provided. As a result, it became less practical in some industries to consider the possibility of delaying entry to foreign markets, for if you did, you might cede the market to a new competitor. In a similar vein, innovation is not restricted to a single country. Entrepreneurs may seek to internationalize as a means of draw closer to industry sources of innovation (Puia & Pretzer-Lin, 2013).

There are other challenges to the evolutionary model. Manufacturing firms tended to start in domestic markets then internationalize by moving to psychologically near markets before attempting distant ones; it was not so for service firms. Service firm internationalization did not follow a traditional evolutionary model (Bell, McNaughton, Young, & Crick, 2003).

Born Global Firms

Born global entrepreneurs are early adopters of internationalization; they apply knowledge-based resources to sell outputs in multiple countries from at or near their founding (Knight & Cavusgil, 2004). Several features make these entrepreneurs unique. They have a global focus; a commitment to explore proactively international markets, and they have a knowledge base that facilitates these activities. Not surprisingly, born global firms first appeared in countries with relatively small domestic markets, and, despite limited resources, they rapidly progressed to international markets (McDougall & Oviatt, 2000).

Since born global ventures often start with small teams, it makes sense to examine the background of the top management team (Hennart, 2014). The knowledge to become born global comes from a variety of sources. Some knowledge might be industry specific; experience in a particular industry might introduce the nascent firm to foreign market opportunities. Other management teams have academic knowledge. Their formal education and study abroad experiences have exposed them to foreign opportunities (Puia, Hicks, & Stackpole, 2017). Both industry and academic experiences can accelerate an entrepreneur's exploration of foreign markets. Last, opportunity finding is not sufficient for international success; born global entrepreneurs need to have the orientation and skills to exploit cross-cultural opportunities.

The Internet-based Entry Strategies

One of the unique properties of the Internet is that it allows a company to have a presence in foreign markets without having any physical or human resources present in that country. This ability to operate virtually has certainly opened new markets for firms, especially for those that can deliver products and services digitally (Eduardsen & Ivang, 2016). Entrepreneurs that can recognize opportunities across borders and have technology capability can use Internet marketing to grow their exports (Bianchi & Mathews, 2016). A new entrepreneurial industry exists to translate websites and create cultural adjustments to make the sites more attractive to a particular nation.

Management Capacity to Internationalize

Since it takes unique skills to internationalize a venture, it is not surprising that the experience of the top management team is a critical issue. Research has shown that ventures whose managers had overseas work experience influenced the speed and depth of internationalization (McDougall, Shane, & Oviatt, 1996). Students can prepare themselves now for international entrepreneurship careers. Research indicates that firms whose managers studied abroad were far more likely to internationalize (Bloodgood, Sapienza, & Almeida, 1996).

How Entrepreneurship Differs Across Countries

Comparative entrepreneurship is the study of how entrepreneurial practice differs across nations. Comparative entrepreneurship draws attention to two sets of characteristics: *entrepreneurial capacity*—the ability of entrepreneurs to respond to new opportunities—and the *entrepreneurial opportunity environment*—the in-country conditions that create opportunities for entrepreneurs (Amoros & Bosma, 2014).

Government programs influence entrepreneurial capacity through the strength of the educational system, the availability of entrepreneurship training programs, as well as by the general cultural and legal environment. One can think of each country as a laboratory; each laboratory starts with a unique resource endowment and is experimenting to develop a system that creates the most dynamic and entrepreneurial economy. By comparing countries, we can identify best practices for nurturing and supporting entrepreneurship.

Each country has unique environmental characteristics that shape the opportunity set for entrepreneurs. Among the factors that shape opportunities are government regulations, financial resources, commercial and legal infrastructure, market openness, physical infrastructure, and cultural and societal norms. In general, countries with an independent legal–judicial system, open markets, adequate physical and financial resources, and limited regulations generate more opportunities for new business creation.

The Global Entrepreneurship Monitor Studies

One systematic approach to comparing entrepreneurship across nations is the Global Entrepreneurship Monitor (GEM) studies. Operated by a consortium of universities, GEM started in 1999 by exploring entrepreneurship in 10 countries. By 2017, it was conducting over 200,00 interviews per year in over 100 countries. The GEM program has three major goals:

- To measure differences in the level of entrepreneurial activity between countries
- To uncover factors determining the levels of entrepreneurial activity
- To identify policies that may enhance the level of entrepreneurial activity.

At the heart of the GEM study is an adult population survey that explores entrepreneurial attitudes and experiences in the general population. Each national team collects its data in exactly the same manner at the same time of year to ensure comparability findings (Quill, Bosma, & Minniti, 2006). The GEM studies present entrepreneurship as a complex phenomenon, where no one measure or metric can capture its richness or complexity. An overview of GEM studies found that only high potential entrepreneurs had a significant impact on economic growth (Amorós, Bosma, & Levie, 2013).

The GEM data has facilitated a wide range of studies across the globe, which examine entrepreneurial capacity and the entrepreneurial opportunity environment. GEM researchers in New Zeeland, one of the top six countries in the world for entrepreneurial activity, discovered a highly networked context. This level of networking made it easier for entrepreneurs to discover opportunities and engage needed resources (Cruickshank & Rolland, 2006). A practical implication of this finding is that programs that improve entrepreneur networking will positively correlate with their success. While similarities are intriguing, differences between countries are also informative. Most research suggests that larger markets are positively related to new business starts. A South African study using GEM data found the opposite result; smaller markets were more attractive to entrepreneurs (Naudé, Gries, Wood, & Meintjies, 2008). It is hard to overestimate the impact of the GEM studies. As of 2017, Google Scholar identified over 20,000 citations to GEM study articles.

Analyzing the Environmental Context

Scholars have paid much attention to the role regulation plays in shaping business opportunities (Puia & Minnis, 2007). There is a consensus that there is an inverse relationship between business regulation and new venture creation; countries with burdensome regulations stifle entrepreneurship. Several groups have looked at the opportunity environment for entrepreneurs. One of the most widely used sources for comparison is the World Bank data set, Doing Business (World Bank, 2008).

The Doing Business studies track regulations of interest to all businesses but particularly entrepreneurs. Table 1.3 compares five countries on three measures for ease of starting a business. The complete Doing Business annual report covers dozens of measures on more than 180 countries.

Table 1.3	**The Regulation of Entrepreneurial Activity in Five Countries**		
COUNTRY	**NUMBER OR PROCEDURES TO START A BUSINESS**	**DURATION IN DAYS TO START A BUSINESS**	**COST (% OF GROSS NATIONAL INCOME PER CAPITA)**
Brazil	13	119	2.6
China	13	33	2.1
Finland	3	14	1.1
India	12	27	49.8
United States	6	6	1.4

(Adapted from Doing Business: Measuring Business Regulation 2013, World Bank)

Countries differ in the ways in which they regulate or restrict the entry of new business. Some regulation of entry is valuable to both the country and the firm. Official registration or licensing, for example, may make a firm more reputable. Most trade scholars often adhere to an alternative model, referred to as the "tollbooth model" (DeSoto, 1990). In the tollbooth model, politicians and bureaucrats encourage regulation as it adds to their power. Some research has gone as far as to infer that public officials create regulations as means of inducing official bribery; firms will pay the official fees needed in order to receive a permit (Shleifer & Vishny, 1993).

The GEM studies and World Bank share some findings; countries that have liberal trade regimes, government policies that support the protection of intellectual property, and availability of capital providing mechanisms have higher levels of international entrepreneurship. There is also evidence that formal programs can boost high-growth entrepreneurship (Autio & Rannikko, 2016).

Culture and Entrepreneurship

Each day, conversations, radio and television programs, Internet sessions, music, art, and architecture bombard us with information. We would be overwhelmed and unable to function without a framework for interpreting this constant stream of information. Yet, most days, we function pretty well. *We have been taught how to make sense of our context.* We have learned the rules for living in our setting by observing our elders and other successful actors, through our various religions, our language, through the sound of our music, and even through the design of our buildings. We have learned our *culture*.

Defining Culture

Culture is the shared set of beliefs, values, and norms passed from one generation to another that structure a member's perceptions of the world. It is the acquired knowledge that people use to experience and interpret their own behavior and that of others. If our minds are *hardware* of intelligence, then culture is software of the mind (Hofstede G. & Hofstede G. J., 2005). Research has supported the idea that while there is variation in each country, nations have cultures (Minkov & Hofstede, 2014).

In a cultural context, members express culture through the behaviors they exhibit, the artifacts they craft, and the political–economic philosophies they embrace. Members base their expressions on the values and beliefs they hold about the world around them. Social structures such as family, religion, language, and education transmit these values and beliefs from generation to generation. In turn, culture influences a country's business practices. Figure 1.1 provides a graphic representation of the complex interrelated set of cultural characteristics.

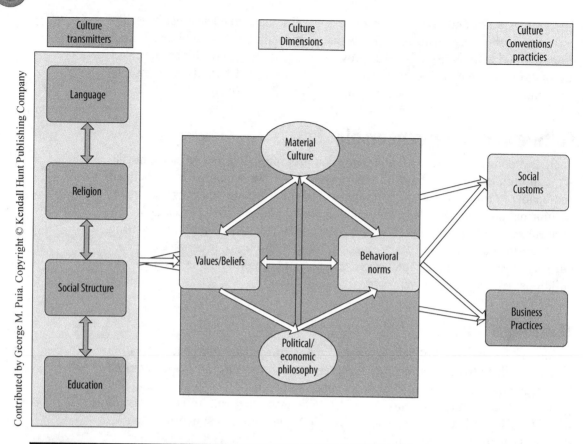

Contributed by George M. Puia. Copyright © Kendall Hunt Publishing Company

Figure 1.1: A model of culture.

Culture's Influence on Management Practices

In addition to finding opportunities and obtaining resources, entrepreneurs must manage in a cross-cultural context. Management texts describe the basic tasks of management as planning, leading, organizing, and controlling. Handling these *basic* management tasks across national borders is complex (Autio, Pathak, & Wennberg, 2013). Recent scholarship, for example, demonstrates the impact of culture on employee attitudes toward benefits and other compensation (Carraher & Buckley, 2005) and on leading complex teams (Chhokar, Brodbeck, & House, 2013). Table 1.4 helps us examine some of the ways that culture influences the four primary tasks of managers.

Table 1.4	Cultural Dimensions of Entrepreneurial Management
MANAGEMENT TASK	**CULTURAL DIMENSION**
Planning	• Controls whether planning will be undertaken • Influences which stakeholders are involved in planning • Influences the time horizon of the process
Leading	• Greatly influences the communication process • Established standards for motivation • Determines the accepted role of leadership • May limit the number of leaders
Organizing	• Influences the structure of organizations • Relates the natures of tasks to the types of individual who can perform those tasks • Determines the appropriateness of certain types of alliances or partnerships
Controlling	• Determines the extent to which groups or individuals are responsible for organizational control • Influences the corporate governance system
Risk Assessment	• Influences which behaviors one considers "risky" • Introduces emotional moderation or implication of perceived risks (e.g., the concept of fate)

While only a partial list, it is easy to see that culture greatly influences the management process.

In addition to shaping management practices, national culture influences a nation's level of innovation. Understanding how culture shapes innovation can help the entrepreneur be more effective in cross-border settings. Further, there is emerging research that suggests that cultural diversity also has a positive influence on innovations. Culture shapes the processes by which international entrepreneurs identify opportunities, organize resources, and manage the implementation of new ventures. By definition, entrepreneurs are innovators; they must learn to work in a culturally diverse setting (Shane, 1993).

Summary

International entrepreneurship is the discovery and evaluation of opportunities and the organization of resources to exploit opportunities across national borders to create fundamentally new goods and services. Opportunity entrepreneurs form new ventures because they see the opportunity for potential rewards. Necessity entrepreneurs create ventures for self-employment to make up for the lack of other job opportunities in their environment. There are also family-based entrepreneurs who create businesses with a view to employing family members and social entrepreneurs who create ventures with the primary goal of creating public good. The study of global entrepreneurship is important because it is a driving force in the creation of new jobs, it improves the quality of life and economic opportunities where it operates, and provides better quality goods and services to customers worldwide.

Two important streams of research in understanding international entrepreneurship are the internationalization literature and comparative entrepreneurship. The internationalization model has two competing theories. In one, firms gradually evolve from domestic firms, undergoing a process of internationalization. In the other, firms are born global and able to exploit knowledge resources in ways that help them enter overseas markets from nearly the point of their founding.

Comparative entrepreneurship helps us identify emerging trends and techniques that make our businesses more competitive. Two large scales studies dominate the comparative landscape: the GEM studies and the World Bank research. The GEM studies help us understand why and how people from different countries become entrepreneurs. The World Bank studies focus our attention on the contextual environment within which international entrepreneurs must operate. Lastly, no study of international entrepreneurship would be complete without exploring the role of cultural difference. Culture shapes the processes by which we identify opportunities, organize resources, and manage implementation of new ventures.

Discussion Questions

1. What changes have taken place in world markets in the last twenty years that make it easier for domestic entrepreneurs to spot opportunities in foreign markets?

2. Can an entrepreneur afford to internationalize slowly, or must their firm be "born global?"

3. How does the level of regulation within a country affect the creation of new ventures?

4. In what ways is the study of international entrepreneurship unique from the study of international business?

5. In what ways do the GEM and World Bank studies improve our knowledge of international entrepreneurship?

References

Alvarez, S. A., & Barney, J. B. (2014). Entrepreneurial opportunities and poverty alleviation. *Entrepreneurship Theory and Practice, 38*(1), 159–184.

Amorós, J. E., & Bosma, N. (2014). *Global Entrepreneurship Monitor 2013 Annual Report*. London: London Business School.

Amorós, J. E., Bosma, N., & Levie, J. (2013). Ten years of Global Entrepreneurship Monitor: Accomplishments and prospects. *International Journal of Entrepreneurial Venturing, 5*(2), 120–152.

Autio, E., & Acs, Z. J. (2010). Intellectual property protection and the formation of entrepreneurial growth aspirations. *Strategic Entrepreneurship Journal, 4*(3), 234–251.

Autio, E., Pathak, S., & Wennberg, K. (2013). Consequences of cultural practices for entrepreneurial behaviors. *Journal of International Business Studies, 44*(4), 334–362.

Autio, E., & Rannikko, H. (2016). Retaining winners: Can policy boost high-growth entrepreneurship? *Research Policy, 45*(1), 42–55.

Baily, M. N. (2012, February 12). The state of American small business (Brookings Brief).

BBC. (2016). Japan tuna nets a high bid at new year Tokyo auction. BBC, 5 January 2016.

Bell, J. McNaughton, R,, Young, S. & Crick, D. (2003). Toward an integrative model of small firm internationalization. *Journal of International Entrepreneurship, 1*(4), 339–362.

Bestor, T. C. (2004). *Tsukiji: The fish market at the center of the world* (California studies in food and culture, Vol. 11). Berkeley, CA: University of California Press.

Bianchi, C., & Mathews, S. (2016). Internet marketing and export market growth in Chile. *Journal of Business Research, 69*(2), 426–434.

Bloodgood, J. M., Sapienza, H. J., & Almeida, J. G. (1996). The internationalization of new high potential US ventures: Antecedents and outcomes. *Entrepreneurship Theory and Practice, 20*(4), 61–76.

Burgal, O., & Murray, G. C. (1998). The international activities of British start-up companies in high-technology industries: Differences between internationalizers and non-internationalizers. In P. D. Reynolds, W. D. Byrave, N. M. Carter, S. Manigart, C. M. Mason, G. Meyer, & K. Saver (Eds.), *Frontiers of Entrepreneurship Research* (pp.447–463). Babson College: Wellesley, MA.

Cano-Kollmann, M., Cantwell, J., Hannigan, T. J., Mudambi, R., & Song, J. (2016). Knowledge connectivity: An agenda for innovation research in international business. *Journal of International Business Studies, 47*(3), 255–262.

Carraher, S. M., & Buckley, M. R. (2005). Attitudes towards benefits among SME owners in Western Europe: An 18-month study. *Journal of Applied Management and Entrepreneurship, 10*(4), 45–57.

Case, S. (2013, January 31). A jobs council report card on US Entrepreneurship.

Chhokar, J. S., Brodbeck, F. C., & House, R. J. (Eds.). (2013). *Culture and leadership across the world: The GLOBE book of in-depth studies of 25 societies.* London: Routledge.

Constable, G., & Rimalovski, F. (2014). *Talking to humans: Success starts with understanding your customers.* New York, NY: Gif Constable Press.

Coviello, N. E., McDougall, P. P., & Oviatt, B. M. (2011). The emergence, advance and future of international entrepreneurship research: An introduction to the special forum. *Journal of Business Venturing, 26*(6), 625–631.

Cruickshank, P., & Rolland, D. (2006). Entrepreneurial success through networks and social capital: Exploratory considerations from GEM research in New Zealand. *Journal of Small Business & Entrepreneurship, 19*(1), 63–80.

Desmaris, M. (2004, July 1). Devarajan's Gotham Entertainment swings deal for Spider-Man in India. *India Business Journal, 2*(1).

DeSoto, H. (1990). *The other path.* New York, NY: Harper & Row.

Drucker, P. (1974). *Management tasks, responsibilities, practices.* New York, NY: Harper & Row.

Eduardsen, J. S., & Ivang, R. (2016). Internet-enabled internationalization: A review of the empirical literature and a research agenda. *International Journal of Business Environment, 8*(2), 152–175.

Foley, J. F. (2013). *The global entrepreneur* (3rd ed.). Jamric Press International: Peoria, IL.

Hennart, J. F. (2014). The accidental internationalists: A theory of born globals. *Entrepreneurship Theory and Practice, 38*(1), 117–135.

Hofstede, G., & Hofstede, G. J. (2005). *Cultures and organizations: Software of the mind.* New York, NY: McGraw-Hill.

Johanson, J., & Vahlne, J. (1977). The internationalization process of the firm: A model of knowledge development and increasing foreign market commitment. *Journal of International Business Studies, 8*, 23–32.

Johanson, J., & Vahlne, J. (1990). The mechanism of internationalization. *International Marketing Review, 7*(4), 11–24.

Jones, M., & Casulli, L. (2014). International entrepreneurship: Exploring the logic and utility of individual experience through comparative reasoning approaches. *Entrepreneurship Theory and Practice, 38*(1), 45–69.

Knight, G. A, & Cavusgil, S. T. (2004). Innovation, organizational capabilities, and the born-global firm. *Journal of International Business Studies, 35*(2), 124–141.

Lew, J. J. (2016). America and the global economy. *Foreign Affairs, 95*(3), 9.

McDougall-Covin, P., Jones, M. V., & Serapio, M. G. (2014). High-potential concepts, phenomena, and theories for the advancement of international entrepreneurship research. *Entrepreneurship Theory and Practice, 38*(1), 1–10.

McDougall, P., & Oviatt, B. (2000). International entrepreneurship: The intersection of two research paths. *Academy of Management Journal, 43*(5), 902–906.

McDougall, P. P., Shane, S., & Oviatt, B. M. (1996). New venture internationalization, strategic change, and performance: a follow-up study. *Journal of Business Venturing, 11*(1), 23–40.

Minkov, M., & Hofstede, G. (2014). Clustering of 316 European regions on measures of values: Do Europe's countries have national cultures? *Cross-cultural Research, 48*(2), 144–176.

Naudé, W., Gries, T., Wood, E., & Meintjies, A. (2008). Regional determinants of entrepreneurial start-ups in a developing country. *Entrepreneurship & Regional Development, 20*(2), 111–124.

Osterwalder, A., & Pigneur, Y. (2010). *Business model generation: A handbook for visionaries, game changers, and challengers.* New York, NY: John Wiley & Sons.

Potts, M. D., & Puia, G. M. (2017). Conviviality and knowledge management in learning communities. *Proceedings of the International Forum on Knowledge Asset Dynamics*, St Petersburg, Russia.

Puia, G. M., Hicks, H., & Stackpole, R. (2017). Knowledge acquisition in new international ventures: How global entrepreneurs find their way. *Proceedings of the International Forum on Knowledge Asset Development.* St Petersburg, Russia.

Puia, G. M., & Minnis, W. (2007). The effects of policy frameworks and culture on the regulation of entrepreneurial entry. *Journal of Applied Management and Entrepreneurship, 12*(4), 36–45.

Puia, G. M., & Ofori-Dankwa, J. (2013). The effects of national culture and ethno-linguistic diversity on innovativeness. *Baltic Journal of Management, 8*(3), 349–371.

Puia, G. M., & Pretzer-Lin, N. (2013). The influence of lifestyle advantages on inbound foreign direct investment: An exploration and research agenda. *Alternative Quarterly Journal of Economics* (Armenia), *4*(11), 69–81.

Quill, M., Bosma, N., & Minniti, M. (2006). *Globe Entrepreneurship Monitor: 2006 data assessment.* Babson College: Wellesley, MA.

Reuber, A. R., & Fischer, E. (2011). International entrepreneurship in Internet-enabled markets. *Journal of Business Venturing, 26*(6), 660–679.

Ries, E. (2011). *The lean startup: How today's entrepreneurs use continuous innovation to create radically successful businesses.* Crown Business: Chicago, IL.

Shane, S. A. (1993). Cultural influences on national rates on innovation. *Journal of Business Venturing, 8*(1), 59–73.

Shleifer, A., & Vishny, R. W. (1993). Corruption. *Quarterly Journal of Economics, 108*(3), 599–617.

Terjesen, S., Hessels, J., & Li, D. (2016). Comparative international entrepreneurship: A review and research agenda. *Journal of Management, 42*(1), 299–344.

UN Comtrade (2017). Results of data query, UN Comtrade Statistics Division.

Wolfensohn, J. D. (2000). *World development report, 1999–2000* (p. 33). Washington, DC: Oxford University Press.

World Bank. (2008). *Doing business, 2008: Comparing regulation in 178 countries.* Washington, DC: Author.

World Trade Organization. (2016). *International trade statistics, 2015.* Geneva: WTO.

Wright, R. W. (1994). Trends in international business research: Twenty-five years later. *Journal of International Business Studies, 25*(4), 687–701.

Zahra, S. A., & George, G. (2002). International entrepreneurship: The current status of the field and future research agenda. In M. A. Hitt, R. D. Ireland, S. M. Camp, & D. L. Sexton (Eds.), *Strategic entrepreneurship: Creating a new mindset* (pp. 255–288). Oxford: Blackwell Publishers.

Some Key Determinants of Entrepreneurship

Nir Kshetri

The University of North Carolina—Greensboro

Key Terms

Economic factors

Institutional factors

Demand-side perspective

Supply-side perspective

Culture

Political stability

Learning Objectives

Upon completion of this chapter, students should be able to:

1. Provide a review of environmental and contextual factors affecting entrepreneurial activities in an economy by focusing both on the demand and supply sides

2. Examine the demand and supply sides of entrepreneurships in the international context

To achieve the above goals, we divide environmental and contextual factors as discussed above into two major categories: economic factors and institutional factors.

Contributed by Nir Kshetri. © Kendall Hunt Publishing Company.

Abstract

This chapter examines economic and institutional factors affecting entrepreneurial activities. Factors analyzed include entrepreneurial opportunities, skills, access to capitals, incentives, culture as well as overall macroeconomic environment and institutional contexts. The focus is thus on the demand- as well as supply-side perspectives of entrepreneurship. We also discuss examples of measures taken by various governmental and nongovernmental agencies to change some of the institutional factors to stimulate entrepreneurship.

Introduction

A number of trends and indicators point toward the fact that entrepreneurship has become a truly global phenomenon. One such indicator concerns the appetite for entrepreneurial ventures. Highly successful entrepreneurial firms are found across the world. In the 2013 Forbes' global list of the 2000 biggest public companies, 63 countries were represented (Schaefer, 2016). In addition, the 2016 list of the world's largest companies has been updated. Moreover, companies from emerging markets such as Brazil, Chile, China, Mexico, and India were represented in the 130 Global High Performers in the Forbes' global list, which were described as "fast growing, nimble and well-managed companies" and grew 28% annually in the average. Various forces and events have shaped this global entrepreneurial revolution. While the general trend suggests a growth in entrepreneurial ventures worldwide, significant cross-country variation exists in entrepreneurial success and a number of features of entrepreneurship (Kshetri, 2014b).

A constellation of factors linked economic and institutional environments influence a country's entrepreneurship trajectory. The Danish National Agency for Enterprise and Construction's Division for Research and Analysis (FORA) has proposed five main categories related to business environment indicators that affect entrepreneurial activities in a country: opportunities, skills, capital, incentives, and culture (FOR, 2006). In addition, FORA also argued that contextual factors such as those related to the macroeconomic environment and institutional context like unemployment rate and GDP growth are tightly linked to a country's entrepreneurial landscape. These factors can be studied under the demand- and the supply-side perspectives of entrepreneurship.

The supply-side perspective of entrepreneurship focuses on the individual traits, attrbiutes, and characteristics of entrepreneurs (Thornton, 1999). Some of the important issues examined under the supply-side include how culture (Weber, 1904), social class, and ethnic group (Aldrich & Waldinger, 1990) are related to individuals' entrepreneurial behavior. According to this logic, differences in entrepreneurship depend on the differences in individuals. Put differently, personality or social group of an individual entrepreneur determines how, why, and where new businesses are founded (Thornton, 1999).

The demand-side perspective of entrepreneurship, on the other hand, focuses on "rates, or the context in which entrepreneurship occurs" (Thornton, 1999) and thus deals with sources of opportunities and the entrepreneurial roles that need to be filled in an economy (Shane & Venkataraman, 2000). According to the demand-side perspective, some of the important ways to examine entrepreneurship include creation of new ventures by organizational hierarchies (Freeman, 1986), the activity of the professions (Wholey, Christianson, & Sanchez, 1993), the policy of nation states (Dobbin & Dowd, 1997), the development of markets (White, 1981) and the advent of technological change (Shane, 1996).

Economic Factors

Economic factors influencing entrepreneurship in an economy are related to indicators such as physical and financial infrastructures, access to capital, gross national product, balance of payment and balance of trade situation, debt and servicing costs, inflation rate, interest rate, exchange rate, and exchange rate stability. We discuss some of these indicators in this section.

Physical and Financial Infrastructures

Availability of physical infrastructures such as roads, ports, water, telecommunications, and power play a critical role in facilitating entrepreneurial activities. Most industrialized countries have well-developed physical infrastructures in place to support entrepreneurial activities. In United States, for instance, the government has played a central role in infrastructure such as roads, rural electrification, and public schooling, which led to increased productivity among small businesses (Plastrik). A lack of well-developed physical infrastructures has been a barrier hindering entrepreneurship development in many developing countries. Among developing countries, China's entrepreneurial performance has been phenomenal, which can be partly attributed to the country's investment in infrastructure. An interesting observation is that every year following the 1978 political and economic reform, China built more modern highways than India had done in the whole period since it achieved independence in 1947 (Overholt, 2009/2010). As of the early 2013, China had 93,000 km of railway track (Rabinovitch, 2013). The investment and infrastructure spending in the rail network has been a key factor in China's economic recovery following the global financial crisis.

Financial infrastructures such as stock exchanges, credit guarantees, payment systems, insurance companies, banks and microfinance organizations, and other lending institutions are equally important in promoting entrepreneurship. It is argued that due to increasing globalization of capital markets, finance is no longer a big problem for promising entrepreneurs in emerging economies. The real problem concerns the lack of channels linking finance with potential entrepreneurs (Florence, 2006).

Access to Capital

Research has indicated that only a small proportion of latent entrepreneurs, or those who would prefer to be entrepreneurs rather than being paid employees, can start their own businesses. A lack of access to capital is often the biggest roadblock for latent entrepreneurs to materialize the goal of starting their own business (Blanchflower, Oswald, & Stutzer, 2001). For most potential entrepreneurs in many developing countries, a village loan shark is the only available source of capital, whose interest rate is 200–300% a year (Gross, 2008).

A Country's Credit Rating

A country's credit rating captures most of the economic indicators discussed above. Note that credit rating agencies (CRAs) analyze and evaluate the creditworthiness of corporate as well as sovereign issuers of debt securities (Elkhoury, 2008). A sovereign rating is aimed at "measuring the risk that a government may default on its own obligations in either local or foreign currency. It takes into account both the ability and willingness of a government to repay its debt in a timely manner" (Moody's Special Comment, 2006). Standard and Poor's ratings, Moody's ratings and Fitch's ratings are among the most widely used credit ratings.

Studies conducted by international economists for both developed and developing economies have indicated that a small number of variables explain 90% the variation in the ratings (Bhatia, 2002). They include GDP per capita, GDP Growth, inflation rate, the ratio of nongold foreign exchange reserves to imports, the ratio of the current account balance to GDP, default history and the level of economic development (Elkhoury, 2008).

In the mid-1990s, some European economies such as Italy and Belgium spent over 12% of their GDP for debt servicing. CRAs and investors perceived the situation as a symptom of major financial weakness hindering entrepreneurship (Fairlamb, 1995). Likewise, in January 2008, the credit rating agency, Moody's warned that the United States was at a risk of losing its triple-A credit rating, which was held since 1917 (Moody's Puts U.S. on Credit Watch, 2008). The January 11, 2008 issue of *Financial Times* noted that "the credit crisis triggered by the growth in risky mortgage lending, which has affected banks and investors around the world, has dispelled the myth that a triple-A credit rating is a guarantee of security."

Institutional Factors

Granovetter (Granovetter, 1985) argued that "the anonymous market of neoclassical models is virtually nonexistent in economic life and that transactions of all kinds are rife with the social connections described" (p. 495). Note that economic actors are embedded in formal and informal institutions. An examination of relevant institutional factors thus would shed some light on the growth of entrepreneurship in a society. We discuss some of the important institutional indicators from the standpoint of entrepreneurship development in this section.

Laws, Policies, and Regulations to Promote Entrepreneurship

Countries differ significantly in their regulations to support entrepreneurial development. For instance, according to the World Bank's Ease of Doing Business 2013 Report (http://www.doingbusiness.org/reports/global-reports/doing-business-2013), India ranked 132 out of the 185 economies considered in terms of the regulatory climate for entrepreneurship. To start a business, 12 procedures are needed to be completed which take 27 days and cost 50% of the country's per capita income. According to the World Bank, it takes 7 years to close a business in India compared to the OECD average of 1.7 years. Likewise, the average time to register property in South Asia is 106 days compared to the OECD average of 25 days. Moreover, companies with over 100 employees require government permission to dismiss workers (Deloitte, 2006). Likewise, in Central African Republic, which had the world's worst regulatory climate according to the World Bank's Ease of Doing Business 2013, eight procedures are needed to be completed to start a business which take 22 days and cost 173% of the country's per capita income. In Sierra Leone, to pay all taxes due, firms need to spend about three times their profits. Likewise, to enforce a contract in Angola, a firm needs to complete 47 procedures, which take over 1000 days. These conditions contrast sharply with Singapore, where starting a new business requires three procedures, which can be completed in 3 days and costs 0.6% of the country's per capita GDP.

Some developing countries, however, have made a considerable progress in establishing regulative institutions that are conducive to entrepreneurship development. The four Visegrad countries (Czech Republic, Hungary, Poland, and Slovakia) are remarkable examples of economies that have successfully promoted the growth of small- and medium-sized enterprises (SMEs). In the early years of transition programs related to SME promotion got higher priority in these countries' national strategies, which led to the development of entrepreneurship in these countries (Forst, 1996). The Visegrad countries have more favorable environment for entrepreneurship compared to other economies in Eastern Europe.

Formal institutions associated with policies and regulations in areas such as science, technology, intellectual property rights (IPR), and labor mobility are linked to a country's entrepreneurial performance (Groenewegen & van der Steen, 2006). In the absence of strong property rights, there are little incentives for entrepreneurs.

In many emerging economies, the rule of law is underdeveloped, which hinders entrepreneurship. Most of the wealth in these economies is in the form of "informal" ownership outside the formal legal system, and hence is not recognized or enforced in the form of legal titles (De Soto, 2003). Most obviously, because of the ineffective legal enforcement of private property rights, most entrepreneurs prefer to rely on political and administrative protection or depend on informal networks for security. The absence of institutions to protect property rights and strong judicial system thus hinders the growth of private entrepreneurship. For instance, insecurity of property rights hindered entrepreneurship in China and private entrepreneurs lacked legal protection in the country (Yang, 2002).

Political Stability

External and internal conflicts in a country increase the costs as well as uncertainty for businesses in the country. More to the point, political instability hampers the implementation of coherent policy to foster entrepreneurship (Forst, 1996). For instance, many foreign businesses show little interest in sub-Saharan Africa because of political instability and corruption (Kshetri, 2011). Analysts also argue that Russia needs to gain political stability for the faster development of entrepreneurship (Charles, 1996). On the other hand, the rapid growth of local entrepreneurship in China can be attributed to the country's ability to maintain political stability.

Skills

One of the most important barriers to entrepreneurship in developing countries centers on poorly educated and unskilled labor force (Aworuwa, 2004). Of particular importance is thus educational program to develop entrepreneurial skills in the society (Florence, 2006). For instance, in the post-socialist economies, experience and training gained under the communist system contributes very little for the management and business skills needed for free market entrepreneurship (Warner & Daugherty, 2004). This is powerfully illustrated in many Chinese entrepreneurs' lack of understanding of practical distinctions between various types of financing (Kambil, Long, & Kwan, 2006). Likewise, important concepts of management, such as marketing and consumer behavior are not integrated into Chinese thinking (Borgonjon & Vanhonacker, 1992), which has hindered entrepreneurial development in the country. Beyond all that many Chinese managers' cognitive framework arguably reflects a "government takes care of everything" culture (Lynch, 2005)

Values and Norms

A society's cultural norms and values are tightly linked to the growth of entrepreneurship. Prior researchers have recognized that cultural norms, beliefs, and values influence attributes required for successful entrepreneurial venture such as attitude toward risk taking and hard work (Weber, 1930). These factors also framed as normative institutions that influence the degree to which a country's citizens admire entrepreneurship (Busenitz, Gomez, & Spencer, 2000).

A lack of modern entrepreneurial culture and the prevalence anti-entrepreneurship norms and values are identified as major problems hindering the growth of entrepreneurship in the post-socialist Russia (Kshetri, 2009). In China, entrepreneurship as an occupation was often considered for individuals not able to find other jobs (e.g., those with criminal records). Similarly, until the 1980s, Irish youths were attracted to jobs in the government and financial services. Likewise, accumulating a huge amount of wealth is a "delicate subject" in China (Hoogewerf, 2002).

More entrepreneurship-friendly institutions are developing in many countries. Some entrepreneurially successful economies have demonstrated that entrepreneurship-friendly social norms can emerge. For instance, defaulting on loans was judged as an immoral practice in Ireland. The social norms also stigmatized bankruptcy (Isenberg, 2010). The Irish economy subsequently produced many multimillionaire entrepreneurs. As of 2008, Ireland had over 30,000 euro millionaires and most of them were self-made (Brown, 2008). Entrepreneurs gradually started treating a business failure as a learning opportunity instead of a personal failure or stigma. Societal norms and values related to entrepreneurship are rapidly shifting in other economies (Kshetri, 2014b). In Estonia's case Skype cofounder Taavet Hinrikus noted: "In the 80s every boy in high-school wanted to be a rock star. Now everybody … wants to be an entrepreneur" (economist.com, 2013b). likewise, entrepreneurs in South Korea are overcoming the stigma and fear of business failure. There are also formal and informal supports to failing and failed entrepreneurs. In her meeting with Facebook CEO in June 2013, South Korean President Park Geun-hye praised the company for "taking on challenges without fear of failure" (Nam, 2013). Some noted that her comment would reinforce the idea: "It's OK to fail" (Nam, 2013).

Also a cultural change in respect of entrepreneurship as a career option has emerged in economies such as China, Japan and South Korea. Working in a large corporation or the government was traditionally considered as a prestigious and desirable career route in these countries. Daniel Cho, who quit his job at a multinational firm to start a mobile-application developer, was quoted as saying: "Just a few years back, giving up a high-paying job at an established company to start a venture firm was foolhardy. Risk taking was something to be avoided" (Nam, 2013). The changing attitude toward failure can also be considered as a cause for such a shift. For instance, there was no customer demand for the personal-diary program developed by Cho's company. Despite this failure he was able to secure new investments (Nam, 2013).

One important aspect of societal norms and values that renders it interesting to us is the fact that private businesses can take measures to change some of them. In Sweden, for instance, the think tank, Timbro is working to bring a long-term shift in the "public opinion in favor of free markets, entrepreneurship, private property, and an open society" (Lehrer & Hildreth, 2002). The institute is funded mostly by large Swedish corporations.

Risk Taking Behavior

Entrepreneurial activities inherently involve risk taking behaviors. Societies across the world vary greatly in their risk-taking behavior. In the Arab world, for instance, large corporate bureaucracies are found to be risk averse (Graham, Lewis, De Marino, & Reinsch, 2006). The lack of a tradition of private entrepreneurship in central and eastern European countries is also related to an underdeveloped risk taking culture in the absence of local norms and social networks providing support for such a culture (Kshetri, 2010). For instance, Russian managers with experience in state-owned enterprises tend to avoid risk (Taylor & Kazakov, 1997). Likewise, some observers have suggested that large proportion of the Chinese tend to lack characteristics needed to be a successful entrepreneur such as risk taking (Anderson, Li, Harrison, & Robson, 2003). Consider, for instance, the Chinese venture capital (VC) landscape. Most VC funds in the country are linked to the government and can be considered as a loan (Harwit, 202). Enterprises that are able to obtain VC funds feel an obligation not to lose the resources. Moreover, an incubator losing the government owned money also becomes a target of official criticism. Chinese government VC funds thus cannot accept the Western level of risk taking.

Summary

This chapter provided an overview of environmental and contextual factors affecting entrepreneurial activities. We discussed how economic and institutional factors facilitate and hinder the development of entrepreneurship in an economy. The discussion focused both on the demand and supply side factors.

An important point to bear in mind is that economic and institutional factors related to entrepreneurship are changing in emerging economies. For instance, overseas Chinese with educations and entrepreneurial experience in the industrialized world, who are more similar to managers from the Western world, are returning to China. Likewise, there has been a rapid increase in the inflow of foreign VC to China thanks mainly to dense networks of overseas Chinese (Jahan, 2016) Source has been updated to 2016 report. A similar point can be made about other emerging economies such as India and Russia.

Developing economies have made considerable progress on the institutional front as well. Central and eastern European transition economies, for instance, are creating institutions to promote democracy. At the same time, new social norms, values and beliefs are evolving to support entrepreneurship in these economies. For instance, in a survey, about 80% of young Russians said that they have "successfully adapted to capitalism" (Nikitina, 2004). Likewise, China is arguably "shifting from top-down, state-directed technology policies to more flexible, market-oriented approaches that foster innovation and entrepreneurship" (Segal, 2004). Cetron and Owen note: "On average, institutions are growing more transparent in their operations and more accountable for their misdeeds." Source has been updated to 2010 edition (Cetron & Davies, 20110).

We also provided some examples to demonstrate that societal and institutional actors such as the government and associations funded by private businesses can change most of the factors discussed in this chapter. A related point is that some factors are easier to change than others. From the national policy maker's standpoint, for instance, enactment of financial legislation to develop local linkage to global capital market, development of entrepreneurial skills may be easier than changing the culture of the society.

Discussion Questions

1. Among the various factors discussed above, which one do you think is the most important one in facilitating and hindering the growth of entrepreneurial activities in an economy?

2. Can environmental and contextual factors be changed by the state or nonstate actors?

3. Why is political stability important for the growth of new businesses?

4. Select a developing country and critically examine how various environmental and contextual factors discussed in this chapter have influenced entrepreneurship in the country.

References

Aldrich, H., & Waldinger, R. (1990). Ethnicity and entrepreneurship. *Annual Review of Sociology*, 16, 111–135

Anderson, A. R., Li, J. H. Harrison, R. T., & Robson, P. J. A. (2003). The increasing role of small business in the Chinese economy. *Journal of Small Business Management, 41*(3), 310.

Aworuwa, O. E. (2004). A bootstrap model for microenterprise development of a distressed community. *Journal of Third World Studies, 21*(1), 79–86.

Bhatia, A. V. "Sovereign Credit Ratings Methodology: an Evaluation," *IMF Working Paper 02/170* (2002), IMF.; R. Cantor and F. Packer, "Sovereign Credit Ratings, Federal Reserve Bank of New York," *Current Issues in Economic and Finance* (1995), 1(3); R. Cantor and F. Packer, "The Credit Ratings Industry, Federal Reserve Bank of New York," *Quarterly Review* (1996); N.U. Haque; M. Kumar; D. Mathieson and N. Mark, "The Economic Content of Indicators of Developing Country Creditworthiness," *IMF, Staff Paper* (1996): 43(4); H. Reisen and J. Von Maltzan, "Boom and Bust in Sovereign Ratings," *OECD Technical Papers* (1999): 148, www.oecd.org/pdf/M00006000/M00006204.pdf

Blanchflower, D. G., Oswald, A., & Stutzer, A. (2001). Latent entrepreneurship across nations. *European Economic Review, 45*(4–6), 680.

Borgonjon, J., & Vanhonacker, W. R. (1992). Modernizing China's managers. *The China Business Review, 19*(5), 12–17.

Busenitz, L. W. Gomez, C., & Spencer, J. W. (2000). *Country* institutional profiles: *Unlocking* entrepreneurial phenomena. *Academy of Management Journal, 43*(5), 994–1003.

Cetron, M. J., & Davies, O. (2010). Trends shaping tomorrow's world. *World Future Society*, 35–50.

De Soto, H. (2003). *The mystery of capital: Why capitalism triumphs in the West and fails everywhere*. Random House.

Deloitte. (2006). *China and India: The reality beyond the hype,* Deloitte Development LLC.

Dobbin, F., & Dowd, T. J. (1997). How policy shapes competition: Early railroad foundings in Massachusetts. *Administrative Science Quarterly, 42*, 501–29

Elkhoury, M. "Credit Rating Agencies and their Potential Impact on Developing Countries," *Discussion Paper No. 186, UNCTAD* (January 2008): http://www.unctad.org/en/docs/osgdp20081_en.pdf

Fairlamb, D. (1995). Europe confronts the inevitable. *Institutional Investor, 29*(4), 85–89.

Florence, E. (2006). Private equity finance as a growth engine: What it means for emerging markets. *Business Economics, 41*(3), 7–21.

FOR A. (2006). Quality Assessment of Entrepreneurship Indicators, Version 2, #16 October 2006, The National Agency for Enterprise and Construction's Division for Research and Analysis International Consortium for Dynamic Benchmarking of Entrepreneurship, Denmark.

Forst, M. (1996). Helping small business in Eastern Europe. *OECD Observer, 198*, 51–54.

Freeman, J. (1986). Entrepreneurs as organizational products: Semiconductor firms and venture capital firms. *Advances in the Study of Entrepreneurship, Innovation, and Economic Growth, 1*, 33–52.

Graham, E. M., Lewis, J. A., De Marino, D. N., & Reinsch, W. A. (2006). How can the U.S. reopen for business to the Arab world? *Middle East Policy, 13*(2), 71–89.

Granovetter, M. (1985). Economic action and social structure: The problem of embeddedness, *American Journal of Sociology, 91*(3), 481–510.

Groenewegen, J., & van der Steen, M. (2006). The evolution of national innovation systems. *Journal of Economic Issues, 40*(2), 277–286.

Gross, D. "Poverty: Cheap loans at insanely high rates? Give us more," *Newsweek* (September 20, 2008), http://www.newsweek.com/id/160074

Harwit, E. (2002). High-technology incubators: Fuel for China's new entrepreneurship? *China Business Revie, 29*(4), 26–29.

Hoogewerf, R. (2002). A new breed of Chinese entrepreneur: Louis Zan Shengda is one of China's richest businessmen—and a prime target for private bankers moving into the country. *Wealth Management, 24*(2).

Jahan, S. (2016). *Human Development Report 2016 Team (Rep.)*. New York, NY: United Nations Development Programme.

Kambil, A. Long, V. W., & Kwan, C. (2006). The seven disciplines for venturing in China. *MIT Sloan Management Review, 47*(2), 85.

Kshetri, N. (2009). Entrepreneurship in post-socialist economies: A typology and institutional contexts for market entrepreneurship. *Journal of International Entrepreneurship, 7*(3), 236–2595.

Kshetri, N. (2010) Business perceptions of regulative institutions in Central and Eastern Europe. *Baltic Journal of Management, 5*(3), 356–377.

Kshetri, N. (2011). Institutional and economic foundation of entrepreneurship in Africa: An overview. *Journal of Developmental Entrepreneurship, 16*(1), 9–35.

Kshetri, N. (2014a). Developing successful entrepreneurial ecosystems: Lessons from a comparison of an Asian Tiger and a Baltic Tiger. *Baltic Journal of Management, 9*(330–356).

Kshetri, N. (2014b). *Global Entrepreneurship: Environment and Strategy.* New York: Routledge

Lehrer, E., & Hildreth, J. (2002). Scandinavia's surprising turn from socialism. *The American Enterprise, 13*(8), 42–44.

Lynch, D. J. (2005). "China's management pool is shallow," *USA Today:*1B

Matthews, C. H., Qin, X., McClure Franklin, G. (1996). Stepping toward prosperity: The development of entrepreneurial ventures in China and Russia. *Journal of Small Business Management, 34*(3), 75–85.

Moody's Special Comment, "A Guide to Moody's Sovereign Ratings", (August 2006): 1. "Moody's Puts U.S. on Credit Watch," *Wall Street Weather* (January 11, 2008): http://www.wallstreetweather.net/2008/01/moodys-puts-us-on-credit-watch.html

Nikitina, O. (2004). Changing times, changing attitudes: What do Russians really think about the transition to capitalism? *RussProfile, 1*(4), 26–27.

Overholt, W. H. (2009/2010). China in the global financial crisis: Rising influence, rising challenges. *Washington Quarterly, 33*(1), 21–34.

Plastrik, P. Global competitiveness and small business. *Harvard Business Review, 69*(1), 174–176.

Rabinovitch, S. (January 16, 2013). Rail helps China back on track. http://www.ft.com/cms/s/0/3a2c7c86-5fc1-11e2-8d8d-00144feab49a.html#axzz2Tx53v8Zg

Schaefer, S. (2016, May 25). The World's Biggest Public Companies. Retrieved from https://www.forbes.com/global2000/

Segal, A. (2004). Is America losing its edge? *Foreign Affairs, 83*(6), 2.

Shane, S., & Venkataraman, S. (2000). The promise of entrepreneurship as a field of research. *Academy of Management Review, 25*(1), 217–226.

Shane. (1996). Explaining variation in rates of entrepreneurship in the United States: 1899–1988. *Journal of Management, 22*(5), 747–81.

Taylor, T. C., & Kazakov, A. Y. (1997). Business ethics and civil society in Russia. *International Study of Management of Organization, 27*, 5–18.

Thornton, P. H. (1999). The sociology of entrepreneurship, *Annual Review of Sociology, 25*(1), 19–46.

Warner, M., & Daugherty, C. W. (2004). Promoting the 'Civic' in entrepreneurship: The case of rural Slovakia. *Journal of the Community Development Society, 35*(1), 117–134.

Weber, M. (1904). *The protestant ethic and the spirit of capitalism.* New York: Routledge.

Weber, M. (1930). *The protestant ethic and the spirit of capitalism.* London, UK and Boston, MA: Unwin Hyman Publishing.

White, H. C. (1981). Where do markets come from? *American Journal of Sociology, 87,* 517–47.

Wholey, D. R., Christianson, J. B., & Sanchez, S. M. (1993). The effect of physician and corporate interests on the formation of health maintenance organizations. *American Journal of Sociology, 99*(1), 164–200.

Yang, K. (2002). Double entrepreneurship in China's economic reform: An analytical framework. *Journal of Political and Military Sociology, 30*(1), 134–148.

Global Entrepreneurial Strategy

John A. Parnell

Belk Chair of Management, School of Business, University of North Carolina at Pembroke

Key Terms

Contingency theory

Crisis management

Dynamic capabilities

Economies of (global) scope

Industrial organization (IO)

Intrapreneurship

Outsourcing

Resource-based view (RBV)

Self-reference criterion

Strategic control

World Trade Organization (WTO)

Learning Objectives

Upon completion of this chapter, students should be able to:

1. Understand and explain the theoretical underpinnings of global entrepreneurial strategy

2. Understand how changes in the global landscape and created opportunities for global entrepreneurship

3. Understand how the global landscape influences the mission of entrepreneurial enterprises

4. Understand the nature of corporate- and business-level entrepreneurial strategy formulation at the global level

5. Understand the challenges associated with strategy execution and control—including crisis management—within the context of global entrepreneurship

Introduction

Global entrepreneurial strategy has become more important in recent decades. Entrepreneurial opportunities occur when new products or services can satisfy the needs of a particular market. In its simplest form, entrepreneurship involves identifying these opportunities and mobilizing to pursue them. The prevalence of such opportunities outside of a firm's host country is more prevalent today than ever (Kovios, 2016).

Entrepreneurship is often associated with small business activity but also occurs within large firms, a process known as corporate entrepreneurship or *intrapreneurship*. Successful entrepreneurship in any size organization requires both intellectual capital and an innovative mindset (Koellinger, 2008). While it can be difficult to develop the latter in large firms, the existence of intellectual capital can be a key advantage for them relative to their smaller counterparts, especially in global environments. Hence, the notion of entrepreneurship is salient for all firms, regardless of size.

The international environment offers a number of applications to strategic management in entrepreneurial firms (White, Guldiken, Hemphill, He, & Khoobdeh, 2016). Historically, the reasons for moving toward globalization are clear. Technological advances emanate from across the globe. Many of these developments come from developed nations such as Japan and countries within the European Economic Union, but others come from rapidly emerging economies such as the BRIC (Brazil, Russia, India, and China) nations.

Strategic planning, however, is much more complex in global environments for several reasons. The external environment—including political and economic instabilities—can vary substantially across borders. Competition can be intense and control of the enterprise quite difficult when operations are geographically dispersed.

Culture is a key consideration and has been posited as one of the key determinants of differences in the level of entrepreneurial activity across nations (Koseoglu, Parnell, & Togalogu, 2013; Parnell & Hatem, 1999). Nonetheless, clear links between cultural attributes and entrepreneurial activity are often difficult to identify. For example, countries whose firms are more likely to be entrepreneurial tend to have moderately high levels of individualism. However, extremely high individualism can actually hinder the development of teamwork, a key ingredient in the entrepreneurship process (Liñán, & Moriano, 2016; Morris, Davis, & Allen, 1994).

Following a commentary of theoretical perspectives, the remainder of this chapter examines how globalization affects each step of the strategic management process within entrepreneurial firms: (1) analysis of the external environment, (2) analysis of the internal environment, (3) strategy formulation, and (4) strategy execution and strategic control. Business activity occurring outside of a firm's host country can be viewed as a continuum from international (the most limited) to multinational to global (the most aggressive). These options are discussed in greater detail later within the strategy formulation section.

Theoretical Perspectives on Entrepreneurial Strategy

The theoretical and philosophical underpinnings of entrepreneurship differ somewhat from that of strategic management within less entrepreneurial, mature firms (Parnell, 2006, 2013). Specifically, three theoretical perspectives warrant discussion. First, *industrial organization (IO)*, a branch of microeconomics, emphasizes the *influence of the industry environment* upon the firm. The central tenet of industrial organization theory is the notion that a firm must adapt to influences in its industry to survive and prosper; thus, its financial performance is primarily determined by the success of the industry in which it competes. Industries with favorable structures offer the greatest opportunity for firm profitability (Porter, 1981). Following this perspective, industry selection is viewed as more important than competitive approach (Hawawini, Subramanian, & Verdin, 2003).

IO assumes that an organization's performance and ultimate survival depend on its ability to *adapt* to industry forces over which it has little or no control rather than to *create* change. According to IO, strategic managers should seek to understand the structure of the industry and formulate strategies that feed off the industry's characteristics (Bain, 1968; Scherer & Ross, 1990). Because IO focuses on industry forces, strategies, resources, and competencies are assumed to be fairly similar among competitors within a given industry. If one firm deviates from the industry norm and implements a new, successful strategy, other firms will rapidly mimic the higher performing firm by purchasing the resources, competencies, or management talent that have made the leading firm so profitable. Hence, the IO perspective is more prominent in the strategic management of large firms operating in mature industries (Barney, 1986; Seth & Thomas, 1994).

Contrary to IO, the *resource-based view (RBV)* sees performance primarily as a function of a firm's ability to utilize its resources. Although environmental opportunities and threats are important, a firm's unique resources comprise the key variables that allow it to develop a distinctive competence, enabling the firm to distinguish itself from its rivals and create competitive advantage. Resources include all of a firm's tangible and intangible assets, such as capital, equipment, employees, knowledge, and information (Barney, 1995). An organization's resources are directly linked to its capabilities, which can create value and ultimately lead to profitability for the firm. Hence, resource-based theory focuses primarily on individual firms rather than on the competitive environment, a perspective consistent with the notion of new venture creation and innovation within entrepreneurial firms.

The *dynamic capabilities (DCA)* approach expands the strategic capabilities perspective by emphasizing the transitory nature of both organizational resources and external factors (Ambrosini & Bowman, 2009; Augier & Teece, 2009; Teece, Peteraf, & Leih, 2016). This notion is inherent in the *VRINO framework* helps strategists evaluate the competitive quality of the resources controlled by the organization on the basis of five progressive characteristics (Barney, 1991). The VRINO assessment assumes subjective value, the idea that the same resource can have different values to different organizations.

1. *Value*: Can the resource be employed to exploit an opportunity or neutralize an external threat? Valuable resources can assist the firm in attaining competitive parity with rivals, but not competitive advantage.

2. *Rare*: Is the resource controlled by a few individuals or firms? Resources that are both valuable and rare can produce competitive advantage, but only temporarily. This is worthwhile, but a resource's scarcity tends to erode over time.

3. *Imitability*: Can other firms easily imitate or acquire the resource? If not, then a firm has the potential for achieving and maintaining competitive advantage over the long term.

4. *Nonsubstitutability*: Can other available resources be substituted for the resource? It is best for firms possessing a resource if substitutes are not readily available.

5. *Organization*: Is the firm poised to exploit the resource? Firms that can leverage valuable, rare, and inimitable resources can attain sustained competitive advantage. While firm resources—both tangible and intangible—ultimately constitute the firm's strengths and weaknesses, merely possessing a resource does not always benefit the organization. Resources are translated into desired results by a firm's capabilities (Eisenhardt & Martin, 2000).

Contingency theory represents a third theoretical perspective. According to this approach, the most profitable firms are likely to be those that "fit" with their environments. In other words, a strategy is most likely to be successful when it is consistent with the organization's mission, its competitive environment, and its resources. Contingency theory assumes that an established firm can increase or decrease entrepreneurial activity over time in order to adjust to the characteristics of its environment. Firms can become proactive by choosing to operate in environments where opportunities and threats match the firms' strengths and weaknesses (Zajac, Kraatz, & Bresser, 2000). Should the industry environment change in a way that is unfavorable to the firm, its top managers should consider leaving that industry and reallocating its resources to other, more favorable industries. From the contingency perspective, entrepreneurs should seek to fill market gaps when their strengths and resource base enable them to do so effectively.

Within the strategic management of mature organizations, each of these three perspectives may contribute somewhat equally to the overall strategic orientation of the firm. In contrast, the resource based and contingency views tend to be dominant in entrepreneurial firms bent on innovation and creativity. Entrepreneurial firms, whether small or large, tend to emphasize the firm's unique combination of resources and capabilities to capitalize on unmet market demand or to align the organization with existing external environmental trends.

External Environment

The first step of the strategic management process, analysis of the external environment, includes a look at a firm's industry structure as well as environmental (i.e., political-legal, social, economic, and technological) forces that affect its operations. External analysis creates the context for business activities. The issue of protectionism and free trade is a central concern in the global environment and creates a context for thinking about global entrepreneurship, as shifts toward greater free trade can create a number of business opportunities for entrepreneurial firms (Bjornskov & Foss, 2008; McMullen, Bagby, & Palich, 2008).

At the global level, the period from World War II to the late 1980s was marked by increased trade protection. Many countries protected their industries by imposing tariffs, import duties, and other restrictions. Import duties in many Latin American countries ranged from less than 40% to more than 100%. However, this trend was not limited to developing nations. Countries in Europe and Asia—and even the United States—have imposed import fees on a variety of products, including food, steel, and cars. In the 1980s, the United States also convinced Japanese manufacturers to voluntarily restrict exports of cars to the United States in lieu of a tariff. Interestingly, this particular tariff may be largely responsible for Japanese automobile manufacturers establishing a large number of production facilities in the United States.

During this time, however, many nations desired to eliminate trade barriers. In 1947, 23 countries entered into the cooperative General Agreement on Tariffs and Trade (GATT). Expanding to over 110 nations over several decades, GATT has assisted in relaxing quota and import license requirements, introducing fairer customs evaluation methods, and establishing a common mechanism to resolve trade disputes.

As momentum for GATT grew, a major shift in United States policy occurred in the late 1970s and the 1980s in favor of "deregulation," eliminating a number of legal constraints in such industries as airlines, trucking, and banking, but not all industries were deregulated. By 1990, a reversal of trade protectionism and strong governmental influence in business operations began to take place. In the United States, new economic policies reduced governmental influence in business operations by deregulating certain industries, lowering corporate taxes, and relaxing rules against mergers and acquisitions. This trend has continued into the twenty-first century, although not as forceful as in the late 1990s.

A GATT agreement led to the formation of the World Trade Organization (WTO), an international body designed to supervise and liberalize global trade. Launched in 1995, the WTO has over 150 nation members representing an estimated 95% of world trade. WTO agreements attempt to forge common ground in trading requirements across nations.

The shift toward free trade has also been seen in Europe, where a number of nations banded together to develop a trade-free European Community. Today, Europe is fast becoming a single market of 500 million consumers in 28 member states. The

European Union (EU) represents the largest trading bloc on earth, accounting for about one-fourth of the world's gross domestic product (GDP). Meanwhile, the United States, Canada, and Mexico established the North American Free Trade Agreement (NAFTA) to create its own strategic trading bloc, the largest of its kind in the world.

This trend toward less regulation has even extended to the former communist countries. As new governments formed in the former Soviet bloc nations of Eastern Europe, such as Poland, Czechoslovakia, and Hungary, they began to open markets and to invite foreign investment (Raiszadeh, Helms, & Varner, 1993). In addition, China officially remains a communist nation, but its economic development policies have shifted toward greater market freedom since the late 1990s. With the United Kingdom's vote to leave the EU and the election of Donald Trump as United States President, the pendulum may be shifting from "free trade" to "fair trade."

Trade restrictions have always existed in market economies to some extent, especially in politically sensitive areas. For example, the United States and other Western countries have banned the export of advanced technology in certain circumstances. The United States prohibits the export of certain electronic, nuclear, and defense-related products to many countries, particularly those believed to be involved in international terrorism. Regulations can also restrict competition in nations whose economies are considered to be relatively open. For example, the city of Paris caps the number of taxi licenses it awards and charges 230,000 Euros for each one. Because they are costly and in short supply, their drivers also have a reputation for poor service. Benjamin Cardoso founded VTC Corporation to provide an alternative, Tourist Vehicles with Chauffeurs (VTCs in French). Rather than wait for a taxi, patrons can contact VTC via smartphone with their request for a ride, and usually get a response in a few minutes. Unionized taxi drivers in Paris did not appreciate the competition from VTC, Uber, and others, and lobbied for a mandated two-hour delay before VTCs can respond to such requests. The French government agreed to a 15-minute delay, and the battle continues today (Todd, 2013).

Trade restrictions aside, globalization has gained steam in the last few decades. In *The World is Flat, New York Times* foreign affairs correspondent Thomas Friedman argued that the period of American world economic domination has ended because changes during the last two decades have leveled or "flattened" the economic playing field for those in other countries, most notably India and China (Friedman, 2005). The dot-com boom and subsequent bust around the turn of the century contributed significantly to the emergence of Friedman's "flat world." During the bubble, telecommunications companies were replete with cash and invested hundreds of millions of dollars to lay fiber-optic cables across the ocean floors, cables that currently and inexpensively connect countries like India and China to the United States. The dot-com bust resulted in significant stock market losses, forcing companies to cut spending wherever possible. Hence, many turned to opportunities for cost reductions created by the fiber-optic cables and began to offshore jobs as a means of addressing a new economic reality. As Indian entrepreneur Jerry Rao explained, any work that can be digitized and moved from one location to another will be moved. Indeed, approximately half a million U.S. Internal Revenue Service (IRS) tax returns are actually completed by accountants in India each year (Friedman, 2005).

The notion of a level economic playing field creates a number of challenges for Western firms and societies, one of which is the debate over "free trade." Supporters contend that a flatter world is here to stay and that efforts to thwart it will only stifle growth in economic powers like the United States, an argument Friedman echoes. Proponents charge that the unbridled global trade drives down wages and will ultimately result in a reduced standard of living in developed nations.

Nonetheless, the flat world has created a plethora of global business opportunities for entrepreneurial firms in both developed and emerging nations. Operating across borders can enable a firm to access key resources, develop economies of scale, and lower production costs. It can also create opportunities for mutually beneficial partnerships. The host country's government may even offer tax and investment incentives.

The failure of many dot-coms notwithstanding, the Internet has promoted substantial change in the structure of business. During the past quarter century, organizations have engaged in a process economists refer to as "disaggregation and reaggregation." (Bughin & Manyika, 2013; Malone & Laubaucher, 1998; Tapscott, Ticoll, & Lowy, 2000) The economic basis for this transformation was proposed by Nobel Laureate Ronald Coase in what is called *Coase's law*: A firm will tend to expand until the costs of organizing an extra transaction within the firm become equal to the costs of carrying out the same transaction on the open market (Coase, 1990). Following Coase's law, large firms exist because they can perform tasks such as raw material procurement, production, human resource management, and sales more efficiently than if they were pursued *outsourcing*, contracting out a firm's noncore, nonrevenue-producing activities to other organizations.

Rapid development of Internet and related technologies in the 2000s—coupled with rapid economic development in parts of Asia and Eastern Europe—enabled firms to reorganize work processes and improve efficiency. It is now much easier to share and exchange information, and to "farm out" specific tasks to the most efficient parties across the globe. Today, there are more than a quarter of a million Indians managing call centers and performing telemarketing functions primarily for firms in United States because they can perform the tasks—with the assistance of technology—more efficiently than their American counterparts. This fast-growing service industry in India was virtually nonexistent just a decade ago (Friedman, 2005).

As a result of this change, many progressive firms have placed less emphasis on performing all of the required activities themselves and have formed partnerships—contractual relationships with enterprises outside the organization—to manage many of the functions that were previously managed internally. Whereas *outsourcing* refers to specific agreements associated with a single task, *partnering* implies a longer term commitment associated with more complex activities.

The effects of the Internet on advertising options and effectiveness have also been pronounced, especially for young firms. In 2014, Pandora began offering a new advertising service that enables political candidates to target listeners based on their zip codes and music preferences. In many instances, voting behavior can be predicted with this information, enabling political organizations to target voters more effectively (Dwoskin, 2014). Indeed, digital advertising is a $50 billion global business, but companies must beware of technological changes and fraud. Advertisers typically pay when viewers click to visit their site. According to the Interactive Advertising Bureau trade association, about 36% of all Internet traffic is counterfeit, emanating from computers hijacked by viruses and programmed to visit select sites. Some phony visitors are well disguised, actually spending random amounts of times on different pages while adding items to a shopping cart before vanishing (Vranica, 2014).

From a global entrepreneurship perspective, the disaggregation and reaggregation phenomenon has created massive opportunities, particularly for small firms in emerging economies. By leverage Internet technology, entrepreneurial enterprises now perform a number of traditional business functions previously performed by a consolidated firm. Hence, any activity that can be digitized can be done almost anywhere in the world.

Internal Environment

The mission of an entrepreneurial organization—the reason for its existence—may be closely connected to its international operations in several ways. For instance, a firm operating in one country may require inputs from firms in other nations. Given the nation's small size and limited natural resources, virtually all of Japan's industries would stymie if imports of raw materials from other nations ceased.

A firm's mission and its international operations are also connected through the economic concept of comparative advantage, the idea that certain products may be produced more cheaply or at a higher quality in particular countries due to advantages in labor costs or technology. Chinese manufacturers, for example, enjoy some of the lowest global labor rates for unskilled or semiskilled production. As skills rise among Chinese workers, however, some companies have succeeded in extending this comparative advantage to a number of technical skill areas as well.

For global entrepreneurs, involvement outside of a firm's host country may also provide advantages not directly related to costs. For political reasons, it is often necessary for a firm to establish operations in another country, especially if its products are widely distributed there. Doing so can also provide other advantages, however, such as gaining expertise about local market conditions. Global automakers operate production facilities across borders to leverage the advantages of disparate locations (Amighini, 2012).

Strategy Formulation: Issues at the Corporate Level

The decision to pursue international opportunities is generally made at the corporate level. In a small firm, this level is not easily distinguished from the business or competitive level of the firm. In a large firm, however, the corporate level may be somewhat removed from the business level, potentially stifling international entrepreneurial activity. If a firm is involved beyond its domestic borders, it may compete abroad at one of three levels: international, multinational, or global. Many small, entrepreneurial firms operate successfully at the international level, whereas their larger counterparts often pursue a multinational or global approach. Effective operations at any of these levels often—but not always—necessitates economies of scale and a relatively high market share (Geringer, Tallman, & Olsen, 2000).

International Orientation

The first option is the most conservative of the three. Some entrepreneurial companies choose to be involved on an international basis by operating in various countries, but limiting their involvement to importing, exporting, licensing, or global partnerships with other firms. Exporting alone can significantly benefit even a small company. However, international joint ventures among firms may be desirable even when resources for a direct investment are available. For example, Proctor & Gamble began licensing out hundreds of undeveloped patents, brands, and rights to new products in the late 2000s, often partnering with small companies. Nehemiah Manufacturing has been licensing P&G's Pampers Kandoo line of toddler cleaning products since 2009. P&G's Febreze brand of air fresheners for use with residential air-filter products has been licensed to Imagine One Resources since 2010. The Febreze brand was licensed to Kaz USA for an odor-controlling standing fan in 2012. P&G-licensed products generated billions of dollars in annual revenues, although the portion returned to the firm as fees is not known (Glazer, 2012).

Although firms with global objectives may choose to invest directly in facilities abroad, there are a number of reasons why global strategic alliances may be more attractive, especially among small entrepreneurial firms. Due to the complexities associated with establishing operations across borders, strategic alliances may be particularly attractive to firms seeking to expand their global involvement. Companies often possess market, regulatory, and other knowledge about their domestic markets, but may need to "partner" with companies abroad to gain access to this knowledge as it pertains to international markets.

International strategic alliances can also provide entry into a global market, access to the partner's knowledge about the foreign market, and risk sharing with the partner firm. They can work effectively when partners can learn from each other, when neither partner is large enough to function alone, and both partners share common strategic goals but are not in direct competition.

A number of problems can arise from international joint ventures. These challenges include the potential for disputes and lack of trust over proprietary knowledge, cultural differences between the partnering firms, and disputes over how to share the costs and revenues associated with the partnership.

Other conservative options are also available to a firm seeking an international presence. Under an international licensing agreement, a foreign licensee purchases the rights to produce a company's products and or use its technology in the licensee's country. This arrangement is common among pharmaceutical firms. This arrangement is common in the pharmaceutical industry, where drug producers in one nation typically allow producers in other nations to produce and market their products abroad (Merchant & Schendel, 2000; Powers & Jones, 2001). However, licensing tends to be best in large firms with combinations of strategic activities, as well as firms with standardized products in narrowly defined market niches.

In contrast to international licensing, international franchising is a more extensive arrangement whereby a local franchisee pays a franchiser in another country for the right to use the franchiser's brand names, promotion, materials, and procedures. While licensing tends to be pursued primarily by manufacturers, franchising is more commonly employed in service industries, such as fast-food restaurants. Led by companies such as Burger King, KFC, Avis, and Coca-Cola, American firms now franchise to over 50,000 local entrepreneurs abroad.

Multinational Orientation

The second option, involvement at the multinational level, is more aggressive than the first. Under this approach, a firm pursues direct investments in other countries, and their subsidiaries operate independently of one another. For example, Colgate-Palmolive has attained a large worldwide market share through its decentralized operations in a number of foreign markets.

In some respects, the multinational orientation represents a transition structure as a firm moves from minimal international involvement to a global orientation. For some firms, however, it provides a fixed strategic position, offering the advantage of greater strategic control.

Global Orientation

The third option, global involvement, is the most aggressive of the three. Globally involved firms pursue direct investments and interdependent subdivisions abroad. Effectively, global firms approach the international marketplace with relatively standardized products.

A global orientation is often associated with established, mature firms. For example, some of Caterpillar's subsidiaries produce components in different countries, while other subsidiaries assemble these components, and still other units sell the finished products. As a result, Caterpillar has achieved a low-cost position by producing its own heavy components for its large global market. If its various subsidiaries operated independently and only produced for their individual regional markets, Caterpillar would be unable to realize these vast economies of scale (Parnell, 2017).

Selecting the Proper Orientation

Firms shift from a domestic mindset to a global mindset for numerous reasons. Pursuing global markets can reduce per-unit production costs by increasing volume. A global strategy can extend the product life cycle of products whose domestic markets may be declining. Establishing facilities abroad can also help a firm benefit from comparative advantage, the difference in resources among nations that provide cost advantages for the production of some but not all goods in a given country. For example, athletic shoes tend to be produced most efficiently in parts of Asia where rubber is plentiful and labor is less costly. A global orientation can also lessen risk because demand and competitive factors tend to vary among nations. There are a number of factors to consider, including the similarity of customer needs abroad to those in the firm's domestic market, differences in production and distribution costs, and regulatory and tariff concerns.

A global orientation brings about three key advantages for firms adopting a global perspective, the first of which centers around economic concerns. The multinational corporation (MNC)—contrasted with a firm operating only in domestic markets—can increase production levels, thereby fostering standardization and economies of scale (Llonch-Andreu, López-Lomelí, & Gómez-Villanueva, 2016). When a firm produces more, it may also enjoy greater efficiencies in marketing and distribution, a phenomenon known as *economies of (global) scope*. The importance of scope economies relative to scale economies has increased in recent years.

The second advantage of globalization is related to cultural change. Global media and the pervasiveness of the Internet have created a global consumer culture, one where distinct localized preferences for particular goods and services have been replaced by higher quality and cheaper offerings bearing global brands (Llonch-Andreu, López-Lomelí, & Gómez-Villanueva, 2016). This shift has enabled firms to address the needs of customers in different markets with common products, services, and marketing approaches. Because consumers are more familiar with the products and services available in other countries, they are likely to be more open to uniform offerings, as opposed to those tailored to the specific needs of a given locale.

Third, a globalization perspective can also foster growth outside of a firm's host country. Given the intense competition in most markets in the developed world, organizations seeking to grow must remain abreast of opportunities that may exist, especially in emerging economies. "Thinking global" enables a firm to seek out and recognize and pursue such opportunities with greater effectiveness.

Whether a firm should pursue international involvement and if so to what extent depends on a number of factors (Parnell, 2017). The following questions may shed light on the appropriateness of a global approach for a firm:

1. Are customer needs abroad similar to those in the firm's domestic market? If so, it may be possible for the firm to develop economies of scale (discussed in greater detail in a future chapter) by producing a higher volume of the same good or service for both markets.

2. Are differences in transportation and other costs abroad favorable and conducive to producing goods and services abroad? Are these differences favorable and conducive to exporting or importing good from one country to another?

3. Are the firm's customers or partners already involved in global business? If so, it may be necessary for the firm to become equally involved.

4. Will it be difficult to distribute goods and services abroad? If competitors already control distribution channels in another country, expansion into that country will be difficult.

5. Will government trade policies facilitate or hinder global expansion? For example, NAFTA facilitates trade among firms in United States, Canada, and Mexico. Similar trading blocks, such as the European Union (EU) occur in other parts of the world.

6. Will managers in one country be able to learn from managers in other countries? If so, it is possible that global expansion can improve efficiency and effectiveness, both abroad and in the host country.

Strategy Formulation: Issues at the Business Level

Innovation—transforming an invention into a commercially viable product or service—is central to the development of competitive strategy in the entrepreneurial firm. Global opportunities for innovation are prevalent, but developing a competitive strategy for a business operating in global markets is not easy.

Entrepreneurial businesses often face barriers to entry facilitated by their more established rivals. Single-runway Silver Comet Field—located 30 miles northwest of Atlanta—discovered this when Delta Airlines began fighting its effort to introduce four daily commuter flights on the grounds that doing so would threaten "Atlanta's economy." Hartsfield-Jackson Atlanta International Airport is a Delta hub and operates 922,000 commercial flights with 203 gates and 58,000 employees. Dallas, Georgia's Silver Comet Field has one gate and two employees. But as a Delta representative put it, "a second airport can quickly expand, and the impact on Hartsfield-Jackson would be significant." Atlanta is the only city in United States among the most populous 10 that lacks at least one secondary commercial airport, something that Propeller Investments, the private-equity firm managing Silver Comet, is trying to change. Bret Smith, Propeller's managing director, noted that Delta has "controlled and dominated the Atlanta market in a way that no other carrier has been able to in any other large metro area" (Carey & McWhirter, 2013).

These barriers can be overcome, however, although doing so can require upstarts to compete on a limited or domestic basis at the outset. For example, global shippers like UPS and FedEx are facing a growing threat from small, regional shippers like LaserShip, Inc., Pitt Ohio, and OnTrac. Regional shippers contract with large customers like Amazon.com to deliver packages in certain areas for 20–40% less than national shippers charge. These shippers form networks, with two or more often working together to deliver a given package. They concentrate on high volume in select geographical areas to cut costs below those of the delivery giants. Because they can reduce costs in urban regions, regional shippers account for a growing share of the delivery market (Stevens, 2013).

There is no simple formula for executing successful business strategies across national borders. Broadly speaking, there are two basic approaches to global strategy orientation, the first of which is associated with the common advice, "think globally, act locally." Following this logic, a business organization would emphasize the synergy created by serving multiple markets globally, but formulate a distinct competitive strategy for each specific market that is tailored to its unique situation. Others argue that an alternative approach—consistency across global markets—is critical, citing examples such as Coca-Cola, whose emphasis on quality, brand recognition, and a small world theme has been successful in a number of global markets. These two approaches represent distinct perspectives on what it takes to be successful in foreign markets.

The first approach, localization (i.e., "acting local"), implies that a firm gives its primary attention to issues at the local level. For a domestic firm, this simply means that its managers are concerned only with domestic issues and do not actively entertain activities outside of the host country. Indeed, globalization may not be appropriate for every firm. Demand for the firm's products or services may not be sufficient to justify global expansion. Rivals in other countries may already be serving the relevant markets effectively in those locales. Channel complexities abroad may necessitate packaging, manufacturing, or distribution changes that are too costly for the firm. Even differences in the availability of ingredients or preferences for styles or flavors associated with the firm can create roadblocks (Asher, 2005). Hence, "acting local" is all that is required for organizations whose strategies suggest that managers "think local." For a firm operating across borders, localization suggests that strategies reflect a strong effort to tailor firm activities to the specific needs of each location.

In contrast, a firm can "act global" by adopting a global perspective on strategy. A number of scholars and practitioners have argued for such an approach. Levitt, Ohmae, and others have long contended that international firms can only survive if they develop global strategies that reflect the growing similarities across disparate markets (Levitt, 1983; Ohmae, 1989). Such firms typically have direct investments and interdependent subdivisions abroad. For example, some of Caterpillar's subsidiaries produce components in different countries, while other subsidiaries assemble these components, and still other units sell the finished products. As a result, Caterpillar has achieved a low-cost position by producing its own heavy components for its large global market. If its various subsidiaries operated independently and produced only for their individual regional markets, Caterpillar would be unable to realize these vast economies of scale and enjoy the benefits of a global strategy.

A localization strategy also has its challenges. Tailoring a business strategy to meet the unique demands of a different market requires that top managers understand the similarities and differences between the markets from both industry and cultural perspectives. This can be difficult. For example, when a Western firm seeks to conduct business with one of its Chinese counterparts, managers from both firms must recognize the cultural differences between the two nations. For example, Chinese managers are more likely than Americans to smoke during meetings and less likely to answer e-mail from international partners. In the United States, it is more common to emphasize subordinate contributions to solving problems, whereas Chinese managers are more likely to respect the judgment of their superiors without subordinate involvement.

Consider Coca-Cola's global approach to marketing the popular soft drink, one that has been relatively consistent across borders. Some product differences exist, however, due to availability and cost factors. In Mexico, for example, Coke contains readily available cane sugar. In United States where customers are not believed to perceive a major difference in sweeteners, Coke changed to high-fructose corn syrup, a less expensive alternative (Terhune, 2006). Compared to Coca-Cola, Yum Brands takes a more localized approach with its KFC business unit. KFC's product offerings emphasize chicken, but can vary markedly from one nation to another.

Given the intense competition in most markets in the developed world, entrepreneurial firms often seek opportunities in emerging markets. While emerging economies such as the BRIC nations, South Africa, Mexico, and parts of Eastern Europe are attractive in many respects, poor infrastructure (e.g., telecommunications, highways, etc.), cumbersome government regulations, and/or a poorly training work force can create great challenges for the firm considering expansion. The advantages notwithstanding, growth through global expansion should be considered carefully before pursuing expansion into any emerging market.

China, for example, boasts the world's largest population and has been tabbed as a world economic leader within the next few decades. At present, China remains a mix of the traditional lifestyle based in socialism and its own form of a neo-Western economic development. Nowhere is this friction seen best than on the roads of Beijing, where crowds of bicycles and pedestrians attempt to negotiate traffic with buses and a rapidly increasing number of personal automobiles. American-style traffic reports have even become pervasive in a country where the world's largest automakers are fighting for a stake in what seems to have become a consumer automobile growth phase of mammoth proportions (Leggett & Zaun, 2002; Chen, 2003).

Western manufacturers such as Eastman Kodak, Proctor & Gamble, Group Danone of France, and Siemens AG of Germany have already established a strong presence in China. A number of Western restaurants and retailers have also begun to expand aggressively into China, including U.S.-based McDonald's, Popeye's Chicken, and Wal-Mart. As the CEO of Yum, owner of KFC, Pizza Hut, and Taco Bell, put it, "China is an absolute gold mine for us" (Chang & Wonacott, 2003).

Africa also presents a number of opportunities to assertive, entrepreneurial firms. Yum Brands has amassing over 1000 locations in Africa. CEO David Novak cites the continent's large population, improved political stability, growing middle class, and cultural preference for chicken as reasons for the strategic interest. Although an estimated 61% of its residents currently live on less than $2 per day, Africa's middle class—those earning between $4 and $20 a day—is projected to increase to 1.1 billion, or 42% of the continent's population by 2060 (Jargon, 2010; Maylie, 2011).

Challenges in Africa are complex, however, and vary across nations. The value of the Ghanaian currency (the cedi) declined by about 10% during 2012; however, resulting in higher costs for products imported by KFCs in Ghana from other countries. In Nigeria, government restrictions prevent restaurants from importing chicken, prompting the KFCs there to add fish to their menus. The Kenyan government also prohibits the import of chicken, but KFC must pay a British–Kenyan monopoly $3 above market rates (Hinshaw, 2013).

Strategy Execution & Strategic Control

A number of execution issues are critical to the success of global entrepreneurs. Culture is a key concern in strategy implementation in any organization, but takes on additional importance within entrepreneurial enterprises. Cultural differences generally represent a major consideration for firms operating abroad, especially in strategy implementation efforts. In many respects, an organization's culture can be viewed as a subset of the national culture. Operating outside one's own country must overcome obstacles in areas such as leadership and maintaining a strong organizational culture. For example, leaders of some nations resist innovation and radical new approaches to conducting business, whereas others welcome such change. Such national tendencies often become a part of the culture of the organization in those countries (Pretorius, Millard, & Kruger, 2006).

The *self-reference criterion* also presents a potential problem. Managers often believe that the leadership styles and organizational culture that work in their home country should work elsewhere. However, like each nation, each organization has its own unique culture, traditions, values, and beliefs. Hence, organizational values and norms must be tailored to fit the unique culture of each country in which the organization operates, at least to some extent. This can create special challenges when firms from different countries become partners or even merge their organizations.

Strategic control, an extension of the execution process, consists of determining the extent to which the organization's strategies are successful in attaining its goals and objectives. Within strategic control efforts, adjustments to the strategy are made as necessary. The need for strategic control is brought about by two key factors, the first of which is the need to know how well the firm is performing. Without strategic control, there are no clear benchmarks and ultimately no reliable measurements of how the company is doing.

A second key factor supporting the need for strategic control is organizational and environmental uncertainty. Because strategic managers are not always able to accurately forecast the future, strategic control serves as a means of accounting for last-minute changes during the implementation process. The notion of strategic control has recently added a "continuous improvement" dimension, whereby strategic managers seek to improve the efficiency and effectiveness of all factors related to the strategy. This is particularly important within the realm of global entrepreneurship where uncertainty is high and constant strategic change is often required (Parnell, Lester, & Köseoglu, 2012).

One key strategic control consideration is that of crisis planning. Indeed, any organization can be faced with a *crisis*, any substantial disruption in operations that physically affects an organization, its basic assumptions, or its core activities (Burnett, 2002). Organizational crises can include any low-probability, high-impact event that threatens the livelihood of the organization. Crises are typically characterized by ambiguity of cause, effect, and means of resolution, and a belief that the organization must respond quickly (Crandall, Parnell, & Spillan, 2014; Parnell, 2015). *Crisis management* refers to the process of planning for and implementing the response to a wide range of negative events that could severely affect an organization. Some potential crisis events are more likely than others in certain types of firms. Airlines, for example, may focus crisis preparations on prospective events such as spikes in fuel prices and hijackings, whereas a small hardware store may plan for events such as the abrupt loss of a key employee or a natural disaster. The nature of the global environment, including economic and political instabilities, suggests that crisis planning should be a key concern of global entrepreneurs. Simply stated, entrepreneurial firms can and should prepare for the ones they are most likely to face.

Although the extent to which a firm is involved globally affects its crisis exposure, the link is complex. Ceteris paribus, involvement in global markets can *reduce* political and economic risk by reducing reliance on a single nation or region. However, involvement in countries and markets prone to crises can *increase* risk. For example, with myriad production facilities and approximately 140,000 employees in over 90 countries, Proctor and Gamble's geographical diversification enables the firm to survive crises induced by country- or region-specific factors such as war, political upheavals, currency devaluations, or catastrophic weather events. In contrast, LAN Airlines operates primarily in Peru, Chile and nearby nations. As a result, LAN is particularly susceptible to external triggers associated with South America. During Europe's financial crisis in the early 2010s, companies with a substantial European presence like McDonald's, Heineken and GlaxoSmithKline engaged in contingency planning and took other preventive measures such as reducing local Euro holdings to limit their exposure, especially in struggling nations like Greece, Italy and Spain (Fuhrmans & Cimilluca, 2012).

Summary

Global opportunities abound for entrepreneurial organizations. However, the turbulence, rapid pace of change, and often unpredictability of the global environment can create roadblocks for many firms. Executives in entrepreneurial enterprises, small or large, should take special care to understand the intricacies of the international arena before formulating its corporate and business strategies. Those who do can greatly improve the prospects for their firms' success in the global arena.

Global strategy formulation can be challenging for entrepreneurs. The common advice to "think globally, act locally" has merit, but not all successful firms in global markets have followed this approach. Entrepreneurs should understand both their own resources and the intricacies of their global markets before crafting a strategy.

Discussion Questions

1. What can entrepreneurs and prospective entrepreneurs learn from the resource-based and dynamic capabilities views?

2. How have global economic changes in the last two decades created opportunities for entrepreneurs? How is this changing with the "Brexit" vote in the United Kingdom and the election of President Trump in the United States?

3. What is the thesis of Thomas Friedman's bestseller, *The World is Flat?* What is the link between the flat world and global entrepreneurship?

4. Should global entrepreneurs follow the "think global, act local" advice? Why or why not?

5. How can the self-reference criterion create a challenge for global entrepreneurs? What can be done to overcome this challenge?

References

Ambrosini, V., & Bowman, C. (2009). What are dynamic capabilities and are they a useful construct in strategic management. *International Journal of Management Reviews, 11,* 29–49.

Amighini, A. A. (2012). China and India in the International Fragmentation of automobile production. *China Economic Review, 23,* 325–341.

Asher, J. (2005). Capturing a piece of the global market. *Brandweek, 46*(25), 2.0.

Augier, M., & Teece, D. (2009). Dynamic capabilities and the role of managers in business strategy and economic performance. *Organization Science, 20,* 410–421.

Bain, J. S. (1968). *Industrial Organization.* New York: Wiley.

Barney, J. (1991). Firm resources and sustained competitive advantage. *Journal of Management, 17,* 99–120.

Barney, J. B. (1986). Strategic factor markets: Expectations, luck, and business strategy. *Management Science, 42,* 1231–1241.

Barney, J. B. (1995). Looking inside for competitive advantage. *Academy of Management Executive, 19,* 49–61.

Bjornskov, C., & Foss, N. J. (2008). Economic freedom and entrepreneurial activity: Some cross-country evidence. *Public Choice, 134*(3–4), 307–328.

Bughin, J., & Manyika, J. (2013). Measuring the full impact of digital capital. *McKinsey Quarterly, 4*, 88–97.

Burnett, J. (2002). *Managing Business Crises: From Anticipation to Implementation*. Westport, CT: Quorum.

Carey, S., & McWhirter, C. (18 December 2013). Why is delta afraid of this tiny airport? *Wall Street Journal*, pp. B1,B2.

Chang, L., & Wonacott, P. (9 January 2003). Cracking China's market. *Wall Street Journal*, p. B1.

Chen, K. (2 January 2003). Beyond the traffic report. *Wall Street Journal*, pp. A1, A12.

Coase, R. (1990). *The firm, the market, and the law*. Chicago: University of Chicago Press.

Crandall, W. R., Parnell, J. A., & Spillan, J. E. (2014). *Crisis management: Leading in the new strategy landscape* (2nd ed.). Thousand Oaks, CA: Sage Publications.

Dwoskin, E. (14 February 2014). Pandora ads will tie music to politics. *Wall Street Journal*, pp. B1, B2.

Eisenhardt, K. M., & Martin, J. A. (2000). Dynamic capabilities: What are they? *Strategic Management Journal, 21*, 1105–1121.

Friedman, T. L. (2005). *The world is flat*. New York: Farrar, Straus and Giroux.

Fuhrmans, V., & Cimilluca, D. (1 June 2012). Business braces for Europe's worst. *Wall Street Journal*, pp. B1, B2.

Geringer, J. M., Tallman, S., & Olsen, D. M. (2000). Product and international diversification among Japanese multinational firms. *Strategic Management Journal, 21*, 51–80.

Glazer, E. (20 March 2012). P&G's $3 billion sideline. *Wall Street Journal*, pp. B1, B2.

Hawawini, G., Subramanian, V., & Verdin, P. (2003). Is performance driven by industry- or firm-specific factors? A new look at the evidence. *Strategic Management Journal, 24*, 1–16.

Hinshaw, D. (9-10 February 2013). KFC leads fast-food race to Africa. *Wall Street Journal*, pp. B1–B2.

Jargon, J. (8 December 2010). KFC savors potential in Africa. *Wall Street Journal*, pp. B1, B2.

Koellinger, P. (2008). Why are some entrepreneurs more innovative than others? *Small Business Economics, 31*(1), 21–37.

Koseoglu, M. A. Parnell, J. A., & Togalogu, C. (2013). Assessing the strategic relevance of organizatonal capabilities: Evidence from Turkish hotels. *International Journal of Management & Decision Making, 12*, 96–120

Kovios, P. (2016). Global importance of entrepreneurship. *Journal of Developmental Entrepreneurship, 21*(1), 1–2.

Leggett, K., & Zaun, T. (13 December 2002). World car makers race to keep up with China boom. *Wall Street Journal*, A1, A7.

Levitt, T. (1983). The globalization of markets. *Harvard Business Review, 83*(3), 92–102.

Liñán, F., & Moriano, J. A. (2016). Individualism and entrepreneurship: Does the Patter depend on the social context? *International Small Business Journal, 34,* 760–776

Llonch-Andreu, J., López-Lomelí, M. A., & Gómez-Villanueva, J. E. (2016). How local/global is your brand? *International Journal of Market Research, 58,* 795–813.

Malone, T., & Laubaucher, R. J. (1998). The dawn of the E-lance economy. *Harvard Business Review, 76*(5), 144–152.

Maylie, D. (1 December 2011). By foot, by bike, by taxi, Nestle expands in Africa. *Wall Street Journal*, pp. B1, B16.

McMullen, J. S., Bagby, D. R., & Palich, L. E. Economic freedom and the motivation to engage in entrepreneurial action. *Entrepreneurship Theory and Practice, 32*(5), 875–895.

Merchant, H., & Schendel, D. (2000). How do international joint ventures create shareholder value? *Strategic Management Journal, 21,* 723–737.

Morris, M. H., Davis, D. L., & Allen, J. W. (1994). Fostering corporate entrepreneurship: Cross-cultural comparisons of the importance of individualism versus collectivism. *Journal of International Business Studies, 25,* 65–89.

Ohmae, K. (1989). The global logic of strategic alliances. *Harvard Business Review, 89*(2), 143–154.

Parnell, J. A. (2006). Generic strategies after two decades: A reconceptualization of competitive strategy. *Management Decision, 44,* 1139–1154

Parnell, J. A. (2013). Uncertainty, generic strategy, generic clarity, and performance of retail SMEs in Peru, Argentina, and the United States. *Journal of Small Business Management, 51,* 215–234.

Parnell, J. A. (2015). Crisis management and strategic orientation in small and medium-sized enterprises (SMEs) in Peru, Mexico, and the United States. *Journal of Contingencies & Crisis Management, 23,* 221–233.

Parnell, J. A. (2017). *Strategic management: Theory and practice* (5th ed.). Solon, OH: Academic Media Solutions.

Parnell, J. A., & Hatem, T. (1999). Cultural antecedents of behavioral differences between American and Egyptian Managers. *Journal of Management Studies, 36,* 399–418.

Parnell, J. A., Lester, D. L., & M.A. Köseoglu. (2012). How environmental uncertainty affects the business strategy-performance link in SMEs: Evidence from China, Turkey, and the United States. *Management Decision, 50,* 546–568.

Porter, M. E. (1981). The contributions of industrial organization to strategic management. *Academy of Management Review, 6,* 609–620.

Powers, T. L., & Jones, R. C. (2001). Strategic combinations and their evolution in the global marketplace. *Thunderbird International Business Review, 43*, 525–534.

Pretorius, M., Millard, S. M., & Kruger, M. E. (2006). The relationship between implementation, creativity, and innovativeness in small business ventures. *Management Dynamics, 15*(1), 2–13.

Raiszadeh, F. M. E., Helms, M. M., & Varner, M. C. (1993). How can Eastern Europe help American manufacturers? *The International Executive, 35*, 357–365.

Scherer, F. M., & Ross, D. (1990). *Industrial market structure and economic performance*. Boston: Houghton-Mifflin.

Seth, A., & Thomas, H. (1994). Theories of the firm: Implications for strategy research. *Journal of Management Studies, 31*, 165–191.

Stevens, L. (19 December, 2013). A new threat to UPS and FedEx. *Wall Street Journal, 19*, B1, B2.

Tapscott, D., Ticoll, D., & Lowy, A. (2000). *Digital capital: Harnessing the power of business webs*. Boston: Harvard Business School Press.

Teece, D., Peteraf, M., & Leih, S. (2016). Dynamic capabilities and organizational agility: Risk, uncertainty and strategy in the innovation economy. *California Management Review, 58*(4), 13–35.

Terhune, C. (11 January 2006). U.S. Thirst for Mexican Cola Poses Sticky Problem for Coke. *Wall Street Journal*, pp. A1, A10.

Todd, T. (16 October 2013). France slams brakes on minicabs after taxi pressure. *France 24*, www.france24.com/en/20131016-france-puts-brakes-minicabs-after-taxi-pressure.

Vranica, S. (24 March 2014). Man vs. bot: The online-ad wars. *Wall Street Journal, 24*, pp. B1, B5.

White, G., Guldiken, O., Hemphill, T., He, W., & Khoobdeh, S. (2016). Trends in international strategic management research from 2000 to 2–13: Text mining and bibliometric analyses. *Management International Review, 56*, 35–65.

Zajac, E. J. Kraatz, M. S., & Bresser, R. K. F. (2000). Modeling the dynamics of strategic fit: A normative approach to strategic change. *Strategic Management Journal, 21*, 429–453.

International Business Plan

Joan Gillman and Kira Henschel

Director, Special Industry Programs, Wisconsin School of Business, University of Wisconsin–Madison

CEO, HenschelHAUS Publishing, Inc.

Key Terms

Planning

Logistics

Finance

Investors

Marketing

Culture

Learning Objective

Upon completion of this chapter, students should be able to:

1. Familiarize themselves with the concepts of business planning and the key differences between a domestic plan and an international one.

International Business Plans

You're not just building a business plan to seek funding or get started. You're building a strategic roadmap for your business for years to come. It's a living, dynamic document that you can go back to year after year. It will be adjusted and changed, based on the realities of the marketplace, but it's a great document to work from.

—Don Kuratko, Professor, Ball State University

Planning is the act that makes all subsequent actions go well—whether you're taking a trip, writing a book—building your business internationally. Business plans are not just tools for start-up businesses, they are dynamic documents that serve as guidelines throughout the life of your enterprise, whether you remain domestic or seek to do business abroad.

Business planning is a two-step process: first you do the strategic work of research and planning, *then* you document the plan in writing. The purpose of an international business plan is to prepare your business for entering or expanding in the international market place. Deciding to operate outside the United States adds a whole new level to the business planning. Each section of your business plan has its own research needs, so you can break your plan down into manageable chunks, rather than dealing with the whole daunting process at once. This is particularly important when you become involved in the international arena, for in addition to the global opportunities that may exist, you must now include potential barriers to entry, such as:

- the stability of the government
- language(s)
- cultural differences
- banking and finance systems
- customs (product entry/exit issues)
- international tax issues
- legal and regulatory issues (product registration, environmental compliance, etc.), and
- operational structure (own, lease, subsidiary, branch, utilities, plant and equipment).

Use the Internet to find out more about your prospective country or countries in these categories. There are several practical resources available, such as the Global Entrepreneurship Index and GEM, the Global Entrepreneurship Monitor. Most banks with international branches are also able to provide statistics, facts, and figures on specific countries.

How much is enough when creating your international business plan? A typical plan will run 25–50 pages in length, probably somewhat longer when considering nondomestic information. Back up your narrative with facts and cite your sources. Do your homework and show your audience that you know the business you're in.

Know Your Audience

First and foremost, you are writing this plan for YOU and your company! If you are an entrepreneur with a small company, your plan provides a roadmap for you to follow. Or perhaps you are creating this plan for a larger organization to expand abroad. Whatever the case, other "audiences" for your plan are:

- the financial community, who will want to see the feasibility of your business substantiated by facts and figures, especially if you're seeking funding;
- potential investors;
- potential managers and other key personnel;
- potential joint venture partners;
- potential landlords;
- potential vendors;
- advisors like your accountant, lawyer, or spouse;
- agencies in the country/countries in which you wish to do business.

What Business Are You Really In? Can It Be Taken Abroad?

Answering these questions is particularly important when deciding to become involved in the international business arena. Large or small companies and the individuals who run them are in the same business—figuring out what their customers need and want, and what they can do to provide some portion of that better than any competitor can. Are you also working with other businesses (business-to-business transactions) or business-to-consumer?

Other questions that need to be considered include: Are you importing, exporting, or both? What are the market opportunities for your goods or services? Most importantly, will they be viable over the long term? Becoming an international business takes time, and above all, patience.

Regardless of your product or service, you are also in the technology business. Crossing borders, time zones, and cultures means using today's technology to better serve your business and your customers. Part of your plan must be staying current on technological developments, and maximizing them in your operations.

What are Your Plans for Growth?

Steven Covey's adage "Start with the end in mind" is particularly true in international business. Your plan should include concepts for the evolution of your business. Even in this ever changing world, you may discover strategic opportunities by focusing on your particular strengths and your unique position, product or service. Are you already operating a successful business domestically and wish to expand by going abroad, or is your business internationally oriented from the start? This will play a significant role in your international business plan.

How far into the future should you plan? Like the captain of a ship, you need to keep your eye on a point far enough out that, if you see a threat or an opportunity, you have time to react to it. The planning horizon is the time required to put a strategic plan in place. It is typical for businesses to form detailed plans for the next 12 months, somewhat less detailed plans for the subsequent year or two, and then simply define visions and values that will guide your choices beyond that horizon. International business development may take considerably longer than building the same company or operation domestically. The questions to ask yourself: Where do I want to be in 10 years, 20, 30? Do I want to grow this business to sell? Whether to pass on to future generations? How big do I want to be?

The ancient philosopher Heraclitus once said, "You never step into the same river twice." In a business, like a river, the environment is fluid. Even if your goal is to remain the same, you must work to stay where you are, or you will find yourself swept along by the current.

Components of Your International Business Plan

An international business plan should include the following main components: front matter, marketing, personnel, financials, and a closing.

Front matter

This should be the last part of your plan that you write. It should include:

- A cover letter
- A nondisclosure statement
- A title page
- A table of contents
- An executive summary
- A business description
- Vision and mission statements.

Potential investors, lenders, employees, customers, and vendors all want to know what your vision of the business is. More importantly, you want to know. Because of the complexity of operating internationally, this may be the most important work you do in your business. It will continually guide what you on what to do and what not to do.

Marketing

The marketing section of your international business plan is the blueprint that keeps you building upward toward customer satisfaction and business success. It should cover, at a minimum, a:

- Market analysis (industry analysis, competitive analysis, customer analysis)
- Description of products/services offered
    - o Are your products/services culturally appropriate?
    - o Does the name of your product/service work in the country/countries in which you seek to do business?
- Marketing plan
    - o Discuss the different aspects of marketing with your particular international markets in mind (product, price, packaging, position, presentation)
    - o Are there legal restrictions for your product/service? Some countries are stricter than others with regard to components, packaging, etc. Do your research! Don't assume because your product/service is acceptable in your home country that it will be successful in your target market.

Personnel

An international business plan is only as strong as the people who execute it. The purpose of the personnel section is to build faith in the business's management team. It helps demonstrate that you and your team have the skills to run your marketing, operations, and financial functions domestically and/or abroad. It is important to provide backgrounds for all key personnel. Depending on the country/countries in which you wish to operate, you may also need to include foreign personnel, either from an operational standpoint or to comply with national requirements.

- Management team
- Staff team
- Plans for growth

Financials

Financial data is how the game of business is scored. This important information indicates the life or death of your business. The financial section reports on how the company has done in the past, and projects how it will perform in the future, about 3–5 five years down the road. This section should include some or all of the following:

- Profit and loss statement
- Cash flow forecast
- Balance sheet
- Break-even analysis
- Assumptions and comments

A soundly conceived and well-prepared financial section is crucial to anyone seeking to secure investors or lenders. For international businesses, exchange rate fluctuations and differing banking and accounting systems add an additional level of complexity. Get the advice of professionals who are familiar with the financial culture of the country or countries you with which you wish to be involved.

Summary

This section rounds up the key facts and presents the final statement of purpose for the international business plan. Most bankers will flip to the back of a plan to assess how well thought-out and thorough the plan is. A typical final section of a business plan might include the following:

- Closing summary statement
- Applications and effects of loans
- Supporting documents (personal financial statements, resumes, positive newspaper articles about the business and other credibility builders).

Writing an international business plan requires a substantial investment of your time and thought, even more than a domestic business plan. To help guide the process, a checklist is provided below for you. Involve others in the process. Get advice and feedback on your plan. Share it with your accountant, your banker, and others you feel would contribute valuable information and support.

A word of advice: *Writing* an international business plan is not enough. You've got to move on it, to take action. Plan, write, line up resources, then go! An ideal business plan will, ideally, be accompanied by an ideal presentation in person by the business owner. It's important to have a positive mental attitude and learn how to leverage your best characteristics to make everything come together. It's essential to believe in what you can do, and that confidence needs to come through in the writing of the plan and in its presentation to others.

A closing thought on creating your international business plan, or planning in general: creating a plan forces you to set goals. Remember the Cheshire Cat in Lewis Carroll's *Alice in Wonderland* asking a lost Alice, "Where are you going?" when she asked directions. "I don't know," answered Alice. The Cat replied, "If you don't know where you're going, it doesn't matter which way you go." Defining goals and means of achieving them is what planning is all about.

International Business Plan Outline

I. Cover Sheet

A. Title of the document

B. Presented to

C. Applicant

D. Date

II. Table of Contents

III. Executive Summary (*usually written last; not more than 2 pages*)

This is an important section of the plan because it should provide a concise overview of the complete plan. Often a lender or prospective investor may read only this section and the financial plan.

A. Brief Description of the Business

- Products/services
- Legal structure
- Background/history of the business
- Is business new to international business or this plan for the international expansion of an existing business

B. The Opportunity

- Market
- Industry
- Competition
- Niche/strategy

C. Financials

- Sales projections
- Profit potential
- Growth potential

D. The People; identify owners, officers, and other key personnel, as well as the management team.

E. The Offering

IV. The Business

A. The Nature of the Business (type and legal structure)

- Start-up or existing business
- Type of business (manufacturing, wholesale, retail, service)
- Legal structure (proprietorship/partnership, LLC, corporation)
- General information (location(s), hours of operation)

B. Product/Service
- What is the product/service?
- What are you selling?
  - ○ price
  - ○ selection
  - ○ service
  - ○ quality
  - ○ convenience
- How will the product/service be produced/marketed?
- Who will buy it?
- Proprietary information

C. History of the Business
- Date the business began operations
- Chain of ownership
- Significant changes in the business product/service line, location/facilities, marketing strategy, capitalization
- Summary of sales and profit history

D. The Business Opportunity
- Sales by size/dollars/units
- Profitability
- Market share
- Based on market analysis

V. The Industry

A. Present Status

B. Trends Impacting the Business/Industry
- Technology
- Economy
- Political
- Legal
- Demographic
- Social

C. Characteristics of Firms in the Industry
- Average firm size
- Cost structure
- Typical profit margins, gross and net
- Seasonal sales patterns
- Other important characteristics

D. Industry Outlook/Forecast

E. Data Sources

VI. The Market

A. Define the Market

- Customer category (consumer, business, industrial, institutional, government)
- Define *need* for product/service
- Geographic coverage (distance, time, traffic patterns, topographic considerations, social and cultural considerations)
- Demographic target (age, income, gender, employment, education, residence, family status, race, religion)
- Psychographic characteristics

B. Quantify the Market

- Size
- Trends
- Local issues
- Based on demographic and geographic definition of the market

C. Profile the Competition

- Who are your competitors?
- Where are they located?
- How do they/you compare?
- Nature and status of each competitor

D. Marketing Strategy

- Competitive focus (price, quality, service, selection, convenience)
- Marketing methods
- Marketing channels
- Channels of distribution
- Advertising/promotion plan

VII. Location

A. Site

- Size
- Physical character
- Legal constraints on use

B. Facilities

- Buildings
- Storage

C. Linkages
- Traffic
- Accessibility
- Convenience
- Exposure
- Parking
- Suppliers
- Competitors
- Market

VIII. Business Objectives

A. Annual profit targets

B. Annual sales growth rate

C. Rate of return on investment

D. Rate of return on equity

IX. Technical Considerations

A. Process/Technology
- Present
- State of the art
- Special applications, considerations, constraints
- Trends

B. Raw materials/inventory
- Requirements
- Sources/availability
- Suppliers

C. Proprietary information
- Patents/Tradenames/Trademarks/Copyright
- Process
- Product

X. Management/Personnel

A. Organization
- Organizational chart
- Major responsibilities of key managers
- Ownership structure
- Board of Directors

B. Management Team
- Resumes of key management personnel
- Strengths and weaknesses
- Personnel
- Compensation (wages and salaries, benefits; legal requirements in country(s))
- Level of investment by managers

XI. Potential Risks and Problems
- What potential problems could arise?
- How likely are they to occur?
- Plan to meet or overcome problems/risks

XII. Financial
A. Projected Income Statement
- 3 years minimum
- Assumptions

B. Projected Balance Sheet
- 3 years minimum
- Assumptions

C. Cash Flow Statement
- First year monthly, second and third years quarterly
- Assumptions

D. Business Valuation
- Methodology
- Assumptions
- Estimated value

E. Break-Even Analysis

F. Sensitivity Analysis
- Assumptions
- "What-if" analysis

XIII. The Offering
A. Capitalization

B. Terms

C. Sources and uses of funds

D. Ownership structure

E. Projected Return to Investors

XIV. Supporting Documents

    A. Organization

    B. Credit reports

    C. Letters of intent or sales agreements

    D. Lease and purchase agreements

    E. Options

    F. Copies of leases

    G. Contracts

    H. Permits and licenses

    I. Insurance (domestic, international as appropriate for country/ies)

    J. Letters of reference

    K. Business development schedule

    L. Resumes

    M. Other issues

Discussion Questions

1. Why is a business plan important when moving a client organization international?

2. What is the most important part of the business plan for your client?

3. Why is financial information important in a business plan?

4. How might the triple bottom line of sustainable strategic management comes into play when developing a business plan?

5. What client might you want to work with in this class?

6. Given the introduction to business plans given in this chapter what might you want to focus upon with your client?

7. How might an international business plan differ from one done for a similar domestic firm?

Additional References/Resources

Gillman, J. (2001). *Business plans that work.* Holbrook, MA: Adams Media.

Alterowitz R., & Zonderman, J. (2002). *Financing your new or growing business.* Entrepreneur Press, 2002.

Schroeder, C. *Specialty shop retailing, how to run your own store, revised.* New York: Wiley.

Small Business Administration
WWW Address: www.sba.gov/oit/info
Description: The U.S. Small Business Administration provides a plethora of information on exporting, international business plans, and other aspects of international business
—www.sba.gov/starting/indexbusplans.html

Small Business Advisor—www.isquare.com/
Information and tools for Small Business—www.entrepreneur.com/

U.S. Commercial Service—Department of Commerce
WWW Address: http://www.export.gov
Description: The U.S. Department of Commerce, the U.S. Small Business Administration, and the Export–Import Bank formed a unique partnership to establish Export Assistant Centers, a network of one-stop shops which deliver a comprehensive array of export counseling and trade financing services to export-ready firms in one convenient location. The sole purpose of these offices is the promotion of U.S. exports.

Strategies
WWW Address: http://strategis.ic.gc.ca/engdoc/main.html
Description: Canada's most comprehensive Internet site. This site provides a plethora of information for exporting companies, including trade facts, market research reports, industry sector analyses, trade statistics, and foreign investment information. Strategies offers many of the services that the US Department of Commerce Commercial Service offers and is a useful site concerning doing business in Canada.

North American Industrial Classification System
WWW Address: http://www.census.gov/ftp/pub/epcd/www/naics.html
Description: The North American Industry Classification System (NAICS) is replacing the U.S. Standard Industrial Classification (SIC) system. NAICS will reshape the way we view our changing economy. NAICS was developed jointly by United States, Canada, and Mexico to provide new comparability in statistics about business activity across North America.

2017 Global Entrepreneurship Index. From the Global Entrepreneurship and Development Institute. Retrieved from https://thegedi.org/2017-global-entrepreneurship-index/

Global Entrepreneurship Monitor. (2017). Retrieved from http://gemconsortium.org/
Description: The Global Entrepreneurship Monitor is the world's foremost study of entrepreneurship. Through a vast, centrally coordinated, internationally executed data collection effort, GEM is able to provide high quality information, comprehensive reports, and interesting stories, which greatly enhance the understanding of the entrepreneurial phenomenon—but it is more than that. It is also an ever growing community of believers in the transformative benefits of entrepreneurship.
GEM is a trusted resource on entrepreneurship for key international organizations like the United Nations, World Economic Forum, World Bank, and the Organization for Economic Co-operation and Development (OECD), providing custom datasets, special reports and expert opinion.
These important bodies leverage GEM's rich data, tried-and-tested methodology and network of local experts to promote evidence-based policies towards entrepreneurship around the world.

The White House. *Executive Order—Global Entrepreneurship.* (2016, June 24). Retrieved from https://obamawhitehouse.archives.gov/the-press-office/2016/06/24/executive-order-global-entrepreneurship

Business Opportunities for Global Entrepreneurship

Alvin J. Jackson, Jr.

Centurion American Development Group, Dallas, Texas

Key Terms

E-commerce and technological change

Global market integration

Intrapreneurial culture

Protectionism

Learning Objectives

Upon completion of this chapter, students should be able to:

1. Understand entrepreneurial compatibility.
2. Understand global opportunities for small businesses.
3. Understand corporate culture as it relates to entrepreneurship.
4. Understand economic challenges, including global market integration and inflation.
5. Understand political systems and perspectives.
6. Understand social and cultural differences.
7. Understand technological effects.
8. Understand market entry approaches.

Part One: Introduction

The last decade of the twentieth century has shown that modern changes can occur in a short period of time in our modern economic history. If we take a look in our rearview mirror, we will notice our bridges for travel no longer constrain us to a limited portion of a specific state, county, or governing country. The roadmap has been extended beyond borders, which has changed the scope of our national and global marketplace. Many people have cruised the globalization steering wheel down the information superhighway. Many organizations have sped this journey up through the development and changes of corporate compatibility. Some people have placed their vehicle on cruise control, making sure to stay on the path that leads through each valley, canyon, and causeway.

What is their purpose? Who will be the one behind the wheel establishing the new face of international expansion? The spirit of international entrepreneurship is a major contributing factor that has affected the way people expand their horizons. No longer does one feel that the road to entrepreneurism stops within the borders of their own country. The key elements of entrepreneurial drive and the economic, political, technological, and social changes that have occurred over the last decade have dramatically created business opportunities for global business.

International entrepreneurship has led pioneers and others down the paths of entrepreneurship freedom, stopping at every nook, corner, and valley to find the opportunities that will unfold in today's emerging international markets.

Knowing You Have Entrepreneurial Compatibility

Entrepreneurial drive is a society that is unlike other organization's existence in today's global economies of scale. The entrepreneur's passion is to conquer and seize opportunities that most individuals would not tackle and do not have the emotions to stomach. Their motivation is to be a steward for change through innovative products or services. They have a creative mind that can think independently about ideas of success and failure. Most entrepreneurs are known for their hard work and their dedication to their respective businesses. Entrepreneurs have established themselves as risk-takers and leaders of optimism. These unique men and women make up a strong percentage of today's innovators as the leaders of global expansion in the twenty-first century.

Keys of Entrepreneurial Drive

Entrepreneurs have a unique form of identity from their inception as leaders in our business forefront. These keen attributes lead highly talented individuals to be less resistant to change and provides them with a burning desire for resiliency to succeed. The entrepreneurial drive sets the table for everyone to have the business savvy or opportunity to succeed.

The key ingredients to entrepreneurial drive are:

- Ability to *seize opportunities* for personal and professional benefit
- *Creative* ability to develop business opportunities
- *Independent thinker*
- *Hard worker* and so is their environment
- *Optimistic—uncertainty* does not bother these types of individuals
- *Innovator—the* strongest quality of an entrepreneur
- *Risk taker*
- *Visionary*
- *Leader*

The entrepreneurial drive seizes opportunities that will benefit them both personally and professionally. Entrepreneurs have a tendency to be hard workers, and they carry these same expectations into their environment. Optimism drives their spirit and the uncertainty does not bother these type of individuals. The entrepreneurial spirit establishes one's ability to be a risk taker and have a vision for the success of their idea. They have to be innovators to the products and services they sell and a leader that reflects the environment of their strategic vision.

Multinational Corporations and Global Markets

From the late 1940s through the late 1960s, multinational corporations (MNCs) from the United States had little competition in global markets (Cateora & Graham, 1999). In fact, MNCs were the only forms of organizations allowed to eat in the lion's den of China for several years. Today, smaller firms have the ability to develop business opportunities through smaller companies who take fewer resources and operational cost to secure an opportunity in the global marketspace.

More and more American entrepreneurs are embarking on the road to China, and many have found their fortunes. Over the past two decades, as China has liberalized its economy, several large companies have prospered by moving manufacturing into China or, more rarely, by producing goods for the Chinese market (Kurlantzic, 2004). Investments by major organizations like GM, Volkswagen, and other major automobile manufacturers are drastically expanding their operations in China. The behemoths have faced several roads that are hard to overcome because of their intensive size and labor costs. The corporate streamline of a major multinational organization only absorbs the ideas of a loose idea thinker.

Global Opportunities for Small Businesses

Yet, more than often not, major multinationals have found making money in China considerably harder than expected (Kuratko, Montagno, & Hornsby, 1990). With intensive operational cost, small entrepreneurs and businesses have been able to seize the opportunity in the international markets of China.

Entrepreneurs and Second Chances

In 1990, Tommy Hodinh founded his own logistic company. Hodinh was a Vietnamese refugee who arrived in the United States in 1972. At the tender age of eighteen, with limited English skills, Hodinh managed to put himself through college. He then worked for IBM for fifteen years, first as an engineer and later as a member of the IBM management team. The whole time he worked for "Big Blue" he knew he wanted to do something else. "I always wished I had the money to start my own company. I had the experience, but I didn't have the capital."

By the 1990s, the barriers to starting a small technology company had dropped considerably. Hodinh realized it did not cost that much to start a company anymore. Since small office space was reasonably priced and the cost to become incorporated was a few thousand dollars, he was able to embark on starting his new venture with his savings. In 1990, Hodinh cofounded MagRabbit Incorporated, which is a software duplication and logistics company based out of Austin, Texas. The first six years were considered the growing years of slow and steady growth, which led to securing a commercial bank loan for MagRabbit. Today, MagRabbit now has more than one hundred employees, nearly $10 million in annual sales, and clients around the world.

Hodinh proved to himself to seek an opportunity for his personal and professional benefit. Not only did he overcome the obstacles of cofounding MagRabbit Incorporated, Hodinh was the first person of Asian American descent in the software business in Austin, Texas.

Key Ingredient for Success

Hodinh was concerned about *seizing* opportunities to start his own business and knew he had the talent from management experience with a Fortune 500 company like IBM. In 1990, Hodinh seized the opportunities to develop technology and proved that his strategic window would lead him to entrepreneur success in the southwest region of the United States, which would later be known as "The Silicon Valley of the South."

(Adapted from Kurlantzic, J. About face—the face of entrepreneurship. *Entrepreneur Magazine.* January 2004: 62. See also http://www.magrabbit.com/current/Press_Entrepreneur.htm.)

Many corporations have faced the difficulties of working with multinational corporations and the powers of strategic alliances in the Chinese markets. Small businesses like Robert Kushner's Pacific China Industries, Ltd. have been able to open the gates of China and have been well received in the Chinese market. One contributing factor to their success as small business entrepreneurs is the research and study time placed in the international markets with a smaller team focus and a smaller scales strategy that has captured the short-term audience of the Chinese market (Lee, 2004). Robert's personal savvy led him to China. His professional drive helped him to understand the cultural differences that would lead to the expansion of his company's products and services.

Pacific China Industries, Ltd.

Robert Kushner is the founder and managing director of Pacific China Industries, Ltd. PCI is a fifteen-person company that develops and manufactures novelties in China. PCI is full of tchotchke products from dancing rock stars to dashboard mounts.

(Adapted from Kurlantzic J. Promised Land. *Entrepreneur Magazine.* January 2004: 66–69.)

The Entrepreneurial Test

Entrepreneurial compatibility is influenced by people who think *independently*. The people who are "outside the box" and have difficulty conforming to structure remove themselves from the foundation of a corporation. Some major corporations embrace this spirit and formulate the ideas to be incorporated with their strategic plans and vision. If they are unsuccessful in their environment, the entrepreneurial tendency is to take the optimistic approach and leave the corporate structure and develop a flat structure with the correct environment for business.

Intrapreneurial or Entrepreneurial? That is the Question

The intrapreneurial or entrepreneurial culture is more prevalent today as the world economy becomes more globalized. An *intrapreneurial culture* has formulated strategies with a positive outlook toward global expansion for many MNCs.

A Kindred Intrapreneurial Spirit

The Tokyo Disneyland Success

Multinational organizations that embrace the intrapreneurial spirit have been successful in market globalization in international markets. These tales account for detailed marketing mistakes and successes. Walt Disney has let optimism blind their initiative for value, research, and intrapreneurial cultural stewardship.

Tokyo Disneyland opened in 1983 on 201 acres in the Eastern suburb of Urazasu. The Orientland ownership group would build, own, and operate the theme park while Disney would advise and consult the Orientland group. Orientland borrowed approximately $650 million that would be needed to bring the project to fruition. Disney invested no money but received 10% of the revenues from admission and rides and 5% of sales on food, drink, and souvenirs.

While the Japanese took some time to respond, by 1990 they began flocking to Tokyo Disneyland by the millions. By 1990, some 16 million a year passed through the turnstiles, about one-fourth more than visited Disneyland in California. In the fiscal year of 1990, revenues reached $988 million with profits of over $150 million. Indicative of the Japanese preoccupation with things "American," the parks serve almost no Japanese food and the live entertainers are mostly American.

As success heightened in Tokyo, Disneyland executives were soon to realize they had been successful in expanding into global markets, but could have gained a significant portion of revenue generation by taking a substantial amount of ownership in Tokyo Disneyland.

Optimism

The intrapreneurial culture directed by Michael Eisner and the Disney executive team provides a close relationship between the executive management team and the board of directors of Walt Disney. These similar qualities or interests led the intrapreneurial culture that established significant strategic initiatives for Walt Disney from the early eighties through the end of the 1990s with Euro Disney.

(Adapted from Sterngold, J. Cinderella hits her stride in Tokyo. *New York Times* 17 February 1991: 6.)

If intrapreneurial opportunities decline within the strategic vision of a corporation, many bright minds either become an extension or leave the organization to build their own organization of leadership and vision. This spirit is defined as *intrapreneurial culture* and the environment will develop a strategic vision.

These two types of culture lead to positive organizational communities in small and major business opportunities (Kurlantzic, 2003). MNCs have expanded the spirit of the intrapreneurial vision, which has led to global expansion in their respective industries. The entrepreneurial leader undertakes the mission of defending their vision, which, in return, leads to opportunities that major organizations have not researched and developed. That is why the entrepreneur is able to overcome big business and, more importantly, able to understand the entrepreneurial process at an international level in emerging markets in the United States, Europe, and Asia.

The Economic Challenges of International Entrepreneurship

The economic compatibility that will lead the wave of international expansion through hearts of compassionate and new ventured entrepreneurs will have to adapt and change to the constant economic filters of geographic economics. The issues of foreign trade have produced barriers to entry for all opportunists who would like to expand their business into global markets.

The United States has seen a rise in debt over the past few years. From mid-2000, the US and global economies have weakened significantly following one of the largest stock market declines in the postwar period, the terrorist attacks of September 11, 2001, major internal combustion in major corporations leading to corporate failure, and the wars in Iraq (Layman, 1991).

These economic events have had a significant impact on the judgment of idealists to produce opportunities in the national and global markets. The economic picture in the United States has played a major role in the impact on the emerging markets in Eastern Europe, Asia, and Latin America. The US budget deficit, global interest rates, and the U.S. dollar have been exposed by the debt linked to the US government and policy (Layman, 1999). It has developed adverse effects on short- and long-term interest rates. The traditional distribution structures in Japan, Europe, and other countries have seen rapid changes to barriers into key markets for small businesses that offer products and services.

The United States has been a major player to the world economic outlook. The high levels of foreign currency denominated debt, as such countries have become extremely sensitive to global real interest rates (European Communities, 1995–2003).The outcome has left the opportunity for global markets to accelerate. This phase will withdraw the fiscal stimulus over the next decade, leading to economic global expansion, in a manner that pays due attention to incentives to work and invest in the United States. Many corporations now seek nonintensive labor markets to secure employment to reduce overhead costs and make their organization more profitable for their short- and long-term economic goals.

Entrepreneurs understand that countries will have to increase the flexibility of their economies through structural reforms and speed up their economies through their own integration into the global economy.

Global Market Integration

The economic picture today is one of several bundled hot buttons. Each geographic region of the world has now been integrated to the advancement in technology and services. This threshold has developed several key communication channels that have broken down the environment of semantics and sparked the interest for organizations to consider global integration.

Though many U.S. consumers associate globalization with leading multinationals like Coca-Cola or GE that have huge operations in many countries, small businesses have actually been one of the main drivers of global integration. According to the U.S. Department of Commerce, between 1987 and 1999, the number of small and mid-sized U.S. exporters more than tripled to 224,000 (Astrachan & Carey Shanker. (2003). By 1999, 97% of American exporters were small businesses, though smaller exporters still only accounted for one-third of total U.S. export sales (Miller & Friesen, 1985).

Entrepreneur's Venture

It is apparent that venture capitalist may worry that too much cash is chasing too few good deals. Entrepreneurs in key sectors are realizing the opportunity is changing seasons. The springtime for funding by venture capitalists would support this statement since there have been significant contributions to specific industry sectors over the last seven years.

Entrepreneurs who have focused in these industry sectors have seen the cash come their way from venture capitalist organizations. Based on numbers listed by 2003 amount invested, these are the key areas that venture capitalists have been far from bean counting:

1. **Connectivity/Communication Tools**—Accel Partners, Intel Capital, and Microsoft are sharing this round of funding with some $38 million for Groove Networks, Beverly, Massachusetts, whose peer-to-peer technology creates secure, virtual workspaces that can be used by widely dispersed people.

2. **Biotechnology**—Favrille, a four-year-old San Diego-based biotech that has developed personalized cancer treatment made from a patient's own tumors, secured $44 million in funding in April. Two days later, the company registered with the SEC for an initial public offering.

3. **Non-Financial Business Services**—Menlo Ventures, NEA, Alloy Ventures, and Deutsche Post Ventures handed over $20 million plus in funding to an organization called Open Harbor. The San Carlos, California based company's software helps global businesses deal with the ever-changing worldwide trade regulations. DHL is standardizing its custom processes with Open Harbor's software.

(Adapted from Florian, E. The venture rebound. *Fortune Magazine* 3 May 2004: 115–116.)

Global Inflation

According to *Grolier's* online encyclopedia, *inflation* is a process in which the average level of prices increases at a substantial rate over a considerable period of time. In short, more money is required to buy a given amount of goods and services. An understanding of *global inflation* is key to building opportunities in international entrepreneurship simply because it is a foothold to your revenue stream in your international venture(s) of business. For the first time in the history of the world, inflation is a universal phenomenon with all currencies tied together. Global inflation outlines the environment for which you formulate certain strategies as they affect different segments of the global marketspace.

Emerging Global Markets

Emerging markets in Eastern Europe, Asia, and Latin America are where more than 75% of the growth in world trade over the next twenty years is expected to occur (Cateora & Graham, 1999). The *reunification* of Hong Kong, Macau, and China has placed all Asians under the control of the same Asian leaders for the first time in over a century.

After more than four centuries, the final remnant of European occupation of Chinese territory was repatriated. The handover of Macau was an event of great importance to the Chinese leadership in what is viewed as the major struggle of this century. The outcome has restored the Chinese territory and sovereignty from outside occupation and exploitation. The country has been a hot spot for the last five years since the Chinese systems have wanted to integrate the key economic financial systems from the one country (Layman, 1999). The significant importance for international entrepreneurship is that the value of their monetary system holds limited complexity in the pursuit of valuations toward currency, which could develop a critical thinking system toward your organization's entrance into the marketplace.

The *European Monetary Union* and the switch from local country currencies to one monetary unit for Europe illustrate the global integration movement of the twenty-first century. In 1978 the community decided to re-launch monetary integration at the Brussels European Council by creating a *European Monetary System* (EMS), with the objectives of stabilizing exchange rates, reducing inflation, and preparing for monetary integration (European communities, 1995–2003). *Euro* is the currency of twenty-seven European Union countries, stretching from the Mediterranean to the Arctic Circle. Euro banknotes and coins have been in circulation since January 1, 2002, and are now a part of daily life for over 300 million Europeans living in the euro area (European communities, 1995–2003).

China as the Engine of the Global Economy

It has been speculated that, because of accumulated debts, the United States is losing its ability to provide a strong source of demand that supports the growth of the global economy. This is considered structural incompatibility putting global growth at risk, which goes further and concludes that an unsustainable potential deficit in global demand now exists as a consequence of the way in which the monetary and financial systems of major East Asian economies are managed—a deficit which the United States has temporarily filled by creation of credit.

The United States has compensated for the East Asian demand deficit by providing the main source of global demand growth for a decade, but the United States has also experienced financial imbalances as a result (a large current account deficit and accumulated debts). And this has only been able to continue because changes to the global financial system in the early 1970s permitted sustained trade deficits to be financed by creating money (rather than balanced with gold reserves).

At the same time, high levels of public spending have been needed to sustain demand in other major economies (i.e., China, France, Germany, Italy, Japan), resulting in some cases of public debt levels that are also becoming critical considering the costs and benefits of common currencies and, by implication, the relative desirability of fixed versus flexible exchange rates.

Economic Outlook for Global Markets

In 2003, strong global economic growth has been anticipated, with an initial expectation that growth would be sustained by US demand.

However, the US economy suffers fiscal imbalances (namely large current account deficits and foreign debts), which many observers have seen as a threat to the sustainability of US and global growth.

(From Center for Policy and Development China's Development: Assessing the Implications, Queensland and Australia. September 2002–October 2003.)

The *International Monetary Fund* (IMF) and the World Bank Group are two global institutions created to assist nations in becoming and remaining economically viable (Cateora & Graham, 1991).

To balance the inadequate monetary reserves and unstable currencies, the IMF was formed to resolve these issues. So long as these conditions exist, world markets cannot develop and function as effectively as they should. The IMF helps overcome these particular market barriers, which plagued international trading before World War II (Cateora & Graham, 1999). Originally, the IMF was an agreement signed by twenty-nine countries. Today, over 181 countries are members of the IMF.

Entrepreneurs must understand the importance of this economic environment because it plays an important role in international trade by helping maintain the stability in the financial markets and by assisting countries that are seeking economic development and restructuring.

Microsoft Evaluates the International Price Challenges

Gartner, Inc., Market Research Reports Microsoft Dealings in Emerging Asian Markets

The Microsoft Corporation recently lowered the cost of a package that includes its Windows operating system and Office suite of software in Thailand to $40, according to a report from market research firm Gartner, Inc. The move, according to Gartner, is in response to the increasing use of the Linux operating system. Gartner indicates that the company may take similar price cuts in China as well. The cost of the same package in the United States starts at about $380.

1. Will the cost differentiation change Microsoft's market share in the Thailand environment?
2. Was this a good decision on Microsoft's entry into the Thailand software market?
3. Explain why you feel Microsoft made the cut back in the international region?
4. Do you feel Microsoft's decision was right in making this move in Thailand?
5. How do you feel it will affect their revenue in China versus the United States?

(Adapted from Technology and Newsbytes, *Biz Education*, November-December 2003 and complete history and description from Gartner, Inc., http://www3.gartner.com/Init.)

The International Entrepreneur Political Perspective

The emerging global economy brings together unity and global nations, which provides outlets of competition. Worldwide competition gives an opportunity for entrepreneurs as well as the buying consumer population. The roadways that open also creates a market capitalization which endorses free enterprise in new markets and small markets that are considered large enough to become viable opportunities.

The main concern of the twenty-first century will be the geopolitical forces that monitor and issue policy for the exchange of goods and services in the global markets. As competition develops in certain markets, the contingency for *protectionism* will become the hot button in most respective markets. The passions for trade will grow, which has already been established in the last decade of the twentieth century. The economies of the industrialized world have entered their mature state of the product life cycle and will be more than modest over the next twenty years.

Protectionism

Protectionism helps nations utilize legal barriers, exchange barriers, and psychological barriers to restrain entry of unwanted goods.

Protectionism on trade maintains these rules for barriers to entry for government restrictions on trade to:

1. protect infant industries
2. protect home markets
3. keep money in home country
4. encourage capital accumulation
5. maintain the standard of living and real wages
6. conserve natural resources
7. industrialize a low wage nation
8. maintain employment and reduction of unemployment
9. increase national defense
10. increase business size for respective industry
11. increase retaliation, bargaining, and negotiation power.

Protectionism is established to make global markets conscious of their worldwide shortage of raw materials and natural resources.

(Adapted from Woellert L. Why do nations tariff? *The World and I* July 1997: 64.)

The Organization for Economic Cooperation and Development (OECD) estimates that the economies of the OECD member countries will expand about 3% annually for the next twenty-five years, the same rate as the past twenty-five years (Robbins, 2003). Organizations like the World Trade Organization (WTO) were formed to help the social, political, and economic changes that will lead the global economy to the future victories in international trade and policy.

The World Trade Organization (WTO)

The United States was a catalyst in the expansion of the definition of trade issues. At the signing of the Uruguay Round trade agreement in Marrakech, Morocco, in April 1994, US representatives pushed for an enormous expansion on trade which resulted in the creation of the WTO, which encompasses the General Agreement on Trades and Tariffs (GATT) structure and extends to new areas not adequately covered in the past few policies for trade.

The WTO is an institution that sets the rules for trade between its 132 members, provides a panel of experts to hear the rule on trade, and disputes between members, leading to binding decisions on trade policy.

(Adapted complete history and description of WTO visit http://wto.org/.)

The European Union (EU)

The European Union is a unique, treaty-based, institutional framework that defines and manages economic and political cooperation among its twenty-seven European member countries. The Union is the latest stage in a process of integration begun in the 1950s by six countries—Belgium, France, Germany, Italy, Luxembourg, and the Netherlands—whose leaders signed the original treaties establishing various forms of European integration.

These treaties gave life to the novel concept that, by creating communities of shared sovereignty in matters of coal and steel production, trade, and nuclear energy, another war in Europe would be unthinkable. While common EU policies have evolved in a number of other sectors since then, the fundamental goal of the Union remains the same: to create an ever-closer union among the peoples of Europe.

(Adapted from http://www.eurunion.org/infores/euguide/Chapter1.htm.)

General Agreement on Tariffs and Trade

The United States and twenty-two countries signed the General Agreement on Tariffs and Trade (GATT) shortly after World War II. This agreement paved the way for the first effective worldwide trade agreements to be conducted into policy. The agreement provides a process to reduce tariffs and created an agency to serve as a watchdog over world trade.

(Adapted from Complete description and history of GATT visit http://www.wto.org/wto/about/about.htm.)

When an entrepreneur is formulating a strategic decision to enter a global market, you should keep in mind the different geopolitical challenges. You should know your state of controllable and uncontrollable initiatives when entering a market. With the continued strengthening of opportunities in international entrepreneurship one must focus on the continued strengthening and creation of regional market groups:

European Union (EU)

North American Free Trade Agreement (NAFTA)

ASEAN Free Trade Area (AFTA)

Free Trade Area of America (FTAA)

Southern Cone Free Trade Area (Mercosur)

Asia-Pacific Economic Cooperation (APEC)

The market groups have enabled entrepreneurs in emerging markets and helped to protect policy and practices of business worldwide. Entrepreneurs will constantly have to examine the way they conduct business and remain flexible enough to react to the rapidly changing global trends to be competitive.

When an entrepreneur seizes an opportunity in global markets, there are several factors he or she should consider to entering an emerging market for global business. Key areas for an entrepreneur to understand when researching opportunities in global markets include:

1. Understanding the balance of trade relationship between merchandise imports and exports in prospective target markets.

2. Extensively researching the political forces of the global environment to have alternative outlines for strategy and implementation for barriers to enter market(s).

3. Understanding the development of domestic industry and how countries will protect existing industry: establishing tariffs, quotas, boycotts, monetary barriers, non-tariff barrier, and market barriers (Cateora & Graham, 1999).

The market groups and research techniques will be explored in later chapters of experimental exercises and the areas of study chapters of this book. The political and legal issues for an entrepreneur will be a challenging process for one to win in their quest for international emergence for global markets.

Social and Cultural Differences in International Markets

Social policy covers a great number of issues which do not stand on their own but, as is increasingly recognized, are both diverse and interlinked. For example, tackling social exclusion involves simultaneously addressing barriers to labor market re-integration, health care issues, and educational aspects and their perception by different countries. Entrepreneurs must evaluate social indicators to provide the broad perspective needed for any international comparison and assessment of social trends and policies.

Social culture is very valuable in our professional and personal cultures. These indicators help set standards and practices that we implement in our daily activities, whether we are in a professional or personal environment.

Corporate Culture and Entrepreneurship

Since the 1990s, the need to pursue corporate entrepreneurship has arisen from a variety of pressing problems including technological changes, innovations, and improvements in the marketplace (Miller & Friesen, 1985).

The corporate culture has also formed a relative deprivation toward many entrepreneurial spirits that exist in this organizational culture. The spirit of the entrepreneur has perceived weakness in the traditional methods of corporate management (Hayes & Abernathy, 1980). Most of this is caused by power and influence from top-level management and corporate streamlining. The chain of command takes control and the end result is the loss of entrepreneurial-minded employees who are disenchanted with bureaucratic organizations (Cisco Systems, 2001).

The bureaucracy enables other organizations to find opportunities and opens the door for organizations that possess a flatter structure. The world globalization has helped open doors that used to be closed. New technologies and the pursuit of core competencies has led to growing levels of international competition.

The pursuit of corporate entrepreneurship as a strategy to counter these problems, however, creates a newer and potentially more complex set of challenges on both a practical and a theoretical level. On a practical level, organizations need guidelines to direct or redirect resources toward establishing effective entrepreneurial strategies. On a theoretical level, researchers need to continually reassess the components or dimensions that explain and shape the environment in which corporate entrepreneurship flourishes.

Workforce Diversity and Globalization

Organizations understand that they are no longer constrained to their natural national borders. A British firm owns Burger King, and McDonald's sells burgers in many different eastern countries. American companies receive almost 75% of their revenues from sales outside the United States (Kanter, 1985). These examples illustrate that the world has become a global outlet and community. In return, entrepreneurs have become capable of working with people from different cultures. *Globalization* has led many organizations to *adapt* to working with people of different ethnic descent and understanding the opportunities to work with managers in different markets representing different cultures. To work effectively in different cultures, entrepreneurs must understand the significance of the cultures they wish to build relationships and customer rapport with as well as adapt their management style to their differences.

Workforce diversity must be addressed among people within given countries. Workforce diversity means that organizations are becoming more heterogeneous in terms of gender, race, and ethnicity. Workforce diversity is an issue in Canada, Australia, South Africa, Japan, and Europe as well as the United States. Managers in the United States and Canada are no longer in work groups that represent their country population (Kanter, 1985). Today, many of these countries have offices established in eastern parts of Asia and Europe, which develops an integration of different cultures working for the same purpose and mission.

Cultural Orientation and Integration

The increasing diversity of American society only enhanced small businesses' willingness to look abroad. As rising numbers of immigrants came to the United States in the 1990s from Latin America and South Asia and started businesses; a large number of those foreign-born entrepreneurs naturally looked to their homelands for export markets. In 2000, studies found that nearly one-third of all startups in Silicon Valley were led by a person of South Asian descent, many of whom outsourced a percentage of their companies' work to India or Pakistan (Kurlantzic, 2003).

Accelerated Vision to Value— An International Entrepreneurship Passion

i2 Technologies

i2 was founded in the late eighties by Sanjiv Sidhu and Ken Sharma, two visionaries in what was later to be known as supply chain management. Sanjiv and Ken's passion was to apply technology and best practices to eliminate inefficiencies in business. From humble beginnings in a two-bedroom Dallas apartment where the first program was created, i2 has grown today to over $1 billion in revenues with more than 1,000 customers and 500 deployments in the last year alone.

i2 recognizes the vast potential waiting to be unleashed in the value chain through value chain management, allowing collaboration across functions in a company as well as across companies in the value chain. This is the next frontier for increasing productivity, and the philosophy to which i2 is applying its expertise, passion, and technology.

i2 Technologies has stuck by this mission since its inception. The i2 philosophy basically believes if you take care of your customers, they will take care of themselves, which will lead to relationship development between i2 and the organization.

Sanjiv Sidhu founded i2 Technologies, Inc. in 1988 with the vision of helping businesses make more intelligent decisions by using information resources.

Under his leadership, i2 has grown to become a market leader, serving such powerhouse clients as Texas Instruments, 3M, IBM, Johnson & Johnson, Lipton, Ford Motor Company, Dell Computer, Toshiba, Warnaco, and Coca-Cola. In March 2000, he led the company through a merger with Aspect Development, the largest software industry merger to date. His multinational team of nearly 5,000 employees is one of the most experienced and highly educated workforces in the business.

Sidhu's overriding concern and the central tenet of his business philosophy is providing optimum value for i2's customers through value chain management. To that end, i2 goes beyond just pioneering and establishing e-business process optimization technology, to tie the technology directly to the value that customers will receive in savings and efficiencies in running their business.

Before starting i2, Sidhu was an engineer working in the world-renowned artificial intelligence laboratory at Texas Instruments in Dallas. Based on his observation that even the smartest people can juggle no more than nine variables when making decisions, he proposed a design for computer software based on artificial intelligence and advanced simulation techniques. The software he proposed enabled planners at Texas Instruments to dramatically improve the management of the production process by taking real-life constraints and variables into account when making planning decisions.

(Adapted from i2 Technologies Website http://www.i2.com/Home/Services/index.html.)

Elements for entrepreneur analysis on culture global markets focus on: (Herskovits, 1992).

1. Material culture—technology and economics
2. Social institutions—social organization, education, and political structures
3. Humans—their belief systems and values
4. Aesthetics—graphic and plastic arts, folklore, music, drama, and dance
5. Language—language barrier(s) and semantics

Understanding culture deals with a certain individual, group, or country's design in living. This is one of the most crucial research elements for opportunities in international entrepreneurship. One must analyze certain factors when evaluating cultural compatibility to meet the expectations of consumer needs for maximum profitability.

The Technological Effect on International Entrepreneurship

Technology has been a key to help move products from manufacturer to end-user, providing local inventory, technical product support, sales, and service. Technology moves at a record pace and sometimes, once obtained, is already obsolete. In today's world, technology is a challenging and ever-evolving field. New computer technologies, increased competition, and continued growth in global markets make today's opportunities for entrepreneurism remarkably different from what they were only a few years ago.

How It Affects Global Competition

The global competition challenge for entrepreneurs requires them to adapt with broad skills and an incredible ability to learn at faster paces than in previous decades of the technology workforce. The range for technology helps in the automating tasks for manufacturing, plant maintenance, construction operations, accounting, sales and marketing, purchasing, inventory, and profit management. The computer systems that are designed to carry the logistics of pinpoint tracking for packages have definitely helped cultivate the direction in distribution services. E-logistics and system integration makes an attractive force that will present an accurate tracking system in a distribution delivery environment.

The Information Superhighway

Since the mid-1990s, the Internet has become a technology phenomenon where there has been a strong beginning; however, there are no predictions on where it will end. It is a full-force market tool that has helped innovate the way we work, how we think, and how we deliver products and services. The Internet has also created extra value to our value chain. It helps us have direct access to goods and services, while also providing us updated current information on where the company's vision will be tomorrow.

With the growth in the use of the Internet, businesses more and more become e-businesses handling many transactions on the Web. Electronic mail and communication barriers are now more accessible than ever. New business ventures can communicate domestically as well as internationally. This has led to increased production and less expense to a company portfolio for small, medium, and major corporations. It has also led to more home-based businesses and a new way of how we view entrepreneurship.

The knowledge and software have been an intangible benefit to how entrepreneurs can conduct business. The Java programming language is one of the main drivers that have led to this e-commerce expansion. For an entrepreneur to understand that Extensible Markup Language (XML) and trans-coding are among the technologies supporting the infrastructure for e-business can be an essential advantage to their competition. From "bricks and mortar" companies to online e-commerce services, no one can get ahead without having the Internet in their market strategies for how they conduct business worldwide.

E-commerce: The Entrepreneur Tool of Technology and Production

E-commerce helps you compete in an increasingly demanding marketplace with a wide scope of domestic and international exposure. E-commerce has helped provide support to many of the major elite corporations that are publicly and privately traded. It has also been a major contributor to many small businesses and their business venture foundation. The production levels and expectations have helped balance the data analysis and implementation efforts that many organizations have had to commit to in order to landscape their e-commerce and Internet infrastructure.

Integrating e-commerce into your company means improved operations, decreased costs, increased sales, and facilitated communication with customers, partners, and employees. The recommendations are high, and the demand from consumers is to make sure that you have a gateway via the Internet. This helps create confidence in products and services that already have traditional value and help keep a relationship with efficient channels of production that establishes a legacy between business-to-consumer (B2C) and business-to-business (B2B) companies.

The Rate of Technological Change

In the early 1990s, Congress passed laws that helped enable the benchmarking in e-commerce. Technology has played a major role in all opportunities for entrepreneurism. The effects of e-commerce helped entrepreneurs exchange information plus provide products and services to local, national, and global markets.

Companies like Cisco Systems helped create a value chain to make networking products that could handle an enormous amount of data and route it from one computer to thousands of other locations within an intranet and Internet infrastructure. The company sits atop a $12 billion Web-enabled value chain. Cisco sits as the front-runner in providing core technologies that help build the network infrastructure (Cisco Systems, 2001).

Most companies today need these transmission facilities to exchange information and goods on the Wide Access Networks (WAN). Broadband systems generally are fiberoptic. Telephone companies are retrofitting their toll and exchange fibers to tie their networks into one synchronous optical network. The main challenge that all participants have experienced in placing this architecture is making the network capable of flowing freely and synchronously. It will take time because of how much money is involved. The telecom cannot keep spending at the rate they have been in years past because of the incredible amount of funding that is needed and the scarcity of resources. Broadband will arrive, but personally even two years is much too optimistic.

The roadmap for extending direct fiber connections to smaller business and residential customers will tie networks and communities together. This same architecture has potential application for residential customers. The industry is in the deployment of new technologies that make it economical for the first time to provide the virtually unlimited bandwidth of fiber to smaller customers, supporting new broadband service applications targeted to small businesses and all consumers. Consider this analysis:

In 1990, people discovered the capability of Windows and personal computers became a phenomenon. The value chain extended these links with the introduction to pathways and channels that have connected an estimated 200 million people in only ten years. Food for thought: it took television three times that long just to have 50 million in market penetration. This is one of the most effective management tools for aspiring entrepreneurs for global expansion.

Rate of New Product Introductions

The rate of new product introductions has moved faster than the rate of the Internet and e-commerce combined. This chain links all highly integrated companies to form alliances to see who can help innovate and re-innovate the technological products the fastest.

Companies are pouring millions of dollars to provide each link that connect these pieces of technology. The old technology phrase that comes to mind, "we are only two years from failure," that has definitely sent a message across the globe to all companies who want to contribute in new business innovations in technology.

Effect of the Internet on International Entrepreneurship

The Internet has changed the way the industry distributes goods and services. A major effect is how distribution companies evaluate their services for allocating and distributing goods. The customer today has much more emphasis on how their roles will affect the distribution industry. An efficient network that will facilitate the exchange and delivery for goods and services has had distribution companies. Distribution companies have had to create network optimization to obtain and control the flow process between the whereabouts and exact location of their goods and services through information. They have also had to implement and enhance logistics on their technology for product tracking. These are key elements that help keep their network alive and mobile for service production.

What Can Brown Do for You?

United Parcel Services

The UPS e-Logistics solution enables these online enterprises to leverage core UPS strengths—global delivery network, extensive IT systems, and supply chain management experience—to outsource the difficult "back-end" processes of running an e-business. It's a quick and cost-effective supply chain solution for small- and medium-sized B2B and B2C companies.

In an interview with UPS chairman James Kelly, he discusses how information technology has helped create new businesses from its delivery service. The company invested $1 billion a year, ten years ago. The focus of this investment was to try to make UPS available to receive and exchange information with customers.

Kelly's executive team wanted to re-engineer a company objective to meet the needs of the customer worldwide. In this way, he could exchange information with the customer and maintain fluent continuity with the transportation and logistics system networks. The average packages that are delivered from the industry are 13.5 million. The upgrade in their logistics system provided top-notch services that in return gave UPS the ability to tell their customers where their packages were and to use this information to provide broader services across the supply chain.

(Adapted from www.usps.com/archives/newsreleases/, United Parcel Services. June 2001.)

What Can Be Learned

Successful Business Opportunities in International Entrepreneurship

Most people understand the challenges they face when they opt to go into business for themselves. Everyone knows the road of having success in the corporate environment of small, medium, and large corporations. *Free enterprise* has been an incredible advantage to Americans in our national democracy. The freedom of private business to organize and operate for profit in a competitive system without interference by government beyond regulation necessary to protect public interest and keep the national economy in balance only exists in democratic forms similar to the United States. So how does that affect pursuing opportunities in our global society? Our assumption must take us back to the most important questions that anyone pursuing or seeking a business opportunity must face. Do you know if you are entrepreneurial compatible?

Entrepreneurial Savvy

The professional benefit of being successful with an international business opportunity will depend on one's self, as well as enabling others to act and share in the creating of the organization's mission. The entrepreneurial drive must lead others to understand the importance of ownership and empowerment in the organization. They must act as stewards who understand the organizational culture and environment. The organization as a whole must be optimistic and look for the opportunity to produce results. The entrepreneurial leader must model the way for the organizational community to understand their vision and purpose. A lot of soul searching will transpire for the entrepreneurial drive to catch on like a fever that is burning hot through their entire organizational community. Encouraging others and building an organizational environment that shares the optimistic uncertainty with a vision in mind will lead to a successful organization in today and tomorrow's global society.

Alternative Approaches of International Entrepreneurship

The international entrepreneur must know that he or she will place a lot of emphasis on the work ethic through the power of a vision or growth image, even if it is only an illusion. This is perhaps the most crucial strategy that must be set in motion early for a business opportunity to be successful from its embryonic beginnings.

The opportunities for business opportunities in the international marketplace for an entrepreneur are not as challenging as they were just one decade ago. There are several alternative approaches that can be utilized as a competitive advantage for the emergence into global markets.

- The Internet and its expanding role in international markets.
- The political and social integration of big emerging markets (Asia, Eastern Europe, Japan, and China).
- The economic spurt evolving in global middle-income households.
- The collaborative qualitative and quantitative research conducted by organizations through strategic alliances and corporate and functional development in major corporations and small businesses.
- Trends in channel structures in Europe, Japan, and developing structures.
- Ethics and social responsibility in today's global environment (Pride & Ferrell, 2000).

These different areas need to be evaluated by an idealist to formulate strategies for a successful road in breaking the international ground barriers. Many have attempted to examine particular factors associated with success in entrepreneurship such as the following:

- Financial Factors that Provide Opportunities for Entrepreneurs
  Lack of records is a main major contributor to the failure of a small business in the first ten years. Records are a major component and a major asset to the financial agenda. One must also remember the value of exchange rates as they are implementing strategies in the global environment.
- Incentive and Control Systems

Understanding the five P's,

1. *The purpose behind the opportunity*—This includes the leader's vision, mission, goals, and objectives, as well as strategies for achieving the mission and vision in a global market.

2. *The principles behind entering the market*—The principles, assumptions, philosophy, and attitude that the entrepreneur embraces through their organizational community.

3. *The processes for succession*—The organizational structure and procedures to make the products or services compatible in the organizational infrastructure to support the system and international structure.

4. *The outcome or performance that is expected*—If the leaders of the organizations have enabled all members of their organizations to buy into their mission and vision, the organizations' results will maximize profitability, which will lead to additional incentives and rewards based on performance.

5. *The people behind the idea* (Pryor, White, & Toombs, 1998)—The people are the most crucial foundation to the channels of your road to international embryonic success. These people are committed to believing in the purpose, the principles, and the process for the organization to succeed in the twenty-first century as we enter the globalization era.

- Market and Entry Approaches
  Examine cases of success and failure utilizing different marketing strategies to introduce products, services, and ideas into the marketplace. The entrepreneurial drive will lead to research in the areas which are barriers to entry in a global emerging market. The high barriers and/or expectations of swift retaliation from existing competitors lead to seven major barriers that develop the strategic windows for an entrepreneur to enter an emerging market.

  Economies of scale—For which the decline of unit costs of a product or service that occurs as the absolute volume of production in a given time period increases.

  Product differentiation—Established organizations may enjoy strong brand identification and customer loyalties that are based on actual or perceived product and service differences.

  Capital requirements—The need to invest large financial resources at the outset. This could become an important factor to your organization entering the emerging global market space.

  Switching costs—Referring to the one-time cost that buyers of the industry's outputs incur as they switch from one company's product or service to another. These are uncontrollable barriers that must be reviewed by an entrepreneur entering a major market that is uncharted by business outside the respective country(ies).

  Access to distribution channels—In some countries, entering existing distribution channels or country structures requires a new firm to entice distributors through price incentives (breaks), cooperative advertising allowances, or sales promotions.

Cost disadvantage independent of scale—Established organizations in globalization may possess cost advantages that cannot be replicated by new ventures and the threat of competition.

Government policy—The governing bodies of the respective countries will help control entry to certain types of industries that could affect the internal structures of cultures of business in the respective countries. Countries must pay close attention to policy and government regulations for aspiring entrepreneurship (Parnell, 2001).

Summary

An entrepreneur must understand all of the facts and assumptions for entering their idea into the global marketspace. Once this steward has assessed their organizational core competencies, they must evaluate the alternative approaches to make a successful launch into the twenty-first century with their newfound business product or services. These strategies will be discussed in later chapters of this book. The macroenvironments, economic, political, social, and market-driven/ technology demands need to be examined as possible causal factors in the success or failure of international entrepreneurship. The right drive, the right passion, and the right strategic window will lead unique men and women to be the revolutionary business leaders of global expansion in the twenty-first century.

Discussion Questions

1. What role do organizations like the International Monetary Fund, World Bank, and European Monetary System play in international trade?

2. What are some reasons a country would employ protectionist measures? What types of groups or organizations are in place in the global arena to mediate issues between countries with regard to protectionism?

3. Give an example of each of the three key areas that an entrepreneur should understand while researching global market opportunities: (1) balance of trade relationships; (2) political forces that affect entry to market; and (3) domestic industry development and how countries will protect their own existing industry.

4. Describe the five elements for analysis on culture that entrepreneurs should focus on when considering global markets according to Herskovits.

5. What effects has the Internet had on international entrepreneurship and how does it relate to its future?

References

Astrachan, Joseph H. & Melissa Carey Shanker. (2003) Family Business Review, 16 (3), 211–219.

Cateora, P., & Graham, J. (1999). *International marketing*. 10th ed. Boston, MA: McGraw-Hill.

Cisco Systems. (June 2001). www.cisco.com/archives/newsreleases/.

European Communities. (1995–2003). Legal notice. http://europa.eu.int/geninfo/ disclaimer_en.htm.

Hayes, R. H., & Abernathy, W. J. (1980, July-August). Managing our way to economic decline. *Harvard Business Review*, 67–77.

Herskovits, M. (1952). *Man and his works*. New York: Alfred A. Knopf, 634.

Kanter, R. M. (1985). Supporting innovation and venture development in established companies. *Journal of Business Venturing* 1:47–60.

Kuratko, D. F., Montagno, R. V., & Hornsby, J.S. (1990). Developing an intrapreneurial assessment instrument for an effective corporate entrepreneurial environment. *Strategic Management Journal* 11:49–58.

Kurlantzic, J. (2003, February). International success in today's world economy. *Entrepreneur Magazine*.

Kurlantzic, J. (2004, January). Promised land. *Entrepreneur Magazine*, 66–69.

Kurlantzic, J. (2003, February). Stay home? *Entrepreneur Magazine*, 66–69.

Layman, J. (1999, August-September). *Macau's handover to mainland China*. CSIS Hong Kong Update.

Lee, C. (2004, April). The global implications of the U.S. fiscal deficit and of China's growth. *World Economic Outlook*, 63–66.

Miller, D., & Friesen, P. (1985). Innovation in conservative and entrepreneurial firms: two models of strategic management. *Strategic Management Journal* 3:1–25.

Parnell, J. A. (2001). *Industry Competition. Strategic Management Concepts*. Texas A&M University Commerce: 23–26.

Pride, W., and Ferrell, O. C. (2000). *Marketing and its environment. Marketing concepts and strategies*. Boston: Houghton Mifflin Company, 79–107.

Pryor, M., White, J., & Toombs, L. (1998). Organizational variable and the five P's. *Strategic Quality Management*. Houston, TX: Dame Publications: 1–3.

Robbins, S. P. (2003). Challenges and opportunities of organizational behavior. In *Organizational Behavior*, 10th ed. New Jersey: Prentice Hall: 14.

Global Entrepreneurial Leadership Competencies

Denise M. Cumberland

University of Louisville, Louisville, KY

Key Terms

Competency

Ethnocentric firm

Geocentric enterprise

Global entrepreneurial leader

Global Mindset

Global perspective

Intellectual capital

Polycentric firm

Project GLOBE

Psychological capital

Social capital

Universal leadership attributes

Learning Objectives

Upon completion of this chapter, students should be able to:

1. Identify the common competencies entrepreneurs need

2. Understand what it means to be a global entrepreneurial leader

3. Understand the Global Leadership and Organizational Behavior Effectiveness (GLOBE) project's identification of universally positive, universally negative, and culturally contingent leadership traits

4. Define Global Mindset, the additional competencies the Global Mindset entails, and understand why these matter to global entrepreneurs

5. Understand how to foster a Global Mindset

6. Identify instruments that assess whether individuals have a Global Mindset

Contributed by Denise M. Cumberland. © Kendall Hunt Publishing Company.

Abstract

The subject of this chapter focuses on the specific competencies global entrepreneurial leaders must possess when their businesses expand across borders or are initiated as a global enterprise. This discussion of how global leaders *think* and *act* may help explain why some entrepreneurs succeed in a global environment and others do not.

Introduction

The three core dimensions of entrepreneurship include innovativeness, risk-taking, and pro-activeness (Covin & Slevin, 1991). Hence, entrepreneurs must be able to recognize opportunity, assume calculated risks with their career, their money and their time, have the ability to assemble an effective venture team, and the creative skill to acquire the needed resources (Kuratko, 2007). A key distinction between the domestic and global entrepreneur is the location of the firm's operations, suppliers, and/or customers. While some firms have chosen to remain domestically focused, a new breed of entrepreneur is venturing past familiar borders far earlier in the life cycle, and in some instances the venture is international at inception. The number of these "born global" firms continues to increase due to new technological breakthroughs, new transportation capabilities, and an increasing number of strategic alliance partnerships (Nummela, Saarenketo, & Puumalainen, 2004; Srinivas, 1995).

Where the venture operates, supplies are secured, and customers located allows for distinction between a domestic versus global enterprise. A subtler, yet critical difference between domestic and global firms is how the entrepreneurs who are navigating these organizations *think* and *act*. Though still limited in number, recent empirical studies have connected the presence of having a Global Mindset to the speed of internationalization (Nummela et al., 2004) and to positive financial performance (Felício, Caldeirinha, & Rodrigues, 2012). It is readily acknowledged that success in a domestic venture may not translate to success on the global stage and that management practices that are acceptable in one country may not be acceptable in a different country (Javidan, Dorfman, deLuque, & House, 2006; Jokinen, 2004). These realities create the need for entrepreneurs to understand the individual characteristics needed for gaining competitive advantage in the global marketplace.

The subject of this chapter focuses on the specific competencies global entrepreneurial leaders must possess when their businesses expand across borders or are initiated as a global enterprise. This discussion of how global leaders *think* and *act* may help explain why some entrepreneurs succeed in a global environment and others do not.

The Entrepreneurial Leader

The management literature recommends that leaders need to incorporate an "entrepreneurial mindset" to gain competitive advantage (McGrath & MacMillan, 2000). Certainly not all leaders will be considered entrepreneurs, but it can be argued that all entrepreneurs are leaders. Global entrepreneurial leaders are discovery-oriented individuals who can operate in a highly uncertain environment where they must continually reposition the organization to capture new opportunities (Gupta, MacMillan, & Surie, 2004).

Over the last 20 years, an explosion of scholarly work around the topic of global leadership competencies has emerged. Two critical questions that have surfaced include:

1. Do global leaders need a higher degree level of the skills they already possess, or

2. Do global leaders need additional competencies beyond what is required of their domestic counterparts? (Jokinen, 2004)

Most scholars of global leadership and most practitioners in the multinational arena collectively agree that the answer to both questions is "yes" (Brownell, 2006; Cant, 2004). The global context is more intense and those who operate on this stage need a higher degree of leadership skills than those operating domestically (Jokinen, 2004). Yet, just having more of the same skill is not enough; leaders must also possess an additional set of competencies to navigate the global firm (Brake, 1997; Felício et al., 2012; Javidan, Steers, & Hitt, 2007; Mendenhall, Osland, Bird, Oddou, & Maznevski, 2008; Nummela et al., 2004) (see Figure 6.1).

Following a discussion of core entrepreneurial competencies, this chapter explores the universal leadership attributes needed for global endeavors, and reviews the extra ingredient needed for global entrepreneurs, the presence of a Global Mindset. The chapter concludes by offering ideas for cultivating a Global Mindset and tools for assessing whether entrepreneurs demonstrate the global leadership competencies that comprise this mindset.

Figure 6.1　Visualization of interrelationship of leadership competencies

Core Entrepreneurial Competencies

Competencies describe underlying characteristics of an individual, which helps predict success at a task or on the job (Boyatzis, 1982). This broad term can also be defined as the knowledge, skills, and abilities (KSA's) that individuals possess, as well as personal traits that help them succeed in their endeavors (Tubbs & Schulz, 2006). In other words, competencies represent who an individual is as well as what they know (Brownell, 2006).

Understanding which competencies lead to superior entrepreneurial performance has been widely examined by researchers. Core competencies needed by entrepreneurial leaders include the ability to:

1. Identify opportunities
2. Create and articulate a vision
3. Mobilize resources
4. Negotiate deals
5. Build alliances (Isenberg, 2008)

Universal Leadership Competencies

During the 1980s and 1990s, the breakdown of market barriers due to technological advances, political upheavals, and especially the liberalization of trade policies, resulted in an increased level of global business activity (Bouquet, 2005; Srinivas, 1995). This rising global economy precipitated dialogue on the topic of global leadership. By the start of the twenty-first century, human resource managers were clamoring for competency-based models of global leadership that would identify the characteristics of leaders who could effectively operate in diverse cultures (Morrison, 2000).

One of the most comprehensive studies designed to understand the impact of specific cultural influences on leadership was the multiphase, multimethod project known as Global Leadership and Organizational Behavior Effectiveness (GLOBE; Morrison, 2000). Initiated as a longitudinal study, this research set out to answer, among others, the following fundamental questions:

1. Are there universally accepted leadership traits?
2. Are there universally unacceptable leadership traits?
3. Are there culturally contingent leadership traits? (House, Javidan, Hanges, & Dorfman, 2002)

The GLOBE project, led by Robert House, involved over 150 researchers and drew on the input of 17,000 managers across 62 countries working in different industries. Project GLOBE has identified three sets of competencies, including a list of 22 leadership traits that are universally perceived as positive, a list of 8 leadership traits that are universally perceived as negative and a list of 34 leadership traits that are culturally contingent (meaning these traits work in some cultures, but not in others) (Den Hartog et al., 1999). Tables 6.1–6.3 provide an overview of these characteristics. While the GLOBE study offers a basis for understanding competencies desirable for global leadership, it does not prove that these competencies are linked to effective global entrepreneurship. Rather, these characteristics offer a foundation for beginning research on global leadership competencies.

Table 6.1 Universally Positively Endorsed Leadership Attributes

INTEGRITY ATTRIBUTES	CHARISMATIC QUALITIES	TEAM CHARACTERISTICS	PROCESS TRAITS	OTHER QUALITIES
Trustworthy	Motivational	Team-builder	Plans ahead	Excellence
Just	Confidence-builder	Communicative	Foresighted	Decisive
Honest	Encouraging	Coordinator	Administratively skilled	Intelligent
Dependable	Positive	Win-Win problem Solver	Effective bargainer	Excellence-oriented
	Dynamic			Informed

Source: Adapted from Den Hartog et al. (1999)

Table 6.2 Universally Negatively Endorsed Leadership Attributes

Loner	Ruthless	Nonexplicit	Egocentric
Irritable	Dictatorial	Noncooperative	Asocial

Source: Adapted from Den Hartog et al. (1999).

Table 6.3 Partial List of Culturally Contingent Leadership Attributes

Individualistic	Enthusiastic	Procedural
Sincere	Compassionate	Worldly
Autonomous	Habitual	Ambitious
Orderly	Sensitive	Intuitive
Cautious	Logical	Self-effacing

Source: Adapted from Den Hartog et al. (1999).

The Extra Ingredient: A Global Mindset

The concept of a Global Mindset can be traced back to 1969 when researcher Howard Perlmutter suggested that those running overseas operations needed to develop a whole new mindset to successfully navigate the global market. Perlmutter argued that firms operate from one of three attitudinal states: first is the ethnocentric firm, which is home-country oriented; second is the polycentric firm, which is host-country oriented; and third is the geocentric firm, which is world oriented (Perlmutter, 1969). To become a geocentric enterprise, those leading the organization had to think geocentrically by eliminating cultural superiority (Perlmutter, 1969).

Before the liberalization of trade polices, a limited number of organizations were involved in global operations and Perlmutter's idea of geocentric enterprises lay dormant. As the twentieth century drew to a close, however, the global economy had expanded and it had become evident that success on the domestic front was not a guarantee for success in an international context. Scholars and practitioners alike returned to Perlmutter's thesis that global enterprises must be led by individuals who have distinct competencies above and beyond what it takes to thrive in a domestic setting. Books, practitioner journal articles, and academic research studies began to appear that tackled the subject of global leadership competencies.

One of the first academic works to reignite the discussion around global leadership competencies was published in 1992. In this seminal piece, Adler and Bartholomew (1992) offered the scholarly opinion that to be successful in a global marketplace, business leaders needed a "global perspective," which included the following skills:

1. Knowledge about many cultures
2. Willingness to learn from people from many cultures
3. Ability to live in many foreign cultures
4. Ability to interact with others from different cultures on a daily basis; and
5. Ability to interact with foreign colleagues as equals (Adler & Bartholomew, 1992).

A practitioner perspective at that same time argued that global business leaders needed a Global Mindset that included six distinct competencies:

1. Technical, business, and industry knowledge on a global basis
2. Conceptual ability to analyze issues and balance contradictory forces
3. Flexibility to adjust to global and local demands
4. Sensitivity to cultural diversity that includes a willingness to hearing others and question one's own assumptions
5. Judgment that allows for making decisions on experience not just data; and
6. Reflection that incorporates learning and continuous improvement (Rhinesmith, 1992).

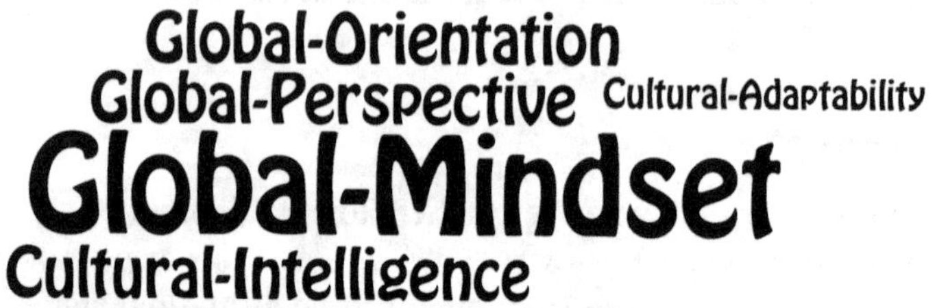

Not surprisingly, during the following decade different terms were used to describe the competencies that global leaders needed to either have, hone, or learn. The terminology ranged from *a global orientation and a global perspective to culture adaptability and cultural intelligence*. The description of having a *"Global Mindset,"* however, has been used most extensively in both practitioner and scholarly literature to describe the extra ingredient a global leader must possess (see Figure 6.2).

Global-Orientation
Global-Perspective Cultural-Adaptability
Global-Mindset
Cultural-Intelligence

Figure 6.2   **Terminology associated with global leadership**

Over the last 20 years, an explosion of work has attempted to define and operationalize what a Global Mindset entails. While the semantics in the 12 definitions in Table 6.4 differ, there is commonality in how Global Mindset is viewed. Across most of these definitional efforts, the core competencies that make up a Global Mindset include:

- A broad world view
- Knowledge about global business

- Cultural awareness and sensitivity
- Adaptability to different cultures
- An ability to influence others from diverse cultures; and a
- Cosmopolitan outlook.

Table 6.4	Definitions of a Global Mindset

WHAT IS A GLOBAL MINDSET?
Rhinesmith (1992): A Global Mindset means scanning the world from a broad perspective, always looking for unexpected trends and opportunities to achieve personal, professional, or organizational objectives. Individuals accept contradictions, trust process, value diversity, are adaptable, and rethink boundaries (Rhinesmith, 1992).
Srinvas (1995): A Global Mindset is a way of approaching the world—a tendency to scan the world from a broad perspective. Experience from practicing managers suggests that eight components form the base for competencies needed to meet the challenges in entering a global environment. These are: curiosity and concern with context, acceptance of complexity and its contractions, diversity consciousness and sensitivity, seeking opportunities and surprises, faith in organizational processes; focus on continual improvement, and extended time perspective and systems thinking (Srinvas, 1995).
Kefalas (1998): He suggests that a Global Mindset is a way of seeing the world as a whole, knowing how to search for similarities, exploiting those similarities to discover differences, and using the knowledge gained from the search to design and execute strategies that benefits all stakeholders (Kefalas, 1998).
Murtha, Lenway, and Bagozzi (1998): Operationalize Global Mindset at the individual level in terms of how managers think about the globalization process with respect to integration responsiveness and coordination (Murtha et al., 1998).
Gupta and Govindarajan (2002): A Global Mindset combines an openness to and awareness of diversity across cultures and markets with a propensity and ability to synthesize across this diversity (Gupta & Govindarajan, 2002).
Begley and Boyd (2003): They define a Global Mindset as the ability to develop and interpret criteria for business performance that are not dependent on the assumptions of a single country, culture, or context and to implement those criteria appropriately in different countries, cultures, and contexts (Begley & Boyd, 2003).
Nummela et al. (2004): A Global Mindset is similar to a global orientation for it describes a manager's openness to and awareness of cultural diversity and the ability to handle it (Nummela et al., 2004).
Levy, Beechler, Taylor, and Boyacigiller (2007): They conclude that a Global Mindset must combine an acute sense of the global business world while simultaneously being culturally adaptable (Levy et al., 2007).
Cohen (2010): A Global Mindset is the ability to influence individuals, groups, organizations, and systems that have different intellectual, social, and psychological knowledge or intelligence form your own. It requires you to know when it is beneficial to have a consistent global standard and when you need to have local elements. It is about openness and awareness of diversity across cultures and markets with a willingness to synthesize across this diversity (Cohen, 2010).
Javidan and Walker (2012): The Najafi Global Mindset Institute at Thunderbird School of Global Management scientifically defined Global Mindset as the set of attributes that help a manager influence individuals, groups, and organizations from diverse cultural, political, and institutional backgrounds. In short, Global Mindset is the capability to influence others unlike yourself, that is, the key difference between leadership and global leadership (Javidan & Walker, 2012).
Smith and Victorson (2012): A Global Mindset means understanding and applying your knowledge about the attitudes, feelings, and perceptions of different cultures and leveraging awareness of various continuums to influence others (Smith & Victorson, 2012).
Felico, Caldeirinha, and Rodrigues (2012): A Global Mindset refers to a set of individual attributes that enable an individual to influence other individuals, groups, and organizations from a diverse, social, cultural, and institutional systems (Felício et al., 2012).

*The author does not intend for this list to be comprehensive.

The Global Mindset Project

One of the more extensive research efforts conducted to empirically determine the scope and components of a Global Mindset began in 2004 at Thunderbird School of Management's Janafi Global Mindset Institute (Javidan & Walker, 2012). Eight professors reviewed the literature on global leadership, conducted interviews with 217 global business executives, and led a conference with 40 academic experts known for their scholarly contributions to the global business field (Javidan & Walker, 2012). Working with a renowned instrument design firm, the Global Mindset Project next operationalized the construct with a survey instrument given to 700 executives working in a global context (Javidan & Walker, 2012). From this work, the Global Mindset was found to have three core elements: intellectual capital, psychological capital, and social capital (Javidan & Walker, 2012). Project GLOBE went on to identify what KSAs comprise each of these three clusters (see Figure 6.3).

Global Mindset

| Figure 6.3 | Three core elements of a Global Mindset |

Intellectual Capital

Intellectual capital reflects an individual's current knowledge of the global environment and their ability to adapt and navigate cultural complexities. The GLOBE project found differences between managers in different countries with respect to performance orientation, power-distance decision-making, and other cultural workplace norms, suggesting that working across cultures is no easy task. Individuals high in intellectual capital, however, are better equipped to mobilize teams operating in diverse cultures. The three elements of intellectual capital include global business savvy, a cosmopolitan outlook, and the ability to work in an environment with more cognitive complexity (Javidan & Walker, 2012). The competencies entailed are listed in Table 6.5.

Table 6.5 Intellectual Capital Competencies

GLOBAL BUSINESS SAVVY	COSMOPOLITAN OUTLOOK	COGNITIVE COMPLEXITY
• Knowledge of global industry	• Knowledge of cultures in different parts of the world	• Ability to grasp complex concepts quickly
• Knowledge of global competitive businesses and strategies	• Knowledge of geography, history, and important persons of several countries	• Strong analytic and problem-solving skills
• Knowledge of how to transact business and manage risk in other countries	• Knowledge of economic and political issues, concerns, hot topics, etc. of major regions of the world	• Ability to understand abstract ideas
• Knowledge of supplier options in other parts of the world	• Up-to-date knowledge of important world events	• Ability to take complex issues and explain the main points simply and understandably

Source: Adapted from Javidan and Walker (2012).

Psychological Capital

Psychological capital enables an individual to have the enthusiasm, energy, and self-confidence to work in the more complex global environment. The GLOBE Project found that this dimension is innate, and, therefore, much harder to teach. The specific elements include a passion for diversity, a quest for adventure, and self-assurance (Javidan & Walker, 2012). The competencies entailed are listed in Table 6.6.

Table 6.6 Psychological Capital Competencies

PASSION FOR DIVERSITY	QUEST FOR ADVENTURE	SELF-ASSURANCE
• Interest in exploring other parts of the world	• Interest in dealing with challenging situations	• Energetic
• Interest in getting to know people from other parts of the world	• Willingness to take risks	• Self-confident
• Interest in living in another country	• Willingness to test one's abilities	• Comfortable in uncomfortable situations
• Interest in variety	• Interest in dealing with unpredictable situations	• Witty in tough situations

Source: Adapted from Javidan and Walker (2012).

Social Capital

Social capital refers to the individuals' ability to behave in a manner that will help build trust relationships with people from diverse cultures. The elements include intercultural empathy, interpersonal impact, and diplomacy (Javidan & Walker, 2012). The competencies entailed are listed in Table 6.7.

Table 6.7   Social Capital Competencies

INTERCULTURAL EMPATHY	INTERPERSONAL IMPACT	DIPLOMACY
• Ability to work well with people from other parts of the world	• Experience in negotiating contracts in other cultures	• Ease of starting a conversation with a stranger
• Ability to understand nonverbal expressions from people from other parts of the world	• Strong networks with people from other cultures	• Ability to integrate diverse perspectives
• Ability to emotionally connect to people from other cultures	• Reputation as a leader	• Ability to listen to what others have to say
• Ability to engage people from other parts of the world to work together	• Credibility	• Willingness to collaborate

Source: Adapted from Javidan and Walker (2012).

Cultivating a Global Mindset

A global entrepreneur, like any leader, must be able to influence individuals, groups, and organizations both inside and outside the boundaries of the organization. The key difference is that the global entrepreneur is also dealing with diverse cultural, political, and institutional systems that require not only a higher degree of leadership skills, but also the presence of a Global Mindset (Beechler & Javidan, 2007). Linked to firm performance (Felício et al., 2012) and to more rapid internationalization (Nummela et al., 2004), the value of a Global Mindset cannot be overemphasized. A Global Mindset begins with the entrepreneur and their recognition that this process is a continual journey as opposed to being developed in one "eureka" educational experience (Herbert, 2000; Lobel, 1990; Smith & Victorson, 2012). Figure 6.4 offers a list of recommendations from practitioners and academic sources that an entrepreneur could use to build the cognitive knowledge and behavioral skills that foster a Global Mindset (Begley & Boyd, 2003; Black, Morrison, & Gregersen, 1999; Brownell, 2006; Cohen, 2010; Gupta & Govindarajan, 2002; Herbert, 2000; Oddoul, Mendenhall, & Ritchie, 2000; Smith & Victorson, 2012; Srinivas, 1995).

Figure 6.4   Recommendations for cultivating a Global Mindset

Assessing Global Competencies

In order to understand if an individual has the global competencies needed for starting or managing a global enterprise, various behavioral assessment techniques are available. These instruments include tests, surveys, and simulations designed to determine whether specific global competencies are present. A comprehensive catalog of instruments includes over 100 common assessments around culture variances pertaining to individualism, power-distance, upward influence, and uncertainty avoidance (Mendenhall et al., 2008). Outlined in the following are three of the more well-known assessment tools that focus on identifying global competencies or cultural adaptability.

Global competency inventory (GCI): Developed in 2000 by Allan Bird, Michael Stevens, Mark Mendenhall, and Gary Oddou, this self-assessment tool is used to measure17 personality predispositions associated with an individuals' effectiveness in environments where cultural variances exist. The three factors of intercultural adaptability assessed include perception management, relationship management, and self-management (Mendenhall et al., 2008).

Global Mindset inventory (GMI): Developed by the Thunderbird Institute, this self-assessment tool consists of nine scales that assess three types of capital intellectual capital, psychological capital, and social capital (Smith & Victorson, 2012).

Intercultural development inventory (IDI): Developed by Mitchell Hammer and Milton Bennett (1993), this self-assessment instrument is used to measure individuals' intercultural sensitivity and intercultural competency. The inventory is divided into ethnocentric stages and ethnorelative stages. Ethnocentric stages suggest that individuals deem their culture the best and prefer to deny differences exist. The ethnorelative stages reflect individuals' acceptance of cultural differences and willingness to adapt and integrate the new culture into their identities (Mendenhall et al., 2008).

Summary

Entrepreneurship is an engine that can power an economy. Not only do new business ventures enable millions of individuals to pursue their dreams, but these ventures also create millions of jobs. Whether an entrepreneurial firm consists of one or 100+ individuals, whether the firm operates across one or 100+ borders, it is how the entrepreneur leading this organization *thinks* and *acts* that can produce a competitive advantage. The willingness to take risks, create products or services marketable to consumers, build strategic business plans, organize resources, formulate a venture team, and recognize new opportunities is considered a necessary skill for entrepreneurs, in general. Because of additional complexities when firms conduct business across borders, however, entrepreneurs who operate on the global stage need to possess, or need to acquire, additional KSAs.

Global leadership requires the entrepreneur to influence people who have different cultural backgrounds. Therefore, it is important to keep in mind the impact of culture on what is considered effective leadership. A recent study of 42 countries found *culture–entrepreneurship fit* plays an important role and suggests that entrepreneurs operating in a global context need to understand cultural leadership ideals and modify their behavior accordingly (Stephan & Pathak, 2016). Project GLOBE, a longitudinal and multicountry study, identified universally endorsed leadership traits, universally undesirable leadership traits, and traits that were contingent on the country.

A well-recognized ingredient for effective global leadership is the presence of a *Global Mindset*. Research has linked a Global Mindset to firm performance and the pace of internationalization. The core competencies associated with a Global Mindset include a global business orientation, knowledge about global business, cultural awareness and sensitivity, adaptability to different cultures, ability to influence others from diverse cultures, and a cosmopolitan outlook.

Entrepreneurs with a Global Mindset are better equipped to lead business and people in a global context. A Global Mindset can be developed through a multidimensional approach that revolves around educational efforts and the opportunity to work with individuals from different cultures. Self-assessment tools are available to help individuals assess their global leadership competencies, including the presence of a Global Mindset. An entrepreneur should recognize, however, that the quest for a Global Mindset is a continual journey as opposed to a destination on a map.

Discussion Questions

1. How do the competencies needed for domestic entrepreneurship differ from global entrepreneurship?

2. What are some reasons a global entrepreneur needs to understand perceptions of leadership?

3. Describe the core competencies associated with a Global Mindset.

4. How does the Thunderbird Institute differentiate the three types of capital associated with a Global Mindset?

5. How can one develop a Global Mindset?

References

Adler, N. J., & Bartholomew, S. (1992). Managing globally competent people. *The Executive, 6,* 52–65.

Beechler, S., & Javidan, M. (2007). Leading with a Global Mindset. *Advances in International Management, 19,* 131–169.

Begley, T. M., & Boyd, D. P. (2003). The need for a corporate global mind-set. *MIT Sloan Management Review, 44*(2), 25–32.

Black, J. S., Morrison, A. J., & Gregersen, H. B. (1999). *Global explorers: The next generation of leaders.* New York: Routledge.

Bouquet, C. (2005). *Building global mindsets.* New York: Palgrave Macmillan.

Boyatzis, R. (1982). *The competent manager: A model for effective performance.* New York, NY: Wiley & Sons.

Brake, T. (1997). *The global leader.* Chicago, IL: Irwin Publishing.

Brownell, J. (2006). Meeting the competency needs of global leaders: A partnership approach. *Human Resource Management, 45*(3), 309–336.

Cant, A. (2004). Internationalizing the business curriculum: Developing intercultural competence. *Journal of American Academy of Business, 5,* 177–182.

Cohen, S. L. (2010). Effective global leadership requires a global mindset. *Industrial and Commercial Training, 42*(1), 3–10.

Covin, J. G., & Slevin, D. P. (1991). A conceptual model of entrepreneurship as firm behavior. *Entrepreneurship Theory and Practice, 16*(1), 7–25.

Den Hartog, D. N., House, R. J., Hanges, P. J., Ruiz-Quintanilla, S. A., Dorfman, P. W., and Associates. (1999). Culture specific and cross-culturally generalizable implicit leadership theories: Are attributes of charismatic/transformational leadership universally endorsed. *Leadership Quarterly, 10,* 219–256.

Felício, J. A., Caldeirinha, V. R., & Rodrigues, R. (2012). Global mindset and the internationalization of small firms: The importance of the characteristics of entrepreneurs. *International Entrepreneurship and Management Journal, 8,* 467–485.

Gupta, A. K., & Govindarajan, V. (2002). Cultivating a global mindset. *The Academy of Management Executive, 16,* 116–126.

Gupta, V., MacMillan, I. C., & Surie, G. (2004). Entrepreneurial leadership: Developing and measuring a cross-cultural construct. *Journal of Business Venturing, 19,* 241–260.

Herbert, P. (2000). Creating a global mindset. *Thunderbird International Business Review, 42*(2), 187–200.

House, R., Javidan, M., Hanges, P., & Dorfman, P. (2002). Understanding cultures and implicit leadership theories across the globe: An introduction to project GLOBE. *Journal of World Business, 37,* 3–10.

Isenberg, D. J. (December 2008). The global entrepreneur. *Harvard Business Review,* 107–111.

Javidan, M., Dorfman, P. W., de Luque, M. S., & House, R. J. (2006). In the eye of the beholder: Cross cultural lessons in leadership from Project GLOBE. *Academy of Management Perspectives, 20*(1), 67–90.

Javidan, M., Steers, R. M., & Hitt, M. A. (2007). *The global mindset.* Oxford: JAI Press.

Javidan, M., & Walker, J. L. (2012). A whole new global mindset for leadership. *People and Strategy, 35*(2), 36–41.

Jokinen, T. (2004). Global leadership competencies: A review and discussion. *Journal of European Industrial Training, 29*(3), 199–216.

Kefalas, A. G. (1998). Think globally, act locally. *Thunderbird International Business Review, 40*(6), 547–562.

Kuratko, D. F. (2007). Entrepreneurial leadership in the 21st century. *Journal of Leadership and Organizational Studies, 13*(4), 1–11.

Levy, O., Beechler, S., Taylor, S., & Boyacigiller, N. A. (2007). What we talk about when we talk about 'global mindset': Managerial cognition in multinational corporations. *Journal of International Business Studies, 38,* 231–258.

Lobel, S. A. (1990). Global leadership competencies: Managing to a different drumbeat. *Human Resource Management, 29*(1), 39–47.

McGrath R., & MacMillan, I. (2000). *The entrepreneurial mindset.* Boston, MA: Harvard Business School Press.

Mendenhall, M. E., Osland, J. S., Bird, A., Oddou, G., & Maznevski, M. L. (2008). *Global leadership: Research, practice and development*. New York, NY: Routledge.

Morrison, A. J. (2000). Developing a global leadership model. *Human Resource Management, 39*(2–3), 117–131.

Murtha, T. P., Lenway, S. A., & Bagozzi, R. P. (1998). Global mindsets and cognitive shift in a complex multinational corporation. *Strategic Management Journal, 19*(2), 97–114.

Nummela, N., Saarenketo, S., & Puumalainen, K. (2004). A global mindset—a prerequisite for successful internationalization? *Canadian Journal of Administrative Sciences 21*(1), 51–64.

Oddoul, G., Mendenhall, G. M. E., & Ritchie, J. B. (2000). Leveraging travel as a tool for global leader development. *Human Resource Management, 39*, 159–172.

Perlmutter, H. V. (1969). The tortuous evolution of the multinational corporation. *Columbia Journal of World Business, 4*(1), 9–18.

Rhinesmith, S. H. (1992). Global mindsets for global managers. *Training and Development, 46*, 63–68.

Smith, M. C., & Victorson, J. (2012). Developing a global mindset: Cross-cultural challenges and best practices for assessing and grooming high potentials for global leadership. *People and Strategy, 35*(2), 42–51.

Srinivas, K. M. (1995). Globalization of business and the third world: Challenge of expanding the mindsets. *Journal of Management Development, 14*(3), 26–49.

Stephan, U., & Pathak, S. (2016). Beyond cultural values? Cultural leadership ideals and entrepreneurship. *Journal of Business Venturing, 31*(5), 505–523.

Tubbs, S. L., & Schulz, E. (2006). Exploring a taxonomy of global leadership competencies and meta-competencies, *The Journal of American Academy of Business, 8*(2), 29–34.

PART TWO

Exporting for Entrepreneurs: Twenty-first Century Strategies, Tools, and Support Services

Nicholas C. Williamson and
Steven M. Cramer

University of North Carolina , Greensboro, North Carolina

Key Terms

Big data

Critical reading

Critical thinking

Electronic database

Entrepreneur

Exporting

Export marketing mix

Import market selection

Learning Objectives

Upon completion of this chapter, students should be able to:

1. Understand the four main components of the export marketing mix

2. Learn how developments in various macro-environments have benefitted entrepreneurs' entry into the exporting domain

3. Be able to specify the functions that the business librarian (BL) can perform for the entrepreneur

4. Be able to specify the functions that the United States Department of Commerce International (USDOCI) personnel can perform for the entrepreneurs

5. Be able to identify the main functions that the freight-forwarding concern (FFCs) personnel can accomplish for the entrepreneurs

6. Understand how personnel of the BL, USDOCI, and FFC sectors perform complementary functions from the entrepreneurs' points of view

7. Comprehend the basic sequence of events that must take place for the entrepreneurs to move forward into the exporting domain

Introduction

Prior to 1980, entrepreneurs had very few prospects for success in exporting. Only large firms had the financial and human resources to successfully engage in all of the different activities that were necessary for such to occur. They had the financial resources to send a highly trained company person to a foreign country market for assessing that market for targeting in exporting. This process used to take weeks or even months to complete. At the time, knowledge that came from printed sources (objective knowledge) was not deemed suitable for assessing an exporting company's commercial prospects for targeting a given country. The person who used to visit the foreign country market would talk to many persons who somehow had some influence on the focal company for the prospects of successful export in the target country. Among these persons were those associated with the companies involved in distribution channels, wholesalers, governmental entities, banks, and other such entities. Conducting and drawing useful meaning from these conversations was something that only experienced and highly paid persons were deemed equipped to do—persons whom only large firms were in a position to hire and keep on-board.

Additionally, voice communications between countries were restricted to telephony that involved cables laid on the ocean floor to connect the telephone systems of countries in different continents. In the 1950s, the cost per minute of transatlantic telephone services exceeded $2.00 per minute—in the 1950s dollars! And these services were not always reliable. Other than classical "snail mail" between countries, the *telex machine* was frequently used by large businesses for written communications between foreign buyers and sellers. The telex machine used to process long strips of a paper-resembling ticker tape and required expensive infrastructure for a company to use. Further, this device only allowed for a single set of "round trip" communications per day between a buyer and a seller.

International ocean transportation was complex, expensive, and unreliable. It was also very intensive in the use of documents, where a given export shipment could require that as many as 50 separate documents be completed. Only a large company could afford to keep in-house highly trained personnel who were necessary to negotiate the complexities involved.

And financing of exports was a perennial problem for all but the very best capitalized large companies. Governmental agencies that specialized in the offer of financing programs were largely unavailable at that time, particularly those serving small- and medium-sized enterprises (SMEs). The rare small firm that somehow got involved in exporting and needed financing almost invariably had to have an understanding, silent "money man" from which to draw financial resources.

Since 1980, there have many developments that addressed the aforementioned problems, thus improving opportunities for SMEs to get successfully involved in exporting. While we will not go into much detail regarding the character of these developments, we will briefly allude to ones that offer particular promise for their use in exporting by entrepreneurs. Electronic databases such as LexisNexis Academic offer key word and code number search opportunities to persons skilled in such searches, with databases offering electronic access to as many as several hundred million pages of electronic documents. The United Nations keeps track of electronically accessible global and bilateral trade flows that are instrumental in enabling the analyst to identify the best country market to target.

Research firms such as Hoovers and InfoUSA (ReferenceUSA) have, in an electronically accessible form, information on upward of about 100 million firms in countries all around the world. Since the electronic records that are used to store information and data on these firms can be key word and code number searchable (more on the latter very soon), the skilled database searcher can identify highly specific types of companies (e.g., all manufacturers of denim in the countries are covered) in just a couple of minutes, rather than many weeks or even months if hard copy sources were searched manually—assuming that they were even available. Internet has enabled persons to access the electronically available data and information from virtually any location on earth, as long as such persons have access to a broadband Internet connection.

Importantly, US Governmental agencies have developed for the offer of different types of export financing to SMEs (e.g. pre-export financing) on very preferential terms. In parallel, the industry of FFCs has developed and become very price competitive in the offer of export logistics and export documentation services. The payment of a modest fee to these firms for their services will enable the entrepreneur to "outsource" these functions entirely. Furthermore, FFCs can perform strategic functions for the exporting entrepreneur such as providing financial interfacing functions between foreign buyers and domestic exporters for little or no out of pocket costs on the entrepreneurial exporter's part.

A problem is that these developments have taken place very quickly, and very few persons have been in a position to incorporate these developments into an organized framework for the entrepreneur to use efficiently. Most academic textbooks on the subject of international marketing/export marketing are not useful for this purpose because their organization tends to follow a "stepping stone" approach, where one chapter might deal with the economic environment of exporting and the next chapter might deal with the cultural environment of exporting. Critically, to the best of our knowledge, no comprehensive, organized operational framework has been made available by the authors of such textbooks. The implicit assumption appears to have been made that the university graduate who has had courses employing such textbooks will have to gain the main functional, strategic and organizing perspectives on the job.

We feel that the careful reading of the contents of this chapter will enable entrepreneurs to get the critically important, organizational operating perspectives by following the advice presented herein. Our critically important advice is that, in order to gain and integrate the advice quickly and effectively, the entrepreneur who wants to export needs to develop some kind of relationship with three types of entities:

- A business librarian (BL) at a local university or a public library
- Personnel with the USDOCI
- Personnel with an FFC

We strongly feel that the entrepreneur who "stands on the shoulders" of the three above types of entities in ways that we will specify will be able to engage in twenty-first century exporting activities at the very highest level. We predict that this person who follows our advice will come to view the export market as not only a strategically important market for the entrepreneur, but, in many cases, will view the export market as *the most strategically and even financially important market to serve*. And, in the process of using the framework described herein, the entrepreneur in no way cedes strategic control to any one of these three entities. The three entities jointly perform activities that are vitally important to the entrepreneur to succeed in exporting, but not one of them will have the "big picture" that the entrepreneur alone will have.

The reader may wonder concerning our ability to make such claims. These claims are justified based on our experience over the past 26 years concerning teaching students at a regional public university (University of North Carolina at Greensboro) on the subject of international marketing/export marketing by (a) initially teaching the students the fundamentals of export marketing by using textbook readings and lectures on the theory and environment of exporting, and, subsequently, (b) having the students apply this knowledge *while they were still enrolled in the export marketing course!* Student teams have been successfully involved in making real export sales of the following products to real foreign buyers in the following countries noted in Table 7.1:

Table 7.1	Export sales made through Export Odyssey	
HOST MANUFACTURING CONCERN	**PRODUCT EXPORTED**	**FOREIGN BUYER**
Finzer Roller Company	Industrial rollers to impart ink onto beverage cans	Malaysian buyer
Performance Textiles, Inc.	Parachute cloth	Polish buyer
Mojo Musical Supply	Musical components	Norwegian purchaser
Plasticard Locktech International	Magnetized cards for hotel room entry	Australian hotel chain
Noni Bacca Winery	Wine	Australian retailer
J. A. King & Co.	Yarn classifier equipment	Indian trading company
Archer Advanced Rubber Components	Industrial component	Canadian buyer
Miss Jenny's Pickles	Pickles	United Kingdom

An administrator at the level of Vice Chancellor at UNCG performed a survey several years ago to determine how many instructors in export marketing at the postsecondary educational level in the United States employed projects that called upon students to actually become involved in exporting while still enrolled in the course. The answer: none. The instructional initiative which we have named the "Export Odyssey" © initiative apparently has no parallel in colleges or universities throughout the United States. And we have not been able to locate a similar instructional initiative in any foreign college or university as well. The results of our collective decades of successful instructional experience in transforming ordinary undergraduate students at a regional public university into successful exporters enable us to present to you in just one chapter the basics of successful twenty-first century exporting.

Twenty-first century exporting is, to us, captured in the following mantra:

The more internet intensive, the more electronically intensive, the more database intensive, the more key word and code number search intensive the export marketing activities are, the faster, the less expensive, and the better that the export marketing activities are for the exporter!

Further, we claim that the export marketing technologies presented herein actually give the entrepreneur a structural advantage over many exporters in large companies! The reason is that many large companies are still run like twentieth century exporting concerns, and do not incorporate into their export marketing activities the items alluded to in the preceding mantra. The result is that such large concerns are, we claim, less cost efficient and less market effective in key ways in comparison with entrepreneurs who employ the technologies presented herein.

The structure of the balance of this chapter is now presented. Part II provides some fundamentally important perspectives regarding marketing mix factors (Product, Price, Promotion, Place or channel of distribution) in exporting that either have no parallel in domestic U.S. marketing domains, or are much less important. Parts III, IV and V give, respectively, insight into the specific kinds of assistance that the BL, USDOCI personnel and FFC personnel can provide to the entrepreneur at little or no out of pocket cost. Part VI concludes the chapter with insights into how the entrepreneur with no experience in exporting can move forward in a sequence of activities involving these three entities, ones that, we claim, have a high likelihood of leading to exporting success for the entrepreneur. The *Export Odyssey* research guide, http://uncg.libguides.com/mkt426, provides links to many of the research tools discussed in what follows.

Key Marketing Mix Issues in Exporting for the Entrepreneur to Consider

We now provide insights regarding the marketing mix that are fundamentally important to the manufacturer entrepreneur. (This chapter is *not* targeted at the export of services.) While the basics are presented here, the reader is advised to find, by way of the Internet, download (for free), and read the identified chapters in the following text when more insight is needed: *A Basic Guide to Exporting—12th Edition*. This document was written by personnel with the USDOCI division. Texts of approximately 17 chapters span approximately 60 pages. Thus, they are very concise and useful, we might add. When needed, we will refer to a given chapter in this text (ABGE), and will provide quotes from that.

Product

Perhaps the most basic product-related question in exporting concerns whether or not the entrepreneur needs to adapt the product for sale to the export market. While there is no "pat" answer to this question, the following issues frequently come into play.

Labels frequently need to be translated into the prevalent language of the targeted country market. This is true even for our close neighboring country Canada that increasingly requires that labels for consumer products be translated into French as well. Furthermore, *measurement units* need to employ the metric system (e.g., gram). And *packaging* frequently needs to be reinforced for what is typically a trip of many thousands of miles to the targeted export market. Additionally, one should carefully regard the *colors* that are used in packaging, for instance, white is the color of death in China. Specific *numbers* have bad connotations in certain countries. The number "four" in Japanese is "shi," which also relates to death.

Product contents and *country of origin* are increasingly required for a product to pass customs of many foreign countries. Regarding the sale of capital goods such as equipment, the *installation* of the product and its *servicing* needs to be established well in advance of the sale of the product. And a product's *warranties* need particular attention since the customary terms of a warranty may be more comprehensive in the export market than is the case in the United States.

Chapter 8 of ABGE gives helpful advice in the product adaptation domain. Regarding specific product regulations imposed by a foreign government, it may be useful to contact personnel at the federally funded Trade Information Center (1-800-872-8723). These persons can provide insights into where to go to receive concrete advice based upon the nature of the product and the identity of the foreign country into which the product will be imported.

Price

One pricing factor in exporting that has no real parallel in domestic pricing activities concerns the use of pricing *incoterms*. Incoterms specify the terms of sale regarding the exporter's obligation to ship the product to a specific geographic point and pay all costs to get the product to that point. For instance, if an exporter sells product "Ex-works," as many US exporters do, then this means that the exporter is not obligated to do anything other than make the product available to the foreign buyer at what is typically the location of manufacture in the United States. While this is very convenient for the US exporter, this may not at all appeal to the foreign buyer who would prefer the convenience of having the product shipped all the way to the buyer's premises, with all expenses paid (delivered duty paid).

A possible issue concerns the very material difference between a product priced "ex-works" and one priced "delivered duty paid" (DDP). For many products such as luxury products, developing countries may assess an import duty that leads to the DDP dollar price being *more than double* the ex-works dollar price. Without the exporter's specifying pricing incoterms in the price, the foreign buyer might claim that the pricing incoterms were assumed to be DDP. The exporter could, thus, be looking at real financial difficulty as a result of not specifying pricing incoterms. Chapter 13 of ABGE provides a wide variety of pricing incoterms that are available to the exporter.

A related pricing issue concerns that of *price escalation*. Specifically, there are all kinds of factors that lead to added costs to the exported price. Among these are: international transportation costs, marine peril insurance costs, import tariff costs, and many others. These sources of "price escalation" can cause the fully "landed" price of the product (the DDP price) to be 3–4 times the ex-works price of the product. The result of price escalation is frequently having a price in the foreign market that is prohibitively high, and not at all appealing to the foreign buyer.

In order to have the "landed" price of the product competitive with the product offering of other marketers in the targeted foreign market, many US exporters are advised to take out of the export price as many "fixed cost allocations" as possible. Typical fixed cost allocations that might otherwise be "layered" into the export price are the ones for R&D and central office overhead. This might lead to the exporter's using an export price that covers all variable costs and leaves some margin to contribute to fixed costs and profits. The exporter who considers such pricing activities should look for wisdom in the following age-old expression: "It is better to have a half loaf of bread than no loaf at all!"

Promotion

Product promotional activities in exporting typically emphasize personal selling of one form or another about 90% of the time. Advertising is almost never used by SMEs in their promotional activities. In this segment on promotion in exporting, we emphasize two forms of promotion: (a) promotion at foreign trade fairs and (b) promotions targeted directly at the foreign buyer and entailing the use of email with attachments.

Foreign trade fairs are an essential part of promotions for many exporters, particularly those who sell capital goods. The most beneficial trade fairs tend to be product or industry specific. Some countries are known for the world-class trade fairs that they offer, for instance, Germany is known for having in many ways the best trade fairs on earth when it comes to machinery.

There are two basic purposes behind the use of foreign trade fairs. The first concerns the identification and communication with foreign final business buyers of product, buyers who would actually use the product in their operations, and who would buy the product *directly* from the exporter. The second purpose is to locate intermediaries to handle the exporter's product in a given foreign market. A tried and true method for finding foreign trade fairs is to just perform a straightforward Google Web search of the following sort: *apparel trade fair.* The results of this search turned up a variety of trade fairs around the world concerning the sale of apparel. Of course, the entrepreneur should evaluate such fairs carefully prior to booking space.

Promotions Directed at Foreign Buyers and Employing Email

A key aspect of twenty-first century exporting concerns making product promotions targeted directly at foreign buyers. Foreign buyers can be either organizational consumers of the product or intermediaries who resell the product in their country markets. What is typically used is a series of two email sent to specified persons in identified companies. (How to identify these companies, and how to evaluate them as viable going concerns will be the subjects of future parts of this chapter.)

The first email message is entitled the "introductory" message, and it usually consists of two brief paragraphs. The first paragraph consists of one or two sentences that build the *credibility* of the entrepreneur's organization in the eyes of the potential customer. For example, a former student team who had a very large textile producer in the United States as a host concern stated in the first paragraph that their host concern was, in fact, the largest textile producer in the identified industrial group in the United States. Apparently, this was an impressive statement because every single recipient of the fax message responded positively to it.

The second paragraph provides the recipients with some insights into what the exporter envisions as a viable outcome of the communication. Ordinarily, this means either the sale *to* or sale *through* the recipient. In the first case, the recipient is a final organizational consumer; in the second, the recipient is an intermediary for the exporter.

The second email message is entitled the "business proposal" message. In this message, the exporter gives, at a minimum, the following pieces of information:

- The precise specifications of the product (line) that is being offered
- The pricing schedule, as related to quantities sold and incoterms
- The preferred method of payment (typically, an irrevocable letter of credit (LOC); this will be briefed in Part V, concerning the FFC)
- The terms of delivery (e.g., product is shipped 4 weeks from the date of the purchase order)

Other items that the exporter, or the FFC, specifically wants to address can be included as well.

The content of the email messages should reflect at least some knowledge of the business culture of country of the recipient of the messages. Useful sources of such information are web sites and ebooks that describe business culture and etiquette in individual countries. One of the authors maintains a list of such sites at http://uncg.libguides.com/countries. Topics covered by these sites typically include greetings, proper business attire for males and females, how to address a potential client (by first name, or Mr, Ms, and other such items), gift giving expectations, and so on.

Place or Channel of Distribution

Channels of distribution used to sell products to foreign buyers come under two major headings: indirect channels and direct channels. Key aspects of each will now be presented.

Indirect channels: These channels entail the entrepreneur/manufacturer identifying and using a U S-based intermediary known as an export management company (EMC). Most EMCs buy products from the US producers and resell the products with their own mark-up to foreign buyers in their own names. EMCs can perform virtually all export marketing channel functions for their US producers/vendors. All that the US producer has to do is to produce the product to specifications and make available that to the EMC in the specified quantities by the agreed upon date. Functionally, such a sale is just like any other sale of product to a domestic US buyer.

Use of an indirect channel (EMC) is a viable option to small-scale producers who have never been involved in exporting before and who do not want to spend much money investigating foreign markets. The producer frequently enters into a contract with the EMC wherein the rights and obligations of each are specified. In the United States, such contracts can usually be canceled with no more than a year's notice. Such may happen when the US producers become aware of the identities of the foreign buyers of the EMC and decides to sell their products to the foreign buyers directly, eliminating the EMC and absorbing the EMC's margin.

EMCs tend to be product market specialists and support a "portfolio" of an average of 4–5 US producers of complementary product (lines). One EMC well known to one of the authors is an EMC that specializes in selling closed out lines of the US-produced automobile tires to organizational buyers of tires found throughout the 30+ island nations in the Caribbean. These buyers are too small for the tire-manufacturing companies to service directly. In order to stay in a US manufacturer's channel of distribution, thus avoiding being eliminated, many EMC owner principals go to great lengths to nurture personal contacts with foreign buyers.

Direct channels: These channels entail the US manufacturer selling products directly to a foreign buyer. The foreign buyer can be a foreign governmental entity, a final organizational consumer buyer, or an intermediary. The key advantages of exporting directly to the foreign buyer are as follows:

- Greater control over marketing activities in the channel of distribution
- A closer relationship with the foreign buyer
- Potentially greater profits flowing from the absorption of the EMC's profit margin.

There are many different types of direct channels that might be used. Chapter 5 of ABGE provides an excellent summary of these channels.

We now turn to an entity whose importance to the US. exporter, particularly to the SME exporter, is growing rapidly as export marketing activities come to be more and more heavily involved in the use of electronic databases. This is the Business Librarian (BL).

The Business Librarian (BL)

In the twenty-first century export marketing activities that are oriented toward the creation of export transactions (as opposed to the fulfillment of export transactions through export logistics and export documentation), the BL is seen as an increasingly important entity. A key reason is that the BL's profession entails a person's becoming intimately familiar with the content and accessibility of a wide variety of databases that are useful in export marketing. The export marketing transaction creation activities in which the BL potentially excels are the following:

1. Identification of the best export market to target
2. Identification of the best type of downstream customer type in the foreign country to target
3. Identification of specific companies both in the United States and outside of the United States that represent "head on" competitors to the US exporting manufacturing concern.
4. Identification of potential customer companies in the country that is targeted (see point 1)
5. Identification of articles in electronic databases that offer insights into
   a. The character of competition in the targeted foreign market, or
   b. The nature of needs of potential customers in the targeted foreign market

This person's value is intimately intertwined in the "mantra" presented earlier in this chapter. Since "time is money," the BL's value to the exporter, particularly the SME/entrepreneur exporter, will only increase. The more quickly and effectively the identifications alluded to 1–5 above can be made, the more valuable the BL will be to the exporter. We now deal with each of these identifications in turn.

Identifying the Best Export Market to Target

Identifying the best foreign market to target with the exported product is one of the most, if not the most, important steps to establish the process of performing export market research. In the academic literature, many articles have been published on this subject. The BL is in a position to perform this research quite efficiently. The multistep procedure that the BL can follow to make this assessment is as follows.

1. Establish the 10-digit harmonized system (HS) code of the product that you want to export. This can be done by US Census Bureau's Schedule B Search Engine. (This comes up quickly with a direct Google Web search.)

2. Access the United States International Trade Commission Trade DataWeb, which provides access to US exports of each 10-digit HS product category to each importing country for at least the past 10 years, leading up to and including 2013.

3. Generate and use the following Excel worksheet:
   a. First column gives the name of the importing country
   b. Second column gives US exports to the country in 2010
   c. Third column gives US exports to the country in 2011
   d. Fourth column gives US exports to the country in 2012
   e. Fifth column gives US exports to the country in 2013.

4. Choose a base year to work with (e.g., 2011).

5. In the sixth column, for each country importing the 10-digit HS coded product from the US, subtract the figure found in the third column from the figure found in the fifth column.

6. Sort the country observations based on the value of figures in the sixth column. This places at the top the country that experienced the greatest gain in US exports of the 10-digit HS-coded product from 2011 to 2013. Everything else being equal, this gain in the share of that country of US exports of the focal product can be argued to be a good indicator of the country's appeal as a country to target with the focal 10-digit HS-coded product in exporting activities.

Identification of the Best Downstream Customer Type to Target in the Country Selected for Targeting

Identification of the best downstream customer type for you to target, a choice that in many circumstances can be interpreted as the best channel of distribution to choose, is another area in which the BL can excel. To clarify this, we will introduce the IBISWorld database as a device for accomplishing the choice. However, we first need to introduce the "Index of Concordance" as a vitally important instrument in this context.

An "Index of Concordance" can be used to get all three code numbers for the product that you are exporting. These code numbers are the 10-digit HS code number, the 6-digit NAICS code number, and the 4-digit Standard Industrial Classification

(SIC) code number. *You must start with the 10-digit HS code number.* The BL will find an "Index of Concordance" that will give the 6-digit NAICS code number and the 4-digit SIC code numbers for your product. Once you establish the 6-digit NAICS code number for your product, you can go to the IBISWorld database and find the identities of viable downstream customer types (channels of distribution).

IBISWorld reports are reports on the status of industries in the United States at the 5-digit NAICS (industry) code level. (The 5-digit NAICS code number is just the 6-digit NAICS code number with the very last digit removed.) Once you have the 5-digit NAICS code number for your product, you can go to that part of the IBISWorld report that has the main heading "Products and Markets" and go to the subheading that reads "Key Buying Industries." Contained within the "Key Buying Industries" segment is a statement of all 5 digit NAICS code industries that would (or might) purchase your product. Typically, there will be four to six 5-digit NAICS-coded categories of firms that might purchase your product.

This is immensely important information. Once you establish the 5-digit NAICS codes for possible downstream customer types, each potentially viewed as a separate channel of distribution, you can go to a database like Hoovers or ReferenceUSA and identify all of the firms in your targeted country that have the NAICS code number for your chosen customer type/5-digit NAICS code/channel of distribution. Not only that, if one uses Hoovers or ReferenceUSA, one has a wealth of contact information for each identified company, such as fax numbers, CEOs' names, geographic addresses, telephone numbers, and email addresses. With this information in hand, you can move ahead and make export product promotional contact with ones that you identify. (This addresses Items #2 and #4 in the introductory section for Part III, concerning the BL.)

Identification of Companies Both in the United States and Outside the United States That Are "Head On" Competitors of Your Firm

Identification for "head on" competitor companies for your concern is extremely important from a competitive perspective. When you identify such companies, you can, for example, go to their websites and study their product offerings and key aspects of their export marketing strategies. This will help you to either (a) selectively adopt marketing strategies that you feel would be appropriate or (b) gain insights into how to compete against these firms.

For example, if your firm produces denim, then you would want to identify all firms that produce and export denim, both inside the United States and outside United States, and study their respective websites carefully. The BL who has access to Hoovers would enable you to determine that the 8-digit SIC code for denim producers is 22110505. You could then use Hoovers to identify all of the firms in the MI database that (a) had 22110505 as the "Primary" SIC code for their operations and (b) were exporters. This search currently turns up approximately

40 conforming companies, ones that tend to be located in either the United States or India. Your competitive analysis of their websites can then be conducted with great efficiency and effectiveness. After all, "Time is money"!

Identify Articles in Electronic Databases That Offer Insight into These Companies

You should Nread some articles on these companies; articles taken from databases offer electronic access of these articles to you. These articles can come from many different types of sources, such as foreign magazines, journals, newspapers, annual reports, blogs, and other such sources. Among the databases that offer particularly useful access in this domain are Nexis Uni (NU; formerly known as LexisNexis Academic), Ebsco's Business Source (BS), or Proquest's ABI-INFORM (ABI).

BS's articles tend to focus on *relatively large foreign firms*. Also, BS can be searched by the 6-digit NAICS code number. So, you can identify all articles in the BS database that concern a given firm that exports denim products by using the following key words:

[Firm Name] AND [NAICS Code for denim producers]
AND [export*] AND denim.

The export* code word gives you access to articles that have the following words:

export   exporting   exports   exporter

The BL will show you exactly how to do this.

Similarly, ABI and NU tend to offer articles from international business sources that provide greater coverage to *smaller firms* than is the case for BS. Keyword search strategies for ABI and NU are similar to those for BS, except that NU does not permit searching by the NAICS code number.

Google Web searches give, *by far*, the best coverage of *small* and *very small* firms. However, they can turn up many, many "hits" that do not have anything to do with the export marketing strategy. Google Web searches that turn up millions of "hits" are not at all unusual. In order to bring into clear view articles that are useful to you, use the following key words when performing Google Web searches: **[company name] export strategy.** This tends to place at the top of the Google Web hit list articles that emphasize export and strategy. That is what you want.

United States Department of Commerce International (USDOCI) Personnel

The USDOCI division is the main US Government entity that is charged with enhancing US exports. There are many services that personnel from USDOCI can provide for US exporters, in general. From the point of view of the entrepreneur, we see that there are two main functions that are provided: (1) identifying a source of financing exports and (2) identifying key US Governmental entities that might be useful in the facilitation of exports. We now explore what we feel are the main entrepreneur-relevant topic areas in each.

Sources of Financing for Exports

The Small Business Administration (SBA) is, in many ways, the key US governmental entity offering support to small enterprises. There are three financing programs that offer the small exporting firm significant benefits: the Export Working Capital Program (EWCP), the International Trade Loan Program, and the Export Express Program. Each of these programs requires the participation of an eligible bank. However, personnel with most banks are familiar with these programs. It might be useful for you to first speak with SBA personnel to determine which lender in your area might be the best one to approach.

The EWCP will guarantee up to $1.5 million, or 90% of the loan amount, whichever is less. These loans provide working capital for export transactions and finance export receivables. The loans can be used to support individual export transactions or can support revolving lines of credit. The International Trade Loan Program can be used to guarantee loans of up to $1.25 million in combined working capital loans and loans used to support buildings, construction, and land. A critically important aspect of this program is identified in Chapter 15 of ABGE: "Applicants must either (a) certify that loan proceeds will enable them to significantly expand existing export markets or develop new ones or (b) show that they have been adversely affected by import competition" (p. 3). Export Express loans are capped at $250,000 and can be dedicated to a variety of export-related purposes. A key feature of Export Express loans is that they can be secured in as little as a week's time period.

One critically important financing-related product that is made available by the Export Import Bank of the United States (Ex-Im Bank) is an insurance policy that enables the beginning exporter to export products to foreign buyers on an open account basis, with 90% of the export price being covered in the program. The cost of the insurance policy tends to be approximately 1% of the "Ex-works" sales price of the product. Foreign buyers of product find this to be particularly appealing, since the terms of open account export sales tend to be very flexible.

To contact persons who will help you with using the aforementioned programs, it would be useful to call the Trade Information Center at the following telephone number: 800-USA-TRAD(E) or 800-872-8723. This number can be used as a "portal" for virtually any US Government export promotion program.

US Governmental Entities for Facilitating Exports

Commercial News USA (CNUSA): CNUSA showcases US-made products. Electronic bulletin boards and illustrated catalog magazines are the main devices for accomplishing this. Each issue of the free bimonthly catalog magazines reaches approximately 400,000 readers from approximately 145 countries. Persons at US embassies and consulates around the world are particularly instrumental in ensuring that the promoted products receive maximum coverage.

Featured US Exporters (FUSE): The following is taken from p. 1 of Chapter 6 of ABGE: "Featured US Exporters (FUSE) is a directory of US products presented on the websites of many US Commercial Service offices around the world. It gives your company an opportunity to target markets in specific countries in the local language of business." The service is free to qualified US exporters.

International Buyer Program (IBP): The IBP is involved in domestic US trade shows and is targeted at US industries that have *high foreign market potential.* Exhibitors at IBP events get the opportunity to communicate with potential foreign buyers from all around the world, persons who have been pre-screened and recruited by US Commercial Service personnel in over 150 cities in foreign countries. The very significant resources that are dedicated to qualifying US exporters are justified based on the high export market potential of their products. Again, the proper telephone number to use for further exploration of this program is 1-800-872-8723.

Freight Forwarding Concerns (FFC)

Up until this point, the guidance that you have received has been primarily targeted at the *creation* of export transactions. Companies that specialize in activities that are involved in the *fulfillment* of export transactions, freight forwarding concerns (FFC) will now be addressed. The FFC specializes in export logistics (transportation and warehousing) and documentation. The FFC can be viewed as your "chief of export operations." You need to follow the guidance of the FFC precisely.

One area where the input of the FFC is vital is in the domain of your properly responding to the requirements of a commercial LOC that an importer might use in purchasing your product. Commercial LOCs, particularly those that are "irrevocable" (cannot be changed without the written permission of the exporter), are "opened" by the foreign buyer "in favor" of the exporter, who is deemed the "beneficiary." The LOC is actually offered by a bank that is associated with the foreign buyer (importer) and provides an ironclad guarantee that the bank will pay up to the amount specified in the LOC as long as you, the exporter, *do what you are legally obligated to do*, as specified in the LOC.

Commercial LOC are *extremely exacting* in their requirements and, as such, can be viewed as a kind of "quality control" device used by the importer. The LOC tells (commands) you to do things such as follows:

- Produce the product *precisely* to specifications
- Produce the product in the specified quantities
- Ship the product on the date specified in the LOC
- Ship the product using specified containers or shipping devices
- In your documentation, spell precisely (correctly) the name of the importing company
- Many, many other such items

Not conforming precisely to the stated requirements of the LOC can lead to the nullification of the foreign bank's guarantee to pay the exporter. At best, the exporter can seek to "amend" the LOC to accommodate a misstep on the part of the exporter, but it will cost the exporter to make such an amendment, if such is even available.

The FFC is very familiar with dealing with LOCs. Whatever the FFC tells the exporter to do in that regard, the exporter should do! The exporter typically books space with the FFC for transporting the exported product on a container ship (if it is shipped by ocean freight, which is typical) and using a container that the FFC had previously leased for such purposes. Frequently, the exporter's product, if it is shipped in small quantities, will be shipped in the same "container" as is the product of other exporters who are shipping products to the same foreign country market. The FFC can thus generate cost-saving economies stemming from the consolidation of different shipments of product in the same container. Fortunately, for the individual exporter, the industry of FFCs in the United States is highly price competitive, and the activities performed by the FFC tend to be standardized. This enables the exporter to secure the services of an FFC for a very reasonable price.

Integrating the Activities of the BL, USDOCI, and FFC

We now present to you a sequence of activities that you should follow en route to your becoming (successfully) involved in exporting. It is important for you to note that in this sequence, you, the exporter, are the *dominant or controlling entity*.

1. Locate a competent BL at a nearby university and introduce yourself. Particularly useful to you would be a BL who works for a public university, one funded to a large extent by the taxpayer—you.
2. Describe precisely your product to the BL, and the BL will be instrumental in doing the following for you, as has already been described herein:
   a. Establish the main product and industry codes (10-digit HS code, 6-digit NAICS code, and 8-digit SIC code (using Hoovers or ReferenceUSA database)

  b. Identify the best foreign market for you to pursue

  c. Identify head on competitors, both in the United States and outside the United States for you to study by way of the Internet, using electronic databases

  d. Identify relevant channels of distribution using IBISWorld database documents

  e. Identify potential customers in the chosen channel(s) of distribution and prepare to initiate communications with them

  f. Draw up pro forma "introductory" and "business proposal" email messages to send to these potential customers. You may either use Google Translate to communicate in the language of the potential customer or just send the document in English in hope that someone on the receiving end will speak English.

3. In parallel with the preceding, make a telephone call (800-872-8723) and subsequently communicate with identified personnel with the SBA to establish financing for your exports.

  a. Discuss with the SBA person what the best financing program would likely be for you

  b. Have that person identify a bank in your area that is familiar with handling SBA guaranteed loans.

  c. Make preliminary efforts to secure an SBA-guaranteed loan with the identified bank.

  d. Communicate with the identified bank your intention to use the bank as the "advising bank" regarding your export activities. The bank would, for example, give you advice that a given commercial LOC has been received, one that designates your firm as the beneficiary, and would assist you with following the LOC requirements.

4. Identify with the help of SBA and advising bank personnel an FFC in your area that would be useful to you.

5. Have FFC personnel give you advice on what you need to do when and if you were to receive an order from a foreign buyer, guaranteed by the foreign buyer's bank in the form of a commercial LOC.

6. COMMENCE EXPORTING OPERATIONS by sending email promotional enquiries to identified potential customers in the identified foreign market.

So, there you have it! You now know the essentials that you need to follow to become (successfully) involved in exporting. There has never been as good a time as the present time is to commence involvement in exporting. As a closing word of caution, we feel that we must admonish you to do the following: Always do what your FFC says to do and when the FFC says that it should be done! Good luck!

Discussion Questions

1. What does the "4 P" of "place" really mean in the context of export marketing? Provide some examples.

2. How has the Internet enabled small- and medium-sized manufacturers to compete with larger exporters?

3. In what ways can a potential exporter benefit from the services of government officials?

Global Economics and Finance

Dale R. Funderburk

Texas A & M University–Commerce, Commerce, Texas

Key Terms

Absolute advantage	Currency board	Industrial policy
Banker's acceptance	Derived demand	Law of one price
Bill of exchange	Dollarization	Leontief's paradox
Comparative advantage	Factor endowment	Mercantilism
Contagion	Factoring	Porter's Diamond
Country risk premium	Forex	

Learning Objectives

Upon completion of this chapter, students should be able to:

1. Understand trade between countries as it relates to economic specialization and resource utilization.

2. Understand comparative advantage as a basis for trade between nations.

3. Identify the differences between absolute advantage and comparative advantage.

4. Identify the major theories attempting to explain patterns of cross-border exchange.

5. Understand the relationship between expanding markets, economic efficiency, and the impact on consumers and producers.

    Understand the microeconomic principles of exchange rate determination.

6. Understand the nature and advantages of common currency regimes.

7. Understand the various types and sources of risks involved in trade between nations.

8. Understand the major instruments and techniques available for financing international trade.

9. Identify agencies devoted to the promotion of international trade.

Introduction

Two of the most often discussed and written about topics in business over the past dozen years have been entrepreneurship and globalization. While the term "entrepreneurship" once tended to be associated primarily with small business activity, and "globalization" was more often associated with giant corporate entities, both phenomena are now recognized as highly relevant, even critical, issues for business entities of all sizes. Today's entrepreneur can ill afford to be ignorant of the forces driving, the opportunities afforded by or the threats imposed by, markets that are rapidly expanding on a global scale. These general topics comprise the focus of the present chapter. Specifically, the chapter is divided into two parts: real analysis or trade theory, and monetary analysis and international finance. Trade theory is addressed first, focusing on the basis for international trade and the microeconomic implications of expanding markets and trade. The second part of the chapter focuses on finance issues related to international trade, especially exchange rate determination, risks peculiar to international trade, methods, and instruments used to finance international trade, plus agencies and institutions that promote international trade.

Trade Theory: The Basic Economics of International Trade

It is a bit ironic and more than a bit disturbing that even in the twenty-first century, economists and policy-makers still find it necessary to undertake to educate the public on the advantages of specialization, increasing productivity and free trade. There is scarcely a scheduled meeting of a major trade institution or organization but that it must contend with the disruptive efforts of large, well-organized protests. From Seattle to Washington to Prague to Genoa, meetings involving the World Trade Organization (WTO), the International Monetary Fund (IMF), World Bank, North American Free Trade Agreement (NAFTA), and the proposed Central American Free Trade Association (CAFTA) have all been targets of "antiglobalization" protesters. Terms such as "globalization," "offshoring," and "outsourcing" have become the derisive rallying mantra of those fearing the effects of rapidly globalizing markets. And unfortunately, elective office seekers all too often find it politically advantageous to capitalize on the insecurities and fears of those threatened by the specter of expanding markets and increased competition. In some respects, it is as though much of the world has turned back the calendar two centuries and entered an era that we might call the **New Mercantilism.**

The Basis for Trade

In almost every important respect, globalization is very much like most other facets of basic international economics and finance that have existed and been studied and written about for literally centuries. It is ironic that in the effort to educate today's critics regarding the benefits of free trade, modern economists inevitably turn to the works of two economists of much earlier eras who faced similar tasks, Adam Smith and David Ricardo. Smith, in the late eighteenth century, and Ricardo, in the early nineteenth century, struggled to convince their fellow Britons of the virtues of free trade. In explaining the concept that has come to be known as **absolute advantage**, Smith ridiculed the fear of trade by comparing nations to households. He also refuted the widely held assumption that trade is a zero-sum game, demonstrating that trade is a positive sum game. Smith's argument was that since every household finds it worthwhile to produce only some of the goods it needs and buy others with products that it can sell, the same logic must apply to nations. "It is the maxim of every prudent master of a family, never to attempt to make at home what it will cost him more to make than to buy. What is prudent in the conduct of every private family, can scarce be folly in that of a great kingdom. If a foreign country can supply us with a commodity cheaper than we ourselves can make it, better buy it of them with some part of the product of our own industry, employed in a way in which we have some advantage" (Funderburk, 2018). In short, it simply makes good economic sense to allow Brazil to grow Brazil nuts and Iceland to grow Eskimo Pies, and then trade, rather than have each country waste resources in trying to produce goods for which they have no advantage.

David Ricardo (Funderburk, 2018) refined and extended the analysis of Smith, developing a theory of **comparative advantage**. Ricardo demonstrated that nations can gain from specialization even if they lack an absolute advantage—that trade, including cross-border trade, does not require absolute advantage. In explaining the basis for trade between two countries, such as England and Portugal, Ricardo showed that if a country is relatively better at making wine than wool, then it makes good economic sense for that country to put more resources into wine, and to export some of the wine to pay for the imports of wool. This is true even if that country is the world's best wool producer since with specialization and trade it would have more of both wool and wine than it would have without trade. Thus, a country does not have to be the best (the most efficient, or low-cost producer) at anything to gain from trade. The gains follow from specializing in those activities, which, at world prices, the country is relatively better at, even though it may not have an absolute advantage in them. Because it is relative advantage that matters, it is inaccurate to say that a country has a comparative advantage in nothing.

While there have been newer, more sophisticated theories developed to explain trade patterns between nations, the theory of comparative advantage still constitutes the base on which these theories are constructed, and even today may be considered the key theoretical underpinning of trade theory. Consider, for example, the theory developed by two Swedish economists, Eli Heckscher (Funderburk, 2018) and Bertil Ohlin (Funderburk, 2018) (and later refined, expanded and formalized by MIT economist Paul Samuelson (Funderburk, 2018)), aimed at explaining trade patterns between nations. Noting how prices differed quite substantially between various countries before they opened trade, Heckscher and Ohlin expressed doubt that demand or technological considerations (emphasized by Ricardo) accounted for most of the international price differences existing in the real world. This theory, often referred to as a **factor endowment** model, hypothesizes that countries export the products that use their abundant factors intensively, and import the products using their scarce factors intensively. Thus, as a simple example, a nation with large oil reserves will have a comparative advantage in oil production over another nation with fertile soil, which will have a comparative advantage in agricultural production.

Economists note that while the Heckscher-Ohlin theory is intuitively appealing and was once widely accepted on the basis of mere casual empiricism, it has not held up so well empirically. When the first serious attempt to test the theory was made by Russian-born Harvard economist, Wassily Leontief (Funderburk, 2018) in 1954, the results were surprising. Using the 1947 input-output table of the US economy (for the development and application of which he was awarded the 1973 Nobel Memorial Prize in Economics), Leontief reached the counterintuitive conclusion that the United States, the most capital-abundant country in the world, exported labor-intensive commodities and imported capital-intensive commodities. This result, which came to be known as the **Leontief Paradox**, took the economics profession by surprise and stimulated an enormous amount of empirical and theoretical research on the subject.

Perhaps of greater interest to students of business strategy is the theory of national competitive advantage developed by the Harvard business professor, Michael E. Porter (Funderburk, 2018). Whereas classical theories propose that comparative advantage resides in the technological differences and/or the factor endowments (land, natural resources, labor, and size of the local population) that a country may be fortunate enough to inherit, Porter argues that these theories are inadequate, or even wrong. He contends that a nation can create new advanced factor endowments such as skilled labor, a strong technology and knowledge base, government support, and culture. After conducting a detailed study of 10 nations to learn what leads to success, he developed the concept that has become known as **Porter's Diamond**. According to Porter, a nation attains a competitive advantage if its firms are competitive. Firms become competitive through innovation. These innovations may include technical improvements to the product or to the production process. He differentiates his theory from the traditional trade theories by arguing that national prosperity is not inherited, but created by choices. Thus he contends that national wealth is not set by factor endowments, but created by strategic choices.

According to Porter, four attributes comprise the basis for a country's diamond of national competitive advantage. He uses a diamond-shaped diagram as the pivotal graphic of a framework to illustrate the determinants of national advantage. This diamond then represents the national playing field that countries establish for their industries. These four attributes include (1) factor conditions—the nation's position in terms of factors of production, such as skilled labor and infrastructure, (2) demand conditions—including the degree of sophistication of consumers in the domestic market, (3) related and supporting industries—which includes suppliers and complementary industries, and (4) firm strategy, structure, and rivalry—conditions for organization of companies and the nature of domestic rivalry.

While Porter's theory, much like that of Heckscher-Ohlin, may be intuitively appealing and is supported by considerable anecdotal evidence, Harfield (Funderburk, 2018) points out that Porter is not without critics. "His lack of clear definitions for his 'models' is a matter of agreement rather than debate." Harfield further notes, "…there is a similar large-scale concern with his lack of empirical data." Thus, to what degree can a nation influence, or even engineer, a national competitive advantage? The extensive literature on the concept of **industrial policy** would seem to cast considerable doubt on the prospects of a country's developing a national competitive advantage through strategic planning and public policy.

Expanding Markets and Economic Efficiency

At the root, globalization is merely a manifestation of improving market efficiency. Economists have long understood that improving communication and transportation lead to market expansion, and ultimately, to greater market efficiency. By the term market efficiency, we refer simply to the effects of forces (such as the improving quality and speed of transfer of information and greater mobility) that tend to reduce transactions costs and thus make exchange more efficient. And as markets become more efficient, producers also must respond by becoming more efficient. It is a basic axiom of economics that competition in the marketplace provides the impetus for greater productive efficiency. As more and better information becomes available, and as mobility—both of resources and output—improves, participants in the marketplace are pressed to become more efficient. They must become more sensitive to the state of technology and to least-cost combinations of resources. As larger numbers of buyers and sellers come to interact in the market, overall economic efficiency improves.

Thus it may be concluded that international trade and globalization are not only the results of increasing economic efficiency, they are causative forces as well. However, it is critical to note that while improved economic efficiency increases overall material well-being, markets do not necessarily ensure that the benefits of increased efficiency are shared by all. There is no assurance that expanding markets, increasing competition, and greater market and productive efficiency will lead to what we may consider a more equitable distribution of income. Consequently, some argue that carefully crafted government policies are necessary in order to correct some of the injurious effects of the impersonal marketplace.

The Microeconomic Impact of Expanding Markets

While economic globalization presents a plethora of new managerial challenges and marketing opportunities and threats, the basic microeconomic implications of the trend are relatively straightforward. As transportation and communications improve, the process impacts the nature and scope of competition. As markets expand, there is invariably an impact on producers and sellers, resource suppliers, and consumers. Below we consider the effects of expanding markets and globalization on each these groups.

Producer/Seller Impact. For producers and sellers, the added competition associated with new, expanding markets invariably brings about new pressures for ingenuity and efficiency. Less innovative, less efficient producers wither and vanish in the face of added competition, while more innovative, more efficient producers and sellers prosper and expand. This happens whether the expanding marketplace occurs within the context of a small, local, village economy or in the context of an increasingly integrated and competitive "global village." It must be kept in mind, however, that a firm may be inefficient through no fault of its own. The roots of the problem may be entirely external. A firm may be inefficient because of its own ineptitude, or because of factors (both microeconomic and macroeconomic in scope) outside its control. While a particular producer/seller may be able to be the low-cost provider in a small, restricted market, that same firm may be unable to compete effectively in an expanded market setting. As markets expand, some producers find themselves without access to the best sources of essential raw materials. Also, a firm may not have access to low-cost resources—especially labor. Governmentally mandated cost-increasing measures such as minimum wage legislation, detailed safety regulations, paid leave requirements, and payroll taxes imposed to fund any number of entitlement programs may place a producer at a distinct competitive disadvantage, especially when posited against competitors whose governments impose no such cost-raising requirements.

Finally, it must be kept in mind that producers themselves are also consumers. They must acquire the resources, the technology, and the raw materials used in producing the output they sell. Consequently, globalization and increasing competition may benefit the producer by allowing the firm to buy inputs at lower prices. Along this line, it is interesting to note that when President George W. Bush imposed tariffs on imported steel in March 2002, he did win favor (for a time) with US steel producers, but he also incurred considerable wrath from firms in steel-consuming industries. Thus, while he may have helped himself politically in steel-producing states like Pennsylvania and West Virginia, he did not help himself in steel-consuming states like Tennessee, where auto producers suffered from (and complained bitterly about) the higher steel prices.

Resource suppliers: labor. As is the case with sellers of goods, broadening markets entail both new opportunities and new threats for sellers of labor services. As transportation and communications improve, labor markets also broaden and become more competitive. Consequently, marketable skills become the watchword for labor. It is significant to note that historically, most foreign competition was in the manufacturing sector. Thus the domestic workers who felt most threatened by foreign trade tended to be blue-collar, production workers. Today, however, as we are seeing that more and more services are also tradable, many more highly specialized, technically educated and skilled workers are experiencing the threat of job loss and dislocation.

For many years workers have crossed national borders to work. The United States has used foreign, migrant workers to supply needed manual labor for decades. Among the earlier enacted of these government programs, the H-2A temporary agricultural certification program establishes a means for agricultural employers who anticipate a shortage of domestic workers to bring nonimmigrant foreign workers to the United States to perform agricultural work or services of a temporary or seasonal nature. Construction workers have for years traversed the globe to provide the expertise and skilled labor necessary for both private and public projects. This is a trend that continues to expand in terms of geographic area covered and also in terms of skills and occupations involved. Under a special program instituted in 1999, the United States Department of Labor allows qualifying hospitals (in "disadvantaged" areas) to employ temporary foreign, nonimmigrant workers as Registered Nurses for up to three years under a H-1C visa. And increasingly, highly skilled, technical workers are able to cross national borders to supply critical labor needs in advanced, as well as less-developed, countries. Under its H-1B program, the United States allows an employer to temporarily employ foreign workers (on a nonimmigrant basis) in specialty occupations. Participants in this program must hold a bachelor's degree or the equivalent in the specific specialty (e.g., engineering, mathematics, physical sciences, computer sciences, medicine and healthcare, education, biotechnology, and business specialties). When initially established this program contained a cap at 65,000 workers. Though the program has expanded significantly through exemptions, roll-overs, and alternative programs, many US firms involved in computer and information technology regularly lobby for increases in the cap, arguing that they cannot compete in the global marketplace without the services of increasing numbers of foreign workers. For example, Microsoft chairman Bill Gates appeared before Congress in both 2007 and 2008, arguing for expansion of the program and warning that America's competitiveness in the global economy was at risk.

In addition to H-1B workers involved in computer and information technology employment in high-tech industries, many work as primary and secondary teachers in public schools, as well as university professors and research scholars. Those in educational institutions tend to work primarily in science, technology, engineering and mathematics (STEM) areas, and bilingual education. Also, foreign medical graduates are able to use the H-1B visa to join residency and fellowship programs and practice medicine in the United States.

An additional point should be made with regard to labor in a global market setting with rapidly advancing technology. Historically, the physical location of the worker *vis-à-vis* the employer or "job site" was critical. It was necessary either for the worker to be mobile and go to the job site, or else for capital to migrate to the workers. Increasingly, however, there are more and more jobs for which the physical location of the worker is inconsequential. Because of advances in computers and information technology, an initial phase was that some workers were able to work at home, and to go into the office only occasionally. Following that, the natural progression has been that more and more jobs require the physical presence of the worker rarely, if at all. Thus a worker in Dallas may be bidding against others in Dublin, Delhi, or Dhaka. And while many jobs will continue to require the physical presence of the worker—if a custodian is to wax a floor, he/she must be in that specific room—more and more jobs will not. This is merely another dimension of a globalizing labor market.

Finally, it must be acknowledged that there are invariably significant short-run costs associated with increased specialization and/or increasing productivity stemming from globalizing labor markets. Those who are displaced and who must shift jobs will inevitably experience costs. In addition to direct retraining and/or relocation costs, there may well be spells of unemployment and reduced wages. However, it is important to keep in mind that the same may be said of any improvement in productivity, whether related to international trade or not. By its very nature, productivity improvement entails being able to produce more (or better) output with the same, or lesser, units of labor input. The introduction of the roller and pan, and later the spray gun, instead of a brush to paint buildings was clearly an increase in productivity but was resisted mightily by painters and their craft unions. Invariably, improvements in productivity involve some labor displacement or dislocation. It is an unfortunate, but unavoidable, byproduct of progress.

Given that there are costs (and losers) resulting from the expanding volume of international trade (and the accompanying economic realignment and restructuring), governments at times find it necessary to devise ways of mitigating the harm accruing to the short-run losers. For example, in the United States, Trade Adjustment Assistance (TAA) has been developed in order to help those harmed by international trade by providing extended unemployment benefits, worker retraining, and temporary taxes on imports. And while the concept of compensating workers disadvantaged by trade-related displacement has its primary roots in the Trade Expansion Act of 1962 and the Trade Act of 1974, the program has been amended and expanded numerous times to cover different sectors of the economy and additional workers. As a case in point, the government created a special program for workers laid off because of the North American Free Trade Agreement, the NAFTA-TAA. In 1994, the year that NAFTA went into effect, 17,000 workers qualified for this program.

Resource suppliers: capital. A major determinant of factor market efficiency is mobility. Because funds are much more mobile than is labor, money and capital markets exhibit a higher degree of efficiency than do labor markets and consequently can and will globalize much more rapidly. While physical capital migration may continue to be a relatively slow and expensive process, the process of funding capital accumulation is becoming much more competitive and efficient. Bryan and Farrell (Funderburk, 2018) were noting by 1994 that the **law of one price** was beginning to operate in global capital markets. They pointed out that in the new global markets, participants are increasingly able to price financial instruments more precisely across markets in multiple currencies. They further argued that the global capital market will play an ever greater role in determining the rate of return on capital investments, while the actions of central banks will matter even less.

This has important public policy implications. Perhaps the most important of these is that the global capital market is integrating to the point where the price of government debt is market determined. Increasingly, debt will be priced according to its specific risks and return, independent of the efforts of governments to control their own interest rates. Consequently, governments that issue debt for the purpose of funding entitlements and/or who pursue inflationary policies inevitably will pay ever-increasing costs for such policies. The recent Greek government debt crisis bore out that principle quite convincingly. The downgrading of Greek government debt to junk bond status in April 2010 created alarm in financial markets and sent bond yields rising to such levels that private capital markets were virtually unavailable to Greece as a funding source. Only a series of bailouts by Eurozone ministers prevented Greece from falling into full-scale bankruptcy and economic collapse. Conversely, it could be expected that funds would flow to the developing nations which would then grow and modernize faster as a result. In line with that principle, it is noted that according to its January 2014 Global Economic Prospects report, the World Bank (2014) reports that "The past two decades have seen dramatic changes in private capital inflows to developing countries. These flows have increased substantially both in absolute terms and as a share of developing-country GDP, and have been characterized by large fluctuations in response to changing global financial and economic conditions." Likewise, private investment in the developed world is likely to be even greater.

Consumers. Consumers are the one group that almost universally benefits from the added competition associated with expanding markets. Even during the Middle Ages, as transportation and communication advances moved markets beyond the bounds of small, rural villages, it was the consumer who inevitably reaped the benefits of new and improved products, new and better choices, and lower prices. As international trade has grown and widened, consumers have benefited. In those economies where governments have erected barriers against expanding trade, consumers have suffered from fewer product choices, higher prices, and a stagnant or declining standard of living. Countries such as Myanmar, the Republic of Congo, Cuba, Zimbabwe, and North Korea are cases in point.[1]

---

[1]Organizations such as the Hoover Institution, the Heritage Foundation and the Frazier Institute rank countries in terms of economic freedom. Each of the countries listed here rates very poor in terms of international commerce—having very high levels of protectionism, high barriers to capital flows and foreign investment, and/or little protection for property rights. These rankings demonstrate that countries with higher levels of economic (market) freedom enjoy higher levels of per capita income.

Currency Issues and International Finance

The primary function of money is that it provides an alternative to barter. By serving as a medium of exchange, money reduces transactions costs and makes exchange more efficient. Differences in the currencies or monetary units used by countries engaging in international trade all too often lead, unfortunately, to the introduction of new risks and other inefficiencies. In order for markets to function with maximum efficiency, the framework within which international trade is carried out must be such that all mutually beneficial trade can occur with a minimum of effort. Instead, we permit financial arrangements to become so tangled that some trade that would have benefited trading parties is not carried out at all. Thus, a major challenge is to find and institute sets of arrangements that will promote the free flow of trade.

What determines the rate at which the money of one country can be converted into that of another? In this section of the chapter, we examine first the mechanism by which exchange rates are determined in uncontrolled or free markets. Next, we examine some of the risks associated with international trade and investment, some of the methods and instruments used in making payment as well as financing international trade, and finally, some of the agencies that serve to promote international trade.

Exchange Rate Determination

When we consider the rate at which the currency of one country can be converted into that of another country, the first principle to keep in mind is that we are dealing with a price. For example, the exchange rate between the US dollar and the British pound sterling should be viewed simply as the dollar price of the pound (viewed from the vantage point of the American), or the pound price of the dollar (viewed through the eyes of the British trader). Thus, while we use the specialized term "exchange rate" to describe the price of a foreign currency, it is nonetheless a price.[2] Given that exchange rates are merely prices, then the understanding of how such rates are determined in a free market becomes a straightforward exercise in basic microeconomics. In any free market, prices are determined by the forces of demand and supply, representing the interaction of buyers and sellers. In any given country, supplies of foreign currencies come into the market from the export of goods and services, from unilateral transfers into the country, and from capital movements into the country. Demands for foreign currencies arise from import activities, from unilateral transfers out of the country, and from capital movements out of the country. These form the basis for the determination of relative currency prices, or exchange rates.

---

[2]As a matter of custom, certain prices are referred to by special names. Thus while the price of a car or an ice cream cone is called a price, the price of loanable funds is referred to as an interest rate, the price of a unit of labor is called a wage rate, and the price charged for the use of real property is called rent. Nonetheless, all are prices and as such are determined in a market economy through the forces of supply and demand.

To establish a home country's demand function for a foreign currency, one could think of that currency as though it were a commodity. Alternatively, the concept of **derived demand** is useful. Normally, one does not acquire a foreign currency for the sake of merely owning or holding that currency. The desire to acquire a foreign currency derives from the desire to acquire foreign-produced goods. Thus, the demanders should be thought of as those who want to make payments to parties in the other country. Using a simple two-country example for illustrative purposes, assume that the United States is the home country and Mexico the foreign country. The United States demand for the peso would merely be expressed in terms of the quantities of pesos that people in the United States would be willing to buy at various alternative prices of the peso, other things being equal. A demand curve for the peso would slope downward to the right, reflecting the fact that the lower the dollar price of the peso, the less expensive are Mexican goods in terms of dollar prices (see Figure 8.1).

Given that the US demand for pesos stems from the importation of Mexican goods, transfers to that country and capital movements from the United States to Mexico, it follows then that a change involving any of those variables will have the effect of shifting the peso demand curve. Thus, if Americans develop a stronger taste for Mexican-produced goods, the demand curve for the peso will shift outward to the right. Similarly, say that real interest rates in Mexico rise relative to US real rates.[3] Other things remaining unchanged, this will produce a rightward shift of the demand curve for pesos. Increased direct investment in Mexico by US enterprises also may be expected to shift the curve to the right. The removal of trade barriers between the two countries (such as those covered by NAFTA) also results in an increase in the demand for pesos, again resulting in a rightward shift of the demand curve for pesos.

The supply schedule of a foreign currency, in this case, the Mexican peso, can be established in a similar fashion. Suppliers of pesos are the Mexicans who purchase goods and services from the United States. They supply (or place on the market) pesos through the act of acquiring dollars needed to pay for US-produced goods. The peso supply curve then represents the quantities of pesos that will be placed on the market at alternative dollar prices of the peso, other things remaining unchanged (see Figure 8.2). Thus, as incomes rise in Mexico and Mexicans begin to import more US goods, the effect will be to increase to the supply of pesos entering the exchange market—shifting the peso supply curve outward to the right. If the price level in the United States rises relative to the price level in Mexico, American goods become less attractive *vis-à-vis* Mexican-produced goods, thus decreasing the supply of Mexican pesos placed on exchange markets. This would, of course, be depicted as a leftward shift of the peso supply curve.

---

[3]Real interest rates, like other real (as opposed to nominal) values in economics, have been adjusted for price level effects. A real interest rate would be measured as the nominal (unadjusted) rate of interest minus the rate of inflation.

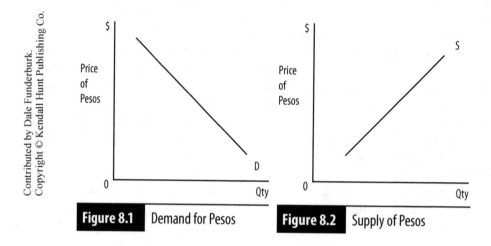

Figure 8.1 Demand for Pesos   **Figure 8.2** Supply of Pesos

As is the case with all market-determined prices, the exchange rate is determined in the market (in this case currency markets) through the interaction of buyers and sellers. Given that the demand curve reflects the preferences of buyers, and the supply curve reflects the preferences of sellers, then it follows that the intersection of the demand curve and the supply curve represents that price (exchange rate) at which the number of pesos placed on the market by suppliers just matches the quantity that buyers are willing and able to take off the market (see Figure 8.3). Thus, point e in Figure 8.3 could be thought of as the market-determined dollar price of the peso.[4] Alternatively, it could be considered the equilibrium exchange rate between the peso and the dollar.

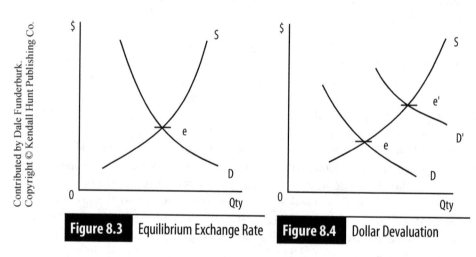

Figure 8.3 Equilibrium Exchange Rate   **Figure 8.4** Dollar Devaluation

[4]Since an exchange rate represents the value or price of one currency in terms of another, then the US dollar price of the Mexican peso and the peso price of the dollar are, mathematically, reciprocals. That is, if the dollar price of the peso is $0.08642 per peso, then the peso price of the dollar is 1\0.08642, or 11.572 pesos per dollar. Similarly, if the dollar price of the pound sterling is $1.7881 per £1, the pound price of the dollar must be 1\1.7881, or £0.5593 per $1.

An exchange rate that is freely determined in international currency markets varies or fluctuates according to changes in international demand and supply conditions. Using our earlier example, assume that Americans begin to import more Mexican products, invest more in Mexico, and take more vacations in Mexico. The combined effect of these changes would be to increase the demand for pesos, meaning that the demand curve for the peso shifts to the right (see Figure 8.4). As the dollar price of the peso rises, the exchange rate would correspondingly adjust, moving from e to e'. This movement could be described as a rise in the dollar price of the peso, or alternatively, as a decline (or devaluation) of the dollar versus the peso.

As another example, assume that a political and economic crisis hits Mexico (such as the so-called "Tequila crisis" of 1994–1995), sending that country's economy into a severe slump. One would expect this to decrease the demand for the peso and, at the same time, increase the supply of pesos coming onto the market. Why? Because of the increased uncertainty and instability associated with doing business in Mexico, Americans (and other internationals) would be less apt to invest in Mexico. That would shift the peso demand curve to the left. At the same time, many of those holding pesos might decide to flee that currency, fearing its loss of value, and move into dollars. This would shift the peso supply curve to the right. The effect? The dollar price of the peso would fall. This could be described either as a decline in the dollar price of the peso, or a peso devaluation *vis-à-vis* the dollar. From the viewpoint of the United States, it would be seen as an appreciation of the dollar relative to the peso.

Control of Exchange Rates

In the section above, our analysis of international currency markets assumed a floating, or flexible, system of exchange in which relative currency values were determined by private demand and supply forces in the market. A floating, flexible, or freely fluctuating exchange rate system is one in which the prices of currencies are determined by competitive market forces. Until around 1971, however, international exchange rates were controlled by governments. Rates were not permitted to move in response to changes in demand and supply. Because rates were fixed for long period of time by government policy, this system is generally referred to as a fixed exchange rate system. A fixed or pegged exchange rate system is one in which the prices of currencies are established and maintained by government intervention. Although the fixed rate system is no longer in use among the major trading nations, there are some advantages to such a system.

Hoping to gain a trade advantage over their trading partners, one nation after another devalued its currency during the Great Depression of the 1930s. This process of competitive devaluation, referred to as "beggar thy neighbor," had a devastating effect on world trade. Following the depression, the United States and other major trading nations sought to reestablish a fixed exchange rate system in order to rebuild international trade and finance. Under the Bretton Woods agreements of 1945, a new system was devised that would have as its key feature the free convertibility of the US dollar into gold. The United States agreed to buy or sell gold as necessary in order to maintain the $35 per ounce price that had been established by President Roosevelt in 1933. The other signatory nations agreed to buy and sell dollars to maintain their exchange rates at agreed-upon levels. This new system was called the "gold-exchange system" or the Bretton Woods system. The IMF was established to police and manage the new system. The primary function of the IMF was to be to offer temporary assistance (loans) to countries that experienced severe balance-of-payments difficulties, thus enabling them to maintain the agreed-upon exchange rate. Only in extreme cases involving "fundamental disequilibrium" in a nation's balance of payments were changes in exchange rates to be permitted. Devaluation was viewed only as a last resort. In general, the Bretton Woods agreements were grounded in the belief that only relatively fixed exchange rates could provide the stability necessary to restore world trade to pre-depression levels.

Two of the major benefits of a fixed exchange rate regime are that it eliminates most exchange rate risk (discussed below) and reduces transactions costs associated with trading in different currencies. The development and spread of the Euro, as well as attempts by various countries to peg their national currencies to some anchor currency through the use of **currency boards** are reflections of the benefits of adoption of a common currency and/or elimination of exchange rate instability. **Dollarization** is but another example of the attempt to gain the advantages of a common currency—elimination of exchange rate fluctuations and reduction of transactions costs.

Whenever any organization makes the decision to engage in international economic activity, it automatically finds itself involved in international financing activities. At that stage, regardless of the prevailing exchange rate regime at the time, they take on additional risks not encountered in domestic trade. The successful global entrepreneur must understand and prepare to deal with such risks. Some of the basics of such risks are considered in the next section.

Country Risk

While all business transactions involve some degree of risk, those involving trade across international borders carry additional risks not present in domestic transactions. These additional risks, collectively called **country risk**, typically include risks arising from a variety of national differences in economic structures, policies, sociopolitical institutions, geography, and currency. When doing business across international boundaries, and especially when investing in foreign countries, it is critical that one understands the nature and extent of such risks, and develops strategies and techniques to mitigate against potential losses stemming from such factors. However, those doing business internationally generally lack the specialized knowledge and/or the data gathering and analyzing ability required to obtain the needed information. Their resources are better utilized attending core business activities. This, of course, gives rise to another market—the market for another type of specialized information. Any number of entities analyze and attempt to quantify country risk. Among those entities that measure country risk are the following providers: Bank of America World Information Services, Business

Environment Risk Intelligence, Euromoney, Institutional Investor, Standard and Poor's Rating Group, and Moody's Investor Services. Country risk analysis is commercially available from a very extensive group of services.

Those who analyze country risk normally decompose the composite risk into several components, identifying certain variables for use in measuring and quantifying the various elements of risk. While the definitions and measurement of the components are not completely standardized, and while the different components sometimes overlap as to measurement criteria, some of the more widely used divisions include:

Economic risk. This element of risk arises from the potential for detrimental changes in fundamental economic goals of the country, or a significant change in the country's comparative advantage. Analysts examine traditional measures of monetary and fiscal policy (inflation/deflation trends, soundness of the financial system, tax policy, government expenditures and transfers relative to income, the government's debt situation), and, for longer-term investments, other real growth factors.

Sovereign risk. This element of risk is associated with a government's becoming of unwilling or unable to meet its loan obligations. Sovereign risk stems from the fact that a private lender faces a unique risk when dealing with a sovereign government. In the event that a government decides not to meet its obligations, the private lender has little or no realistic recourse in the court system—in that it normally requires the permission of the government in order to sue it. A government's debt repayment history, any repudiation of such obligations in the past, and variables reflecting the government's ability to pay are factors used in assessing sovereign risk.

Political risk. This is the risk arising from a change in political institutions stemming from a change in government control, social fabric, or other noneconomic factors. It covers the potential for internal and external conflicts, plus expropriation risk. Since there exist few reliable, quantitative measures to help assess political risk, analysts must examine qualitative factors such as relationships of various groups in a country, the decision-making processes of the government, and the history of the country.

Transfer risk. This element of risk is that arising from a decision by a foreign government to restrict capital movements. Governmentally imposed restrictions can make it difficult or impossible to repatriate profits, dividends, or capital. Given that a government can change capital movement rules at any time, transfer risk applies to all types of investments. Quantifying the risk is difficult because the decision to restrict capital movement may be a purely political response to another problem. However, in economic terms, there are some variables that exhibit predictive value concerning if and when a country might find it necessary and/or advantageous to restrict capital movements. For example, a growing current account deficit as a percent of GDP might signal a more pressing need for foreign exchange to cover that deficit. The risk of a transfer problem increases if no offsetting changes develop in the capital account.

Exchange rate risk. This is the risk associated with any unexpected adverse movement in the exchange rate. Exchange rates fluctuate on a continuous basis as a result of short-run factors such as currency speculation activities, changes in a country's import/export position, fluctuations in interest rates, and normal funds flows. Economic fundamentals determine and bring about adjustments in exchange rates over the longer run. And while it is often possible to eliminate or at least minimize exchange rate risk through various hedging mechanisms, that strategy normally is impractical over the life of a plant or similar direct investment. Factors that reflect the degree of over- or under-valuation of a currency can help isolate and quantify exchange rate risk.

Neighborhood risk. This element of risk, also called location risk, may be associated with spillover effects caused by problems in a region, or even by problems with a country's significant trading partners. When Brazil devalued its real in January 1999, that action had a devastating effect on the Argentine economy, effectively spelling the ultimate doom of that country's "convertibility" regime. The concept of "contagion" is at the core of this element of risk. Factors such as membership in international trading alliances, distance from economically or politically important countries and other aspects of geography provide key indicators of neighborhood risk.

The effects of differences in country risk show up in any number of venues relative to business and economic activity. One clear reflection of the impact of country risk is found in international differences in interest rates. Keeping in mind the law of one price, which suggests that international interest rates will converge until the observed differences reflect only differences in maturities and risks, the concept of **country risk premium** becomes of interest. This concept refers to the increment in interest rates that would have to be paid for loans and investment projects in a particular country compared to some standard. One way of establishing the risk premium of a country is to compare the interest rate that the market establishes for a standard security in the country (say, treasury debt) to the comparable security in the benchmark country (say, US treasury bills, notes, or bonds). If the debt issues involve payment in the same currency (say, US dollars) and have the same maturities, then the difference must be attributable to country risk. There are a number of agencies and institutions that calculate and make available data relative to country risk premiums.

Exchange Rate Forecasting

Because fluctuations in exchange rates can have a significant impact on their costs of operations as well as the value of the revenues they receive from such operations, businesses engaged in the global marketplace often find it important to be able to anticipate such movements. In fact, the entity that can forecast such exchange rate movements is apt to find that information highly valuable. Why do businesses forecast (or purchase forecasts) and what are the uses and advantages of exchange rate forecasts? Whether it involves the firm's hedging decisions, short-term investment decisions, or capital budgeting decisions, information shedding light on the direction (and hopefully, magnitude) of upcoming exchange rate movements can be critical.

Uses and Users of Exchange Rate Forecasts

Hedging: Whenever companies conduct business across borders, they must deal in foreign currencies. They must exchange foreign currencies for home currencies when dealing with receivables, and vice versa for payables. Foreign exchange risk is the risk that the exchange rate will change unfavorably (against them) before the currency is exchanged. A foreign exchange hedge is a method used by companies to eliminate or minimize, or hedge, this risk. Perhaps the simplest way to think about hedging is in terms of insurance. When companies (or ordinary individuals) decide to hedge, they are insuring themselves against some negative event—such as an adverse exchange rate movement. This doesn't prevent a negative event from occurring, but if it does happen and one is properly hedged, the impact of the event is reduced. Hedging techniques generally involve the use of complicated financial instruments known as derivatives, the two most common of which are forward contracts and options. A forward contract locks in the exchange rate at which the transaction will occur in the future, whereas an option sets a rate at which the company may choose to exchange currencies. An important feature to keep in mind is that the goal of hedging is not to make money but to protect against losses. And since every hedge has a cost, before a company decides to use hedging, it must ask itself if the benefits received from the hedge justify the expense. Thus, exchange rate forecasting, which can provide a valuable piece of information needed in making that decision, takes on considerable significance.

Short-term investment decisions: Companies sometimes have excess cash available for short periods of time. In such instances, large deposits can be established in any of several different currencies. The characteristics of the ideal currency for such deposits are (a) that it exhibits a high rate of interest and (b) that it strengthens in value over the investment period. For example, assume that FunderCorp, a US-based multinational corporation, has excess cash that it is considering depositing into a British bank account. If the British pound has appreciated against the dollar by the end of the deposit period when pounds are withdrawn and exchanged for US dollars, then more dollars will be received. If, on the other hand, the pound has depreciated against the dollar, fewer dollars are received. Thus it is important for FunderCorp to be able to anticipate the direction of such exchange rate fluctuations. So, once again, exchange rate forecasting can help the business in deciding whether to invest the short-term cash in a British account or in a US, European, or Japanese account.

Capital budgeting decisions: Consider the decision of a multinational corporation regarding whether to invest funds in a foreign project. The firm will need to take into account the probability that the project may periodically require the exchange of currencies. Sound capital budgeting analysis can be completed only when all estimated cash flows are measured in the parent's local currency. As an example, assume that Commerce Worldwide, another US-based multinational, needs to decide whether to establish a subsidiary in Brazil. The earnings to be generated by the proposed Brazilian subsidiary would periodically need to be converted into US dollars to be remitted to the parent company, Commerce Worldwide. Once again, it is clear that unanticipated currency fluctuations can lead to faulty capital budgeting decisions. Good exchange rate forecasts can mitigate that risk.

Other uses and users of forecasts: In addition to the reasons discussed above, businesses may need to forecast exchange rates when attempting to forecast corporate earnings (which may include earnings from foreign subsidiaries), or when making long-term financing decisions. For example, bond issues may be denominated in foreign currency as well as in the domestic currency, once again placing a premium on being able to anticipate or forecast exchange rate fluctuations. Two other types of entities that routinely engage in foreign exchange transactions—but for reasons very different from those discussed above—and are "power users" of exchange rate forecasts are currency traders and central banks.

The world's largest and most liquid market, with a daily global trading volume of some US $4 trillion—more than the New York Stock Exchange and NASDAQ combined—is **Forex**, the foreign exchange market. Forex is a global over-the-counter, decentralized market for the trading of currencies. The main participants in Forex are larger international banks. Trades between foreign exchange dealers can be very large, involving hundreds of millions of dollars. Most of the Forex transactions are trades between currency pairs, with the Euro, the US Dollar, the British Pound, the Japanese Yen, the Australian Dollar, and the Swiss Franc, the so-called "Majors" comprising the bulk of the traded pairs. Other traits and characteristics of Forex is that it operates continuously (24 hours per day except weekends), allows for very heavy leveraging, and involves very light supervision and regulation vis-à-vis other types of financial markets. And, in addition to being the largest financial market in the world, Forex is also the most volatile. Relative to the direct participants in the market, it is important to understand that unlike other types of businesses (such as those discussed above) for which currency exchange is merely a necessary adjunct to their core business activity, for the currency trader, currency trading is the core business activity. Currency traders flourish or perish based on their ability to function in this fast-paced, high-stakes environment. Because of the very nature of Forex trading, currency traders are among the most voracious and sophisticated users of exchange rate forecasts as well as some of the most proficient and professional forecasters themselves.

And finally, it should be noted that central banks around the world, such as the Federal Reserve and the European Central Bank, are heavily involved in foreign exchange markets. In their efforts to maintain the stability of financial systems and to contain systemic risk that may arise from financial markets, central banks have become highly cognizant of the phenomenon called **contagion**. As the global economy has grown and national economies (especially certain groupings of economies and/or economies within certain geographic regions) have become more correlated with one another, the likelihood that significant changes in one country will spread to other countries has become a threat of increased concern.

For example, one of the more infamous occurrences of this phenomenon was the "Asian Contagion" which started in 1997. This international financial crisis began in Thailand, spread to bordering Southeast Asian countries, and eventually even spilled over to Latin America. One of the vehicles through which contagion can manifest itself is that of sudden, large, and/or unanticipated fluctuations in currency values. To the extent that central banks are able to anticipate destabilizing currency swings, then if they are able to coordinate their efforts and collectively have the financial wherewithal to act on a sufficiently large scale, they may be able to ameliorate the damage. But it is axiomatic that in order to offset a coming future event, one must see it coming. Once again, forecasting is crucial.

Approaches, Methods, and Techniques

Given the broad range of different uses and users of exchange rate forecasts, it is not surprising that such forecasts also entail a broad range of focuses and variables, as well as methods and techniques. For example, short-term exchange rate forecasts generally focus on different variables and employ different techniques as compared to longer-term forecasts. Likewise, real exchange rate forecasts, which tend to be more important to managers planning longer-term investment projects, must include (either explicitly or implicitly) a forecast of relative inflation rates, whereas nominal exchange rate forecasts that tend to be more important for currency traders, may not. So, because there are so many different uses and users of exchange rate forecasts, and because no single approach has proven itself superior to others over a broad spectrum of applications, one finds relatively little commonality regarding the topic and practice—even in terms of textbook classifications and descriptions. Thus, the purpose and limited intent of the discussion that follows is merely to provide a rough, general overview of the main approaches, methods, and techniques employed in order to generate most forecasts.

Technical Forecasting Approach employs the use of historical exchange rate data, mainly that related to volume and price, to predict future values. Such forecasting focuses on recognizing rate patterns and trends and tries to extrapolate those trends. In a very important sense, technical analysis is based on the premise that history repeats itself. The analysis is "technical" in the sense that it does not rely on a fundamental analysis of the underlying economic determinants of exchange rates, but only on extrapolations of past price trends. While there are various methods used by these technicians, a mainstay is the study of price charts, with various moving average and other time-series techniques being widely employed. And while, for example, identifying a trend of successive daily exchange rate adjustments may be helpful for very short-term periods such as day-to-day changes, such patterns may be less reliable for forecasting long-term movements, even no longer than a quarter or a year. It is also often noted that while academicians and their academic studies tend to discredit the validity of technical analysis, many traders nonetheless depend on technical analysis for their trading strategies.

Fundamental Forecasting Approach is generally based on identifying fundamental relationships between economic variables and exchange rates. Whereas short-term exchange rate forecasts could be generated using technical models that do not incorporate economic fundamentals, longer-term forecasts rely on macro-economic models. Fundamental forecasting models tend to employ more sophisticated statistical, econometric techniques of analysis. These forecasters often start with a basic economic model, which is then used to produce forecasting equations. For example, the purchasing power parity (PPP) forecasting approach is based on the theory of one price (discussed earlier in this chapter), which states that identical goods in different countries should have identical prices. However, since price adjustments are by no means instantaneous, PPP may play a more important role in long-term forecasting, but contribute little to shorter-term forecasts. Two major difficulties involved in fundamental forecasting are, first, that one has to forecast a set of independent variables in order to forecast the exchange rates. Forecasting the former will certainly be subject to errors and in fact may not necessarily be easier than forecasting the latter. Secondly, the values that are estimated using historical data may change over time because of the changes in government policies and/or the underlying structure of the economy.

Other Forecasting Approaches used to anticipate exchange rate fluctuations include so-called "market-based" forecasts, efficient market/random walk forecasts, mixed methods, and composite forecasts. While analysis of these various approaches and techniques is well beyond the scope of this chapter, it may be mentioned that in general: (a) market-based forecasting involves the use of a market determined exchange rate (such as the "spot rate" or "forward rate") to forecast the spot rate in the future;[5] (b) the efficient market hypothesis assumes that market prices, including exchange rates, reflect all relevant, publically available information (such as money supplies, inflation rates, trade balances, and output growth), and thus will change only when the market receives new information. Since news is considered to be unpredictable, it follows that the exchange rate will change randomly over time; (c) mixed/composite forecasting involves the development of forecasts based on a mixture of forecasting techniques. Various forecasts of a particular currency value are assigned weights based on their historical reliability, with the actual forecast of the currency being a weighted average of the various forecasts developed. While the relative advantages and weaknesses of the various approaches and techniques continue to be studied, the consensus is that exchange rate fluctuations are very difficult to predict and to date, there is no clear-cut winner in the quest to accurate and useable forecasts.

Payment Terms and Options for International Trade

Every shipment abroad requires some form of financing while in transit. Additionally, the supplier (exporter) needs financing, either internally generated or externally acquired, to buy or manufacture its goods. The buyer (importer) must carry these goods in inventory until they are sold. In some cases, the supplier will have sufficient cash flow to finance the entire trade cycle out of its own funds, and thus be willing to extend credit until the importer has converted the goods into

---

[5]The spot rate refers merely to the current exchange rate of a currency. The forward rate is the rate at which a bank is willing to exchange one currency for another at some specified date in the future.

cash. Alternatively, the buyer may be able to finance the entire cycle by paying cash in advance. Usually, however, some in-between approach is chosen, involving a combination of financing by the buyer, seller, and third parties. Thus, in any international trade transaction, credit is inevitably provided by either the supplier/ exporter, the buyer/importer, one or more financial institutions, or some combination of these.

Relative to the issue of credit, however, one critical aspect of all trade, whether cross-border or domestic, is not really different—and that is the importance of insuring payment. The process of making that determination should start well before any contract is signed. Employing the principles of conservative credit management, the seller should keep in mind that it is up to him to perform "due diligence" in order to arrive at a reasonable assessment of the risks posed by the potential deal. It is a good practice to apply the time-tested caveat of "know who you're dealing with" insomuch as is practical. Even some fairly simple, basic research such as contacting chambers of commerce or better business bureaus (or their equivalent that may be present in many developed countries), freight forwarders, trade associations or banks, larger credit reporting services (such as international affiliates of Dun & Bradstreet and TRW) or even asking the buyer to provide references, can provide at least some information on the buyer. The next step is for the seller to use that information to make a decision based on his or her assessment of his or her own risk tolerance. In this process, it is generally helpful to ask several questions: Can the business afford the loss if it is not paid? Can the sale only be made by extending credit? Will extending credit and the possibility of waiting several months for payment still make the sale profitable? How long has this buyer been operating and what is his credit rating? Are there viable alternatives for collecting if the buyer does not live up to his obligations? Only after completing this process and assessment should the business address issues of payment means and options.

There are five principal means and options for payment in international trade. Associated with each is a different degree of risk to the exporter and the importer. As a general rule, the greater the protection afforded to the exporter, the less convenient are the payment terms for the importer. Thus, when choosing among payment methods to require, the supplier must weigh the benefits in risk reduction against the cost in terms of lost sales. The five basic means of payment used to settle international transactions are briefly discussed below—ranked in order of increasing risk to the exporter.

Cash in advance. Under the prepayment or cash in advance method, the exporter will not ship the goods until the buyer has remitted payment to the exporter. This method affords the exporter the greatest protection and allows it to avoid tying up its own funds. Prepayment is often required of first-time buyers whose creditworthiness is unknown, or where there is political instability in the importing country. Most buyers, however, are unable and/or unwilling to bear all the risk by prepaying the order. Additionally, due to competitive pressures, requiring payment in advance is not something that generally works for exporters unless they have a unique product or market niche. When this method of payment is used, the payments are most often made in the form of an international wire transfer to the exporter's bank account or foreign bank draft.

Letter of credit. This is an instrument issued by a bank on behalf of the importer promising to pay the exporter upon presentation of shipping documents in compliance with a set of stipulated terms. In effect, the bank is substituting its credit for that of the buyer. This method may be viewed as a compromise between the seller and the buyer because it affords certain advantages to each party. The exporter is assured of receiving payment as long as it presents documents in accordance with the agreement. When credit is extended, this method of financing offers the exporter the greatest degree of safety. The advantage to the importer is that it does not have to pay for the goods until shipment has been made and documents are presented in good order.

Drafts. This instrument, also known as a **bill of exchange**, is an unconditional written order—usually drawn by the exporter and addressed to the importer—ordering the buyer to pay on demand (or at a specified future date) the face amount of the draft. The draft represents the exporter's formal demand for payment from the buyer. Inasmuch as banks are not obligated to honor payments on the buyer's behalf, the draft affords the exporter less protection than does the letter of credit. However, the draft does enable the exporter to use its bank as a collection agent. The bank forwards the draft or bill of exchange to the foreign buyer (either directly or through a branch or correspondent bank), collects on the draft, and then remits the proceeds to the exporter.

Drafts may be either sight drafts or time drafts. Sight drafts must be paid on presentation. Time drafts are payable at some specified future date and as such become a useful financing technique. A **banker's acceptance**, discussed below, is a time draft that has been accepted by the drawee, the bank to which the draft is addressed.

Consignment. Under this arrangement, goods are only shipped, but not sold, to the importer. The exporter ships the goods to the importer while still retaining actual title to the merchandise. The importer has access to the goods but does not have to pay for them until they have been sold to a third party. The exporter is thus placed in a position of having to trust the buyer to pay once the goods are sold, with very limited recourse in case of default. Because of the high risk, consignments are infrequently used except in special cases such as affiliated or subsidiary companies trading with the parent company.

Open account. Functionally, open account selling is the opposite of cash in advance or prepayment. The exporter ships the merchandise and expects the buyer to remit payment according to the agreed-upon terms. The seller is relying completely on the creditworthiness, integrity, and reputation of the buyer, meaning obviously that open account terms carry the highest risk of nonpayment. Adding to the risk is the fact that any subsequent collection activities that may be necessary will be guided by the laws and customs of the buyer's country. Historically, this method of financing normally has been used only when the buyer and seller have mutual trust and considerable experience in dealing with each other. However, as world markets become more competitive, open account terms are gaining in usage and are sometimes the only means of entry. Thus, despite the risks, open account transactions today are widely used, especially among industrialized countries in North America and Europe where the overall volume of trade is very high, and credit information is readily available.

Financing Techniques in International Trade

Due to the additional risks and complications involved in international transactions, banks today play a critical role in financing such trade. As the volume of trade has grown in recent years and financing has become such an integral part of international transactions, banks have progressed from financing individual trade deals to providing comprehensive solutions to trade needs. This is especially true of large US banks located in major money centers. These services may include combining bank lending with funds from government export agencies, international leasing, and even risk insurance. However, in addition to straight bank financing, there are a number of other techniques available for trade financing. Some of the more important ones are discussed below.

Bankers' acceptances. A banker's acceptance is an order to pay a specified amount of money to the bearer on a given date. Bankers' acceptances have been in use since the twelfth century, though they were not a major money market security until the volume of international trade ballooned in the 1960s. They are used primarily in international trade with the purpose of financing goods that have not yet been transferred from the seller to the buyer. The great strength of the banker's acceptance is that it can allow an exporter to receive funds immediately, yet allow an importer to delay its payment until a future date. Keeping in mind that the banker's acceptance is a time draft drawn on a bank, it follows that whenever the bank "accepts" the draft (by stamping "accepted" across the instrument), it makes an unconditional promise to pay the holder of the draft the stated amount on the specified date. Thus, the bank effectively has substituted its own credit for that of the borrower. In the process, it has created a negotiable instrument that is traded freely in money markets, typically denominated in multiples of US $100,000. Maturities on bankers' acceptances are typically 30–180 days, with the average being 90 days. Maturities can be tailored, however, to cover the entire period needed to ship and dispose of the goods financed.

Accounts receivable financing, or factoring. Factoring, which involves the sale of the seller's accounts receivable to a third party, is becoming increasingly popular as a trade financing vehicle. The third party, or factor, buys a company's receivables at a discount from face value, thereby accelerating their conversion to cash. As with any debt-like claim, there will be charges for the time value of money and the credit risk associated with the receivables. Most factoring is done on a nonrecourse basis, meaning that the factor assumes all the credit and political risks (except those involving disputes between the transacting parties). The factor performs its own credit approval process on the foreign buyer before purchasing the receivable. For providing this service—which can be relatively expensive—the factor purchases the receivable at a discount and also receives a flat processing fee.

Though becoming more widely used in international trade, factoring of foreign accounts receivable is less common than factoring of domestic receivables. Most international factors or factoring houses are subsidiaries of a major bank or commercial finance company, having the knowledge and expertise to collect in their own country. Factors often utilize export credit insurance to mitigate the additional risk of a foreign receivable.

Forfaiting. Because capital goods tend to be quite expensive, meaning that importers may not be able to make payment for the goods within a short time period, longer-term financing becomes necessary. To deal with this problem, a special variant of factoring called "forfaiting" is sometimes used. Forfaiting is the discounting, without recourse to the original holder, of medium-term export receivables (such as a promissory note or bill of exchange). These are normally very large transactions (in excess of $500,000) with the receivables being denominated in fully convertible currencies such as the US dollar, the Euro, or the British pound sterling. The technique is most often used in cases of capital goods exports with a 5- to 7-year maturity involving semiannual installment payments. Since the forfaiting institution (usually a subsidiary of a large international bank) assumes the risk of nonpayment, it must assess the creditworthiness of the importer just if it were extending a medium-term loan. As is the case with many international transactions, the critical nature of country risk analysis is readily apparent.

Agencies that Promote International Trade

Due to the inherent risks associated with international trade, government institutions, as well as the private sector, offer various forms of export credit, export finance, and guarantee programs to reduce risk and stimulate foreign trade. Three prominent agencies that provide these services in the United States include the Export-Import Bank of the United States (Eximbank), the Private Export Funding Corporation (PEFCO), and the Overseas Private Investment Corporation (OPIC). These institutions are briefly described in turn.

Export-Import Bank of the United States. The Eximbank is the only US government agency dedicated solely to financing and facilitating US exports. Established in 1934 with the original goal of facilitating Soviet-American trade, its current mission is to finance and facilitate the export of American goods and services and maintain the competitiveness of American companies in overseas markets. Operating as an independent agency of the US government, it has financed, guaranteed, or insured over $400 billion in US exports. Eximbank's programs are generally designed to encourage the private sector to finance export trade by assuming some of the underlying credit risk and providing direct financing to foreign importers when private lenders are unwilling to do so. Pursuant to these objectives, the Eximbank offers programs that are classified as (1) guarantees (the two most widely used of which are the Working Capital Guarantee Program and the Medium-Term Guarantee Program), loans (two of the most popular being the Direct Loan Program and the Project Finance Loan Program), and insurance (the most widely used of which is the Bank Letter of Credit Policy).

Private Export Funding Corporation. PEFCO, a private corporation, is owned by a consortium of commercial and industrial companies. It was created in 1970 by the Bankers' Association for Foreign Trade to mobilize private capital for financing the export of big-ticket items (such as aircraft or power generation equipment) by US firms. It purchases the medium- to long-term debt obligations (usually 5–25 years) of importers of US products at fixed interest rates. PEFCO finances its portfolio of foreign importer loans through the sale of its own securities. These bonds are readily marketable since they are in effect secured by Eximbank-guaranteed loans.

Overseas Private Investment Corporation. OPIC, formed in 1971, is a self-sustaining federal agency that provides US investors with insurance against loss due to the specific political risks of expropriation, currency inconvertibility, and political violence, that is, war, revolution or insurrection. Since 1971, OPIC has supported over $145 billion in US investment overseas. To qualify, the investment must be a new one or a substantial expansion of an existing facility and must be approved by the host government. Coverage is generally restricted to a maximum of 90% of equity participation. OPIC also provides business income coverage, which protects a US investor's income flow if political violence causes damage that interrupts operation of the foreign enterprise. While the cost of the coverage varies by industry and risk insured, these costs are not based solely on objective criteria. They also reflect subsidies geared to achieve certain political gains, such as fostering development of additional energy supplies

Summary

This chapter was divided into two major focuses: the microeconomic foundations and principles explaining and surrounding the development, expansions, and patterns of international trade, and the financial considerations associated with carrying out trade between nations. The first portion of the chapter deals with the various microeconomic explanations of cross-border trade. Adam Smith's attention to the concept of absolute advantage was reviewed and assessed as representing merely an extension of the basic economic principles of specialization and efficient resource allocation. Next, David Ricardo's theory of comparative advantage is the most widely accepted explanation for specialization and trade. Additionally, some of the newer, more sophisticated theories aimed at explaining trade patterns between nations were examined. Among these was the factor endowment theory, which hypothesizes that countries tend to export the products that use more intensively their abundant resources, and import goods that call for more intensive use of their scarce resources. Finally, consideration was turned toward Michael Porter's theory in which he argues that national competitive advantage is not necessarily a condition that merely stems from the bundle of natural resources, land, labor, and entrepreneurial ability that a country may be fortunate enough to inherit, but rather is something that can be created and developed by strategic choices.

Also in the microeconomic portion of the chapter, we focused on the impact of expanding cross-border trade as it affects different groups in an economy. Consumers constituted the largest group in this regard, and they are perhaps the one group that almost universally benefits from expanding markets and intensifying completion. They reap the benefits of wider product choice and lower prices. Producers, on the other hand, may benefit or suffer as a result of expanding markets and increased competition. Some thrive in the climate of expanding markets and competitive challenges, while others wither under the sting of increased competition and the associated need to improve efficiency and control costs. Labor and especially organized labor often resist trade expansion on the grounds that it costs jobs. Generally that "job loss" is actually "job displacement" as opposed to a net loss of employment, but the impact on the displaced worker (or even an industry, business or region) can be devastating all the same.

The second portion of the chapter examines how exchange rates are determined in a free market environment. Factors affecting the demand for and supply of national currencies were examined and used to illustrate how relative currency values respond to market conditions. Next, certain of the regimes and strategies for dealing with fluctuating currency values as well as other elements of risk peculiar to cross-border trade were identified and examined. The impetus for and advantages of common currency regimes, such as Europe's adoption of the euro as a common currency and the Americas' experimentation with "dollarization," were also examined.

Particular attention was paid to the fact that international trade presents special difficulties and involves significantly greater (and different) challenges and risks than does trade within national boundaries. The nature and causes of country risk factors, including exchange rate risk, were explained and analyzed. And because of the potentially devastating effects of unanticipated exchange rate fluctuations, the techniques and uses of exchange rate forecasting were examined. Further, the means and instruments required to provide for a climate of confidence and to ensure timely payment between parties that do not have long, established trading histories, and who may operate under different trading customs and laws, are explained and analyzed.

Finally, for any business interested in availing itself of many of the numerous opportunities provided by globalizing markets, it was noted that there are private entities as well as federal agencies devoted to the promotion of international trade and which offer programs and assistance specifically targeted at these endeavors. These include the Export-Import Bank, the Private Export Funding Corporation, and the Overseas Private Investment Corporation.

Discussion Questions

1. Explain the various types and sources of risks involved in trade between nations.

References

Funderburk, D. (2018). Global Economics and Finance. *International Journal of Family Business.*

The World Bank. (2014). The World Bank Group. *Global Economic Prospects.*

Cross-Cultural Customs and Communication Styles

Anatoly Zhuplev

Hilton Center for Business, Loyola Marymount University, Los Angeles, California

Key Terms

Achievement vs. ascription

Body language

Communication

Content vs. context in communication

Cross-cultural management

Cross-cultural/intercultural communication

Cultural competencies (GLOBE project)

Cultural dimensions/variables

Cultural values and norms

Culture

Culture shock

Direct vs. indirect communication

Ethnic culture

Ethnocentric vs. polycentric cultural orientation

Formal vs. informal communication

Hofstede's cultural dimensions

International management

International negotiations

National culture

Negotiations

Neutral vs. emotional cultures

Nonverbal communication

Organizational culture

Universalism vs. particularism

World Values Survey variables

Work/organizational culture

Learning Objectives

Upon completion of this chapter, you should be able to:

1. Understand the essence of culture, cultural customs, their role, and applications in three key areas of international entrepreneurship: marketing, negotiations, and management

2. Comprehend cultural dimensions and their impact on international entrepreneurship

3. Explore cross-cultural aspects of communications, negotiations, and marketing in international entrepreneurship

4. Develop cross-cultural awareness through self-assessment

5. Gain cross-cultural knowledge and skills in international negotiations

Introduction

Globalization, political-economic liberalization, falling barriers for travel, foreign trade, and investments, with obvious variations, ups and downs, facilitate business opportunities worldwide. In the "flat world" (Friedman, 2007) business playing field becomes more even, mitigating vast competitive advantages that large corporations have been enjoying due to their economies of scale or other size-related strategic advantages. At the same time, globalization intensifies entrepreneurial competition on an unprecedented scale. In this sense, a small "mom and pop" business operating somewhere in the heartland of the American mid-West may be knowingly or unknowingly competing with the likes of Wall-Mart, Amazon, a foreign-based corporate giant, or a small/medium-size overseas retailer taking advantage of inexpensive global communication such as e-mail, Skype, cost-efficient electronic commerce that levels the playing field in the global market-place, and low shipping rates and precision in UPS delivery. Often, international expansion of a business enterprise or its business alliance overseas is triggered by some unplanned chance events and encounters, resulting from personal or business travel, reading, or mass media impacts. Sometimes, contemplating and initiating international business venture is stimulated by personal, family background and experiences, international ethnic connections or by conscious pursuits of marketing opportunities, and emotional decisions that are just hard to resist.

Increasingly, many enterprises driven by forces and dynamics of globalization are being pushed to the international arena in order to survive or stay competitive through outsourcing or strategic alliances overseas. Innovations in transportation (ocean, air, land) create ease, efficiency, and lower cost/risk affordability in international shipping, massive-scale travel and tourism, thus enabling international commerce and investment. Crucial improvements in information technologies (computers, the Internet, e-mail, Skype, Wikipedia, Facebook, Twitter, electronic foreign language translation, or video imaging to name a few) dramatically expedite personal, business and political communications, cross-cultural interactions, and exchange in a truly global scope. Intensified political-economic dialog among nations on the bilateral, multilateral, regional, and global basis, as well as diminishing barriers for international commerce and investment, amplify these processes. In this environment, international entrepreneurial engagement for both small and large companies not only creates opportunities but also becomes imperative: internationalize or bust. Under these forces, large and small companies are exposed and, in fact, compete internationally even if their untended thinking and mode of operation are domestic.[1]

Whatever the entrepreneurial motivation or situation, going international means facing immense diversity and interdependence in political, economic, sociocultural, technological, and other conditions. Understanding, interpreting, and translating these conditions into business success unfold in a cultural context through communication.

In essence, entrepreneurial drivers and fundamentals of business are similar across the world: start-up dynamics, product/service development, market research and the 4Ps (product, pricing, place, and promotion) in marketing mix, soliciting financing and keeping business above the water, finding and retaining good employees, ensuring compliance with the home and host country regulatory requirements, and so forth. Human and business behaviors, however, vary in a myriad of cultural values and norms, organizational forms, and styles and patterns of communication. In some cultures, it takes persistent effort, long time, and skills to develop personal relations and trust first: later that may come to fruition in a successful business transaction or a long-lasting business alliance. In other cultures, entrepreneurs take care of business in the first place, focusing on "hard" variables—product/service, pricing, deadlines, or financials. There, they treat human dimension, personal relationships, as a mere by-product of business transaction. In some cultures, a person's age, gender, ethnic origins, affiliation with his/her social class, or religious orientation are key priorities in his or her organizational status and role in business decision-making; therefore, these persons should be paid major attention in negotiations, marketing, or management. In other cultures, while these characteristics play role, other factors—educational qualifications, professional competence, business efficiency, technical expertise, or personal assertiveness and ability to "get things done"—are more crucial in ultimately defining this person's status, role, advancement, and have different priorities and implications for negotiations, marketing, and management.

Fundamentally, cultural diversity around the world and cross-cultural variations in international entrepreneurship stem from differences in geography, climate, religion, historical patterns, language, family traditions, government, law, economics, technology, and other conditions.[2] In turn, culture—through values and norms—permeates and impacts behavioral patterns for individuals, groups, organizations, and societies. The latest annual Global Entrepreneurship Monitor (GEM) 2016–2017 report that includes 66 economies worldwide reveals wide variations of entrepreneurial patterns across the world. The GEM Conceptual Framework

---

[1]Additional details are available from Zhuplev (2017, Chapter 1). *Internationalization of the Company* (Vol. 1 of this book) discusses strategic benefits, costs, and risks of international expansion, as well as analytical tools, practical applications, sources of information, and assistance for such an expansion.

[2]In strategic analysis, these environmental conditions are often operationalized in the PEST (political, economic, social, and technological) or PESTEL (political, economic, social, technological, environmental, and legal) analytical frameworks.

argues that the existing national and entrepreneurial framework conditions, as well as basic requirements, efficiency enhancers, innovation, and business sophistication comprise the national, social, cultural, political, and economic contexts. Along with social values about entrepreneurship and individual attributes (psychological, demographic, and motivation), they impact outcomes of the national socio-economic development, entrepreneurial output) and generate entrepreneurial activities. For example, according to the report, total early stage entrepreneurial activity measured as a percentage of adult population, 18–64 years, participating in entrepreneurship, driven by opportunity or necessity, varies from as high as 33% for Burkina Faso in the group of factor-driven economies and Ecuador in the group of efficiency-driven economies to as low as 4% for Malaysia in the group of efficiency-driven economies, and Italy and Germany in the group of innovation-driven economies. Cross-cultural customs and communications comprise a fabric connecting the above business aspects of the entrepreneurial process in entrepreneurial behavior, trends, and patterns (Global Entrepreneurship Monitor, 2017).

Cross-cultural behavioral patterns in international entrepreneurship experience multiple interdependent effects of national, ethnic, regional, organizational, and individual culture. Hofstede (1980, 2008), F. Troompenaars and C. Troompenaars (2012), Inglehart (2009), Minkov (2007), and other experts in their work portray cultures across the world through a dozen or so cultural dimensions or variables that categorize trends and patterns of business thinking and behavior in the cultural context. These dimensions provide entrepreneurs with useful cultural orientation and outline implications for conducting international communication, marketing, management, and negotiations. Cross-cultural knowledge and skills comprise an important "soft" power platform in entrepreneurial survival and success under globalization.

Culture and Its Role in International Entrepreneurship

The process and outcomes of international entrepreneurship are affected by many factors, conditions, and circumstances intertwined in specific business situations and transactions in innumerable ways. While "hard" factors and variables—product characteristics, financial ratios, business strategy, law, or regulations—are at the core of the entrepreneurial process, culture plays crucial but often "soft," intangible role in this process.

Culture is the collective programming of the mind, which distinguishes the members of one human group from another. Culture, in this sense, includes systems of values, and values are among the building blocks of culture. Culture is also viewed as a system of ideas and norms that are shared among a group of people and that, when taken together, constitute a design for living (Hill & Hult, 2016). Values and norms that develop in consistent attitudes result in certain trends and patterns of organizational and business behavior. In a broad sense, cultural uniqueness in mental programming, the "software," embraces three levels: personality, culture, and human nature. All these levels are inherited and universal (human nature), learned and specific to group or category (culture), inherited and learned, and specific to individual (personality) (Hofstede, Hofstede, & Minkov, 2010).

Cultural values, norms, attitudes, and patterns encompass and permeate life, work, the way people think, behave, and conduct business, although normally, as part of the day-to-day routine, individuals do not specifically attribute their thinking and behavior to culture in a rational, linear way. At any given time and place, a multitude of the intertwined natural, economic, legal, technological, social, and other forces and conditions interacting with personal traits, demographics, ethnicity, family, religious preferences, educational level, and other characteristics result in certain cultural effects, outcomes, and changing patterns on different levels, from individual to global (Figure 9.1). Likewise, cultural forces and forms affect the surrounding natural environment, economic dynamics, legal system, technological developments, social fabric, and other aspects of human reality. Existing simultaneously as causes and outcomes of a myriad of interactions and interdependent transactions in business, culture manifests itself as an integrative factor on the international, national, subnational, regional, industry, and corporate levels (Zhuplev, 2017).

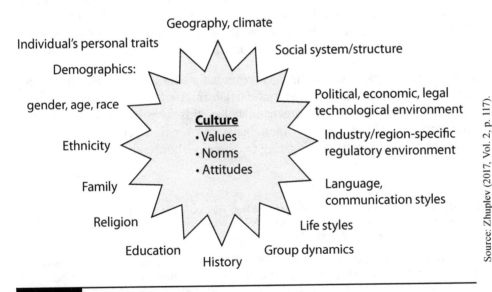

Source: Zhuplev (2017, Vol. 2, p. 117).

Figure 9.1 Determinants of Culture

Business in some cultures (e.g., Japanese or Arabic) becomes possible only after establishing reasonably close personal relationships where securing trust and engaging "soft" factors come first as prerequisites. It is particularly true about business involving foreign partners and alliances. On the contrary, in other cultures (e.g., the US or UK culture), it is customary to pick up a phone, start "shopping around," looking for "best value for the money," discussing, and doing business with strangers in a speedy manner, without first establishing sufficient personal bonds, trust, or mutual empathy.

Three areas in international entrepreneurship stand out as key frontiers in cultural applications: international marketing, international negotiations, and international management. Forces of globalization facilitate market expansion beyond traditional geographic and political boundaries by creating attractive cross-border *opportunities* for domestic companies or *pushing* domestic companies overseas in their quest for survival and escape from high domestic competition or strict regulations. Increased global integration, improvements in computing and information technologies, as well as generally improving global climate for trade and investment mitigate strategic risks associated with international business.[3] Technological advances in communication and transportation make international business more cost-effective and easier not only for large corporations but also for a broad range of small- and medium-size companies.

The falling trade barriers and proliferation of freedom in exchange of information and people tend to make products and marketing strategies more homogeneous on a global scale. However, *international marketing* mix (product, price, place, and promotion components) continues to vary across nations, depending on regional and local cultural patterns.[4] *International negotiations*, particularly crucial for the international entrepreneurial venture initiation process, are also strongly affected by culture. And finally, *managing international* subsidiaries, international joint business ventures, maintaining various other kinds of business alliances, or simply managing domestic company comprised of multicultural workforce requires comprehensive multicultural understanding and practical managerial action.

In international entrepreneurship, it is common for entities from different national cultures to establish and maintain interaction in cross-border business transactions. With a certain degree of generalization, this form can be categorized as *inter-national culture* where business behavior over time tends to blend into a more homogeneous pattern mitigating cross-national differences.

---

[3] One illustration to this is the World Trade Organization (WTO), the major global body facilitating and regulating international trade that has been in existence since 1995. As of July 2016, WTO included 164 member nations whose trade policies and flows abide by the WTO rules. Together they accounted for 98% of world trade (Hill & Hult, 2016).

[4] Despite the remaining national differences in consumer demand and government regulations on a wide variety of consumer products, food, clothing, and other culturally bound items, many commodities (e.g., oil, agricultural products), industrial products (aircraft, equipment), technological gadgets ("iPad," cell phone), and other products and services tend to be increasingly global. Obviously, notwithstanding global similarities, even global products vary in their regional and national specifications, depending on the climate, electric frequency and voltage, product-safety requirements, and other conditions. On top of that, regional cross-cultural differences should be an integral part of international business research and market strategy. Regional analysis is particularly important when it comes to large countries characterized by multifaceted demographics and complex politico-economic landscape. For example, Japan is one of the world's major markets and most ethnically homogenous countries. Ethnic Japanese comprise 98.5% of the nation's total population of 127 million people). From the distance of New York or Los Angeles, Japan may well seem just that—a large and very homogenous marketplace. However, two of Japan's major metropolitan districts with the capitals of Tokyo and Osaka that are only 246 miles (396 km) apart are quite different in their market dynamics, business practices, and strategic approaches. Variations in market dynamics require different approaches to formulating a company marketing mix, the 4Ps (Consumer Lifestyles in Japan, 2017). Such variations in the marketing mix are also common in Belgium, a small, ethnically diverse European country with a population of 11.3 million (58% Fleming, 31% Walloon, and 11% mixed, or other). Yet another example is Singapore, a small Asian country-city of just 5.7 million people. Despite its small geographic size, Singapore is also ethnically diverse—74% Chinese, 13% Malay, 9% Indian, and 3% comprised of other ethnic groups (Central Intelligence Agency, 2016). In large but ethnically homogenous countries such as Japan or small but demographically diverse countries such as Belgium and Singapore, there is an evident need for differentiation in marketing strategies and business practices.

A participant in a business transaction may be representing a certain nation, but his/her individual cultural profile may differ from this nation's general cultural profile, depending on this person's religious affiliation, ethnic origins, position in the national social stratification, and other cultural traits. *National culture* is a convenient operational term, although sometimes it distorts reality; in multiethnic countries, national culture often comprises different subcultures along the lines of their ethnic groups, regions, industries, firms, social/interest groups, business firms, and individuals. Thus, the categories of national character and national culture reflect this level in a very integrated form.

Ethnic culture characterizes distinctive ethnic groups populating a nation: many nations comprise different ethnic groups, often quite distinctive in their language, religion, beliefs, values, and other cultural characteristics. For instance, there are three major ethnic groups in Canada (English speaking, French speaking, and native Canadians), two major ethnic groups in Turkey (Turks and Kurds), several dozen relatively sizeable distinctively different ethnic groups in Russia, and a "melting pot" in the ethnically diverse United States of America.

Regional culture often correspond with the ethnic cultural boundaries (people of the same ethnic group tend to live in geographic/regional clusters), but can be a mix of several ethnic cultures populating the region and differentiating themselves on the basis of local climate, geographic landscape, historical events (wars, political unions), or an industry dominant in the area. A good example would be regional cultural differences that exist between northern and southern regions of some large countries (e.g., the United States, Italy, or Germany).

Culture specific to a particular *industry* or an economic sector may also have its unique impact on business. Sometimes industries within the national borders have very distinctive differences in business culture. For example, informality, fluidity, and personal relations play an important role in the Hollywood film production. On the other hand, business procedures and etiquette in the banking industry are more formal, transparent, and strictly regulated. Due to strategic importance for a national economy or other reasons, some industries operate under preferential treatment, financial support, and control from the national government under industrial policy. For instance, industrial policy affects agriculture, railroads, and aircraft production in the European Union (EU), oil industry in Russia, Venezuela, Mexico, or some export-oriented "national champions" in Japan.

Organizational culture (sometimes this term is used interchangeably with corporate culture) resulting from a juxtaposition of many previous types comprises a culture of a specific organization. The dynamics of corporate culture include routine behavior when people interact such as organizational rituals and ceremonies and the commonly used language; norms that are shared by work groups throughout the organization such as "a casual Friday"; dominant values held by the organization such as "commitment to quality" or a "customers come first" attitude; certain philosophy as a driving force behind organizational policies toward employees, customers, shareholders, and other groups of stakeholders; patterns in "organizational politics," and the perception of organizational climate by its major stakeholders through the physical layout, the way employees interact, resolve their conflicts, and so on. Often, organizational culture reflects personalities of its founders (Disney, Ben & Jerry's, Google, or Dell Computer Corporation in the United States; Li & Fung in Hong Kong; or Toyota in Japan), a type of industry and product, evolutionary stage in organizational life cycle, and other factors. Corporate size also has strong impact on business culture, suggesting significant differences between large and small business organizations.

In a broad sense, entrepreneurial culture in a nation is a contributing factor and at the same time an outcome of the business macro-environment comprised of religious effects, political forces, legal system, economic conditions, socio-demographic structure, and technological environment earlier referred to as the PEST or PESTEL frameworks. Under these frameworks, the individual's cultural profile and behavior are shaped by the family, educational systems and institutions (schools, universities), profession, gender, age, race, community, friends, personal networks, and other conditions.

Over the past few decades, there have been several global studies on national culture of major importance; their key findings are summarized in what follows. Geert Hofstede of the Netherlands in his seminal cross-cultural study from 1967 to 1973 surveyed 116,000 respondents from over 70 different countries around the world working in IBM's local subsidiaries in 50 countries and 3 regions. Subsequent studies validating the earlier results have included commercial airline pilots and students in 23 countries, civil service managers in 14 counties, "up-market" consumers in 15 countries and "elites" in 19 countries (Hofstede, 1980). The Hofstede study abridged the world's vast cultural variety to four universal dimensions allowing for international comparisons in managerial patterns: power distance, individualism, masculinity, and uncertainty avoidance. Building on the ever evolving stream of cultural research, Hofstede later added two new dimensions to his original framework: *long-term orientation* and *indulgence versus restraint*.

In the 1980s, Fon Trompenaars, another Dutch researcher, studied over 15,000 people in organizations in 47 countries and came up with seven cultural characteristics: universalism vs. particularism, individualism vs. collectivism, neutral vs. emotional, specific vs. diffuse, achievement vs. ascription, perception and use of time, and perception of physical environment (Trompenaars & Trompenaars, 2012). In 1991, a group of international researchers conducted a study among students in 23 countries, using a survey instrument developed with Chinese employees and managers. The results from this study led Hofstede to add to his model the fifth dimension of long-term orientation initially called Confucian dynamism (Minkov, 2011). In the early 1990s, Robert House and associates (2004) initiated another major study—a cross-cultural project—Global Leadership and Organizational Behavior Effectiveness (GLOBE)—focusing on leadership and societal culture. The study involving 170 researchers in 62 societies and 951 organizations with some 17,000 managers culminated in nine characteristics—"cultural competencies"—performance orientation, assertiveness orientation, future orientation, human orientation, institutional collectivism, in-group collectivism, gender egalitarianism, power distance, and uncertainty avoidance (Javidan & Dastmalchian, 2009). The latest influential cross-cultural study is the World Values Survey, a worldwide investigation of sociocultural and political change, being conducted by Ronald Inglehart and associates. The World Values Survey completed so far five waves of survey builds on the European Values Surveys first carried out in 1981. Together these amount to representative national surveys of basic values and beliefs in 97 societies on all six continents, containing 88% of the world's population. World Values Survey's cultural variables include: support for democracy, tolerance of foreigners and ethnic minorities, support for gender equality, the role of religion and changing levels of religiosity, the impact of globalization, attitudes toward the environment, work, family, politics, national identity, culture, diversity, insecurity, and subjective well-being. Two major dimensions of cross-cultural variation in the world are: *traditional values vs. secular-rational values* and *survival values vs. self-expression values* (The World Values Survey, 2017).

Among the major global comparative studies of national culture as mentioned earlier, the Hofstede and Trompenaars research studies are particularly instrumental as applied educational tools in international entrepreneurship. Although, as with any scholarly research and applied tool, the Hofstede and Trompenaars studies have methodological and practical limitations, they provide a useful framework for cross-cultural generalization and practical guidance. An integrated summary of the Hofstede and Trompenaars findings and their cross-cultural impact on business are presented in Table 9.1 and Figure 9.2.

Table 9.1	Dimensions of National Culture

CULTURAL DIMENSIONS AND COUNTRIES	DESCRIPTION OF THINKING AND BEHAVIOR
Power distance *Countries with highest power distance:* Malaysia, Guatemala, Panama, Philippines, Venezuela. *Countries with lowest power distance:* Austria, Israel, Denmark, New Zealand, Ireland.	The extent to which people accept unequal distribution of power. In higher power distance cultures, there is a wider gap between powerful and the powerless.
Individualism vs. collectivism *Individualistic countries:* USA, Australia, Great Britain, Canada, the Netherlands. *Collectivistic countries:* Guatemala, Panama, Colombia, Venezuela, Pakistan.	Individualism leads to reliance on self and focus on individual achievement; the extent to which individuals or closely knit social structures such as the extended family (collectivism) are the basis for social systems.
Masculinity vs. femininity *Countries with highest masculinity:* Japan, Austria, Switzerland, Ireland, Mexico. *Countries with lowest masculinity:* Sweden, Norway, Denmark, Costa Rica, Finland.	The extent to which assertiveness and independence from others is valued. High masculinity leads to high sex-role differentiation, ambition, and material goods.
Uncertainty avoidance *High uncertainty avoidance countries:* Greece, Portugal, Guatemala, Uruguay, Belgium. *Low uncertainty avoidance countries:* Singapore, Jamaica, Denmark, Costa Rica, Sweden.	The extent to which the culture tolerates ambiguity and uncertainty. High uncertainty avoidance leads to low tolerance for uncertainty and to a search for absolute truth and predictability.
Long-term orientation (based on limited data) *Countries with long-term orientation:* Mainland China, Hong-Kong, Taiwan, S. Korea. *Countries with short-term orientation:* West Africa, Philippines, Canada, UK, USA.	The extent to which people focus on past, present, or future. Present orientation leads to a focus on short-term performance achievements.
Universalism vs. particularism *Universal cultures:* USA, Switzerland, Germany, Sweden. *Particular cultures:* France, Italy, Spain, the Middle East.	Universalistic cultures develop rules that apply to all relationships and situations. Particularistic cultures focus on the uniqueness of each situation.
Neutral vs. emotional *Neutral cultures:* Japan, UK, Indonesia *Emotional cultures:* Italy, France	Interactions are based on objectivity and neutrality, or they are based on emotional bonds.
Specific vs. diffuse *Specific cultures:* USA, Australia, the Netherlands. *Diffuse cultures:* France, Italy, Japan, Mexico.	Relationships are specific to situations or generalize to different situations.
Achievement vs. ascription *Achievement-based cultures:* USA, Canada, Norway, Sweden, UK. *Ascription-based cultures:* the Middle East, Eastern Europe, France.	People's worth is judged by their recent performance and achievement, or by an ascribed status based on other factors such as birth or social class.
Perception and use of time *Present-oriented and linear:* USA, Germany. *Past-oriented:* Mexico.	Focus and value are placed on the present, past, or future.
Perceptions of physical environment *Environment to be used:* Brazil, Portugal, S. Korea. *Environment to be respected:* Japan, Egypt, Singapore, Sweden.	Either the individual or the environment is seen as dominant; the environment is either used or respected.

Source: Adopted from Hofstede (1980) and Trompenaars (1994).

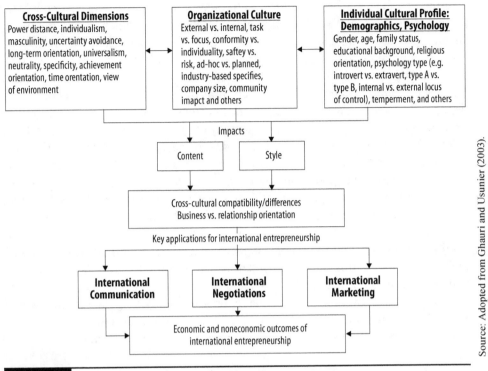

Figure 9.2   Cross-Cultural Impact on International Entrepreneurship

Cross-Cultural Aspects of International Communication

Communication is a heart of business. It involves initiating, transmitting, and sharing meaning by messages through media such as words, behavior, or material artifacts. Unlike R&D or engineering that heavily relies on technology (computers, manuals, experiments, etc.) and causality, business is well grounded in human behavior-based interactions that tend to be more loosely correlated with each other. That implies higher uncertainty and dissonance in various aspects of business communications compared to the fields of engineering and technology.

International entrepreneurs engage in communications in many ways. Initiation of international business venture requires complex research of products, markets, technologies, financing, cost analysis, legal issues, global positioning, entry strategy, and other issues. These activities involve reading, listening, speaking, writing, interacting with other people, traveling, and negotiating internationally; altogether they may eventually lead to a successful business transaction. International marketing includes collecting information on products, prices, promotion, and channels of distribution networks, where personal connections and other informal aspects are paramount. Finding a reliable international distributor or a client, building trust, requires strong motivational, communication, and other human skills. Managing a foreign subsidiary, a joint venture, or maintaining an international business alliance requires complex knowledge and applications in international management where the human aspect of communication is a key.

Communication in a cross-cultural entrepreneurial environment is graphically presented in Figure 9.3. *Communicator:* In the global business environment, an entrepreneur from culture A (for example, the United States) may initiate his/her international business venture by sending ideas, enquires, intentions, descriptions, samples, etc. to an individual from culture B, for example, Japan. *Encoding/sending:* Using his/her own cultural frame of reference, level of education, professional knowledge, and previous business experience, the US entrepreneur transforms his/her business ideas, enquires, etc. into a certain content related to buying, selling, pricing, product-related information, a joint project proposal, etc., and transmittable format (verbal, written, audible, graphic, nonverbal, etc.) that the Japanese counterpart should understand. *Message:* The US entrepreneur sends a verbal, written, or nonverbal message with a definite intended content (e.g., a business proposal or a pro-forma invoice). A purpose of the message may be to have the Japanese counterpart to understand an idea, accept a product for distribution, or verify some regulatory requirements related to importing this product to Japan. However, this intended content is transmitted in a certain environment that also includes unintended factors and effects: emotions, a tone of voice (in the case of a verbal communication), facial expression, body language (in the case of a face-to-face communication), a writing style, or relevant situational business circumstances. The message may be composed in English or Japanese.

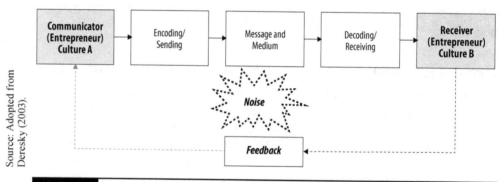

Source: Adopted from Deresky (2003).

Figure 9.3   A Cross-Cultural Communication Process Model

Medium: This is a channel through which the message is sent. The US entrepreneur can choose from several options: a formal letter on a company letterhead, e-mail, fax, telephone, face-to-face meeting, Skype videoconference, the Internet, personal meeting, etc. Each communication channel has its own effectiveness and efficiency, pros and cons, including those grounded in a cross-cultural acceptance. For example, making an unsolicited (cold) call is a very common practice in the United States.[5] However, in many Asian cultures, including Japan, this practice is often less tolerable from the cultural standpoint, so using an intermediary is a common way of initiating business communication/transaction. The e-mail format may seem efficient and easy logistically, but can be perceived in some countries as

---

[5]This has been amplified by the proliferation of electronic media, robocalls, smartphones, advances in artificial intelligence, and other IT innovations.

culturally unacceptable, thus leading to a negative business outcome. *Decoding/ receiving:* Using his/her own cultural frame of reference, level of education, professional knowledge, and previous business experience, the Japanese counterpart receives, interprets, and understands the message in the cultural and business situational context. The receiver then may decide to react and respond to the enquiry. That provides feedback to the communicator, indicating a confirmation that the message was received and had an effect on the receiver. Again, maintaining an effective two-way communication is a very common cultural norm in the US business, but often much less spread in other cultures, frustrating American entrepreneurs who are waiting in vain to receiving a response/feedback from their overseas contacts. *Noise:* At every stage, the communication process is distorted by various environmental impacts. In addition to noises typical for mono-cultural communications in a domestic business, there are numerous kinds of noises/distortions related to international communications. It can be an unintended linguistic barrier resulting from a biased translation of message from English into Japanese, misinterpretation, or misperception,[6] or it can be caused by technological incompatibility between a transmitting and a receiving fax machines because of the differences in electric voltage and frequency, or outdated copper telephone lines and switches. Sometimes, communication breakdowns happen for economic reasons: a receiver in a poor country may me hesitant to respond to a message sent by a sender from a rich country because of the high international telephone/fax or Internet connection rates. Failure in receiving a timely response may cause interpretation or misinterpretation on the sender's part via feedback, leading to a positive or negative business action. Many problems and breakdowns in international communication happen due to cultural differences and misunderstandings.

Cross-cultural differences in international entrepreneurship are caused by variations in the balance between *content* and *context* in communication among individuals affiliated with different national cultures. Cultures with *high content/low context* stress a straightforward exchange in facts and emotions in communication. Information is given primarily in words, and meaning is expressed explicitly, often in writing; the entrepreneur says what is meant and means what is said. In other words, the entrepreneur in the high content culture tends to emphasize an intended content and put it in a structured, explicit, and straightforward format. Typical examples of national cultures with high communication content are the United States or Germany. On the contrary, many national cultures such as Japan, China, or nations in the Arab world have a tendency to exhibit *high context/low content* in communication style. In this type of communication, shared experience and established personal relations make certain things well understood without them needing to be stated explicitly (people involved in communication can "read between the lines" and understand the "body language." Rules for speaking, keeping silence, and behaving are implicit in the context. For example, the relationship-based Japanese culture tends to avoid "losing face." In this context, to sidestep embarrassment and for other cultural reasons, the Japanese counterpart in his/her negotiation with the US counterpart is not likely to say "no," should there

---

[6]For example, depending on the context, the English word "cool" can mean chilly/cold or indicate a good, positive feeling about something.

be a need. He/she (mostly he because women's participation in business, government, and public life is limited) more likely to express it indirectly by saying something like: "It will be difficult," or "I will think about your proposal." The Japanese use of language is particularly unique and very different from other cultures. What is actually said has no meaning or significance whatsoever. Japanese use their language as a tool of communication, but the words and sentences themselves give no indication of what they are saying. What they want and how they feel are indicated by the "way," in effect, style, they address their conversational partner. Smiles, pauses, sighs, grunts, nods, and eye movements convey everything (Bergenthal, 2014; Garten, 2015; Roquet, 2016). The Japanese leave their fellow Japanese perfectly well aware what has been agreed, no matter what was said. Foreigners leave the Japanese with a completely different idea. Usually, they think that everything has gone swimmingly, as the Japanese would never offend them by saying anything negative or unpleasant (Lewis, 2006). In dealing with high-context cultures, the US entrepreneur should pay much more attention to the body language, surrounding events and circumstance, facial expression, and other unintended and informal communication aspects beyond the message itself.

Other important cross-cultural characteristics in international communication include: *direct* (preference for explicit one- or two-way communication, primarily in words, including identification, diagnosis, and management of a conflict) *vs. indirect* (preference for implicit communication and conflict avoidance); *expressive* (emotive and personal communication style with a high degree of subjectivity, stress on relationships) *vs. instrumental* (unemotional, impersonal, high degree of objectivity); *formal* (high emphasis on following protocol and social order) *vs. informal* (stress on dispensing with ceremony and rigid protocol) (Brake, Walker, & Walker, 1995). Solid knowledge and operational skills in using these cross-cultural characteristics in international entrepreneurship may help in avoiding blunders in communication, negotiations, and marketing. It may also facilitate greater effectiveness and efficiency in these areas of international business.

Cross-Cultural Aspects of International Negotiations

International business negotiations as part of cross-cultural communication take place at every stage of the entrepreneurial process, from venture initiation to the termination of business relationships. Culture is an important component in international business as a whole, but it is particularly critical during the initial stages of a business venture where parties learn about the venture itself, the surrounding business environment, and of utmost importance are building relationships and trust while trying to strategically protect themselves. On a very general level, the key steps in the international negotiation process include but not limited to: (1) preparation (collecting task-related information, forming the negotiating team, preparing the agenda), (2) building the relationship (establishing rapport, entertaining an international counterpart's team, learning about personalities, gaining trust), (3) first round of task-related information exchange, (4) persuasion (applying strategies, tactics, and arguments to strive in achieving the set goals), (5) concessions (making and discussing counterproposals resulting from the first round of information exchange), (5) reaching and legitimizing agreement, and (6) post-agreement activities, including the verification of progress toward the achievement of the set goals, as well as the resolution of disagreements and conflicts. As can be easily seen from this simple list of negotiation activities, all of them are strongly immersed in culture and culturally bound communication style.

Cultural impacts on negotiation vary depending on a managerial perspective (Table 9.2).

Table 9.2	**Negotiation Factors and Cultural Responses: A Managerial Perspective**	
NEGOTIATION FACTORS	**RANGE OF CULTURAL RESPONSES**	
Definition of negotiation	Contract	Relationship
Negotiation opportunity	Distributive	Integrative
Selection of negotiators	Experts	Trusted associates
Protocol	Informal	Formal
Communication	Direct	Indirect
Time sensitivity	High	Low
Risk propensity	High	Low
Groups vs. individuals	Collectivism	Individualism
Nature of agreements	Specific	General
Emotionalism	High	Low

Source: Lewicki (2006, p. 420).

Although it is difficult to categorize the world's rich cross-cultural mosaic into specific boxes related to the entrepreneurial process or the international negotiation process, certain useful generalizations can be made (Table 9.3) on the basis of the aforementioned cultural variables. Due to a limited space, cultural impacts on negotiations are summarized only on the high end of the cultural dichotomies.

Table 9.3   Cultural Impacts on International Negotiations

CULTURAL VARIABLES	KEY POTENTIAL IMPACTS ON NEGOTIATING WITH REPRESENTATIVES OF THIS CULTURE
High power distance	Reliance on intermediaries, at least at initial stages. Negotiating teams are split into participants with high decision-making power and those with no power. Several initial rounds of negotiations with low-power negotiators may be required before final decision involving high-ranked negotiators can be reached. Establishing personal rapport is extremely important. Situations causing the other side to "lose face" should be avoided.
High individualism	Expression of independent judgments, opinions in negotiation, and decision-making. An advance study of strong and weak points on negotiators' background (personal, educational, professional, business), as well as their positions in the decision-making process is advised. Business (task-related) aspects vs. relationships are emphasized. Using individual negotiators and small teams as opposed to large teams. Preference for structure and priorities in presenting information according to negotiators' individual profiles and roles in negotiations. Taking into account individual motivations and responsibilities for the outcome of negotiations in developing your negotiation strategy and conflict resolution can increase leverage in negotiation.
High masculinity	High priority is placed on effectiveness and efficiency of the business under negotiations, lesser emphasis on issues beyond the bottom line. Explicit presentation of information and high assertiveness on all stages of negotiations. Lesser likelihood for female negotiators to be involved in key decision-making roles. Situations causing the other side to "lose face" should be avoided. The opposite party's "macho" propensity can be exploited.
High uncertainty avoidance	Restraint toward entrepreneurial business ideas and bold projects that are not backed up by information and/or resources. Risk avoidance. Abundance of supporting information, feasibility studies, and references required in order to back up the major points under negotiations. Slower pace of negotiations and decision-making, possibility of several rounds of negotiations. High reliance on formal rules and procedures in dealing with complex and uncertain matters.
High long-term orientation	Be prepared to deal with adherence to traditional, forward-oriented priorities. Reservations toward product, technological, and business innovations. Certain role played by nonbusiness considerations (e.g., community, nation-wide issues) beyond the bottom line.
Universalism vs. particularism	Universalism presumes the reliance on formal rules and procedures universally applied toward various situations. Merit-based promotion and remuneration. Egalitarianism. Particularistic types entail reliance on personal relationships, taking into account specific cases and individual circumstances rather than general categories. Inclination toward revising conditions that have been already agreed upon.
Neutral vs. emotional	Neutral types tend to operate with and appeal to the logic, methods, facts, statistics, structures, and priorities in negotiations. They lean toward putting business aspects first. On the contrary, emotional types emphasize personalities and interpersonal relationships on various stages of the negotiation process.
Achievement vs. ascription	Achievement-oriented type in negotiations tends to have characteristics similar to those associated with high individualism, masculinity, and short-term orientation. Greater likelihood for young negotiators with professional knowledge and skills to be included in a team. On the contrary, ascriptive cultures are likely to be associated with the characteristics of collectivism, femininity, and long-term orientation. Team composition and negotiating power may be based on age, hierarchical status, or the length of tenure in the firm. Nepotism vs. professionalism may also play a role.
Cooperation vs. competition	Negotiation is a give-and-take game, and there is always something to gain and something to lose. Cultures with high propensity for cooperation are more likely to pursue non-confrontational strategies in a lieu of the long-term mutual benefits with a "win-win" outcome. On the opposite, cultures oriented toward competition often emphasize a "go it alone" strategy and short-term "the winner takes all" orientation.

Lalita Manrai and Ajay Manrai (2010) developed a general conceptual framework capturing culture's influence in international business negotiations. Their framework includes 12 relationships among the 6 key constructs (Figure 9.4). International entrepreneurship requires cross-border interactions with business partners, government officials, employees, suppliers, distributors, etc. They involve a range of issues from sale of goods and services to setting up manufacturing operations, strategic alliances, joint ventures, etc., all of which require negotiation. Apart from the mastery of the subject matter, a manager must also have an understanding of the partner's culture to avoid cultural blunders and ensure successful outcomes.

The constructs and relationships presented in the L. Manrai and A. Manrai framework provide useful cultural insights for international negotiations. The framework suggests that negotiation behaviors are influenced by the *negotiator's characteristics*: qualifications (knowledge, experience, skills, and decision-making power in negotiations), inclinations (personality, attitudes), and goals that can vary broadly. The interrelationships among the three categories of negotiation behaviors also suggest the importance and impact of *non-task activities* (developing a personal rapport, socializing, or family entertaining) and specifics of the aforementioned *negotiation process* (key components, stages, their sequence, and interconnections), both of which are highly influenced by culture. Of the three categories of negotiation behaviors identified in the conceptual framework, the negotiation outcome is influenced by all other five constructs in the Manrai framework including the three negotiator characteristics and two other negotiation behaviors, namely, non-task activities and the negotiation process. The negotiation process is influenced by four other constructs including the three negotiator characteristics and one negotiation behavior, namely, non-task activities. The non-task activity behavior is influenced by the three negotiator characteristics, namely, negotiator's goals, negotiator's inclinations, and negotiator's qualifications. This understanding can be useful in training the negotiators in terms of developing cultural sensitivity, development of effective negotiation strategies, monitoring the progress of negotiations, detecting the signs of trouble, and adaption of strategy as needed to achieve mutually satisfying solutions (L. Manrai & A. Manrai, 2010).

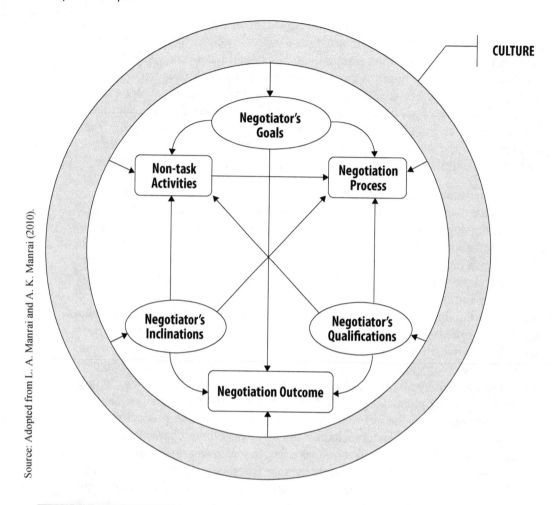

CULTURE

Source: Adopted from L. A. Manrai and A. K. Manrai (2010).

Figure 9.4   A Conceptual Framework of Culture's Influence in International Business Negotiations

What traits distinguish successful negotiators from average negotiators in practical terms? Although specific answer to this question may vary and depend on the context and assessment criteria that are complex and culturally driven, one study of the British negotiators offers some insights. According to this study, both average and successful negotiators spend the same amount of time in planning. The difference is *what* planned.

- Good negotiators develop twice as many alternatives as less effective negotiators. This leaves them with more options when negotiations deviate into uncharted waters.

- While the main objective of negotiations is to reduce and reconcile different interests, experienced negotiators spend much more time on areas where there is a common ground and agreements are possible, rather than devoting excessive time to topics where obvious differences exist. Experienced negotiators also "nibble away" at differences rather than tackling head on.

- Skilled negotiators spend more time exploring long-term issues and their effects than do average negotiators. This practice puts companies emphasizing short-term objectives at a negotiating disadvantage.

- Good negotiators are flexible in setting goals. They define goals within ranges (e.g., a return on investment of 10–20%) rather than as definite targets (We must get a minimum 14% return.).

- Unskilled negotiators have definite sequences of points to cover, ranked usually by their order of importance. Skilled negotiators go into meetings with a series of issues to tackle but do not have a predetermined sequence. The second method makes it more difficult for the other side to determine what the opposite negotiating team considers as the critical issues. This method also maintains a balance among the issues, thereby minimizing the chances that either side will hurt the negotiations by applying pressure on sensitive issues.

- Successful negotiators generally go through four phases: (1) building up rapport, (2) learning about the proposed agreement, including its technical, legal, and business aspects, (3) bridging differences through reason, persuasion, and, occasionally, argument, and (4) making concessions and drawing up agreements (Hill, 2005).

Cross-Cultural Aspects of International Marketing

International marketing involves a number of cultural considerations. *Product* decisions, including brand name, quality, scope of the product line, warranties, and packaging are often culturally bound either directly or indirectly. For example, a beautiful gift packaging in Japan sometimes means more than the gift itself. Americans, on the other hand, are often tend to be driven by product's functionality. *Pricing*, although a key economic component of marketing, also varies depending on culture in such aspects as list price, discounts, bundling, payment terms, and financing alternatives. The rising global middle class is increasingly willing to pay premium price for the quality product and brand. *Place* (distribution) is intertwined with culture through such components as distribution channels (fragmented or concentrated), motivating the channel (long-term vs. short-term; monetary vs. intangible), criteria for evaluating distributors, locations, logistics (transportation, warehousing, and order fulfillment). *Promotion*/advertising includes such culturally bound items as choosing the right media, public relations, promotional programs, budget, and projected results of promotional programs. Compared to other components of the entrepreneurial process (e.g., creativity, product development, technological innovation, or financing), culture is relatively more conservative and less receptive to change. Globalization tends to make entrepreneurship and marketing more international and integrate previously distinctive national markets into more homogenous, whether the company expands overseas or stays domestically, competing with both domestic and foreign firms on its home turf.

Other things being equal, a standard, uniform promotional message on an international scale is more attractive to businesses because of its cost-efficiency; it does not require expensive country-by-country modifications and because the uniform promotional strategy is easier to design and manage. However, in the majority of real circumstances, localization in product attributes and marketing are dictated by technical standards government regulatory requirements in a local country on imported products and services, or simply by a limited spending power among the local population. Along with that, a need for localization may often be driven by cultural differences in consumer behavior. In the international marketing context, countries differ in a multitude of ways along a range of dimensions, including social structure, language, religion, education, role of the family, and government in shaping and modifying consumer behavior.

In highly stratified societies (India with its cast system is perhaps the most extreme example of social stratification), market segmentation and other elements of marketing can be drawn along the lines dividing societal layers. Members of society affiliated with specific strata commit themselves to abiding certain life styles, norms, and rituals that stay relatively stable, making marketing strategies and methods more uniform and consistent within the same strata.

Among many characteristics of the cultural impact of language on international marketing the "content vs. context" dyad deserves particular attention. In the high-content/low-context cultures, such as that of the United States or Germany, marketing should emphasize a rational approach, logic, facts, numbers, etc. focusing on cost vs. functionality and quality. On the contrary, low-content/high-context countries, such as Japan, require more emotional, "irrational" appeal by referring to images, family, friendships, traditions, or group relationship. Many countries, based on their cultural traditions, restrict marketing of alcohol, tobacco, weapons, but are relatively more flexible on pornography, nudity in advertising, or using substances (e.g., the Netherlands in Europe). Some countries restrict hostile and comparative advertising, or using children in advertising.

Islamic religion strictly forbids charging and receiving interest in conducting business. In Hinduism, the cow is a sacred animal, and devoted religious Indians do not eat beef.

There are numerous striking examples of cultural blunders committed in international marketing by US firms with strong international reputation that cost them dearly. For example, S.C. Johnson Wax, a manufacturer of waxes and polishes, encounters resistance to its lemon-scented Pledge furniture polish among older consumers in Japan. More careful market research revealed that the polish smelled similar to a latrine disinfectant used widely in Japan in the 1940s. Nike had to recall thousands of products when a decoration intended to resemble fire on the back of the shoes resembled the Arabic word for Allah. Pepsi's slogan "Pepsi Brings You Back to Life" was debuted in China as "Pepsi Brings You Back from the Grave." Cheetos, a bright orange and cheesy-tasting snack from PepsiCo's Frito Lay unit, do not have a cheese taste in China. Chinese consumers generally do not like the taste of cheese because it has never been a part of traditional cuisine and because many Chinese are lactose-intolerant. One of the famous examples was Disney's 1992 expansion to Paris, France, where the famous entertainment firm committed a litany of cultural blunders, from trying to restrict the use of alcohol in the theme park to serving croissants and coffee, a typical French breakfast, while patrons wanted bacon and eggs, US style (Hill & Hult, 2016).[7]

Due to historical, political-economic, and other reasons, different countries have different structures in the distribution systems, depending on the industry. For instance, in Asian countries, where family connections and personal relations come first, distribution systems often fragmented, hard to penetrate for an outsider, let alone foreigner, and distribution channels tend to be long. A US exporter may have difficult time trying to penetrate distribution networks there on his/her own. Under the circumstances like this, at initial strategic stages, an effort should be made to form an alliance with a local company and invest time and effort in long-term relationships to develop personal trust, a precondition to business success.

Cross-Cultural Aspects of International Management

As the entrepreneurial venture grows, expands globally, and matures, sound management as opposed to purely entrepreneurial drive becomes increasingly important. Along with many advantages of operating internationally, comes cross-cultural organizational complexity. Whether taken in a more traditional perspective, as a set of managerial functions (planning, organizing, influencing, and controlling), or viewed as a set of roles that managers play in organizations (interpersonal, informational, and decisional), international management experiences the strong cultural impact.

Under different situational circumstances, US-based international entrepreneurs face cross-cultural managerial challenges in two typical settings: (1) when international business venture is being initiated/managed on American soil by a foreign company in partnership with a US firm and (2) when a US firm initiates/manages its fully owned subsidiary or a joint venture overseas. Although not an international business venture in a strict sense, a purely domestic business venture in the United States employing culturally diverse labor force also requires a lot of cross-cultural sensitivity and managerial savvy.

With significant breadth and complexity of cross-cultural issues in management, some of the major managerial applications are presented in Table 9.4. Obviously, reducing complex and fluid entrepreneurial reality to an academic scheme reflecting this reality is incomplete and static.

---

[7]Additional examples of cross-cultural blunders in international promotion can be found in "Cross Cultural Marketing Blunders" by Kwinesssential, a UK based consultancy

http://www.kwintessential.co.uk/cultural-services/articles/crosscultural-marketing.html.

Table 9.4   Cross-Cultural Implications for International Management

IMPLICATIONS OF POWER DISTANCE		
MANAGEMENT PROCESSES	**LOW POWER DISTANCE**	**HIGH POWER DISTANCE**
Human resource management		
Personnel selection	Educational achievement	Social class; elite education
Training	For autonomy	For conformity/obedience
Evaluation/promotion	Performance	Compliance; trustworthiness
Remuneration	Small wage difference between management and worker	Large wage difference between management and worker
Leadership styles	Participative; less direct supervision	Theory X; authoritarian, with close supervision
Motivational assumptions	People like work; extrinsic and intrinsic rewards	Assume people dislike work; coercion
Decision making/ organizational design	Decentralized; flat pyramids; small proportion of supervisors	Tall pyramids: large proportion of supervisors
Strategy issues	Varied	Crafted to support the power elite or government
IMPLICATIONS OF UNCERTAINTY AVOIDANCE		
MANAGEMENT PROCESSES	**LOW UNCERTAINTY AVOIDANCE**	**HIGH UNCERTAINTY AVOIDANCE**
Human resource management		
Personnel selection	Past job performance; education	Seniority; expected loyalty
Training	Training to adapt	Specialized
Evaluation/promotion	Objective individual performance data; job switching for promotion	Seniority; expertise; loyalty
Remuneration	Based on performance	Based on seniority or expertise
Leadership styles	Nondirective; person-oriented; flexible	Task oriented
Motivational assumptions	People are self-motivated, competitive	People seek security, avoid competition
Decision making/ organizational design	Smaller organizations; flat hierarchy; less formalized, with fewer written rules and standardized procedures	Larger organization; tall hierarchy; formalized; many standardized procedures
Strategy issues	Risk taking	Averse to risk
IMPLICATIONS OF INDIVIDUALISM		
MANAGEMENT PROCESSES	**LOW INDIVIDUALISM**	**HIGH INDIVIDUALISM**
Human resource management		
Personnel selection	Group membership; school or university	Universalistic, based on individual traits
Training	Focus on company-based skills	General skills for individual achievement
Evaluations/promotion	Slow, with group; seniority	Based on individual performance
Remuneration	Based on group membership/ organizational paternalism	Extrinsic rewards (money, promotion) based on market value

IMPLICATIONS OF INDIVIDUALISM (CONTINUED)		
MANAGEMENT PROCESSES	**LOW INDIVIDUALISM**	**HIGH INDIVIDUALISM**
Leadership styles	Appeals to duty and commitment	Individual rewards and punishments based on performance
Motivational assumptions	Moral involvement	Calculative: individual cost/benefit
Decision making/ organizational design	Group; slow; preference for larger organizations	Individual responsibility; preference for smaller organizations
IMPLICATIONS OF MASCULINITY		
MANAGEMENT PROCESSES	**LOW MASCULINITY**	**HIGH MASCULINITY**
Human resource management 　Personnel selection 　Training 　Evaluation/promotion 　Remuneration	Independent of gender, school ties less important; androgyny Job oriented Job performance, with less gender-based assignments Less salary difference between levels; more time off	Jobs gender identified, school, performance and ties important Career oriented Continues gender tracking More salary preferred to fewer hours
Leadership styles	More participative	More theory X; authoritarian
Motivational assumptions	Emphasis on quality of life, time off, vacations: work not central	Emphasis on performance and growth; excelling to be best; work central to life; job recognition important
Decision making/ organizational design	Intuitive/group; smaller organizations	Decisive/individual; larger organization preferred
IMPLICATIONS OF LONG-TERM ORIENTATION		
MANAGEMENT PROCESSES	**SHORT-TERM ORIENTATION**	**LONG-TERM ORIENTATION**
Human resource management 　Personnel selection 　Training 　Evaluation/promotion 　Remuneration	Objective skill assessment for immediate use to company Limited to immediate company needs Fast; based on skill contributions Pay, promotions	Fit of personal and background characteristics Investment in long-term employment skills Slow; develop skills and loyalty Security
Leadership styles	Use incentives for economic advancement	Build social obligations
Motivational assumptions	Immediate rewards necessary	Subordinate immediate gratification for long-term individual and company goals
Decision making/ organizational design	Logical analysis of problems; design for logic of company situation	Synthesis to reach consensus; design for social relationships
Strategy issues	Fast; measurable payback	Long-term profits and growth; incrementalism

Source: Adopted from Hofstede (1980, 1991) and Cullen (1999).

The above cultural categories, however convenient cognitively, are always intertwined and have blurred borderlines in a real organizational setting. Additionally, all such kinds of cultural categories across the world, from national to organizational, are subject to change under advances in technology, communication, transportation, falling trade barriers, and proliferation of freedom in exchange of information and people. The former, seemingly monolithic Soviet Union with its almost 300 million people is no longer in existence, Eastern, Central European and Baltic countries have been integrated into the EU, China and India are transforming into formidable global players, and even traditional Japan shifting its distinctive cultural patterns as generational cultural norms and values evolve.

Business ventures, cases, and actors in international entrepreneurship are unique in their own ways, requiring a situational approach. A great deal of practical experience and skills are needed in international entrepreneurship in the cross-cultural context.

Discussion Questions

1. Define culture, its role, and key practical applications for international entrepreneurship in terms of international marketing, international negotiations, and international management.

2. Explain national and corporate culture and discuss main points of their interrelationship.

3. Explain the meaning of cultural dimensions identified by Hofstede and Trompenaars in their studies.

4. American business communication style is commonly characterized as high content/low context; in contrast, Japanese business communication style has high context and low content. Explain this difference and possible cross-cultural implications for the US–Japanese international business negotiations.

5. According to Hofstede, American culture is characterized by a high level of individualism. On the other hand, Latin American countries such as Ecuador, Guatemala, and Venezuela have a low level of individualism and, respectively, a high level of collectivism. What cultural impacts is such a contrast in cultures likely to have on business negotiations between Americans and their counterparts from these Latin American countries?

6. What are the major impacts of high-power distance and high social stratification on market segmentation?

Case: Cross-Cultural Communications

Large Baltimore, the manufacturer of cabinet hardware, had been working for months to locate a suitable distributor for its products in Europe. Finally, it invited to present a demonstration to a reputable distributing company in Frankfurt; it sent one of its most promising young executives, Fred Wagner, to make the presentation. Fred not only spoke fluent German but also felt a special interest in this assignment because his paternal grandparents had immigrated to the United States from the Frankfurt area during the 1920s. When Fred arrived at the conference room where he would be making his presentation, he shook hands firmly, greeted everyone with a friendly *guten tag*, and even remembered to bow the head slightly as is the German custom. Fred, a very effective speaker and the past president of the Baltimore Toastmasters Club, prefaced his presentation with a few humorous anecdotes to set a relaxed and receptive atmosphere. However, he felt that his presentation was not very well received by the company executives. In fact, his instincts were correct, for the German company chose not to distribute Fred's hardware products.

Discussion Questions

1. What went wrong?

2. How would you approach this problem?

3. Review German vs. United States comparative cultural profile at https://geert-hofstede.com/germany.html and Germany's business culture guide at http://www.executiveplanet.com/germany-2/ .

4. Offer recommendations to Fred on developing his presentation.

Source: Adopted from Hill (2013)

Memo

To: **Team FMC**

From: **Instructor**

Date: **[   ]**

Re: ***Skill development exercise: International negotiations***

Goal: cross-cultural skill development in international entrepreneurship

Your FMC team is in charge of the development of an international negotiation strategy (background below).

Background: FMC, a US-based automaker (http://en.wikipedia.org/wiki/Ford_Motor_Company), is contemplating its international expansion to China. FMC has contacted Dongfeng Motor Corp. (DMC http://en.wikipedia.org/wiki/Dongfeng_Motor) to propose negotiations in [*date*]. FMC's proposed agenda for the first round of negotiations includes general acquisition-related issues: DMC market valuation, due diligence, management, financials, government regulatory framework, contingencies, etc. At this first stage, there is no intention to discuss more specific details of the proposed acquisition.

Assignment

- Develop/design strategy and tactics for a 3-day long business visit/negotiation for FMC. Defend your work by presenting to the audience (FMC presents first, DMC second).

Negotiation aspects/issues to be considered in your design:

Introduction
The Team
Preparation
Time
Relationships
Opening
Discussions
Agreement

Memo

To: **Team DMC**

From: **Instructor**

Date: **[   ]**

Re: **Skill development exercise: International negotiations**

Goal: Cross-cultural skill development in international entrepreneurship

Your DMC team is in charge of the development of an international negotiation strategy (background below).

Background: Dongfeng Motor Corp. (DMC http://en.wikipedia.org/wiki/Dongfeng_Motor), a China-based automotive company, has been contacted by FMC (http://en.wikipedia.org/wiki/Ford_Motor_Company), a US-based automaker, which is contemplating its international expansion to China. FMC has contacted DMC to propose negotiations in [*date*]. The FMC's proposed agenda for the first round of negotiations includes general acquisition-related issues: DMC market valuation, due diligence, management, financials, government regulatory framework, contingencies, etc. At this first stage, FMC has not indicated any interest to discuss more specific details of the proposed acquisition

Assignment

- Develop/design strategy and tactics for a three-day long business visit/negotiation for DMC. Defend your work by presenting to the audience (FMC presents first, DMC second).

Negotiation aspects/issues to be considered in your design:

Introduction	
The Team	
Preparation	
Time	
Relationships	
Opening	
Discussions	
Agreement	

References

Amorós, J. E., & Bosma, N. (Eds.). (2013). *Global entrepreneurship monitor.* http://www.gemconsortium.org/docs/download/3106 (accessed March 15, 2014).

Bergenthal, K. (2014). *Essential business culture guides. Guide to Japan.* Executive Planet. http://www.executiveplanet.com/index.php?title=Japan

Brake, T., Walker, D.M., & Walker, T. (1995). *Doing business internationally: The guide to cross-cultural success.* New York: Irwin.

Brinkmann, U., & Weerdenburg, O. V. (2014). *Intercultural readiness: Four competencies for working across cultures.* London: Palgrave Macmillan.

Cellich, C., & Subhash, J. (2012). *Global business negotiations across borders: Practical solutions.* New York, NY: Business Expert Press.

Central Intelligence Agency. *World Factbook.* (2016). https://www.cia.gov/library/publications/resources/the-world-factbook/index.html.

Chang, L.-C. (2003, March). An examination of cross-cultural negotiation: Using Hofstede framework. *Journal of American Academy of Business, 2*(2), 567–570.

Chang, L.-C. (2002, March). Cross-cultural differences in styles of negotiation between North Americans (U.S.) and Chinese. *Journal of American Academy of Business, 1*(2), 179–187.

Consumer lifestyles in Japan. (2017). Euromonitor International. http://www.euromonitor.com/consumer-lifestyles-in-japan/report (accessed October 26, 2017).

Curry, J. E. (1999). *International negotiating. Planning and conducting international commercial negotiations.* San Rafael, CA: World Trade Press.

Derecky, H. (2008). *International management. Text and Cases* (6th ed.). Upper Saddle River, NJ: Pearson/Prentice Hall.

Ehanee, M. N., Kirby, S. L., & Nasif, E. (2002). National culture, trust, and perceptions about ethical behavior in intra- and cross-cultural negotiations: An analysis of NAFTA countries. *Thunderbird International Business Review, 44*(6), 799.

Garten, F. (2015). *The international manager: A guide for communicating, cooperating, and negotiating with worldwide colleagues.* Boca Raton, FL: CRC Press.

Faure, G. O. (1999). The cultural dimension of negotiation: The Chinese case. *Group Decision and Negotiation, 8*(3), 187–215.

Francesco, A. M., & Barry A. G. (1998). *International organizational behavior. Text, readings, cases, and skills* (pp. 187–215). Upper Saddle River, NJ: Prentice Hall.

Fraser, C., & Zarkada-Frazer, A. (2002). An exploratory investigation into cultural awareness and approach to negotiation of Greek, Russian and British managers. *European Business Review, 14*(2), 111–127.

Friedman, T. (2007). *The world is flat.* London: Penguin. https://www.penguin.co.uk/books/55443/the-world-is-flat/.

Gestenland, R. R. (2002). *Cross-cultural business behavior: Marketing, negotiating, sourcing and managing across cultures.* Hendon, VA: Copenhagen Business School Press.

Ghauri, P., & Usunier, J.-C. (Eds.). (2003). *International business negotiations* (2nd ed.). https://books.google.com/books?hl=en&lr=&id=YdLV7JpM-90C&oi=fnd&pg=PR9&dq=Ghauri,+P.+and+Usunier+J-C.+(1996)+International+Business+Negotiations&ots=byKKUgqrQ_&sig=yUrM-K3ECxm556Qg3HDiTNX_HNU#v=onepage&q&f=false (accessed April 13, 2017).

Harris, P. R., Moran, R. T., & Moran, S. V. (2004). *Managing cultural differences: Global strategies for the twenty-first century* (6th ed.). Burlington, MA: Elsevier Buttenworth-Heinemann.

Hill, C. (2013). *Global business today* (8th ed.). New York, NY: McGraw-Hill/Irwin.

Hill, C., & Hult, T. (2016). *Global business today* (9th ed.). New York, NY: McGraw-Hill/Irwin.

Hill, J. (2005). *World of business: Globalization, strategy, and analysis.* Mason, OH: Thompson/South-Western.

Hofstede, G. (1980). *Culture's consequences: International differences in work-related values.* Beverly Hills, CA: Sage Publications.

Hofstede, G. (2008). *Geert Hofstede analysis.* http://www.cyborlink.com/besite/hofstede.htm (accessed October 28, 2008).

Hofstede, G., Hofstede, G. J., & Minkov, M. (2010). *Cultures and organizations: Software of the mind: Intercultural cooperation and its importance for survival* (3rd ed.). New York, NY: McGraw-Hill.

House, R.J., Hanges, P.J., Javidan, M., Dorfman, P.W., & Gupta, V. (eds.). (2004). Culture, Leadership, and Organizations: The GLOBE Study of 62 Societies. Thousand Oaks: Sage Publications.

Javidan, M., & Dastmalchian, A. (2009). Managerial implications of the GLOBE project: A study of 62 societies. *Asia Pacific Journal of Human Resources, 47*(1), 41.

Lewicki, R. J., Saunders, D. M., & Barry, B. (2006). *Negotiation* (5th ed.). New York, NY: McGraw-Hill/Irwin.

Lewis, R. (2006). *When cultures collide. Leading across cultures* (3rd ed.). Boston, MA: Nicholas Brealey International.

Manrai, L. A., & Manrai, A. K. (2010). The influence of culture in international business negotiations: A new conceptual framework and managerial implications. *Journal of Transnational Management, 15*(1), 69−100.

Marks, R. H. (2005). Launching a consumer product in China. *Multinational Business Review, 13*(3), 107−122.

Mattock, J. (Ed.). (2003). *Cross-cultural communication: The essential guide to international business* (3rd ed.). Sterling, VA: Kogan Page.

Metcalf, L. E., Bird, A., Peterson, M. F., Sharmahesh, M., & Lituchy, T. R. (2007). Cultural differences in negotiations: A four country comparative analysis. *International Journal of Cross-Cultural Management, 7*(2), 147–168.

Minkov, M. (2007). *Cultural differences in a globalizing world.* Bingley, UK: Emerald Group Publishing.

Mintu-Wimsalt, A. (2002). Personality and negotiation style: The moderating effects of cultural context. *Thunderbird International Business Review, 44*(6), 729.

Rackham, N. (2005). The behavior of successful negotiators. In J. Hill (Ed.), *World of Business. Globalization, Strategy, and Analysis.* Reston, VA: Huthwaite Research Group.

Roquet, P. (2016). *Ambient media: Japanese atmospheres of self.* Minneapolis, MN: University of Minnesota Press.

Salacuse, J. W. (2003). *The global negotiator: Making, managing and mending deals around the world in the twenty-first century.* New York, NY: Palgrave/McMillan.

Salacuse, J. W. (1999). Intercultural negotiation in international business. *Group Decision and Negotiation, 8*(3), 217–236.

Song, Y.-J., Hale, C. L., & Rao, N. (2004). Success and failure of business negotiations for South Koreans. *Journal of International and Area Studies, 11*(2), 45–65.

The World Values Survey. 2017. http://www.worldvaluessurvey.org/ (accessed April 13, 2017).

Trompenaars, A. (1994). *Riding the waves of culture: understanding diversity in global business.* Burr Ridge, IL: Irwin Professional Pub.

Trompenaars, F., & Trompenaars, C. (2012). *Riding the waves of culture: Understanding diversity in global business.* New York, NY: McGraw-Hill.

Wade, J. (2004). The pitfall of cross-cultural business. *Risk Management, 51*(3), 38–42.

Wigley, C. (2006). Asian marketing: East meets West. *Brand Strategy,* 38.

Zhu, Y., Nel, P., & Bhat, R. (2006). A cross-cultural study of communication strategies for building business relationships. *International Journal of Cross-Cultural Management, 6*(3), 319–341.

Zhuplev, A. (2017). *Doing Business in Russia: A Concise Guide.* New York, NY: Business Expert Press.

A Knowledge Approach to Developing Global Entrepreneurs

Madeline M. Crocitto and Sherry E. Sullivan

State University of New York
College at Old Westbury
College of Business at Bowling Green State University

Key Terms

Action learning

Cultural entrepreneurs

Financial competency

Global entrepreneurship

Greening

Knowing how

Knowing whom

Knowing why

SCORE

Service learning

Small Business Administration

Learning Objectives

Upon completion of this chapter, students should be able to:

1. Assess the major trends contributing to the increased interest in global entrepreneurship.

2. Identify and understand the theoretical approaches to education in global entrepreneurship.

3. Explore three forms of knowing competencies and how they apply to starting and maintaining a global business.

4. Recognize types of competencies and characteristics necessary for international entrepreneurship.

5. Learn about government and other resources for career planning and business start-up activities

6. Explore methods to develop cultural awareness with and without travel

Special thanks to book editors Shawn M. Carraher and Dianne Welsh for their useful comments and to Michael R. Gavencak for his helpful feedback.

Universities recognize that the global economy offers unique learning experiences in a variety of ways. They are continually expanding their repertoire of opportunities for students to meet their peers from other countries and learn about how business is conducted in other countries. Typically, this is accomplished through study abroad programs, with recent figures showing about 15% of American undergraduates participating in such programs. On the other hand, students from other countries are steadily increasing their enrollment in U.S. universities, comprising 5% of students in US classrooms. These students are primarily from China, India, and Saudi Arabia. This exposes US students to the reality of the global economy, the need to think globally about their careers, and encourages both visiting and US students to build stronger business associations (Witherell, 2016). Thus, in our technology-driven, interconnected global economy, universities can play a pivotal role in educating students to participate in business across borders.

There is a renewed recognition by governments and universities that entrepreneurship is the key to competitiveness in today's global business arena (Friedman, 2005). The U.S. Small Business Administration (SBA, 2017) reports that small businesses, defined as those employing fewer than 500 employees, created 62% of net new jobs between 1993 and 2016, comprised 47.8% of the private sector's payroll, and constituted 97.6% of exporters. Small firms are highly innovative, registering more patents per million dollars of R&D stock than larger firms, irrespective of industry (Plehn, 2013). Yet, small business owners may lack the skills and knowledge necessary for doing business internationally, be intimidated by the prospect of international dealings, and miss the opportunity to reach the 96% of the world's customers who are outside the United States (Office of Advocacy, 2004; SBA Take your business global, n.d.).

More so now than in the past, new generations of workers find the career path of an entrepreneur to be especially attractive and rewarding, constituting a clarion call to university educators. Members of Generation M "Millennials" (born between 1977 and 1992) are highly familiar with technological-mediated communications across global borders and value individualism and work-nonwork balance (Glass, 2007). Generation Z members (born between 1995 and 2005) are particularly interested in learning about entrepreneurship. They are very concerned about financial literacy and safety; almost half plan to be self-employed in the future, especially African Americans and Hispanics (Northeastern University innovation imperative series, 2014). These younger generations are inspired by, and aspire to be like those described in Forbes "Thirty under Thirty" yearly evaluation of successful young people across twenty industries. These include such examples as 17-year-old Rohan Suri who developed a low-cost method to diagnose concussions; Keiana Cave, a 19-year-old college student whose method of detecting toxins has received over $1.2 million dollars from Chevron to continue her research; and Sean Pettersen who developed an exoskeleton to protect construction workers from injury (Howard & Sportelli, 2017).

There are other trends that are contributing to the increasing interest in entrepreneurship. First, technology continues to fuel the growth of many entrepreneurial endeavors that span the globe. The successes of Google founders Larry Page and

Sergey Brin, Facebook's Mark Zuckerberg, and Twitter's Noah Glass and Jack Dorsey (Carlson, 2011), are well known and inspired others to explore entrepreneurial opportunities in technology. Some individuals are driven to create a new smartphone "app" (Streitfeld, 2012) while others seek new ways of connecting individuals with needed services. For example, Uber came about in 2008 when its founders, Travis Kalanick and Garrett Camp, could not catch a cab ride (Hartmans & McAlone, 2016). Today its global reach is expanding, despite a bumpy ride in some countries; it is considered the most valuable start-up of all times (MacMillan, 2016).

Second, entrepreneurship continues to offer opportunities to individuals with a unique vision about sustainability and social responsibility, but who prefer to avoid what they perceive is the staid and slower nature of corporate life (Mainiero & Sullivan, 2006). Many small business owners are already capitalizing on interest in "greening." They are building businesses with sustainable products and services in such areas as food, packaging, and printing, or are using fair trade ingredients and products (Small Business Sustainability Report, 2013). These entrepreneurs include people like Izhar Gafni and Martin Riddiford. Gafni admired the green nature of bamboo bikes but found their price too high for people in developing countries needing an inexpensive form of transportation. Over the course of several years, Gafni invented a $30 cardboard bike made of recycled packaging, bottles, and car parts which is treated to withstand the elements (Choi, 2013). Gafni transformed his love of cycling into a green product to help people improve their daily lives. Likewise, Riddiford wanted to create a cost-effective alternative to the kerosene used by over 780 million people to light their homes. With his partner Jim Reeves, Martin developed a $10 light that is fueled by a falling bag of rocks, similar to how a falling weight runs a grandfather clock. Riddiford and Reeves' invention offers not only a cheaper light source but also reduces deaths caused by accidents associated with the use of kerosene lights (Tust, 2013). Gafni and Riddiford's stories illustrate how an individual in one country can use green business practices to provide cost-effective solutions to the problems of people in different parts of the world.

Third, there has been a steady growth in what we call "cultural entrepreneurs." Cultural entrepreneurs recognize that people from all parts of the world have migrated to other countries for better opportunities, but still desire a taste of their homeland. Cultural entrepreneurs develop businesses to meet the needs of growing ethnic groups within a foreign nation. For example, in the United States, Hispanics are the largest minority, comprising 17% of the population. From 2002 to 2007, there was an increase of 43.6% in the number of Hispanic-owned businesses. Goya Foods, Inc, founded by Prudencio Unanue and his wife Carolina, both from Spain, grew to be the largest Hispanic-owned food company in the United States. The company was successful because it met the demand for quality Latino cuisine while also capitalizing on the growing demand for foods which are part of a healthy diet (PRNewswire, 2014). Like the growth in the number of Hispanic business owners, the number of businesses owned by Asians increased 40.4% during the same time period (U.S. Census, 2012). For example, H Mart is a Korean grocery that started with just one store in Queens, New York in 1982.

Today, H Mart has 45 stores in the United States and 8 in Canada; over half its customers are not Asian (Kwon, 2013). Goya and H Mart are just two examples of how entrepreneurs began by offering products targeted to a select ethnic group only to see their businesses grow as their products became popular with individuals outside their target demographics.

A report issued by the Global Entrepreneurship Monitor illustrates the important role government can play in encouraging entrepreneurship, finding that entrepreneurship training is most effective in countries which makes it possible to actually move entrepreneurial knowledge into concrete action (Martínez, Levie, Kelley, Sæmundsson, & Schøtt, 2010). The report also noted that across the 38 countries examined, 80% of people who learned about starting their businesses gained their knowledge through formal education. Universities have also responded to the increased interest in formal entrepreneurial training by creating degrees focused on global entrepreneurship and the growing use of international exchange student programs, particularly in the United States (Fischer, 2009) and the United Kingdom (Rae & Woodier, 2012).

In sum, given the major factors contributing to the growth in global entrepreneurship, the purpose of this chapter is to present educators, especially those teaching in universities without a stand-alone entrepreneurship program, with a systematic approach to guide the development and enhancement of international courses and programs with an emphasis on global entrepreneurship. We chose to use a knowledge-based approach in developing this chapter, drawing from the scholarship on global entrepreneurship. A review of the global entrepreneurship literature identified five theories as the basis of international entrepreneurship education. These five theories are: (a) the resource-based view that considers knowledge as crucial in evaluating and using resources; (b) the knowledge-based view that focuses on individual and organizational learning; (c) the dynamic capabilities view that concentrates on knowledge creation and flow; (d) the network theory of interpersonal connections that explores how people connect at various stages of organizational growth; and (e) the theory of value creation which is based upon market knowledge (Peiris, Akoorie, & Sinha 2012). The common bases of these theories point to knowledge as vital to an entrepreneur's awareness of global opportunities and his/her ability to innovate and take action within today's global market. Because of the focus of entrepreneurship research on knowledge creation and development, in this chapter we use a knowledge approach to explore best practices in global entrepreneurship education.

We begin the chapter by presenting a knowledge-based model as a systematic framework for examining how educators can develop students' interest and capabilities in global entrepreneurship. Next, this framework is applied to present various methods and techniques which educators can use to help students learn more about managing international ventures and partnerships. Finally, we conclude the chapter by recommending strategies for the further advancement of global entrepreneurship education.

A Knowledge-Based View of Global Entrepreneurship Education

Global entrepreneurship is defined as the activities which create and process value through opportunities across national boundaries (Styles & Seymour, 2006). Because of this broad definition, faculty may find it difficult to create student awareness of entrepreneurship outside of a stand-alone course or program. Furthermore, many university career counseling centers and courses which discuss career options tend to focus on organizational employment, leaving students with relatively little exposure to self-employment, small business ownership, and entrepreneurship as a career path. Even students enrolled in an entrepreneurship course may be taking it as an elective and may not perceive it as a career option.

In keeping with the finding that knowledge is the key component of global entrepreneurship, we suggest faculty and students collaborate to develop college students' knowing competencies so that they may identify and act upon entrepreneurial opportunities. One such framework that focuses on individual knowing competencies is DeFillippi and Arthur's (1996) intelligent career model.

Well-known scholars DeFillippi and Arthur (1996) posit that knowledge and its accumulation changes in response to shifting environmental, employment, and personal variables; it is not dependent on or subordinate to a single organization or country. They advocate a learning-centered approach that reflects the shift away from organizational employment to a model of occupational excellence, wherein employees seek to continually upgrade their skills valuable in the global marketplace. We think this framework may be effectively used as a model for teaching entrepreneurship. It suggests that an individual takes ownership of his/her career and invests in it guided by the intelligent careers concepts of knowing how, knowing why, and knowing whom (Korotov, Khapova, & Arthur, 2010). This framework may be especially relevant to educating students who are already aware that their interests and preferences are not conducive to organizational employment and for challenging the naïve view that if someone starts a small business locally, then global markets are out of reach.

Applying a Knowledge-Based Approach

DeFillippi and Arthur (1996) identified three forms of knowing as manifested in people's beliefs and identities (knowing why), knowledge and skills (knowing how), and network or relationships (knowing whom). The *knowing why* competency reflects a person's values and motivation. *Knowing why* relates to the person's identity and the fit between this identity and choices made relative to tasks, projects, and organizations and countries. *Knowing how* refers to the skills and knowledge needed for performance on the job. It is the person's level of expertise. Individuals may use their various employment settings and experiences on different projects to both apply and expand the skills and knowledge they possess. *Knowing whom* refers to the relationships or links which contribute to an individual's networking activities. The friends, colleagues, and professional associations with whom individuals network can help build a reputation, provide needed visibility and access to opportunities, as well as present new sources for learning outside of the person's organization and country. Table 10.1 provides a summary of the knowing competencies of university students.

Table 10.1	The Knowing Competencies of Students
KNOWING WHY	Individuals have different career goals and will seek situations that support their preferences and identity. Early in their academic career, students are exposed to different fields of study and from this exposure, they begin to learn what they enjoy, are good at, and identify with. Their identity is then translated into choices about their college major and what types of organizations they wish to work in. Once in their first job after college graduation, the knowing why competency continues to be tested and developed. Was the right organizational and career path chosen? Is the work satisfying?
KNOWING HOW	Upon completion of their college programs, these newly-minted graduates are sometimes placed in job situations that are more trials by fire than an application of their educational experiences. Their organizations may be more diverse and spread across many countries, being much different than the individuals they interacted with at university. Moreover, even as proficiencies are developed, requirements shift, requiring a need for continuous learning.
KNOWING WHOM	The need to develop the knowing whom competency becomes readily apparent to students seeking jobs. Students network with more senior students and alumni to learn more about job openings and organizational cultures. They also learn to join professional associations to make contacts with others doing similar work or who might have job positions available.

DeFillippi and Arthur's ideas on knowing competencies have been applied to the study of such topics as mentoring (deJanasz & Sullivan, 2004), leadership (Scandura & Williams, 2002) and networking (Scandura & Williams, 2002). Drawing from the ideas of intelligent careers (Arthur, Claman, DeFillippi, & Adams, 1995; Baker & Aldrich, 1996; Bird, 1996; DeFillippi & Arthur, 1996), we will examine how developmental experiences, exercises, and sources of information can be used to enrich students' knowing why, how, and whom competencies, thus suggesting a systematic approach to educating global entrepreneurs. Given the interrelated nature of these knowings, our recommendations may apply to one or more "knowings" competencies.

Knowing Why

It is an exciting time to start a business because one may think expansively as suppliers and customers can be anywhere in the world. It is important that a potential global entrepreneur be aware of why he or she will be involved in global markets and what needs to be known in order to be successful. According to the Small Business Administration, 97% of U.S. exporters are small businesses (Delehanty, 2015) as are 31% of importers (U.S. Census Bureau, 2012). This offers opportunities to learn more about other cultures as well as participate in expanding international economies as a manufacturer, distributor or agent for buyers and sellers (Capela, 2016).

Major reasons for becoming involved in global business, especially importing and exporting, are to be competitive and increase sales. International trade offers a means to increase sales by expanding to other markets, reducing the costs of labor and materials, and taking advantage of currency fluctuations. It is also a viable alternative to those in a stagnant economy with prospects of under or no employment.

Students' education about global issues can be examined on both cognitive and behavioral levels. Assessment on a cognitive level of their beliefs and identities may be accomplished by a self-test or classroom test of the factual and cultural aspects of doing business globally. Assessment on a behavioral level would occur when a student is placed in another culture or actually engages in international commerce. For example, there are assessments to determine suitability for international study and global intelligence. However, for various reasons, many students are unable to experience an international exchange or internship programs which would increase their knowing why (individual's beliefs and identities), knowing how (knowledge and skills), and knowing whom (network or relationships) competencies. Thus, the behavioral and networking features of students' knowing competencies may provide the biggest challenge to university professors, especially when students have not traveled or worked internationally, and the university offers few international exchange programs.

Self-Assessment

Faculty should emphasize to students that intelligence, motivation, and adaptability are characteristics of successful managers and entrepreneurs, regardless of country context (Baruch, 2002). There is an entrepreneurial "mindset" which we have studied in terms of personality characteristics such as extraversion, goal-setting, confidence, tolerance for ambiguity, and risk orientation. While some attitudes may be changed through university programs (Peltier & Scovotti, 2010), we believe students should start by examining their own characteristics and participate in efforts to change their perspectives about starting, failing, or restarting their own business.

One method to attune students specifically to their entrepreneurial potential and develop their knowing why competency is to have faculty administer a measure of entrepreneurial orientation, such as Grant's (1996) personality scale, (for other measures, see Lyon, Lumpkin, & Dess, 2000). The Small Business Administration (SBA) also offers some assessments including those that ask questions about characteristics such as independence and creativity along with more specific questions which focus on small business ownership (SBA Learning Center, n.d.). Faculty members can also make use of assessments similar to those used by the UN's EMPRETEC entrepreneurship training program. The UN program screens participants for behaviors such as persistence, goal-setting, risk orientation, planning, and acquiring information (Mugione, 2013).

Self-assessments may be especially important for future entrepreneurs because many students have not considered entrepreneurship as a career option. Often students have not had sufficient exposure to entrepreneurial activities. Although parents or other family members who are entrepreneurs can serve as important role models for interested students (Grant, 1996), not all students have such role models. Moreover, students may lack confidence or may be unaware that they possess the aptitude for starting a business (Ede, Panigrahi, & Calcich, 1998). Generally, the self-assessment process is similar to the first stage of preparing oneself for an international assignment. Individuals must engage in serious self-evaluation and become self-aware (Tu & Sullivan, 1994), because both are necessary before any action should be taken.

Given that students may be risk-aversive and/or lack confidence, they should understand that competencies associated with entrepreneurship can be developed. One study found that personal attitudes, self-efficacy in recognizing opportunities, awareness of social norms, and especially resilience, are related to entrepreneurial intention (Perez-Lopez, Gonzalez-Lopez, & Rodriquez-Ariza, 2016).

Career Planning

Students who find themselves in a global entrepreneurship class by decision or default may not have considered entrepreneurial activity or may not consider it as a career option due to lack of knowledge. Other courses such as Organizational Behavior and Human Resource Management which include career topics in general, may not spark the student's proclivity for independence and creativity. Students may not realize they may earn a sufficient amount of income turning a hobby or activity they enjoy, such as personal training, cooking, writing, or making various products, into a career. Typical sources of information may be of little help. For example, visiting the O*NET website (http://www.onetonline.org) and entering entrepreneurship as an occupation produces little information. Another entry for small business results in a list of occupations such a sales engineers, veterinarians, aviation inspectors, and general managers with no reference to starting a business as an occupation.

Career planning and self-assessment may be particularly important for diverse students and women. One study found that while Black Americans were more aware of business opportunities and more likely to start a business, they were less likely to bring their efforts to completion or remain in business over time as compared to White Americans (Köllinger & Minniti, 2006). However, these numbers are changing according to the latest report from the SBA (SBA Office of Advocacy, 2017). Likewise, in a large-scale study of women in 30 countries, the degree of women entrepreneurs varied by cultural tolerance of gender segregation (Pathak, Goltz, & Buche, 2013) and how family situations, especially motherhood, influenced women's entrepreneurial effort (Brush, de Bruin, & Welter, 2009).

Minority students and women should be aware of these findings and thus educated in knowing how to develop their ideas into successful businesses while overcoming societal and personal barriers.

Travel

Ideally, students would learn cultural and language skills best by immersion in another country for an extended period of time. For the past 15 years, however, the percentage of US postsecondary students studying abroad has stayed close to 35%, with mostly undergraduate seniors studying in another country for a semester or summer term (National Center for Education Statistics, 2015. In total, only 10% of U.S. undergraduates will have the opportunity to study in another country despite the growth of international programs (Witherell, 2016). Larger universities such as Columbia, Duke, University of Southern California have Centers for International Business Education and Research (Martin, Heppard, & Green, 2011); New York University has one of the largest exchange programs of varying lengths with a choice of studying in one of 14 countries (New York University, n.d.). In addition to the benefits of cultural and language immersion, studying in other countries which participate in the principles for responsible management education (PRME) program builds leadership skills when students work to develop sustainable business outcomes (Sroufe, Sivasubramaniam, Ramos, & Saiia, 2015).

Developing Cultural Awareness without Travel

Technology may also assist less ambitious programs. The virtual cross-cultural experience uses software such as Skype to develop team projects and meetings between classes in different countries. Professors develop assignments and schedules which are effective in creating an international experience without the travel costs. Students enjoyed the experience and used technology to learn more about their fellow students (Luethge, Raska, Greer, & O'Connor, 2016).

Simulations can help overcome the lack of entrepreneurial and actual international experiences and provide students with greater awareness of their own beliefs and identity (knowing why) in general, and in comparison to other cultures. There are simulations and software aids, such as one for a business start-up, that may help students gain virtual experience in small business operations (EntreEd, n.d.). MIT (2017) sponsors Learning Edge, a free learning website, which offers simulations ranging from a green energy start-up to those which help build negotiation and pricing skills. Professors teaching in a functional area such as accounting or management can add an international component to simulations in order to enhance students' understanding of cross-cultural issues.

Harrison and Hopkins (1972) suggest student teams live and work in "microcultures" in order to stimulate the international travel experience. Microcultures may include involvement with groups, organizations, or individuals in a neighborhood dominated by a particular racial or ethnic group and/or with ties to other countries. Cross-cultural experiences may be developed based on any aspect of diversity such as religion (e.g., attending religious services other than those of one's own religion), racial or ethnic diversity (e.g., visiting restaurants, shops, museums, and festivals in various ethnic neighborhoods); or age (e.g., visiting a senior citizens center, retirement complex, or day-care center).

Faculty members may discover activities occurring on their own or a neighboring campus which may expose students to different cultures. For instance, some international business student clubs hold events which showcase food and attractions (e.g., dance demonstrations) from around the globe. Students plan and manage these events, encouraging students from different cultures to work together and learn from each other. The event itself provides entertainment in which both club members and nonmembers gain an appreciation of other cultures. Other opportunities to expose students to other cultures may occur during times in which the communities on campus celebrate holidays. In March, for example, Persians celebrate the New Year Nowruz on the first day of spring. New Year Nowruz often coincides with Lent before Easter observed by Christians and Passover observed by Jewish people. Student clubs often hold celebrations of these holidays and invite members of the college community and guests. Holiday celebrations provide a forum for peer learning; students share the history of these holidays with fellow students in a relaxed atmosphere away from the traditional classroom setting.

In the same way, cultural lessons gained by international travel could be simulated by permitting student teams to create their own cultures. Similar to the 10-week training approach developed for Peace Corps volunteers, students can become responsible for creating a community. The development of norms in this uncertain environment simulated the experiences the Peace Corps volunteers could actually experience in their assigned countries. As the student community evolves in the classroom, students can be encouraged to evaluate the emergent organization and interpersonal relations (Harrison & Hopkins, 1967).

Another exercise that permits the simulation of international experiences requires that the class be divided into two groups, with each group developing its own unique culture or taking on the values and behaviors of a culture unlike their own which the groups have researched in advance of the exercise. After the groups have practiced their new culture, representatives from each group are sent to the other group to learn about its culture. The groups then meet as a whole for a debriefing session. Each group presents what it learned about the other culture; the accuracy of their findings is checked by the other group (Zacur & Randolph, 1993). This exercise provides students with the opportunity of trying to decipher another culture. It emphasizes the value of observation and thoughtful interaction for understanding cultural diversity. Just as openness is linked to the knowledge transfer necessary for organizational learning, it is salient to the environmental scanning necessary for successful entrepreneurship. Students will discover that intercultural sensitivity, in terms of both sending and receiving messages among different cultures, is necessary toward understanding another culture (Taylor & Osland, 2003).

Faculty should be vigilant in seeking opportunities to internationalize business education. For example, some colleagues have students in various functional business courses (e.g., finance, human resources, economics) act as consultants to their fellow students in an international business course. In these circumstances, students can understand the contribution of each functional area to a successful business and how functional knowledge can be used to conduct business in various international settings (Palocsay, White, & Zimmerman, 2004). In fact, with the growing diversity of our college students in racio-ethnicity, national origin, religion, and gender, opportunities exist within the class to discuss cultural differences. Some classes may constitute cultural microcosms. In one class, we discussed a news report of a young woman's account of how she was treated differently when she covered her hijab with winter hats due to the cold weather. This opened a dialogue in class where some female students explained their decision to cover their heads and whether people had responded differently to them (CBS, 2014).

In sum, faculty members may be especially challenged when teaching future entrepreneurs who lack exposure to other cultures and countries. There are various ways to overcome this obstacle. One method is the use of high-quality simulation experiences either virtually or in person. The use of simulation exercises can increase students' knowing why competencies by providing opportunities for them to examine their own ideas and beliefs in comparison and contrast to the beliefs and norms of other cultures. Another method is make use of on-campus events to encourage students to interact with students who have different culture backgrounds or who come from different countries. Such interactions may enhance both knowing why and knowing whom competencies and help student forge relationships that extend well beyond their time as students. Similarly, the use of in-class discussions encourages peer-to-peer learning as students share their own stories of growing up in a different country and what it is like to study far away from home. Even discussions about the diversity amongst students from the United States, such as the experiences of students who have lived in different parts of the country, can create lively interactions which may improve awareness of others who are different and help students become more self-aware.

Knowing Why and Knowing How

Students' "knowing why" competency will become more salient as they develop their "knowing how" competency. This may be especially true for U.S.-born students whose families have been in the United States for several generations. These students have grown up unfamiliar with a non-US culture and without hearing a foreign language spoken at home. Further, the U.S. education system often does not require foreign language until the upper grades, if at all. Thus, the nuances of another culture gained by living with relatives and friends from another country as well as by long-term study of another language, which includes its literature and history, are missed. Below we detail the Knowing How competencies to prepare students to seek and act on entrepreneurial opportunities in the global arena.

Foreign Language Competency

Knowledge of another language helps one understand its structure and, to a certain extent, the thinking behind it. In business, a foreign language competency opens up foreign investment in terms of assessing customers and competitors. A study of 53 managers in Thailand found that knowledge of another language was important in import and export negotiations as well as for effective communication with customers and others, such as suppliers. For these managers, being able to communicate effectively in another language is a competitive advantage; it helps them to better understand the cultures of others and to avoid conflict (Thitthongkam, Walsh, & Bunchapattanasakda, 2011). Knowledge of another language may create a better understanding when working in one's native country for a company based in another country, may help one work in cross-national virtual teams, and may help one obtain expatriate assignments.

Faculty input into curriculum development and individual student advising should encourage studying another language and study abroad, especially if student visits to business start-ups and intensive language study are offered in these programs. Alternatively, faculty may encourage students to volunteer or work in another country to learn more about how culture influences the operations of small businesses. For example, students can volunteer for as short a time as one week to teach English or work on a conservation project (Work anywhere, 2017). In addition to offering a service, students can understand the concept of fair trade in cultivating, purchasing products, and consumer preferences by immersion in activities in other countries.

Such activities help students build their knowing why competencies (their beliefs and identities) as they gain greater awareness of who they are in terms of the types of environments in which they would prefer to work and for what purpose. By comparing their own cultures to other cultures, students learn not only about similarities and differences, but also about who they are in comparison to others. Likewise, such activities help build students' knowing how competencies (skills and knowledge) as they gain specific knowledge about working and living in other countries and how to manage cultural differences.

Financial Competency

Much has been written about the reasons for small business failures, with financial issues as one of the major reasons cited. Most small employer businesses carry debt and dip into personal savings. Crowdfunding was recently permitted by the Securities and Exchange Commission, with some restrictions, as of 2016 (SBA, 2016).

Financial issues that led to the closing of small businesses include problems with cash flow, accounting errors, high costs, borrowing, and inability to determine pricing and profit (Goltz, 2011). Universities should ensure that financial literacy, defined as the triangle of financial knowledge, financial behavior, and financial attitude in handling money to produce beneficial long- and short-term decisions, is a part of the entrepreneurship curriculum (Garcia, 2011).

Education in entrepreneurship should include topics such as debt, equity, financing, sales projection, and tax issues (Carland & Carland, 2010). Students who take an entrepreneurship course as an elective, as part of a minor, or for personal knowledge may not remember or have sufficient knowledge of basic finance and the awareness of the fluctuating dollar and currency exchange rates of other countries. Reinforcing the basics of international finance by applying these concepts in class should be part of a basic entrepreneurship course.

Students should also be aware of financial differences across the globe. A study of people's financial knowledge in 14 countries found country-based differences in such activities as calculating interest, risk, and inflation as well as financial behavior involving evaluating buying, setting long-term goals, saving, and comparison shopping. Despite these across country differences, there were demographic patterns that were common across countries. For instance, across the 14 countries, women had lower levels of financial knowledge and behavior than men but were more likely to think long term. Across the countries, middle-age people were likely to be more financially literate than were older or younger people; education was positively related to financial literacy (Atkinson & Messy, 2012). Understanding differences and similarities in financial behaviors of people in diverse countries can be a valuable learning experience to budding global entrepreneurs.

In the United States, the Office of Entrepreneurship Education Division of the Small Business Administration strongly supports the inclusion of finance as part of students' college education (U.S. Small Business Administration, 2008). Further, it found that emerging entrepreneurs who used crowd-funding for their start-up were more likely to receive external funding to continue their venture.

Organizations, such as the nonprofit Operation HOPE offer training on how to start, develop, and maintain a business to create new wealth (SBA, 2017) and improve one's quality of life (Bryant, 2010). Universities and educators can utilize the information and services provided by these organizations to support students' interest in starting and maintaining their own enterprises.

Trade Competencies

Whether as an importer, exporter, agent, or distributor, the global entrepreneur must be familiar with trade agreements in order to proceed with a business plan. These agreements minimize problems in intellectual property, application of rules and procedures, and promote familiarity with paperwork. Guidebooks such as *Import/Export for Dummies* (Capela, 2016) explain the nuts and bolts of how to research opportunities, register a business, evaluate suppliers, and determine markets. The book defines basic terms such as freight forwarder, customs broker, letter of credit, bill of lading, and describes the process of researching and conducting international business transactions (Capela, 2016). Similar information may be obtained from the Small Business Administration Office of International Trade, which describes the State Trade and Export Promotion Program (STEP) to provide assistance in training, translation, and grants to support small businesses involvement in international trade (SBA, 2014). The SBA supports SCORE which provides free or low cost assistance in advice, mentoring, and workshops including international trade (Score, n.d.). Faculty can require students to consult these and other reliable sources when students develop their business plans.

Knowing How Through Action Learning

Service Learning. Even the most astute person with an entrepreneurial bent may still be perplexed by how to begin a global entrepreneurial career. One way to build students' confidence is to have them apply the skills they have developed in college to service learning projects. Service learning is a form of experiential learning in which students, often working in teams, use their business skills to benefit the community (Kolenko, Porter, Wheatley, & Colby, 1996). Although the usual context is a nonprofit organization or an identifiable community need, we extend this notion to small businesses in the community. We have discovered that small businesses are often founded by people from other countries and/or diverse racio-ethnic groups. Working with these business owners, our students must immediately communicate effectively and become familiar with different ways of doing things.

Assistance with projects that have students apply their business skills and develop their interests in types of businesses can be gained by joining organizations such as Enactus (formerly Students in Free Enterprise) which promotes worldwide gains through the "entrepreneurial spirit." With university and business executive partners around the world, students work to create business models to improve health, food distribution, and energy use among others (ENACTUS, n.d.). Although not specifically aimed at entrepreneurship, Campus Compact (2016) joins university students with their communities to develop social responsibility. We have found students better understand how their skills can be applied in an entrepreneurial-like approach to developing innovative solutions for nonprofits or to help their communities. One study found that business students' attitudes toward sources of economic inequality changed after participating in a year-long service learning project, although they maintained belief in a just world (Seider, Gillmor, & Rabinowicz, 2011). We have found shorter assignments to be insightful to students about economic justice and the role of entrepreneurship in human development and cultural adaptation. One recent placement was with a local community church promoting economic development within the community. Students researched basic information such as how to write a resume, develop a business plan, secure sources of funding, and use social media to be posted on the community website. The information was reviewed by the professor and then translated into Spanish by another professor. Other students participated by helping at information sessions hosted by a local bank on obtaining funding to start a business. Our students enjoyed this active learning with a purpose, developing confidence in their judgments, gaining interpersonal, team-building, and communication skills, and sharpening their business acumen.

Activities to Enhance Cultural Intelligence

One relatively simple exercise to create cultural awareness is to permit each student or student team to choose a country to research. Student research should capture the rapidly changing global environment and myriad sources of information available (Haynes, 1998). Students investigate and report back to the class about the country's business environment, ethical standards, and culture. Attitudes toward entrepreneurial activities and work in general, should also be included in these types of assignments. Such research experiences can be further improved by the use of virtual tours, interviews with entrepreneurs and government officials about doing business in that country, and examining entrepreneurial opportunities in that environment.

Students may team up with students from the countries examined, sharing digital pictures, knowledge, and personal experiences. Enhancing country research through contact with entrepreneurs, government officials, and students from another country would also increase a student's networking skills (knowing why competencies). Using technology for this type of communication should also help students realize the increasing ease in entering new international markets and running a business (Jagersma & van Gorp, 2003), thereby further supporting their entrepreneurial interests. In fact, some colleagues report success with hands-on projects for graduate students which require them to consult to small businesses and their small business development agency. Students interact continuously with the business owner and use the resources of the agency. Having students interact with government officials and agencies is especially important, because it helps students to realize that many international efforts would not be operational without extensive government support (Dlabay, 1998). A similar project can be used for undergraduate students which relies on technology and secondary information (Bell, Callaghan, Demick, & Scharf, 2004).

Another highly useful technique for enhancing students' awareness of other cultures is to have them read the fiction of other countries. Students are provided with a list of the cultural values of the country of interest and assigned a story to read in which they search for evidence of these values. This process usually causes students to react to the values of the countries more intensely than they normally would when reading a textbook description of the country's culture (Harris, 1991). For even greater student involvement and development of the knowing why competency, students can be asked to find a story, novel, or book representative of a country of special interest to them. Each student then makes a short, oral presentation about the content of his or her reading and how it reflects the values and customs of the chosen country. Students often choose stories from countries of their ancestry and report insights from parents or grandparents about life in that country. Similarly, recent immigrants and exchange students often chose stories from their home countries and provide a much richer description of their countries beyond what would be available in any textbook. These students are in a position share their comparisons of the cultures of their own countries with that of the United States. U.S. born students may find local groups which offer programs about their ancestry. Talks about how their grandparents or great-grandparents were perceived accompanied by drawings and photographs of previous times help students see how contemporary attitudes about race and ethnicity and the ingenuity of self-employment are similar to those of many years ago. The National Endowment for the Humanities funds scholars in these areas to give talks for educational purposes and they may visit classrooms as well.

In addition to using fiction to learn about other cultures, television news programs like 20/20, Nightline, and 60 Minutes often feature interesting reports on life in other countries. Cable channels (e.g., A&E, History, Discovery) and public television often run documentaries about the history and culture of other countries, which may be assigned or shown in class. These professional productions capture students' attention and provide a comprehensive amount of information.

Likewise, watching news reports from other countries can also help U.S. students realize that such agencies as the BBC, unlike US news agencies, tend to emphasize world news rather than news of their own country. Major motion pictures, and films made in other countries often shown on cable television networks, can also be used to illustrate cultural differences and similarities as well as provoke examination of one's own stereotypical views of other cultures. Similarly, foreign-made films (e.g., Slumdog Millionaire; Crouching Tiger, Hidden Dragon; The Lives of Others) may bring to life what students have studied (Glenn, 2002), offering cultural and political allegories, with enlightening views of values, customs, and attitudes while challenging common stereotypes.

In addition to television programs and movies, specific exercises can be used to better understand common stereotypes of other countries while increasing knowledge about those countries. For example, faculty can present the class with "Strange Facts" about a certain country. These facts are used to provide students with a very mild sense of culture shock. Students are presented with a list of statements that indicate the "strangeness" of another culture. For example, statements about Japan could include: "Dependency is a sign of health; independence is considered a kind of sickness," and "Bosses often introduce their subordinates to prospective marriage partners." Items listed are discussed and students are asked to describe what it would be like to be a manager in a company in which workers held these attitudes (Van Buskirk, 1991). Such exercises usually produce much discussion, especially about differences in ethical standards or the impact of business policies on workers' personal lives. Sullivan and Tu (1995) reported that when conducting the exercise, international students criticized the Western students for implying that the Japanese culture was wrong. They detailed idiosyncrasies about Western cultures that, from their perspectives, were strange or illogical. This exercise helps student learn more about themselves (knowing why) and about other countries. Similar exercises include "Number Superstitions" or "Directional Differences." The Number Superstitions exercises translate English numbers into a Chinese dialect, for example, four = death. The Directional Differences exercise asks students to point to the future and past. Students will learn that Westerners tend to view the future as being in front of them and past behind them, whereas Asians believe the past is in front of them as it has been lived and is known, whereas the future is behind them as it is unknown and yet unseen. These are simple but useful ways to increase cultural awareness (Sullivan & Tu, 1995).

An important, but overlooked, aspect of gaining awareness of cultural differences is examining the influence of nonverbal communication. In Western countries, individuals tend to rely heavily on the spoken word, whereas in countries like Japan, China, and in the Middle East, the external environment, situation, and nonverbal behavior are crucial elements in communication. A failure to understand the importance of nonverbal and environmental cues can dramatically reduce the effectiveness of international relationship building. There are a number of exercises that focus on communication. One interesting role-playing exercise that illustrates the importance of the context of communications is called "Outside Expert" (McGarvey, 1992). Students pretend that their companies have sent them overseas. Their task is to ask host country nationals questions in order to develop future business plans. However, unbeknownst to the students, their questions are answered according to the following rules: (a) if the student is smiling when he/she asks a question, the question is answered "yes," and (b) if the student is not smiling, the question is answered "no." Thus, most students will find the responses to their questions confusing. Although these rules may seem odd to U.S. students, Asians, and many people in the Middle East place a higher value on the context of the question than on the content.

A useful technique that challenges student to think about their own cultural identity as well as the thinking patterns of those of other cultures is having students play the games of other countries. For example, the ancient Chinese board game call "Go" is especially useful, as it requires students to think in nontraditional, non-Western ways. The strategy of Go is to move around your opponent's weak spots and gain control of territories. This strategy of Go is much different from the strategy of chess, which is the game most Westerners learn, in which one confronts opponents head on and captures playing pieces (Byrne, 1992).

Correspondingly, a simulation that can be used to illustrate the differences in cultural values is the Model United Nations program, which is hosted on many university campuses. For the Model UN, students act as ambassadors to discuss current issues actually being discussed in the real United Nations (UN). Students studying entrepreneurship should be encouraged to participate in such programs as they inform students about current international issues, especially in business, and build the skills necessary to function effectively in global business (Phillips & Muldoon, 1996). Sessions of the student UN could be observed, taped, or downloaded to be used as the basis for class discussions.

Exercises, TV programs, and movies can be used to increase students' knowing how and why competencies as they challenge stereotypes and examine situations from different perspectives. These types of culturally-laden activities can also provide information and insights about how entrepreneurship is viewed in a society and help students gain a better understanding of the global business environment.

Knowing Whom

The previous knowing why and knowing how activities require students to connect with faculty, other students, and business people to help with their decision making and entrepreneurial career plans. The student should feel empowered by the knowledge and support of their university to take the necessary steps to explore global markets and make global and local connections. Technology and social media such as the LinkedIn professional network can be developed to assist with introductions and negotiations in international trade. Mentors from SCORE, colleagues from training programs, and students from the local and host university exchange programs should be viewed as a means of building long term networks of information and relationships. Although technology may nurture and sustain social relationships, many cultures rely on personal face-to-face relationships in order to do business. Generation Z members also value personal contact and interaction (Howard & Sportelli, 2017). Social capital helps the entrepreneur develop a network and build a reputation, provides access to more information, and has been linked to higher levels of performance (Baron & Markman, 2000).

Faculty members should also consider field trips and/or hosting speakers from multinational organizations and small businesses that operate across country borders so that students have access to knowledgeable people experienced in global business. Ideally, faculty and administrators could develop a collaborative learning environment for students. Such an approach was successful when small- and mid-sized firms partnered with a university to advise on the MBA program (Doll, Sharkey, & Beeman, 1996). Having students serve as mentors to other students and retirees interested in entrepreneurship creates a positive learning environment and self-efficacy in applying academic knowledge to real life decisions (Gimmon, 2014).

Our experience has been that students who may not have considered entrepreneurship or have great ideas but aren't sure how to connect with others to implement them will have a foundation of support and confidence-building activities.

Global Knowledge

The Intersections of Knowing Why, Knowing How, Knowing Whom

Academic internships and travel, study abroad, and student exchange programs have the greatest impact in developing all three of a student's knowing competencies. There is no better method to learn about another culture than to experience it "in person." Exchange programs can help students learn more about whom they are (knowing why), specific skills about living and adapting to different cultures (knowing how), and interacting with host country nationals and developing an international network (knowing whom). Despite the popularity of technology, perhaps nothing may replace the social capital developed with face-to-face contact.

International experiences provide students with a "realistic job preview" of what a longer term international assignment might entail and what issues are particular to doing business in another country. Because most universities sponsor some form of these programs, we will not discuss them in detail but will instead focus on methods and techniques that faculty members can introduce in their own classrooms. (For more information on international programs, see Sullivan & Tu 1995).

As more U.S. universities develop exchange programs with universities in other countries, greater opportunities exist now than in the past. US students with minimal foreign language skills may be limited to studying in schools abroad where instruction is solely in English which explains why the UK is the most popular destination for U.S. students (Sullivan & Tu, 1995). This language deficiency along with the growth in the nontraditional student population in the United States, which often means older students with more family responsibilities, suggests that the possibility of studying in another country for an extended period of time is less likely for U.S. students.

These obstacles, however, can be overcome with university support. It is important that networking with entrepreneurs be included in these types of study abroad arrangements. For example, the State University of New York has created the Collaborative Online International Learning (COIL, 2014) program which promotes collaboration among faculty and students in other countries. (More details about a recent conference program may be obtained at http://coil.suny.edu/). An entrepreneurship class paired with a similar class in Canada critiqued one another's business plans and provided feedback throughout the semester. The conference room was equipped with a large screen and audio so the Canadian professor could speak directly to the American students. The semester culminated with a trip to Canada for live presentation of completed business plan. One student commented, "This was the highlight of my college education." There are 118 universities from 18 countries currently participating in this program. Faculty can encourage their university to participate or informally partner with a colleague at another university to try this type of collaboration.

International Team Assignments and Service Learning Projects

In perhaps the most entrepreneurial aspect of business education, students visiting another country may work in teams, perhaps with students of the host country, to develop business plans (Kish, 2003). Although some of the service learning projects described earlier in this chapter do not require travel, planning a service learning project with entrepreneurial learning on site in another country would be ideal and could be coupled with an international exchange program. This type of assignment often requires students to encourage entrepreneurial ventures as a means of economic and personal development by supplying helpful information and using their business expertise outside their native country. As an added learning experience, students learn about the culture, perspectives, and particular issues related to entrepreneurial activity and economic growth in other parts of the world. Following this idea, students may work with an organization which offer a wide range of choices in addition to developing private enterprise in all parts of the world (www.usaid.gov). Faculty should be vigilant in developing relationship with colleagues who may take students on summer programs as well as counterparts in other countries to develop community service projects as part of the general business exchange program.

Self-Awareness for International Study

We have come fully circle in discussing developing competencies for international learning by returning to self-assessment for an international internship or other forms of international learning. With over 14% of U.S. undergraduates studying outside the United States, with business the second most popular area of study, students have a great opportunity to study abroad (www.usaid.gov). To maximize the success of this option, students should seriously consider the cost and benefits in the context of their own interests and abilities.

The first step in determining student readiness for an international assignment is self-assessment. One way for budding entrepreneurs to learn about global business opportunities is to gain experience by seeking an internship, especially if it involves travel, with a multinational corporation. Some students may complete one or two assessment exercises and decide that international internships and travel do not currently match their personality or needs. Other students may struggle for a longer period of time before they reach their decisions. Because of differences in the timing of decision-making, students should be provided with self-awareness and evaluation techniques as they learn throughout their university education. Students may work in organizations as expatriates and after that experience, use their learning to turn to entrepreneurship later in their lives as a means to self-development and economic progress.

An important, but often neglected aspect of an international education is helping students carefully evaluate long-term expatriate assignments, international relocations, and the impact of short- and long-term international assignments on careers. Gaining international experience may be especially important to future entrepreneurs, who will not have the support of an international management department on which some employees of large firms often rely.

Overall, study abroad and international assignments help today's workers gain knowing competencies. Building knowing competencies increases marketability in our contemporary business environment, a worthwhile approach with workers often moving across industry, organizational, occupational, and country boundaries (Arthur & Rousseau, 1996; Sullivan & Arthur, 2006). This is necessary for individual learning which cumulatively creates organizational knowledge. Future entrepreneurs should be exposed to international experiences either virtually or ideally in person as another means of gaining a competitive advantage and building social and intellectual capital (Crocitto, Sullivan, & Carraher, 2005).

Global Entrepreneurship Education—Looking Forward

The area of entrepreneurship is receiving increased attention as a valid area of study, and deservedly so, given its impact on the economic and social well-being of our society. In the past, the study of international business has tended to focus on expatriate managers and the structures of multinational organizations, which is reflected in international business education. Likewise, there has been little consideration of the need for global skills in entrepreneurship education.

Increased knowing why, how, and whom global competencies are important not only for the highest level executives and expatriate managers, but also for managers and employees who may interact frequently with individuals from other countries via email, teleconferencing, and other virtual technologies. Both the self-employed and workers in today's global environment will need competencies that go beyond those expected of a typical expatriate manager. Those with entrepreneurial inclinations to start a business will have fewer resources to learn about the complexities of doing business with firms in other countries, unless our pedagogy emphasizes the global aspects of entrepreneurship. Whether individuals are organizationally employed or become entrepreneurs, they all will be working with diverse groups or individuals. Students (and faculty) need to continuously learn the cultural nuances and financial information such as currency and international trade requirements of a society, as culture is imbedded in how business is conducted.

All students should be equipped to function in a multicultural and global world (Haigh, 2002). Research indicates that women and minorities often find entrepreneurship as a means around the glass ceiling and toward upward mobility, with the number of women and minorities owned businesses increasing at a rate faster than the national average (U.S. Census Bureau, 2005). As educators, we have an obligation to raise awareness about entrepreneurial enterprise and to prepare students to develop and grow their global entrepreneurial ventures. In order to successfully accomplish this, we need to be vigilant in keeping ourselves aware of and current in international issues. It is up to us as faculty to provide students, regardless of major, a broader knowledge base along with specific skills necessary for engaging in global entrepreneurship. As global workers, faculty and students must all embrace continuous learning and the ability to adapt to changing circumstances, cultures, markets, laws, and regulations.

The purpose of this chapter was to provide a framework for systematically examining intentional education and techniques for developing students' global competencies to improve their career success through entrepreneurial endeavors. We hope that by considering how teaching methods, tools, and sources of information can be used to develop students' knowing why, how, and whom capabilities, business educators can help students gain the skills necessary to succeed in the global economy. More importantly, however, is to remind ourselves that in addition to providing knowledge and techniques, we need to attend to the psycho-social aspects of the people who are our students. We can enable them to create a vision of their future selves and inspire the self-assurance to work toward its realization.

Discussion Questions

1. Explain why small businesses need to consider themselves as part of the "global economy."

2. Is entrepreneurship more appealing to certain demographic groups compared to others? Why or why not?

3. Can entrepreneurship be taught? What is a good balance of formal and informal preparation?

4. Discuss how each of the five theoretical bases of entrepreneurship can guide someone in the decision to start a business.

5. How can universities create increased awareness and interest in entrepreneurship as a career option?

6. How can education help develop the traits and behaviors important to successful entrepreneurship?

7. How can entrepreneurship increase sustainability and economic growth in the U.S. as well as other countries?

8. What other ways beyond those mentioned in the chapter would you recommend to increase cultural intelligence?

9. What steps can entrepreneurship programs and classes take to foster financial literacy into their course content?

10. Discuss the importance of trade competencies in successful international business exchange.

11. What types of knowledge and skills could beginner entrepreneurship students offer small businesses in their communities?

References

Arthur, M. B., Claman, P. H., DeFillippi, R. J., & Adams, J. (1995). Intelligent enterprise, intelligent careers. *Academy of Management Executive, 9*(4), 7–22.

Arthur, M. B., & Rousseau, D. M. (1996). The boundaryless career as a new employment principle. In M. B. Arthur & D. M. Rousseau (Eds.), *The boundaryless career* (pp. 3–20). New York: Oxford University Press.

Atkinson, A., & Messy, F. (2012). *Measuring financial literacy: results of the OECD/International Network on Financial Education (INFE) pilot study.* Paris: Organisation for Economic Cooperation and Development (OECD).

Baker T., & Aldrich, H. E. (1996). Prometheus stretches: Building identity and cumulative knowledge in multi-employer careers. In M. G. Arthur & D. M. Rousseau (Eds.), *The boundaryless career* (pp. 132–149). New York: Oxford University Press.

Baron, R. A., & Markman, G. D. (2000). Beyond social capital: How social skills can enhance entrepreneurs' success. *Academy of Management Executive, 14*(1), 106–117.

Baruch, Y. (2002). No such thing as a global manager. *Business Horizons, 45*(1), January/February 36–42.

Bell, J., Callaghan, I., Demick, D., & Scharf, F. (2004). Internationalising entrepreneurship education. *Journal of International Entrepreneurship, 2,* 109–124.

Bird, A. (1996). Careers as repositories of knowledge: Considerations for boundaryless careers. In M. B. Arthur & D. M. Rousseau (Eds.), *The boundaryless career*, (pp. 150–168). New York: Oxford University Press.

Brush, C. G., de Bruin, A., & Welter, F. (2009). A gender-aware framework for women's entrepreneurship. *International Journal of Gender and Entrepreneurship, 1*(1), 8–24. doi: http://dx.doi.org/10.1108/17566260910942318

Bryant, J. H. (2010). Financial literacy and silver rights. *Organisation for Economic Cooperation and Development. The OECD Observer,* (No. 279), 17–18. Retrieved from: https://issuu.com/oecd.publishing/docs/oecdobserver_279_may2010

Byrne, J. (1992, October 26). The best B schools. *BusinessWeek*, Industrial/Management ed; Issue 3290, 60–70.

Campus Compact. (2016). Feature Initiatives Campus Civic Action Planning. Retrieved from: https://compact.org/what-we-do/featured-initiatives/

Capela, J. (2016). *Import/Export kit for dummies* (3rd ed). New York: John Wiley & Sons.

Carland, J. C., & Carland, J. W. (2010). Entrepreneurship education: building for the future. *Journal of Business and Entrepreneurship, 22*(2), 40–59.

Carlson, N. (April 13, 2011). The real history of twitter. *Business Insider.* Retrieved from http://www.businessinsider.com/how-twitter-was-founded-2011-4

CBS local news. (2014). http://chicago, cbslocal.com/2014/02/10how-chiberia-changed-perceptions-for-a-muslim-woman/

Choi, C. Q. (2013, May 7). 2013 Invention awards: Cardboard bike. Retrieved from http://www.popsci.com/technology/article/2013-04/transportation-cardboard-bike

Crocitto, M., Sullivan, S. E., & Carraher, S. M. (2005). Global mentoring as a means of career development and knowledge creation: A learning based framework and agenda for future research. *Career Development International, 10*(6/7), 522–535.

DeFillippi, R. J., & Arthur, M. B. (1996). Boundaryless contexts and careers: A competency-based perspective. In M. B. Arthur & D. M. Rousseau (Eds.), *The boundaryless career* (pp. 116–131). New York: Oxford University Press.

Delehanty, P. 2015 December. Small businesses key players in international trade. SBA Office of Advocacy. Retrieved from https://www.sba.gov/sites/default/files/advocacy/Issue-Brief-11-Small-Biz-Key-Players-International-Trade.pdf de Janasz, S. C. & Sullivan, S.E. (2004). Multiple mentoring in academe: Developing the professorial network. *Journal of Vocational Behavior, 64*(2), 263–283.

Dlabay, L. R. (1998). Integrated curriculum planning for international business education: Analysis of global business trends. *Delta Pi Epsilon Journal*, Summer, 158–165.

Doll, W. J., Sharkey, T. W., Beeman, D. R. (1996). Reengineering the MBA for small and mid-size firms: A business-driven approach. *Mid-American Journal of Business, 11*(2), 19–23, https://doi.org/10.1108/19355181199600008

Ede, F. O., Panigrahi, B., & Calcich, S. (1998). African American students' attitudes toward entrepreneurship education. *Journal of Education for Business, 73*(5), 291–297.

Enactus. n.d. Learn more about starting a program on my campus. Retrieved from: http://enactus.org/who-we-are/universities/

EntreEd: The National Consortium for Entrepreneurship Education. Post secondary resources. Retrieved from: http://www.entre-ed.org/resources/postsecondary/

Fischer, K. (November 15, 2009). Universities offer international resources t help economy at home. *The Chronicle of Higher Education*. Retrieved from https://chronicle.com/article/Universities-Offer/49162.

Friedman, T. L. (2005). *The world is flat: A brief history of the twenty-first century.* New York: Farrar, Staraus and Giroux.

Garcia, L. (2011). *Teaching private equity investment in higher education: An entrepreneurship approach.* Rochester: Social Science Research Network. doi: http://dx.doi.org/10.2139/ssrn.1944809

Gimmon, E. (2014). Mentoring as a practical training in higher education of entrepreneurship. *Education + Training, 56*(8/9) 814–825.

Glass, A. (2007). Understanding generational differences for competitive success. *Industrial and Commercial Training, 39*(2), 98–103.

Glenn, J. M. (2002). Beyond our doorstep: Preparing students for an international business environment. *Business Education Forum, 56*(3), 9–12.

Goltz, J. (January 5, 2011) Top 10 Reasons Small Businesses Fail. Retrieved from http://boss.blogs.nytimes.com/2011/01/05/top-10-reasons-small-businesses-fail/?_php=true&_type=blogs&_r=0

Grant, J. M. (1996). The proactive personality scale as a predictor of entrepreneurial intentions. *Journal of Small Business Management, 34*(3), 42–50.

Gupta, A. K., & Govindarajan, V. (2001). Converting global presence into global competitive advantage. *Academy of Management Executive, 15*(2), 45–56.

Haigh, M. J. (2002). Internationalisation of the curriculum: designing inclusive education for a small world. *Journal of Geography in Higher Education, 26*(1), 49–67.

Harris, C. (1991). Using short stories to teach international management. *Journal of Management Education, 15*, 374–378.

Harrison, R., & Hopkins, R. (1967). The design of cross-cultural training: An alternative to the university model. *Journal of Applied Behavioral Science, 3*(4), 431–460.

Harrison, R. & Hopkins, R. (1972). Training for cultural understanding. *Training and Development Journal*, 8–10.

Hartmans, A., & McAlone, N. (August 1, 2016). The story of how Travis Kalanick built Uber into the most feared and valuable startup in the world. Retrieved from http://www.businessinsider.com/ubers-history

Haynes, T. (1998). Learning activities for international business. *Business Education Forum, 54*(4), 31–33.

Howard, C. & Sportelli, N. (2017). Forbes 30 under 30. Editors. Retrieved from https://www.forbes.com/30-under-30-2017/#57fb15223fcd

Jagersma, P. K., & van Gorp, D. M. (2003). Spin-out management: Theory and practice. *Business Horizons, 46*(2), 15–24.

Kish, V. (2003). Passports to education. *BizEd, 2*(2), 38–43.

Kolenko, T. A., Porter, G., Wheatley, W., & Colby, M. (1996). A critique of service learning projects in management education: Pedagogical foundations, barriers, and guidelines. *Journal of Business Ethics, 15*, 133–142.

Köllinger, P., & Minniti, M. (2006). Not for lack of trying: American entrepreneurship in black and white. *Small Business Economics, 27*(1), 59. doi: http://dx.doi.org/10.1007/s11187-006-0019-6

Korotov, K., Khapova, S., & Arthur, M.B. (October 25, 2010). Career Entrepreneurship ESMT Working Paper NO08-009 R1

Kwon, N. (2013). Asian sensation. *Canadian Grocer, 127*(8), 49–53.

Luethge, D. J., Raska, D., Greer, B. M., & O'Connor, C. (2016). Crossing the Atlantic: Integrating cross-cultural experiences into undergraduate business courses using virtual communities technology. *Journal of Education for Business, 91*(4), 219.

Lyon, D. W., Lumpkin, G. T., & Dess, G. G. (2000). Enhancing entrepreneurial orientation research: Operationalizing and measuring a key strategic decision making process. *Journal of Management, 26*(5), 1055–1085.

MacMillan, D. (2016, March 02). Uber spends big on international expansion; company's international business lost $237 million in 2014. *Wall Street Journal (Online)*

Mainiero, L. A., & Sullivan, S. E. (2006). *The opt-out revolt: Why people are leaving companies to create kaleidoscope careers.* Mountain View, CA: Davies-Black Publishing.

Martin, J. A., Heppard, K. A., & Green, S. G. (2011). Taking international business education programs and pedagogy to new heights: Fundamental questions for educators and students. *Business Horizons, 54*(4), 355.

Martínez, A. C., Levie, J., Kelley, D. J., Sæmundsson, R. J., & Schøtt, T. (2010) A Global Perspective on Entrepreneurship Education and Training. Retrieved from http://www.gemconsortium.org/docs/download/276

McGarvey, R. (1992, June). Foreign exchange. *US Air Magazine*, 58–65.

MIT Management Sloan School. (2017). LearningEdge. Retrieved from: https://forio.com/simulation/mit-sloan-salt/index.htm

Mugione, F. (2013). EMORETEC inspiring entrepreneurship. *International Trade Forum*, 1, 15.

National Center for Educational Statistics. (2015). Digest of Education Statistics, Table 310.10 Retrieved from: https://nces.ed.gov/programs/digest/d15/tables/dt15_310.10.asp

National Endowment for the Humanities. (n.d.) Division of Education Programs. Retrieved from: https://www.neh.gov/divisions/education

New York University, n.d. Retrieved from: http://www.nyu.edu/academics/studying-abroad.html

Northeastern University innovation imperative series: Meet Generation Z. (November 18, 2014). Retrieved from: http://www.northeastern.edu/innovationsurvey/pdfs/Innovation_Summit_GenZ_PollRes_KeyMess.pdf

Palocsay, S. W., White, M. M., & Zimmerman, D. K. (2004). Interdisciplinary collaborative learning: Using decision analysts to enhance undergraduate international management education. *Journal of Management Education, 28*(2), 250–260.

Pathak, S., Goltz, S., & Buche, M. W. (2013). Influences of gendered institutions on women's entry into entrepreneurship. *International Journal of Entrepreneurial Behaviour & Research, 19*(5), 478–502.

Peiris, I. K., Akoorie, M. E. M., & Sinha, P. (2012.) International entrepreneurship: A critical analysis of studies in the past two decades and future directions for research. *Journal of International Entrepreneurship, 10*(4), 279–324.

Peltier, J. W., & Scovotti, C. (2010). Enhancing entrepreneurial marketing education: the student perspective. *Journal of Small Business and Enterprise Development, 17*(4), 514–536.

Perez-Lopez, M. C., Gonzalez-Lopez, M. J., & Rodriquez-Ariza, L. (2016). Competencies for entrepreneurship as a career option in a challenging employment environment. *Career Development International, 21*(3), 214–229.

Phillips, M. J., & Muldoon, J. P. (1996). The Model United National: A strategy for enhancing global business education. *Journal of Education for Business, 71*(3), 142–147.

Plehn, J. (2013). Product innovations by young and small firms. Small Business Research Summary. Retrieved from http://www.sba.gov/sites/default/files/files/rs408.pdf

PRNewsWire. 2014, March 27. Retrieved from: http://www.prnewswire.com/news-releases/goya-foods-expands-global-reach-with-the-opening-of-four-new-facilities-to-support-consumer-demand-of-goyas-healthy-product-lines-252632861.html

Rae, D., & Woodier, Harris, 2012. International entrepreneurship education. *Education + Training, 54*(8/), 639–656.

SBA: Small Business Administration, Office of Advocacy. (2017). What's new with small business?Retrieved from https://www.sba.gov/sites/default/files/Whats-New-w-Small-Business-2017.pdf

SBA: Small Business Administration Office of Advocacy: Small business research summary #241 Costs of Developing a Foreign Market for a Small Business: The Market & Non-Market Barriers to Exporting by Small Firms. Palmetto Consulting, November 2004. Retrieved from https://permanent.access.gpo.gov/websites/www.sba.gov/advo/research/rs241.pdf

SBA: Small Business Administration. (n.d). Take your business global. Retrieved from https://www.sba.gov/sites/default/files/articles/oit_business_global_brochure.pdf

SBA Take your business global. n.d. Retrieved from https://www.sba.gov/sites/default/files/articles/oit_business_global_brochure.pdf

SBA Learning Center. Is Entrepreneurship for you? Retrieved from http://sbaguide.org/IsEntrepreneurshipForYou.html

SBA Office of Advocacy. (2017, January). Annual Report of the Office of Economic Research FY 2016. Retrieved from https://www.sba.gov/sites/default/files/OER_Annual_Report_FY2016.pdf

SBA Office of Advocacy. (2016). https://www.sba.gov/sites/default/files/Finance-FAQ-2016_WEB.pdf

SBA. (2014). Fact Sheet U.S. Small Business Administration Office of International Trade. State Trade and Export Promotion Grant Program. Retrieved from: https://www.sba.gov/sites/default/files/files/STEP2014_program_announcement_factsheet.pdf

Scandura, T. A., & Williams, E. A. (2002). Formal mentoring: The promise and precipice. In R. Burke and C. Cooper (Eds.), *The new world of work* (pp. 241–257). London: Blackwell.

SCORE. (n.d.) Starting your international business: What you must know and where to find it. Retrieved from: https://www.score.org/search/site/starting%20international%20business

Seider, S. C., Gillmor, S. C., & Rabinowicz, S. A. (2011). The impact of community service learning upon the worldviews of business majors versus non-business majors at an American university. *Journal of Business Ethics, 98*(3), 485–503.

Small Business Sustainability Report. (2013). The Big Green Opportunity, 2013. Retrieved from http://biggreenopportunity.org/wp-content/uploads/2013/05/Big-Green-Opportunity-Report-FINAL-WEB.pdf

Sroufe, R., Sivasubramaniam, N., Ramos, D., & Saiia, D. (2015). Aligning the PRME: How study abroad nurtures responsible leadership. *Journal of Management Education, 39*(2), 244

Streitfeld, D. (November 17, 2012). As boom lures app creators, tough part is making a living. New York: New York Times. A1. Retrieved from http://www.nytimes.com/2012/11/18/business/as-boom-lures-app-creators-tough-part.

Styles, C., & Seymour, R. G. (2006) Opportunities for marketing researchers in international entrepreneurship. *International Marketing Review, 23*(2), 126–145.

Sullivan, S. E., & Arthur, M. (2006). The evolution of the boundaryless career concept: Examining physical and psychological mobility. *Journal of Vocational Behavior, 69*(1), 19–29.

Sullivan, S. E., & Tu, H. S. (1995). Developing globally competent students: A review and recommendations. *Journal of Management Education, 19*(4), 473–493.

Taylor, S., & Osland, S. (2003). The impact of intercultural communication on global organizational learning. In M. Easterby-Smith & M. A. Lyles (Eds). *Handbook of organizational learning and knowledge management*. Malden, MA: Blackwell Publishing.

Thitthongkam, T., Walsh, J., & Bunchapattanasakda, C. (2011). The roles of foreign language in business administration. *Journal of Management Research, 3*(1), 1–15.

Tu, H., & Sullivan, S. E. (1994, January/February). Preparing yourself for an international assignment. *Business Horizons, 37*(1), 67–70.

Tust, A. (2013, May 6) 2013 Invention awards: Ballast bulb. Retrieved from http://www.popsci.com/technology/article/2013-04/lighting-ballast-bulb

U.S. Census Bureau. 2012). Retrieved from https://factfinder.census.gov/faces/tableservices/jsf/pages/productview.xhtml?pid=SBO_2012_00CSA01&prodType=table

U.S. Small Business Administration. (2008). SBA broadens office of business and community initiatives to focus on financial literacy, entrepreneurial education. *Real Estate & Investment Week*, 131.

U.S. Census Bureau. (July 28, 2005). Newsroom U.S. Census Bureau News. Press Release. Retrieved from http://www./releases/archives/business

Van Buskirk, B. (1991). Five classroom exercises for sensitizing students to aspects of Japanese culture and business practice. *Journal of Management Education, 15*(1), 96–112.

WorkAnywhere. (2017). Retrieved from: https://anyworkanywhere.com/

Witherell, S. (2016). Open Doors 2016 Executive Summary. Retrieved from https://www.iie.org/en/Why-IIE/Announcements/2016-11-14-Open-Doors-Executive-Summary.

Zacur, S., & Randolph, W. (1993). Traveling to foreign cultures: An exercise in developing awareness of cultural diversity. *Journal of Management Education, 17*(4), 510–516.

International Franchising and Other Forms of Entrepreneurship

*Dianne H.B. Welsh with
Ilan Alon*

University of North Carolina–Greensboro
University of Agder, Kristiansand, Norway

Key Terms

International franchising

Emerging markets

Industrialized markets

Learning Objectives

Upon completion of this chapter, students should be able to:

1. Appraise the extent to which emerging markets account for worldwide business growth

2. Determine the characteristics of an emerging market and how they are measured

3. Evaluate why franchising has had such an impact internationally

4. Analyze what forms franchising has taken in different parts of the world

5. Differentiate between emerging and industrialized markets

6. Appraise the extent of franchising worldwide

7. Describe new franchise industry segments and forms that have emerged

8. Differentiate between industrialized and emerging countries and how franchising has developed in these countries

Much of the franchising sections of this chapter are based on four comprehensive volumes, two emerging markets, and two industrialized markets, edited by Welsh and Alan and published by CCH, Inc, in 2001, 2002, 2003. See reference list for complete cite.

Introduction

Franchising has experienced phenomenal growth in the United States and abroad in recent years. Today, there are more than 28,000 different franchise systems in the world that operate in one or more countries (Alpeza, Erceg, & Peterka, 2015). In the United States, about 40% of all US retail sales can be attributed to franchise units, and franchising is estimated to account for approximately 10% of gross domestic product (GDP; Spencer, 2010). Franchising accounts for approximately 40% of all US retail trade (IFA, 2006). The franchise sector in the US accounts for about 10% of new jobs per year, and the franchise sector directly or indirectly supports more than 18 million jobs (Reynolds, 2013). The US Census Bureau (2010a) reports that franchise businesses accounted for 10.5% of businesses with paid employees in the 295 industries for which franchising data was collected in 2007. Of the 4.3 million total establishments surveyed, 453,326 were either franchisee or franchisor-owned businesses (US Census Bureau, 2010b). Additionally, franchise businesses accounted for nearly $1.3 trillion of the $7.7 trillion in total sales for these industries, $153.7 billion out of the $1.6 trillion in total payroll, and 7.9 million workers out of a total workforce of 59.0 million (US Census Bureau, 2010b). While there are no exact figures for the percentages of franchised businesses around the globe, franchising has an indelible mark on world trade. This chapter examines franchising first in emerging markets around the world, and then in industrialized markets. First, we define what an emerging market is, characteristics of emerging markets, why franchising has had such an impact internationally, and research in emerging markets by the area of the world market. Central and Eastern Europe, Mexico and South America, Singapore, Malaysia and Hong Kong, China, India, and the Middle East. Then, we look at industrialized markets, beginning with North America. We follow with an examination of Japan, Australia, New Zealand, South Africa, and Europe, including Austria, Denmark, Finland, France, Germany, Greece, Italy, and Norway. Finally, we study the United Kingdom.

Emerging Markets

In the United States, Canada, and parts of Western Europe, franchising has reached domestic market saturation, but emerging markets remain relatively untapped. Emerging markets, accounting for 80% of the world's population and 60% of the world's natural resources, present the most dynamic potential for long-term growth to businesses, in general, and to franchisors, specifically. The US Department of Commerce estimated that over 75% of the expected growth in world trade over the next two decades will come from emerging countries, particularly big emerging countries, which account for over half the world's population but only 25% of its GDP. Brazil, Russia, India, China, and South Africa (BRICS), which currently account for more than a quarter of the world's land area and more than 40% of the world's population, are ripe for international trade. The increasing demand for consumer goods, coupled with major infrastructure needs in these markets, underscore their potential as key export destinations for US goods and services (US Department of Commerce).

Emerging markets are among the fastest growing markets for international franchisors. Several surveys conducted by Arthur Anderson showed that more and more franchisors are seeking opportunities in emerging markets. An article in *Franchising World* (Amies, 1999, pp. 27–28) stated, "Franchises are springing up in the most unlikely, and for many of us unheard-of, places … Those franchisors who can establish a beach-head on these wilder shores could do very well, but the risks are great."

The research that has been conducted in emerging economies helps us better understand international franchising opportunities and threats in emerging economies (see Table 11.1).

Summary of US Published Articles in Franchising Research: An International Journal and the *Proceedings of the International Society of Franchising* Pertaining to Franchising in Emerging Markets*

Table 11.1		
YEAR	**TITLE**	**AUTHOR(S)**
1988	Franchising in Asia	Neilson & Yo
1988	International Business Format…	Kaufmann & Leibenstein
1990	Franchise…East Asia	Chan & Justis
1991	Opportunities…U.S.S.R.	Welsh & Swerdlow
1992	The Future…U.S.S.R.…Students	Swerdlow & Welsh
1992	Franchising Opportunities in the Free…	Grimaldi
1992	Pizzas in Mexico…	Willems, English, & Ito
1992	Franchising…Former Soviet Union	Christy & Haftel
1993	Pizza Hut in Moscow…	Christy & Haftel
1993	A Cross Cultural…Russian Hotel	Welsh & Swerdlow
1994	A Survey of Franchising in Singapore	Chan, Foo, Quek, & Justis
1994	Franchising in China	English & Xau
1994	Does Business Format…Russia	Swerdlow & Bushmarin
1995	Franchising in Brazil	Josias & McIntryre
1995	Franchising in India…	Paswan & Dant
1995	Franchising in Indonesia	Chan & Justis
1996	Franchising in South Africa	Scholtz
1996	Franchising into Asia…	McCosker
1996	Local Franchising…Singapore	Goh & Lee
1996	The…Elegant Shoplifter,…Kuwait	Welsh, Raven, & Al-Bisher
1997	Franchising as a Tool for SME…	Sanghavi
1997	An Overview…South African…	Scholtz
1998	NAFTA and Franchising…	Falbe & Welsh

Table 11.1	(continued)	
1998	Franchising in Slovenia...	Pavlin
1998	Case Study...Mexico	Hadjimarcou & Barnes
2000	New Trends in Slovenian Franchising	Pavlin
2000	Franchising in Mexico	Lafontaine
2001	Int'l Franchising in China...	Alon
2001	Int'l Franchising in Emerging Markets...	Welsh
2001	The Emerging Patterns of Franchising...	Dant & Kaufmann
2001	Publication Opinion About Franchising...	Paswan, Young & Kantamneni
2002	An Exploratory Study of Encroaching...	du Toit
2002	A Comparative Analysis of Franchise...	Terry
2002	Brand-Country of Origin Association...	Paswan & Sharma
2003	How Do Franchisors with Int'l...	Elango
2003	A Survey of Franchising in China	Bian & Alon
2003	Retail Franchising As An Entry Mode...	Picot-Coupey & Cliquet
2003	The Role of Franchising in African...	Siggel, Maisonneuve & Fortin
2003	The Franchise Baseline 2002...	du Toit

*The authors do not intend for this list to be comprehensive
Note. For a complete citation, see the Reference list.

Background

What Is an Emerging Market?

While there is no consensus definition of the term "emerging market," Czinkota and Ronkainen (1997) identified three characteristics associated with an emerging economy:

- Level of economic development
- Economic growth
- Market governance

Level of Economic Development

The level of economic development in a country is typically measured in terms of its GDP per capita. GDP per capita is a useful measure of economic development because it is related to the population's wealth, extent of middle class, and level of industrial and service sector development (Alon & McKee, 1999).

Using the level of economic development as a demarcation criteria for distinguishing emerging markets equates with the anachronisms of the World Bank and the United Nations, which include terms such as less developed countries (LDCs), third-world countries, and developing countries. The World Bank divides countries based on GDP per capita into four classes. Three of the big emerging countries (India, China, and Vietnam) fall into the lowest income class. According to the World Bank, only about 16% of the world's population resides in developed market economy countries. The world's population is likely to exceed 10 billion by the end of the 21st century, up from 7.5 billion this year, per research based on United Nations data. Developing countries, notably those in Africa, will experience tremendous growth, whereas the developed world's population will decline or remain flat (Sauter, 2011).

Economic Growth

When dealing with emerging markets, it is important to adjust GDP per capita to purchasing power parity (PPP) to gauge income in relation to the "real" cost of living (Arnold & Quelch, 1998).

Economic growth is usually measured in terms of the country's GDP growth rate. The usage of economic growth is consistent with the concept of "emerging." Emerging and developing markets dominated the period between 2003 and 2013, particularly Developing Asia, which grew at an average annual pace of 8.5% (Pasquali, 2013). In 1997, 1998, and 1999, East Asia, Brazil, and Russia encountered financial crises that set back their economies' growth. Such crises demonstrate that the often-touted high growth rates of emerging markets may not be sustainable over a long period of time.

The level of economic growth in a country is among the most important considerations for international franchising expansion (Alon & McKee, 1999). When examining an emerging market's GDP growth, one must contrast it to the growth in the population. If population growth rates exceed GDP growth rates, then the standard of living in those countries will drop over time. One useful measure that captures both population growth and GDP growth is the GDP per capita growth rate.

Market Governance

The third criteria for judging emerging markets is the country's market governance that includes the extent of free market, government control of key resources, stability of the market system, and the regulatory environment within a country. Countries that are liberalizing their economic institutions and democratizing their political structures are often referred to as transitional economies/countries. These transitions have been welcomed by western economies and are regarded as opportunities for international franchising expansion.

Among the most important of the elements of transition, with respect to international investors, are the political and economic risks that are introduced by the reorganization of economic and political units in the emerging marketplace

(Czinkota & Ronkainen, 1997). Such risks are systematically evaluated by western institutions, such as the Economist Intelligence Unit, Institutional Investor, and International Country Risk Guide (ICRG).

Market governance influences a wide range of country risk elements such as government regulation and red tape, political stability, bribery, ownership restrictions, controls of capital flows, and import restrictions, all of which are important to international franchisors' evaluations of foreign market potential (Alon & McKee, 1999).

Several authors, both industry analysts and academics, have identified emerging markets as a topic that needs further research for the franchise industry. In 1988, Kaufmann and Leibenstein wrote an article for the United Nations when franchising in developing countries was just beginning. In 1990, Welsh conducted the first survey on Russian soil on franchising, at a time when the word franchising had no meaning to the population except when coupled with McDonald's. That was the same year the McDonalds franchise opened in Moscow to a tremendous welcoming by the Russian people and the press (Welsh & Swerdlow, 1991). Since then, franchising in emerging markets has grown dramatically. For example, by 1995, there were 26 more franchisors in Brazil alone than there were in all of South America in 1985 (International Franchise Research Centre, 2000). In 2012, Brazil's franchising industry was expected to grow profits of 15%, while the total number of franchises rose by a further 10% to 2,031 brands (Geromel, 2012).

Academics and practitioners have answered the call for more research and evaluation of franchising in these new markets around the globe. Young, McIntyre, and Green (2000) examined the content of articles that had been published in the International Society of Franchising Proceedings. Out of almost 70 articles between 1987 and 1999, 9 dealt with economies in transition and 14 dealt with developing economies. Practitioners have also published articles on the topic. For example, Swartz (2001) of Arthur Anderson examined the state of franchising in Asia-China, Indonesia, Singapore, and Malaysia, Eastern Europe-Russia, Poland, Hungary, and Greece, as well as the Middle East-United Arab Emirates, Israel, Saudi Arabia, Kuwait, Egypt, and South America-Chile, Uruguay, Brazil, Argentina, Columbia, and Peru.

Practice and Theory Development

Why has franchising had such an impact internationally? What form has franchising taken in different parts of the world? Several authors have addressed these questions. Grimaldi (1992) analyzed the opportunities for franchising in free trade zones. Kaufmann (2001) looked at the issues of cultural and legal differences in the age of the Internet and the impact of franchising on host country development. Specifically, he examined the modes of entry, cultural differences and proven concepts, cultural differences and technology, legal differences, and host country development. Stanworth, Price, and Purdy (2001) looked at franchising as a means of technology transfer for developing economies. Their article explored the background of internationalization of franchising, favorable factors to the growth of franchising, benefits to developing economies, other consequences to developing economies, advantages and risks to franchisors, as well as government action to encourage franchising. The authors gave a special insight into Indonesia, China, and Brazil.

Models are beginning to be developed in international franchising. Thompson and Merrilees (2001) examined marketing with a modular approach to branding and operations for international retail franchising systems. Examples of Australian firms extending their franchise systems into Eastern Europe, Asia, and Latin America demonstrate the applicability of this approach to branding in their article. Other authors cite that new symbiotic relationships are created when franchising expands into developing countries. Franchising allows firms to achieve the expanded reach and efficiencies associated with internationalization more rapidly and effectively than the firms could achieve on their own. Dana, Etemad, and Wright (2001) developed an interdependence paradigm to explain these franchise marketing networks using firms in South Korea and the Philippines as examples.

Research by Areas of the World Market

Central and Eastern Europe

Nitin Sanghavi's (2001) article, "The Use of Franchising as a Tool for SME Development in Developing Economies: A Case of Central European Economics," gave a personal perspective on the use of franchising as an economic development tool from his numerous experiences with those countries. Sanghavi summarized the current state of franchising in Eastern Europe as compared to 1997 when he first looked at the topic (Sanghavi, 1997).

Swerdlow, Roehl, and Welsh (2001), and Alon and Banai (2001), in their respective articles, "Hospitality Franchising in Russia for the 21st century: Issues, Strategies, and Challenges," and "Franchising Opportunities and Threats in Russia," gave a historical review of franchise development in Russia as well as a current and future look at the prospects for franchise development in an area of the world that is barely realizing its full potential as an economic power. Both articles examined the postcommunist economy with a focus on environmental factors associated with international franchise development and entry strategies that potential franchisors would find successful. The articles included practical suggestions for those entering and maneuvering through Russia's huge market. Skip Swerdlow and Dianne Welsh, along with their co-authors, published several articles in the early 1990s examining franchising in the former U.S.S.R. (Swerdlow & Bushmarin, 1994; Welsh & Swerdlow, 1991, 1993). Christy and Haftel (1993) published the only case study on franchising in Russia in the early era: Pizza Hut entering the Moscow market.

Aneta Nedialkova (2001) specifically examined franchising opportunities in Bulgaria, with a focus on the macroeconomic factors of the Bulgarian economy associated with franchising. While international investors have been developing franchises in Bulgaria for over 25 years, the market has remained sluggish due to the government system and bureaucracy. However, many positive developments have come about and recent success stories have given reasons to be optimistic in regard to the future of franchise development in Bulgaria.

Viducic (2001) described the two types of franchise arrangements that are prevalent in Croatia, using the examples of McDonald's and Diner's Club. First, franchising has taken the form of several corporate facilities in operation, where local interaction with the store is limited to employment, not ownership. Second, the form whereby an entrepreneur is taken on as a franchise holder with the understanding that his or her capital involvement will increase over time as well as his or her ownership interest as a full franchisee. Additionally, the article elaborates on the state of Croatian franchise activity and other forms of market expansion that have been successful in Croatia. A few years after McDonald's entered the Croatian market, other franchises began to appear, such as the Hungarian bakery franchise Fornetti and the US franchise, Subway. Institutional support initiatives for franchising development in Croatia started in 2003 when the first Franchising Centers in Osijek and Zagreb were founded (Alpeza et al., 2015). Now, there are about 180 franchise systems in the country, of which 14% are of Croatian origin. The franchise systems operate in some 1,000 locations and employ about 16,500 employees.

Conditions, features, and trends in Slovenian franchising are analyzed empirically in an article by Pavlin (2001). Using the definition of franchising adopted by the European Franchise Federation (EFF), there were over 40 operating franchise systems in Slovenia in 1998 and, in 2009, there were 107 (European Franchise Federation, 2011). Pavlin compares these results to studies he conducted on Slovenian franchising that were published in 1998 and 2000. In 1998, of the 40 franchises operating in his country, 20 participated in his survey on the current state of franchising. The article includes results from a recent survey of prospective Slovenian franchisees identifying their core attributes which include a willingness to follow the franchise manual and guidelines, creativity and ability to cope with a variety of situations, experience with earlier self-employment, and technical experience; and offers a framework for the profitable future development of the industry in Slovenia that might be useful for franchisors and franchisees.

In 2013, Kazakhstan had approximately 450 franchises operating in Kazakhstan with 3,000 franchising outlets (US Department of Commerce, 2013). Akhmetov and Raiskhanova (2001) described franchising from an institutional context and a development perspective, then discussed the economic condition of the country and the reforms that have been established by the government that will enhance business development. Finally, the authors gave their viewpoint on franchise industries that they believe would thrive and ended with a discussion of future research that needs to be conducted. So far, Kazakhstan has more than 350 franchises, opened more than 3,000 franchise companies, which employ more than 17,000 people, and the turnover of the sector reaches $1 billion a year (Sayabaev et al., 2016).

Mexico and South America

Three articles focused on different aspects of Mexican franchising. Teegan (2001) examined foreign expansion and market entry from three different perspectives. The first perspective is that of the Mexican franchisee that might purchase the rights to a US-based franchise. The second perspective is that of the US franchisor that might sell the rights to their business format. The third perspective is that of the host government, namely Mexico, in terms of the economic impact and development within their country. Teegan shared the results of a survey of over 70 Mexican franchisees of US-based franchise systems. Results showed that commonly held beliefs within both the United States and Mexico concerning the desirability of franchising as a mode of market entry, and caution of the part of franchisees, franchisors, and the host governments are warranted. The article painted a realistic view of the risks and rewards of franchising and a bountiful amount of information for those contemplating franchising in Mexico.

Hadjimarcou and Barnes (2001) explained the expansion process of a relatively new and small franchisor, Silver Streak Restaurant Corporation, into Mexico as a case study. The authors detailed the cultural challenges of entering Mexico, the company's efforts to identify a suitable partner in the host country, the adaptation of the concept to address differences in the new market, and the multitude of crucial decisions that need to be made when going international. The authors discussed the recent changes in the law that favor franchising, as well as the role that strategic alliances played in the success of their international franchise efforts. Implications for both research and practitioners are explicated. Silver Streak Restaurant Corporation opened their first franchised restaurant in 1996 in Juarez, a city of 1.5 million on the border of the United States (Hadjimarcou & Barnes, 1998).

Welsh and Falbe (2001) updated their study which was the first to examine the effect, if any, of the North American Free Trade Agreement (NAFTA) on franchisor perceptions of characteristics associated with franchisee success and failure in Canada, Mexico, and the United States (Falbe & Welsh, 1998). The original research addressed two key issues in franchising. The first was the extent the study of franchisee success and failure by analyzing franchise executives' perceptions of the importance of several characteristics associated with franchisee success and failure. Second was to examine differences among the executives' perceptions of these characteristics based on the location of the franchisor: Canada, Mexico, or the United States. Their study found that the respondents' perceptions of the importance of system quality, brand name, local environment and communication, and other scales of franchisor and franchisee activities differed by the country of origin. Additionally, results of the study showed that neither business type nor franchise size had any effect on perceptions of success or failure. The authors examined the research that has been conducted since the study appeared in 1998 and what we know in 2001.

Josias and McIntyre published the first article examining franchising in Brazil in 1995. McIntyre gave us an update in 2001 on what is now the third largest franchising market in the world. In 2001, only the United States and Canada had more franchises than Brazil. However, China has climbed the ladder adding to its franchise total, which has reached 111,477, with the previous countries operating 757,055, 78,000, and 2,031 stores, respectively (Edwards, 2011; Canadian Franchise Association, 2014; Geromel, 2012). The author covered the history of franchising in Brazil, described what is unique about Brazilian franchising, and gave her view of the country's prospects for the future franchise market. McIntyre views Brazilian franchising as ripe for development, evidenced by the size of the domestic franchise industry, demographics of the population, and current economic conditions.

Singapore, Malaysia, and Hong Kong

Researchers began publishing articles on franchising in Asia in 1995. Goh (2001) assessed Singapore's franchise industry by presenting the results from two surveys, one conducted in 1995 and another in 1999. The first survey was mailed to 62 franchisors and found that most were engaged in mass market franchising. The second survey of 140 existing and potential franchisors was conducted in 1999 by the Singapore government. At least half of those respondents already had franchises operating in other countries, particularly in Southeast Asia, but in the Middle East and Africa as well. The author summarized the opportunities and difficulties a franchisor may face when entering Singapore. Since then, about 500 franchise concepts and over 30,000 franchisees conduct businesses in Singapore (Stanford, 2016). Singapore's economy is somewhat unpredictable due to its high dependence on trade. However, the country's opportunities outweigh its risks for franchising.

McCosker (1996) reported on a survey of foreign franchises that desired to enter the Asian markets of Singapore, Malaysia, Hong Kong, and Indonesia. He gathered information from the existing literature, as well as franchisors that had already entered these markets, and interviews conducted during visits to those countries. Chan, Foo, Quek, and Justis (1994) published an article that reported on a survey that identified the major franchises that existed, the different types of franchises, and the nature and characteristics of franchise agreements in Singapore. Since these articles were written, the Malaysian government has taken initiatives to promote franchise business, because they realize that it will boost economic development, create more job opportunities, and establish a variety of business in the country (Hoe & Bhatti, 2013). In 2006, the franchising industry was estimated to make up about 25% of total retail sales in Malaysia. As a strategy for entrepreneurial development in the country, the government has given full support to encourage franchise growth.

English and Xau (1994) explored franchising in China by reporting on the entrance and subsequent experiences of two US-based franchises into the country: Kentucky Fried Chicken (KFC) and McDonald's. They updated his report in a 2001 article. They found that the primary difference experienced by franchisors entering the Chinese market is that the government is the franchisee. English and Xau still believe that the rewards for franchising in China are there and that patience will be rewarded. In 1995, Chan and Justis looked at franchising in Indonesia by investigating the climate for franchising and the perceptions of the Indonesian people toward franchising. In recent years, Indonesia's economic growth, wealth, and size of the local market have seen an increase in demand for foreign brands and a corresponding increase in international businesses entering the market through franchising (Payne & Drakes, 2013).

China

China has the most potential for growth of all markets. Three authors from the Department of Hotel and Tourism Management at the Hong Kong Polytechnic University discussed the rapid expansion of the franchised hotel industry in China and the opportunities that exist for further development (Pine, Zhang, & Qi, 2001). Additionally, they expanded on the creation and growth of indigenous hotel chains. From 1979 to 1999, the number of hotels in China had grown from the ground up, so to speak. There are now 7,035 hotels where there previously were none. In 2007, there were 13,583 star-rated hotels in China (Travel China Guide, 2007). The authors related their understanding of China's cultural, economic, and political background as essential for success in this market. Wilke English, from the United States, teamed up with one of his Chinese students to look at two prominent franchises that entered China early on: KFC and McDonald's. The authors have an update from the early beginning of franchising in 1994, when these franchises were in a joint venture arrangement with the Chinese government, basically as the "franchisee." The articles covered the challenges faced by these early franchising pioneers and the quick-fire success they experienced. His "Y2K Update" looked at these two systems, which now have about 300 outlets in China. Particularly interesting is the lack of competition these two chains have encountered in China. English and his student also covered legislation that was passed in China that contains a similar legal structure to franchising in the United States. This makes franchising much more inviting to potential franchisors who wish to enter this vast and expansive market. With the help of Ilan Alon, Rollins University, who collected the Y2K data, Wilke English compiled price comparisons in US Dollars and in Yuan of the McDonald's menu items as of 1993 and 2000, and compared the data to Belton, Texas (the author's residence).

Han (2001) expanded on the legal issues affecting franchising in China. She pointed out many market segments and diverse populations that are in China and that make the market interesting as well as challenging for the franchisor. She examined China's franchising measures, how they are defined, and what must be included in franchise agreements to be in full compliance with China's contract law. Intellectual property rights and how they should be protected were also covered. She related that care must be given to the selection of Chinese trade names and marks that accompany patents, trademarks, trade names, copyrights, trade secrets, and domain names. She also examined in detail all the laws that franchisors must comply with, including labor laws, land use regulations, and tax laws in addition to specific laws that govern franchising. Dispute resolution, arbitration, and litigation alternatives in franchise agreements and how they are enforced in the Chinese Court of Law are explicated.

In July 2000, Alon (2001) interviewed a Chinese beauty parlor franchisor in Shanghai. Alon uses a standardized interview instrument that consists of 23 questions concerning ownership, franchising, and strategic marketing. Six major findings that are helpful to understand the state of franchising and business development in China emerged and are summarized in the article: 38% of the franchisor's outlets are in Shanghai, all of the parent stores are in downtown Shanghai, 56% of the outlets in Shanghai are owned by the franchisor, the start-up costs are around $20,000, the franchisor relies on tie-in sales instead of royalties for ongoing income, and the company prefers to own the most profitable locations. Nair (2001), who owns a US-based company engaged in joint ventures in China, gave an overview of franchising in China from the perspective of a franchisee. The author painted a picture of the country as it exists today and how it has transformed. He also explored the advantages and disadvantages of franchising in China, the pros and cons of direct and indirect franchising, and the types of opportunities available for foreign firms to invest and establish a foothold in this gigantic market. In 1992 the Chinese government announced the decision to reform the economy through decentralization efforts. This was the beginning of many reforms aimed at privatizing state enterprises. Early pioneers in franchising systems in China encountered many problems working through the new regulations of the state, but franchising flourished and is one of the major franchise markets worldwide today.

Edwards (2011) reported that the China Chain Store and Franchise Association (CCFA)—a quasi-government nonprofit membership association for Chinese and foreign retailers, franchisers, and well-known foreign brands— now has 900 members with 180,000 outlets across China. The total annual sales of CCFA members reached nearly $300 billion in 2010—about 13% of total retail sales in China. CCFA has also monitored the top 120 franchises in China to gain a clearer picture of franchise development. In 2010, these 120 companies operated 111,477 franchise stores, an increase of 17.6% over 2009. Total sales of the top 120 franchisors reached $52.4 billion in 2010, up 8.9% from 2009. Edwards (2011) identifies the following opportunities: the consumer middle class is expanding, brands from the West are highly regarded, established franchises from the West have new and modern business systems, and cities that are in the second and third tiers are opening to franchising. Challenges include: problems with intellectual property protection, lack of management skills by local managers, the challenge of identifying and evaluating candidates for licensing, the size of China makes for many different markets, the regulatory environment is constantly changing, and franchises must adapt to the Chinese market (Edwards, 2001).

India

India is a country with a huge potential for franchising growth. It is estimated that the current market in India is approximately USD 1 billion and has a per annum growth rate of 30%. The U S Government has designated India as a big emerging market (BEM). Paswan and Dant's (1995) study looked at the definitions of franchising by native Indians and compared it to the American concepts of franchising. They offered the first framework for franchising in India. Paswan, Dant, and Young (2001) covered some prospects and caveats for entering this market as a franchisor. Dant and Kaufmann (2001) gave a descriptive account that is given from a 2000 survey of franchisors in the Delhi area. The data is divided into six major categories of findings that include the distribution by sectors, scope and ownership patterns, system age and size, franchisee selection, financial arrangements, and operating procedures. The authors compared and contrasted these findings to technology-based franchise systems that are prevalent in the Delhi area and are considered by some as the future of franchising in India. Paswan et al. (2001) contrasted the other articles by concentrating on the Indian people's opinions of franchising. The results indicated that there are six major dimensions that potential customers use to evaluate a franchise: macro- and socio-economic concerns, social well-being, individual well-being, consumer benefits, quality improvement, and localized development. Paswan et al. (2001) urged further research in emerging markets to also look at the customer side, as well as the franchisor and franchisee sides of the equation when evaluating potential markets.

Today, franchising in India is a popular business model that is increasing at a fast rate. Mehta and Kaushik (2015) believe that franchising could be a significant growth engine for the Indian economy in the next few years. Within the small industries of India, franchising businesses are expanding; these include fast food, retailing, hotel and other services-based businesses. Thus, prospects for Indian retail franchising are high considering the current state of economy and other parameters (Mehta & Kaushik, 2015).

Other Asian Markets

The Middle East

Khan and Khan (2001) specifically analyzed the restaurant industry in the Middle East, concentrating on the major trends and success factors related to franchising. The authors emphasized the political and legal considerations, language, culture and traditions, menu items and service, demographic and economic changes, and availability of resources that must be taken into consideration when entering this market. Khan and Khan (2001) included a table of 22 countries that are differentiated by area, population, annual population growth, and GDP. Additionally, handy assessment checklists are included that can be utilized by franchisors who are considering entering a new market. Raven, two former students, and Welsh presented cases on Starbucks Coffee International and Mercedes Benz in Kuwait (Welsh, Raven, & Al-Bisher, 1996). The latter is a real event that transcribed while the Kuwaiti student worked at his family's dealership. The Starbucks case was written in 1996 before Starbucks entered this market and is quite forward thinking. Interestingly, as predicted in the original article, Starbucks opened its first outlet in Sharq, Kuwait, in 1999, and it has become one of the most profitable stores in the entire region. M. H. Alshaya Co. operates over 350 Starbucks stores in the Middle

East (Starbucks Corporation, 2014). Both cases give excellent insights into the country, the region, the culture, and its people, thanks to the collaboration between the academic authors and the native Kuwaitis.

Industrialized Markets

North America

Franchising began in the United States in the 1850s with the Singer Sewing Machine Company. One of the first and most famous franchisors was Henry Ford, who figured out the value of franchise systems whilst quickly distributing cars to yearning first-time car buyers and not being encumbered with the cost of inventory. Today, franchising encompasses a system that is used around the world to sell over 1 trillion dollars worth of goods and services from Tokyo to New York (Reynolds, 2002). Franchising is powerful and it is here to stay.

Currently, franchising is 40% of retail trade in the United States and 25% in Canada (Fenwick & Strombom, 1998; Scrivener, 2001). In the article, Welsh (2001) covered the definitions of franchising, regulation, survival rates, recent developments and future trends. One trend that was identified is the focus on self-reliance. Young people want higher income, job security, and the self-satisfaction that comes with owning their own business or franchise. This will affect franchising growth positively, especially for women and minorities internationally.

Clarkin (2002) examined the differences in expansion strategies among more than 1,200 North American franchises. International market development continues to be increasingly important. The study examines two major issues: the differences in size, age, and other characteristics between those pursuing international expansion and those not, and the possible motivations for international expansion. The study found similar results to a study done 27 years earlier that found opportunity recognition as a more important motivator for international expansion than market saturation. The reasons for the findings and their implications are further explained in the study.

Multiunit and Master Franchising

Grunhagen and Mittelstaedt (2002), one of the founders of the International Society of Franchising, gave us a historical synopsis of franchising, and a look at the state of the franchise industry and recent developments that have spurred growth and expansion. They described new industry segments that have emerged, including franchisees' mini-chains that cross states and regions. They also discussed the reasons behind the astronomical growth of multiunit franchising from the franchisor's as well as franchisee's perspectives. The major advantages usually cited to a franchise are explicated, with the authors giving some new reasons not previously considered. Grunhagen and Mittelstaedt (2002) also looked at the motivations of multiunit franchisees, which may be different than the usual explanations given for franchising. The literature gave three reasons why individuals choose to franchise:

single-unit franchisees are so eager to get into business for themselves that they become risk indifferent, multiunit operators believe that they can "beat the system" by the advantages of a larger and more geographically dispersed locations, and franchisees are not entrepreneurs, so they need the system that franchising has built-in. The authors argued that entrepreneurship is an important motivator for multiunit franchisee ownership. The article adds to the body of literature by addressing franchisee motivations, and that a reasonable explanation for the growth of multiunit franchising is entrepreneurship.

In his article, "The Organizational Determinants of Master International Franchising," Alon (2000) first defined and explained why master franchising is such a popular form for global expansion. He then goes on to develop a group of propositions as to the impact of certain organizational variables on the use of master franchise agreements overseas. These types of agreements are primarily used for business format franchisors. Alon divides the factors into three explanations: resource based, knowledge based, and strategy based. The resource-based explanation looks at size, age, and brand-name asset specificity. The knowledge-based explanations include know-how and experience in managing global operations. Price, product, and strategies are given as strategy-based reasons. These explanations should be examined before a franchisor enters a host country and decides the level of risk that he/she can tolerate. Ilan Alon gave a theoretical framework for global expansion that can be expanded on and is sorely needed in the field.

Coompanthu and Roth's (2002) study focused on international services and explores the various organizational forms that are possible and their impact on profitability. The article focused particularly on the use of plural management. Plural management can be defined as using a combination of company-owned or company-operated, and franchised forms. Unit growth, uniformity, local responsiveness, and system-wide adaptation are all affected by using plural management. As a result, when there is high performance ambiguity, or when it is difficult to determine employee job performance, firms are more likely to use franchised forms for international expansion. When there is a great deal of outcome uncertainty, company-owned/operated forms are more likely. The authors urged franchisors to look at the nature of the industry and the organizational forms that have worked best to achieve a higher performance level in the future. Plural management is offered as a strategic solution to the problems of achieving tight control if there is high performance ambiguity and the need to respond effectively to local markets.

Erramilli, Agarwal, and Dev (2002) also looked at global entry modes in the service industry. The article focused on nonequity modes of entry that feature minimal or no investment requirements. These nonequity modes are popular among consumer-services firms, such as hotels and restaurants. Professional services firms like consulting businesses, for example, rarely use this form. The study looks at the reasons for choosing between two nonequity modes: franchising and management-service contracts. The perspective taken in the article is that the form that most effectively transfers organizational capabilities is the one that should be adopted rather than the one that provides the most effective control over the subsidiary. The latter is most recommended by international business theories. An international sample of hotel firms was used to find that capabilities that are difficult to imitate cannot be effectively transferred through franchising. In such cases, a management-service contract is preferable. Infrastructure was found to be critical to the type of mode chosen and the success of the franchise. Additionally, the level of development of the country had an effect. In countries where customers are more service conscious, and there is ample supply of talented managers and investors, franchising worked better. The authors warned that firms focus mostly on the transfer characteristics of their business when making these modal decisions. If they are not perfectly imitable, there will be problems with franchising, and more calling for management-service contracts.

Global Franchise Relationships

Sydow (2002) examined the service sector also, but looked at network leadership. He argued that, strategically, franchise systems need to link to interorganizational networks and be more relationship oriented. He also covered the management practices that are necessary for this to happen and anchored his recommendations in the theories that have been developed on structure. Sydow illustrated the application of this theory with six business format franchise networks in Germany: McDonald's (fast food restaurants), OBI (retail superstores), Aufina (real estate agencies), Schulerhilfe (tutoring providers), ComputerLand (retail sales and computer services), and Hyper Services (service providers). Jorg Sydow offered concrete suggestions for the industry to follow, as well as implications for management that have global applications.

In the article, "International Growth of US Franchising: Cultural and Legal Barriers," Hawkes and Bandyopadhyay (2002) built a framework that examined the cultural and legal barriers that American franchisors could face as they expand globally. Their framework is built on two dimensions: the cultural distance of the potential market from the United States and the extent of legal barriers in that market. Strategies that should be taken by the franchisor given these barriers are explicated. For example, Italy and Spain have many legal barriers but are culturally similar, so the business format needs adapted more. In Japan, there are fewer legal barriers, but it is culturally distant, so more product adaptation should occur. In the Gulf Region (Middle East), a great deal of adaptation of the product and the business format would be necessary because many legal barriers exist in these countries and they are culturally distant. In all, this article offered practical advice that can be easily understood and implemented.

The United States

Fred DeLuca (2002) created the world's largest franchise operation when he created Subway (Jones, 2011). In North America, they have surpassed McDonald's with the most number of locations. With Annie Smith and Les Winograd, Fred told his story of how Subway conquered America and then spread worldwide. It all began in 1965 with the help of a family friend, who loaned him $1,000 to help pay for college tuition. By 2002, it had more than 16,000 franchised restaurants in 74 countries. As of 2013, there are 25,549 Subway franchise stores in the United States, with more than 37,000 franchises in 99 countries and territories worldwide (Morran, 2013; Subway, 2014). The article by DeLuca covered the management challenges facing the franchise as it has expanded globally, as well as a summary of its growth in certain counties, including Australia, Venezuela, India, and China. The article concludes with a summary of future endeavors on the horizon.

Alon (2002) in his article, "The Organizational Factors of US International Franchising: A Comparative Study of Retailing, Hotels, and Professional Business Services," analyzed how these industries have expanded globally through the number of outlets, including size and scale, the growth rate, the pricing strategy, and the geographical dispersion. These factors aid in explaining why franchisors have gone global and differences between the three industries that are discussed. For instance, the age of the franchise was insignificant for the hotel and professional business service categories and had a negative relationship on internationalizing in the retailing sector. One of the most interesting findings of the study was the fact that younger franchisors in the retail sector were more likely to franchise. Ilan Alon provided clear evidence that the decision to go international should be studied at the industry level. This study cleared the way for the development of a complete model of internationalization that is sorely needed by the franchise industry to make better decisions on where, when, and why to go global.

Canada

With a population of 30 million, its proximity, and culture, Canada is often the first stop for US franchisors to expand internationally. Jones and Wong (2002) described the state of the Canadian market, including currency, banking, legislation at the federal and province levels, and regulations. Additionally, the authors discussed the numerous factors to consider in adapting franchise agreements to the Canadian market, especially the enforcement of contracts from one province to the next. Franchise legislation is currently in force in five Canadian provinces: Alberta, Ontario, New Brunswick, Prince Edward Island, and Manitoba. The legislation for Manitoba came into action on October 1, 2012 (Floriani & Liebman, 2014). Canada has followed the lead of the European Union and enacted the Personal Information Protection and Electronic Documents Act which protects all personal information collected in the private sector during commercial activities of companies. Quebec has had such legislation in place since 1994, while Ontario prepared a draft of its own privacy legislation and two other provinces were in the process of doing the same. In 2004, the federal legislation extended to the provinces that had not passed their own legislation concerning privacy. By 2014, there were 76,000 franchises operating in Canada (Canadian Franchise Directory, 2014). In all, Jones and Wong's article comprehensively covered all basic aspects of what a franchisor needs to know to enter the market. It would benefit potential and existing franchisees to read the article as well as to get a total understanding of the entire franchise system in Canada.

The Pacific Rim

This vast area of the world is an open door to franchisors looking for densely populated consumer markets that are receptive to new opportunities. Despite the critics' misgivings, Western fast food chains first entered East Asian markets with a great deal of success. KFC average sales per store in Asia are US $1.2 million, compared to per store revenues in the United States of US $933,000 (Oches, 2011). Choo (2002) chose three franchisors with different capabilities and levels of internationalization to illustrate the critical success factors needed to enter the East Asian market. Dome Coffees from Australia, The Coffee Bean & Tea Leaf Company from the United States, and Royal Copenhagen Ice Cream from Australia are qualitatively analyzed using the techniques of Yin (1994), and Miles and Huberman (1994). Results showed that there were mainly six key success factors in the East Asian market: distance management, contract enforcement, cultural adaptability, host country risk management, marketing approach, and partnership management. The greater the cultural differences between the franchisor and franchisees in East Asia, the more important these success factors become in transferring a profitable franchise system. Choo made a significant contribution in providing any potential or current franchisor a useful insight into approaching and competing successfully in this market.

Japan

In his article, "Franchising as a Growth Strategy in the Japanese Retail Market," (2002b) Nitin Sanghavi reviewed the opportunities and challenges for companies that use franchising as a growth strategy in the Japanese market. He covered the developments in the Japanese and retail consumer markets, the effect of the stock market, and what it would take to be profitable in this densely populated country. Compared to other industries, franchising has done relatively well in Japan, maintaining a growth rate of 6–8%. In terms of the number of stores, service-related franchises showed the most growth, although sales per store were not as significant as food services or retail commerce franchises. Seventy percent of the total increase in sales of the franchise industry was in retail commerce franchises. The author engaged the reader to understand the effect of various business customs and lifestyle trends on franchise success in Japan and how the franchise should include these factors in its overall business strategy and structure to be successful.

Australia

Frazer (2001) explained the franchise market on this unique continent that is regarded as a leader in franchise practices. The current legislation on franchising in Australia dates back to 1998. Overall, their Franchising Code of Conduct has been declared effective in making franchising more professional and since it was passed, growth in franchising has occurred. As of 2010, there were approximately 1,025 business format franchisors in Australia (WhichFranchise Australia, 2014); in 2014, that number increased to 1,160. In fact, Australia has more franchisors per capita than the United States. As per the Franchise Council of Australia

(2017), there are about 79,000 franchise units in the country, reflecting an increase of 8.2% since 2012. Individual franchise systems have grown from a median of 18–23 units per system, so there is still the potential for expansion in this country. Frazer gives us an optimistic view of the future of franchising in Australia.

New Zealand

Paynter (2002) summarized the history of franchising and the results of the annual Franchise Association of New Zealand survey. A total of 111 systems are analyzed in terms of the number currently operating in the country, the number of people employed, the number of franchised and company-owned units, the percentage increase in sales growth, the industry groupings by percentage, the number of native franchise operations, and the median start-up costs, among other statistics. In 2012, there were over 440 franchise systems operating 22,000 units in New Zealand (Franchise Association of New Zealand, 2014). Paynter's results of the number of systems that have websites (84%) and the failure rate data are particularly interesting. Over a three-year period, only 6% failed, and a miniscule 16% of franchisors (6% of franchisees) considered franchising as a bad return on their investment. A hardy 77% rated their system excellent or above average. These results are good news for the industry.

Dana (2002a) encapsulated the New Zealand franchise market, which has the highest number of franchises per capita, one franchise per 186.5 citizens (Lord, 2013). Additionally, three quarters of these franchises are New Zealand-based franchisors. Foreign franchisors are primarily from Australia. Dana gave a detailed description of both, as well as possible legislation that may be enacted in the future. New Zealand does not have any franchise legislation, but may enact similar legislation in the future that mirrors the one passed in July of 1998 in Australia.

Leo Paul Dana also discusses initiatives that the government should consider to aide in franchise development as well as future challenges in the industry. Specifically, Dana identified that future research should explore why New Zealand franchisors tend not to expand globally.

Israel

Dana (2002b) analyzed the current state of franchising in Israel, explained why franchising has gained popularity quickly, and the reasons for its accelerated growth in his article, "Israel's Experience with Franchising." He gave two basic reasons for this phenomenon. First, Israel is a country composed of many immigrants. In the 1990s, there were a million new immigrants. Second, thousands of defense military personnel retired in their early forties with a lump sum payment from the government of $250,000 and were looking for investment opportunities—many bought franchises. That fueled the growth of home-grown franchises in banking, financial services, fashion, and fast food. Interestingly, Israeli franchisors have not ventured abroad, except for a couple of notable exceptions. Burger Ranch has done well entering the Hungarian and Romanian markets, while Reliable Rent a Car has done well expanding into the Mediterranean region-Cyprus, Egypt, Italy, Malta, Portugal, Spain, and Turkey. Dana also summarized the legal environment in Israel and what he sees as possible franchise legislation and protection in the future.

South Africa

In his 1996 and subsequent 1997 articles, Scholz described the state and penetration of franchising as a form of business in South Africa. He included an overview of the environment for franchising, the population, and the legal regulations concerning franchising. In 1997, he reported there were 170 franchise systems and 6,000 outlets operating in the country and that the market was ripe for more entry of international franchises. Growing 13% annually, South Africa now has over 400 franchise systems and 23,000 franchise outlets (Smit & Van Wyk, Inc., 2013).

Anita du Toit's (2002) study of franchising in South Africa focused on the issue of encroachment in multibrand franchises by using in-depth interviews of franchisors who had operated a business format franchise and had two or more franchised brands. About 10% of the franchisors in South Africa met the criteria. Qualitative analysis with the use of themes to give a larger, consolidated picture was utilized following the suggestions of Creswell (1994). Eight themes emerged and are described in detail in the article: brand management systems, achieving economies of scale, brand positioning, cultural divergence, conflict between stakeholders, policies on geographical proximity, failure of acquisitions, and separation of brands. Du Toit concluded by making recommendations for future research based on her results, and theorized that perhaps multibrand franchises may not be able to be managed successfully to avoid encroachment. She also included some great recommendations that, if incorporated, would improve brand management of multibrand franchises and assist in avoiding encroachment problems, good suggestions wherever the franchise is located worldwide.

Europe

Most of the world's international business, trade, and investment occur among three regional markets, Europe, North America, and Asia, also known as the Triad. Rugman (2001) advanced the thesis that globalism—the existence of a single market unified by economic and political forces—is a myth; triad-based international business is the past, present and future reality of international trade. More profound is the fact that most trade occurs within the triad. For example: 90% of all cars produced in Europe are sold in Europe and over 60% of EU countries' exports go to other EU countries. However, bike sales actually overtook car sales in 23 of the 27 European Union member states, except for Belgium and Luxembourg in 2012 (data was not available for Cyprus and Malta) (Marks, 2013). This is the first time since World War II that bikes outsold cars in Italy and Spain hit a record in bike sales for the first time in their history (Marks, 2013). This could be attributed to the global recession, since the EU economy was, and is, still recovering. European car sales were at a twenty year low for the first half of 2013. In Romania, bikes outsold cars five to one (380,000 to 72,000 cars) and Germany sold the most bikes to cars (3,966.000 to 3,083,000 cars) (Marks, 2013).

Rugman's research also suggested that national governments regulate most service sectors, limiting market forces, and that business needs to: *think regional, act local, and forget global* (Rugman, 2001, p. 11).

In Europe, the EU is the central economic organization that drives the region, the world's largest economic superpower, a huge consumer market of 370 million people, and a union of 15 nations that continues to attract prospective members. In 2000, the European Union was the world's leading exporter—with a total value of $814 billion, 20% of the world's trade volume—and the second largest importer (Wright, 2000). As of 2011, Europe's exports of manufactured goods reached nearly US $5 trillion (World Trade Organization, 2012). The Euro, the official currency of the EU, has so far shown to be stable, convertible, and has increasingly become an internationally viable alternative to the US dollar for business transactions and central bank operations.

While economically many of the European countries are integrated, the history, language, and culture of individual countries is unique. The plurality of cultures and languages in Europe makes complete standardization more difficult, if not impossible, for franchising systems. For example, a consistent image and a single brand formula can fail abroad as Eddie Bauer, Marks and Spencer, and Wal-Mart can attest.

A study of more than 1,500 consumers and 40 retail grocery and clothing brands in France, Germany and the UK found appreciable differences in buyers' motivations. The French wanted service and quality; the British wanted affinity; and the Germans desired price/value. In Germany, discount-food market accounts for 32% of franchises, compared with 8% in France. Thus, companies need to adjust their product offering, pricing, brand image, or service and tailor their image at the national level (Child, Heywood, & Kliger, 2002). The European market is much more heterogeneous than the U.S., and a careful strategy of adjusting the franchising concept to national differences is advisable.

In the section that follows, the franchising conditions in 12 European countries are reviewed. Table 11.2 provides some descriptive statistics for these countries taken from the International Franchise Association's website. According to the statistics, in 2002, these countries accounted for over 347 million consumers with an average GDP per capita exceeding $24,500 with a combined market of about $7.8 trillion. In 2014, these countries accounted for 373 million consumers and the average GDP per capita was over $36,000. Additionally, franchising in Belgium, Ireland, Netherlands, and Sweden is covered.

Table 11.2	European Countries Examined					
COUNTRY	LANGUAGES	CAPITAL CITY	POPULATION 2002	PER CAPITA GDP 2002	POPULATION 2014	PER CAPITA GDP 2014
Austria	German	Vienna	8,078,000	$25,655	8,221,000	43,100
Denmark	Danish	Copenhagen	5,300,000	$32,000	5,560,000	37,700
Finland	Finnish	Helsinki	5,130,000	$16,000	5,266,000	36,500
France	French	Paris	58,000,000	$23,000	65,950,000	35,500
Germany	German	Berlin	82,000,000	$25,000	81,147,000	39,100
Greece	Greek	Athens	11,500,000	$11,305	10,770,000	25,100
Italy	Italian	Rome	56,900,000	$20,000	61,482,000	30,600
Norway	Norwegian	Oslo	4,400,000	$33,300	4,722,000	55,900
Portugal	Portuguese	Lisbon	9,900,000	$10,901	10,800,000	23,800
Spain	Spanish	Madrid	40,000,000	$13,200	47,370,000	31,100
Switzerland	German	Bern	7,110,000	$35,614	8,000,000	46,200
United Kingdom	English	London	59,100,000	$24,300	63,400,000	37,500

Source: International Franchising Association, www.franchise.org (retrieved Feb, 24, 2014)

Overview of Franchising in Europe

Stanworth and Purdy (2002) gave a review of the European markets from the perspective of UK franchisors and discussed the expansion plans of British franchisors who planned to penetrate the markets of the European Union. Forty-one percent of their sample claimed to either operate in another European country or planned to become active in the EU shortly. Stanworth and Purdy suggested that companies aspiring for international expansion may underestimate the real cost of expansion, need to develop linguistic skills, and plan to develop some company-owned outlets, if they want to emulate what the UK international franchisors are already doing. The EU markets can be ranked by the number of franchisors in descending order: Spain, Germany, UK, France, Italy, Portugal, Netherlands, Sweden, Austria, Greece, Belgium, Ireland, Denmark, and Finland.

Mendelsohn (2003) reviewed the comparative legal environment for franchising in Europe, discussing the European Commission regulations relating to franchising and several key franchising cases heard before the European Court of Justice, including Yves Rocher, Computerland, Pronuptia, ServiceMaster, and Charles Jourdan. The assertion in these cases is that the market sharing arrangements inherent in franchising may violate EC competition law. The legal environments of franchising are examined in nine countries: Austria, Belgium, Finland, Germany, Italy, Netherlands, Portugal, Spain, Switzerland, and the United Kingdom.

Sherman (2003) offered final suggestions to European franchisors wishing to internationalize their operations by discussing key trends. While international franchising has been mostly US led, European franchisors are expanding overseas in increasing numbers. Sherman advised European franchisors wishing to expand into the United States to thoroughly understand their strengths and weaknesses, potential target markets, partners, trademarks, products and services, company resources, and rationale for expansion.

Two international franchising lawyers, Mazero and Martyn (2002a, 2002b), provided an analysis and a checklist for due diligence in international franchising. This topic is increasing in importance because of new requirements and renewed focus on money laundering, corruption, and terrorism internationally. The authors advised franchisors to investigate prospective franchisees thoroughly by reviewing prospective franchisees publicity, credit history, corporate affiliations, civil and criminal reports, real property, bankruptcy records, liens and judgments, and regulatory authorities.

Unlike the United States, Europe is much more cosmopolitan, consisting of a variety of nations and cultures with differing and often conflicting histories. European franchisors have one distinct advantage over American franchisors in Europe. That is, they are often multilingual and they understand the cultural variations within their markets better than Americans. American franchisors' transaction costs can be high in terms of translating materials, adapting manuals, brochures and advertising, overcoming cultural and geographical distance, and controlling local operations.

American franchisors should ask themselves the following questions: Can the company's core competency and brand travel? Are the company's abilities and know-how valued in foreign cultures? Are there economies-of-scale or first-to-market advantages in entering the European market? Are there entrenched competitors with more acceptable brand recognition? What adjustments do they need to make to the standard formula? The answers to these questions lie in franchisors' ability to recognize opportunities and threats in the environment and strengths and weaknesses in their organization.

The implications of cultural and environmental diversity to franchisors wishing to do business in Europe is twofold: (1) franchisors need to adapt their franchising concept and management style to local cultures and (2) franchisors need to find ways to cooperate with local partners and governments to promote entry into a variety of service sectors that are sometimes restricted or regulated. Such cooperation can happen if the two sides understand the benefits and limitations of franchising as they relate to the host market economic and social goals and needs.

Austria

No special franchising law exists in Austria and franchise agreements typically fall under the civil law that regulates contracts, consumer protection, competition, and intellectual property. Austrian and European antitrust regulations are important determinants of case law. Details on applicable laws of franchising in Austria are given by Marco Hero in his 2003 article.

Denmark

Sanghavi (2002a) discussed retail franchising in Denmark. Denmark is one of the most affluent members of the EU, and franchising has much potential there. His chapter on Denmark reviewed the franchising development in the country, the infrastructure and legal environment, the franchising market, the financial environment, and the marketing environment. As an appendix to the article and as a reference to the reader, Sanghavi (2002a) attaches the European Code of Ethics for Franchising to which Denmark subscribes. The article concluded that opportunities for retail franchising in Denmark are abundant.

Finland

Tuunanen (2002) presented and analyzed data on franchisors in Finland from 1999 to 2002. His research indicated that there are 164 franchisors in Finland, employing 38,000 people, and generating gross annual sales of about $3.25 billion. Currently, Finland is home to about 300 franchising systems with over 6,000 operating units accounting for over $6 billion in sales (US Department of Commerce, 2012). Tuunanen reviewed the key definitions of franchising, created a framework for identifying business format franchising in Finland, and collected and analyzed the data with a variety of methods.

While Tuunanen's analysis provided a franchisor perspective, Torikka and Tuunanen (2002) examined franchisee-training programs. In Finland, the government participates in the education of franchisees through economic development centers. In recent years, many programs have emerged to train current and prospective franchisees. Torikka and Tuunanen evaluated the effectiveness of these programs by describing careers shifts of the trainees. They report the results from a sample of 100 graduates of the first five programs and found that one-sixth bought a franchise. These results showed that government agencies can promote franchising and economic development through focused educational programs. These programs had a major effect on the success rate of the trainees.

France

Penard, Raynaud, and Saussier (2003) presented an overview of franchising in France, with detailed statistics and discussed the current legal environment. The authors found that franchisors in France attempt to establish a balance between company-owned stores and franchisee-owned stores, and that this balance is sector specific. Furthermore, domestic franchisors charge higher royalties as compared to foreign franchisors, which often require fixed fees.

Cliquet and Perrigot (2003a) answered the call of Penard, Raynaud, and Saussier for industry-specific franchising research. They examined variations to franchising in French hotel chains. Half of the chains have at least 15% franchisee ownership. Dual distribution, using both company-owned and franchisee-owned outlets, simultaneously has accelerated the growth of the French hotel sector, ensured territories are adequately covered, lowered the financial burdens of expansion, and maintained control over operations and renovations. Plural forms of organization stimulated competition among members of the organization (multiunit franchisees, franchisees, and company-operated units), and provided operational flexibility to adjust to economic cycles and changing client behavior or legislative guidelines. Drawbacks to this system included most notably the possibility of network conflict, particularly between the company-owned outlets and the franchisee-owned outlets, which sometime compete directly with one another. Multiple-unit franchising is growing rapidly in France.

Perrigot and Cliquet (2003b) further investigated the French hotel sector in relation to the franchising sector. This sector is motivated in part by increases in travel and tourism to France. The authors examined the survival, growth and stability of French hotels for the period 1995–1998 and argued that franchisors using a dual distribution strategy or a franchising strategy are more competitive than company-owned hotels in the long run, and predicted that national companies will outlast foreign companies in the French hotel sector.

Germany

Germany is the largest economy in Europe. Flohr (2002) examined the legal environment to franchising in Germany by outlining relevant laws concerning contracts, consumer protection, antitrust and competition, intellectual property, and labor. On a higher level, the EEC Block Exemption for Vertical Restraints of 1999 is discussed in the context of German franchising.

Schlamp (2003) described franchising as it applies to women in Germany. General conditions for women in Germany, startup businesses by women, women-based businesses, and their role in the economy are discussed. Franchising is a way for women to mobilize their business ventures and a solution to some of the problems they face.

Greece

Dimou and Ikkos (2003) presented the climate for franchising in Greece, the economy, business environment, and the overall profile of Greek franchising. Greece is a member of the European Monetary Union, and its economy improved appreciably in the 1990s. The retail sector was significantly restructured due to changes in real incomes, a substantial urbanization, and an inflow of capital from the European community. According to the authors, Greece had 400 franchisors with over 4,000 outlets. Greek franchisors recently have expanded into the Cyprus and the Balkan countries because of their physical and cultural proximity. The authors provided detailed analysis of environmental and industry factors affecting franchising in Greece.

With the current economic crisis, Greece seems to be one of the countries that was hit the worst. Franchising may be one of the most viable, low risk business models with high potential to re-ignite entrepreneurial activity in the country.

Italy

Luca, Majocchi, and Pavione (2003) examined the Italian economy from a franchising perspective in detail. The authors provided a history of franchising, present conditions for growth statistics, as well as offered their thoughts on the prospects of different industries.

Vianelli's (2003) article compliments Luca et al. by examining Italian franchising as a mode of entry into international markets. While Italian franchisors have limited experience with internationalization, a few have achieved considerable success, most notably the Benetton group. Positive country-of-origin effects of the *made in Italy* image has helped the Italian fashion industry gain recognition and acceptance internationally. This is evident by the presence of Italian high fashion outlets in the most exclusive streets of European capitals. About 80 Italian franchisors are presently franchising abroad. Half of the Italian franchisors overseas operate in the personal items category, which includes clothing, intimate wear, footwear and accessory type products, followed by hotel, restoration, and household article sectors. Benetton, for example, sells most of its clothes through its international franchised outlets. Franchising has paved the way for the country to export Italian made products. The 10 largest destinations for Italian exports are Germany, France, USA, UK, Spain, Switzerland, Belgium, Netherlands, Austria and Greece; Italy mostly trades with European countries.

Norway

Singh (2003) described the franchising environment in Norway. Norway is an industrial, oil-rich country, with a high standard of living. Norway, however, is not part of the E U. As of 2002, there were 184 franchisors with a network of over 7,253 outlets. There is little statistical material on franchising in Norway; however, as of 2004, there were 242 franchise systems in operation (Nilssen, 2004). Franchising was relatively new to Norway in 2002, but the country has made strides in developing the sector and franchising is poised for growth. The political environment in Norway is stable, labor laws and taxes are demanding on employers, and franchising enjoys no specific restrictions. Singh explained the social, economic, legal, and consumer environments of franchising. She then examined franchising from the standpoint of price, promotion, and place considerations.

Portugal

Dahab, Cunha, and Cardim (2002) discussed international franchising in Portugal. By looking at how McDonald's entered into the country, the authors attempted to shed light on the need for adaptation to local circumstances. They analyzed the factors leading to international franchising in Portugal, addressed the organizational structure of franchising, and presented empirical evidence from the McDonald's case, which is discussed in detail.

United Kingdom

The United Kingdom is an important international market for international franchisors. The retailing and service sectors are highly developed and about one-third of British retailing is franchised.

Cross, Burton, and Rhodes (2002) employed the transaction cost approach to franchising to explain the use of intermediaries, such as a master subfranchisor, in international franchising development. These intermediaries are more likely to be used when the market is geographically and culturally distant, smaller, less experienced franchisors internationalize, markets are less developed, a larger number of foreign markets are served, and more extensive host country operations are established. Direct franchising is more likely to occur with franchisors that have more resources and more experience in international markets. Diseconomies of scale, associated with managing the franchisor–intermediary relations, discourages franchisors from using intermediaries in international expansion.

Stanworth, Brodie, Wotruba, and Purdy (2002) utilized a sample of 673 independent contractors in direct sales franchising to examine this low-cost, low-entry barrier business that attracts mostly women who are interested in part-time and self-employment opportunities. Their study looked at changes in self-employment in a variety of countries (mostly European), presented a typology of direct sales franchising based on two dimensions: product/service and home-based/external premises, and compared and contrasted franchising to direct selling.

Unlike Cross et al. (2002) and Stanworth et al. (2002), who utilized survey methodology, Quinn (2003) examined international franchising using a qualitative, ethnographic approach. This approach provided an in-depth explanation for the internationalization of one UK franchising firm from 1987 to 1995. The author explained the company's initial market entry, patterns of internationalization, and the changing nature of expansion efforts. Keys to successful international franchise expansion were new product development and aggressiveness in obtaining qualified franchisees.

Conclusion

The advent of franchising is a worldwide phenomenon, and the importance of franchising cannot be overlooked. In countries around the globe, franchising effects the economy substantially and every day, it becomes a larger percentage of the retail trade. It accounts for US $1 trillion in retail spending per year and employs one out of 16 workers in the United States. In 2010, the US Census Bureau reported that franchise businesses accounted for "nearly $1.3 trillion of the $7.7 trillion in total sales for these industries, $153.7 billion out of the $1.6 trillion in total payroll, and 7.9 million workers out of a total workforce of 59.0 million." If we add direct and indirect jobs through the supply chain, franchises support 7.9 million workers. This report is based on 2007 US census data (US Census Bureau, 2010).

In some countries, franchising accounts for about half their total retail sales. Although franchising has its critics, and there are franchises to avoid, it is here to stay. The more we know about franchising, the better off the public and the industry will be. Franchisors, franchisees, those studying franchising, the governments of countries interested in furthering economic development and employment, and the massive populations who desire the opportunity to try franchising themselves through purchasing a franchise, starting their own franchise or tasting its fare, all need this information.

Areas ripe for future research include what various forms of franchising exist and the ability to adapt to the ever-changing global marketplace. Franchising is becoming more complex in order to adapt to a world marketplace that is increasingly becoming more accessible with technological advances. There are more forms of franchising, and there is an increasing symbiotic relationship among the various stakeholders of franchising: franchisors, franchisees, host markets, and consumers. What has not been addressed is the addition of franchisee associations in these symbiotic relationships and that they are becoming at least as powerful, if not more powerful in some spheres, as associations worldwide that have been traditionally composed of franchisors. These influential organizations will continue to wield an increasing share of power in the future. Furthermore, it is likely that such franchisor and franchisee organizations, respectively, will join in associations of their counterparts by region or mirror political associations, such as the European Franchise Federation (EFF) which formed as the European Union (EU) became a reality. In a larger part, these organizations will eventually exert a major influence on supplier networks, legislation, regulatory standards and safeguards, and shared technology and communication. They will transcend language and cultural barriers to create networks that are user-friendly. John Naisbitt, author of *Megatrends*, predicted that the future of franchising would benefit from an increasingly service-based economy, an increasingly convenience-oriented society, a more specialized workforce, more participation by women and minorities, and an increasingly globally-based marketing strategy. His future trend analysis is coming true sooner than originally predicted. Research will only help us to understand where these trends are and where the industry is going.

Family business franchises are now in their second generation, and a small number are even entering third generation franchises. This is particularly true of franchises in the United States, as it has the longest history of franchising. However, other parts of the world where franchises first developed, such as hotel and restaurant industries, are also experiencing "trans-generational franchising." Trans-generational franchising, as defined by Welsh (2003), is the "on-going operation of a franchise or franchises that have gone from the original franchisee(s) to another generation of franchisee(s) that are connected either by family membership or ownership." When the international component is added to a trans-generational franchise or network of franchises, a more complex form of franchising emerges. This has major implications for the franchisor who is trying to maintain positive relationships with franchisees. Additionally, the franchisor may be trans-generational. Welsh calls this the "blind date" phenomenon in franchising. The ability of the franchise system to sustain these long-term relationships could have a major impact on the future of franchising.

The Raymond Family Institute conducted a survey on U.S. family businesses and family business franchises participated (*IFA Insider,* 2002). Understanding the impact of family businesses on franchising and the actual size of this population that is predicted to keep growing in the future is a major research phenomenon. Since franchising accounts for 5% of the 8 million small businesses in the United States, and two-thirds of these small businesses are considered family businesses, the impact of this combination is profound in real terms today. Unfortunately, this report is no longer done. In some parts of the globe, such as the Pacific Rim, the percentage of family businesses is even higher, up to 90% or more. Tomorrow, the way we do business from a management, marketing, and legal stand point may be very different based on these changing demographics. This area is ripe for research and methodologically should be studied using longitudinal data analyses.

Franchising, more than any other time in our history, is facing many new challenges. That is why leadership, vision, and strategic decision-making applied to the franchise industry is so important (Welsh, Adler, Falbe, Gardner, & Rennick, 2001). If the industry is to continue to grow, it needs to transform itself into a 21st century learning organization. Technology can be compared to a moving treadmill, with the speed of information continually ramping up to the next level. Communication is of utmost importance in this age. The environment must be continually scanned for relevant information on the market and its customers. The franchisor and the headquarters staff must provide leadership to communicate their vision to the franchise community. In turn, the franchisees, customers, and associations must communicate their vision of the future to the franchisor. Strategic decision-making must evolve from this interaction. It is important that the vision is clear to all stakeholders. The world marketplace demands it.

Discussion Questions

1. What is an emerging market?
2. What are the two types of franchise arrangements in Croatia?
3. In Mexico, what are the three different ways to enter the market?
4. What is the third largest franchise market in the world?
5. What country has the most potential for growth of all markets?
6. What six major findings were uncovered by Alon with a Chinese beauty parlor franchise that tells us much about franchising in China?
7. Where did franchising begin, what year and what company?
8. How big is franchising in Australia?
9. What questions should American franchises ask themselves?
10. What are the cultural and environmental impacts to franchises wanting to do business in Europe?

References

Akhmetov, A., & Raiskhanova, R. (2001). Franchising in Kazakhstan. In I. Alon & D. H. B. Welsh (Eds.), *International franchising in emerging markets: China, India, and other Asian countries.* Riverwoods, IL: CCH, Inc.

Alon, I. (2000). The organizational determinants of master international franchising. *Journal of Business and Entrepreneurship, 12*(2), 1–18.

Alon, I. (2001). An interview with a Chinese franchisor in Shanghai: XiangXiangShanShouShen—A beautification parlor. In I. Alon & D. H. B. Welsh (Eds.), *International franchising in emerging markets: China, India, and other Asian countries* (pp.105–108). Riverwoods, IL: CCH, Inc.

Alon, I., & Banai, M. (2001). Franchising opportunities and threats in Russia. In D.H.B. Welsh & I. Alon (Eds.), *International franchising in emerging markets: Central and Eastern Europe and Latin America* (pp.131–148). Riverwoods, IL: CCH, Inc.

Alon, I., & McKee, D. I. (1999). Towards a macro-environmental model of international franchising. *Multinational Business Review, 7*(1), 76–82.

Alon, I., & Welsh, D. H. B. (Eds.). (2002). Organizational factors of U.S. international franchising: A comparative study of retailing, hotels, and professional business services. *International franchising in industrialized markets: North America, the Pacific Rim, and other countries* (pp.223–232). Riverwoods, IL: CCH, Inc.

Alpeza, M., Erceg, A., & Peterka, S. (2015). Development of Franchising in Croatia—Obstacles and policy recommendations. *Review of Innovation and Competitiveness, 1*(1). Retrieved from http://hrcak.srce.hr/155592?lang=en

Amies, M. (1999, Jan/Feb). The wilder shores of franchising. *Franchising World*, pp. 27–28.

Arnold, D. J., & Quelch, J. A. (1988, Fall). New strategies in emerging markets. *Sloan Management Review*, 7–20.

Canadian Franchise Association. (2014). *Fast franchise facts*. Retrieved from http://www.cfa.ca/Publications_Research/FastFacts.aspx

Canadian Franchise Directory. (2014). *Franchise guide*. Retrieved from http://www.canadianfranchisedirectory.ca/franchiseguide.aspx

Chan, P. S., Foo, J. K. S., Quek, G., & Justis, R. T. (1994, February). A survey of franchising in Singapore. *Proceedings of the International Society of Franchising, Las Vegas, NV.*

Chan, P. S., & Justis, R. T. (1995, February). Franchising in Indonesia. *Proceedings of the International Society of Franchising, San Juan, Puerto Rico.*

Christy, R. L., & Haftel, S. M. (1993, February). Pizza Hut in Moscow: Post-coup system development and expansion. *Proceedings of the International Society of Franchising, San Francisco, CA.*

Child, P. N., Heywood S., & Kliger M. (2002). Do retail brands travel? *The McKinsey Quarterly, 1*, 11–13.

Choo, S. (2002). Valuable lessons for international franchisors when expanding into East Asia. In D. H. B. Welsh & I. Alon (Eds.), *International franchising in industrialized markets: North America, the Pacific Rim, and other countries* (pp. 249–268). Riverwoods, IL: CCH, Inc.

Clarkin, J. E. (2002). Market maturation or opportunity recognition? An examination of international expansion by U.S. and Canadian franchise systems. In D. H. B. Welsh & I. Alon (Eds.), *International franchising in industrialized markets: North America, the Pacific Rim, and other countries* (pp.65–94). Riverwoods, IL: CCH, Inc.

Cliquet, G., & Rozenn P. (2003a). Plural form development in the French franchise networks. In I. Alon & D. H. B. Welsh (Eds.), *International franchising in industrialized markets: Western and Northern Europe* (pp.207–226). Riverwoods, IL: CCH, Inc.

Cliquet, G., & Rozenn P. (2003b). Survival analysis of French hotel franchising. In I. Alon & D. H. B. Welsh (Eds.), *International franchising in industrialized markets: Western and Northern Europe* (pp.227–254). Riverwoods, IL: CCH, Inc.

Coompanthu, S., & Roth, K. (2002). International services: The choice of organizational forms and plural management. In D. H. B. Welsh, & I. Alon (Eds.), *International franchising in industrialized markets: North America, the Pacific Rim, and other countries* (pp.137–158). Riverwoods, IL: CCH, Inc.

Cresswell, J. W. (1994). *Research design: Qualitative and quantitative approaches.* Thousand Oaks, CA: Sage Publications.

Cross, A. R., Burton, F., & Rhodes, M. (2003). International expansion of UK franchisors: An investigation of organizational form. In I. Alon & D. H. B. Welsh (Eds.), *International franchising in industrialized markets: Western and Northern Europe* (pp.419–448). Riverwoods, IL: CCH, Inc.

Czinkota, M. R., & Ronkainen, I. A. (1997). *International business and trade in the next decade: Report from a Delphi study* (Working Paper No. 1777-25-297). Washington, DC: Georgetown University.

Dahab, S. S., Cunha, M. P. E., & Cardim, R. L. (2002). Internationalization of franchising: Juggling local tastes and brand consistency. In I. Alon & D. H. B. Welsh (Eds.), *International franchising in industrialized markets: Western and Northern Europe* (pp. 373–390). Riverwoods, IL: CCH, Inc.

Dana, L. P. (2002a). Franchising in New Zealand. In D. H. B. Welsh & I. Alon (Eds.), *International franchising in industrialized markets: North America, the Pacific Rim, and other countries* (pp.313–324). Riverwoods, IL: CCH, Inc.

Dana, L. P. (2002b). Israel's experience with franchising. In D. H. B. Welsh & I. Alon (Eds.), *International franchising in industrialized markets: North America, the Pacific Rim, and other countries* (pp.325–332). Riverwoods, IL: CCH, Inc.

Dana, L. P., Etemad, H., & Wright, R. W. (2001). Franchising in emerging markets: Symbiotic interdependence within marketing networks. In D. H. B. Welsh & I. Alon (Eds.), *International franchising in emerging markets: Central and Eastern Europe and Latin America* (pp.119–130). Riverwoods, IL: CCH, Inc.

Dant, R. P., & Kaufmann, P. J. (2001). The emerging empirical patterns of franchising in India. In I. Alon & D. H. B. Welsh (Eds.), *International franchising in emerging markets: China, India, and other Asian countries* (pp. 159–172). Riverwoods, IL: CCH, Inc.

DeLuca, F., Smith, A., & Winograd L. (2002). The Subway story: Making North American franchising history. In D. H. B. Welsh & I. Alon (Eds.), *International franchising in industrialized markets: North America, the Pacific Rim, and other countries* (pp. 209–222). Riverwoods, IL: CCH, Inc.

Dimou, I., & Ikkos, A. (2003). The status quo of Greek franchising opportunities for future growth. In I. Alon & D. H. B. Welsh (Eds.), *International franchising in industrialized markets: Western and Northern Europe* (pp. 279–298). Riverwoods, IL: CCH, Inc.

du Toit, A. (2002). An exploratory study of encroachment in multi-brand franchise organizations. In D. H. B. Welsh & Ilan Alon (Eds.), *International franchising in industrialized markets: North America, the Pacific Rim, and other countries* (pp. 333–362). Riverwoods, IL: CCH, Inc.

Edwards, W. (2011, July 01). *The pros and cons of franchising in China*. Retrieved from http://www.chinabusinessreview.com/the-pros-and-cons-of-franchising-in-china/

English, W. (2001). Franchising in China: Y2K update. In I. Alon & D. H. B. Welsh (Eds.), *International franchising in emerging markets: China, India, and other Asian countries* (pp. 57–65). Riverwoods, IL: CCH, Inc.

English, W., & Xau, C. (1994, February). Franchising in China: A look at KFC and McDonald's. *Proceedings of the International Society of Franchising, Las Vegas, NV.*

English, W., & Xau, C. (2001). Franchising in China: Y2K update. In I. Alon & D. H. B. Welsh (Eds.), *International franchising in emerging markets: China, India, and other Asian countries* (pp. 64–65). Riverwoods, IL: CCH, Inc.

Erramilli, M. K., Agarwal, S., & Dev, C. S. (2002). Choice between non-equity entry modes: An organizational capability perspective. In D. H. B. Welsh & I. Alon (Eds.), *International franchising in industrialized markets: North America, the Pacific Rim, and other countries* (pp.159–184). Riverwoods, IL: CCH, Inc.

European Franchise Federation. (2011). Retrieved from http://www.eff-franchise.com/

Falbe, C. M., & Welsh, D. H. B. (1998). NAFTA and franchising: A comparison of franchisor perceptions of characteristics associated with franchisee success and failure in Canada, Mexico, and the United States. *Journal of Business Venturing, 13*(2), 151–171.

Fenwick, G. D., & Strombom, M. (1998). The determinants of franchisee performance: An empirical investigation. *International Small Business Journal, 16*(4), 28–45.

Flohr, E. (2003). The legal environment of franchising in Germany. In I. Alon & D. H. B. Welsh (Eds.), *International franchising in industrialized markets: Western and Northern Europe* (pp. 255–270). Riverwoods. IL: CCH, Inc.

Floriani, B., & Liebman, M. (2014). Canada. In P. Zeidman (Ed.), *Franchise in 30 jurisdictions worldwide*. Retrieved from http://www.franchise.org/uploadedFiles/F2014 Canada.pdf

Franchise Association of New Zealand. (2014). *What is franchising?* Retrieved from http://www.franchiseassociation.org.nz/what-is-franchising-.html

Franchise Council of Australia. (2017). *Franchising: An introduction*. Retrieved from https://www.franchise.org.au/franchising-an-introduction.html

Frazer, L. (2001). The effect of regulation: An analysis of the Australian franchising code of conduct. *Proceedings of the society of franchising, Las Vegas, NV.*

Geromel, R. (2012, July 27). *Franchising: The best way of investing in Brazil.* Retrieved from http://www.forbes.com/sites/ricardogeromel/2012/07/27/franchising-the-best-way-of-investing-in-brazil/

Goh, M. (2001). Singapore's local franchise industry: An assessment. In I. Alon & D. H. B. Welsh (Eds.), *International franchising in emerging markets: China, India, and other Asian countries* (pp. 187–208). Riverwood, IL: CCH, Inc.

Grimaldi, A. (1992, February). Franchising opportunities in the free trade zones of developing countries. *Proceedings of the Society of Franchising, Palm Springs, CA.*

Grunhagen, M., & Mittelstaedt R. A. (2002). Multi-unit franchising: An opportunity for franchisees globally? In D. H. B. Welsh & I. Alon (Eds.), *International franchising in industrialized markets: North America, the Pacific Rim, and other countries* (pp. 95–116). Riverwoods, IL: CCH, Inc.

Hadjimarcou, J., & Barnes, J. W. (1998). Case study: Strategic alliances in international franchising—the entry of Silver Streak Restaurant Corporation into Mexico. *Journal of Consumer Marketing, 15*(6), 598–607.

Hadjimarcou, J., & Barnes, J. W. (2001). Strategic alliances in international franchising—the entry of Silver Streak restaurant corporation into Mexico. In D. H. B. Welsh & I. Alon (Eds.), *International franchising in emerging markets: Central and Eastern Europe and Latin America* (pp. 293–306). Riverwoods, IL: CCH, Inc.

Han, A. M. (2001). Legal aspects of franchising in China. In I. Alon & D. H. B. Welsh (Eds.), *International franchising in emerging markets: China, India, and other Asian countries* (pp. 83–104). Riverwoods, IL: CCH, Inc.

Hawkes, C. K., & Bandyopadhyay, S. (2002). International growth of U.S. franchising: Cultural and legal barriers. In D. H. B. Welsh & I. Alon (Eds.), *International franchising in industrialized markets: North America, the Pacific Rim, and other countries* (pp. 199–208). Riverwoods, IL: CCH, Inc.

Hero, M. (2003). Legal aspects of franchising in Austria. In I. Alon & D. H. B. Welsh (Eds.), *International franchising in industrialized markets: Western and Northern Europe* (pp. 93–110). Riverwoods, IL: CCH, Inc.

Hoe, C. H., & Bhatti, M. A. (2013). Factors influencing university students' decision to select franchise business as career option. *International Postgraduate Business Journal, 5*(1), 67–79.

Homata, A., Mihiotis, A., & Tzortzaki, A. M. (2016). Franchise management and the Greek franchise industry. *In Factors affecting firm competitiveness and performance in the modern business world.* Hershey, PA: IGI Global.

International Franchising Association (2014). Retrieved from www.franchise.org.

International Franchise Research Centre (2000). *World wide franchising statistics.* Retrieved from www.wmin.ac.uk/~purdyd/.

Jones, B. (2011, March 08). *Subway passes McDonald's as the world's largest franchise.* Retrieved from http://theurbantwist.com/2011/03/08/subway-passes-mcdonalds-as-the-worlds-largest-franchise/

Jones, P., & Wong, M. (2002). Franchising in Canada. In D. H. B. Welsh & I. Alon (Eds.), *International franchising in industrialized markets: North America, the Pacific Rim, and other countries* (pp. 233–248). Riverwoods, IL: CCH, Inc.

Josias, A., & McIntyre, F. S. (1995, February). *Franchising in Brazil. Proceedings of the International Society of Franchising, San Juan, Puerto Rico.*

Kahn, M. A., & Khan, M. M. (2001). Emerging markets for restaurant franchising in Middle Eastern countries. In I. Alon & D. H. B. Welsh (Eds.), *International franchising in emerging markets: China, India, and other Asian countries* (pp. 209–227). Riverwoods, IL: CCH, Inc.

Kaufmann, P. J. (2001). International business format franchising and retail entrepreneurship: A possible source of retail know-how for developing countries-Post-script. In D. H. B. Welsh & I. Alon (Eds.), *International franchising in emerging markets: Central and Eastern Europe and Latin America* (pp. 80–86). Riverwoods, IL: CCH, Inc.

Lord, S. (2013, November 13). *Is New Zealand becoming too franchised?* Retrieved from http://www.franchise.co.nz/article/1258

Luca, P. de, Majocchi, A., & Pavione, E. (2003). Franchising in Italy: Trends and development. In I. Alon & D. H. B. Welsh (Eds.), *International franchising in industrialized markets: Western and Northern Europe* (pp. 299–330). Riverwoods, IL: CCH, Inc.

Markins, C. (2002, July 22). Businesses needed for national survey. *IFA Insider, 7*(15), 4.

Marks, J. (2013, Oct. 30). *More bikes were sold than cars last year in 23 European countries.* Retrieved from http://inhabitat.com/more-bikes-sold-than-cars-last-year-in-23-european-countries/

Mazero, J. G., & Martyn, I. G. (2003a). Due diligence for international franchisors: Practical considerations to avoid criminal and civil liabilities. In I. Alon & D. H. B. Welsh (Eds.), *International franchising in industrialized markets: Western and Northern Europe* (pp. 499–510). Riverwoods, IL: CCH, Inc.

Mazero, J. G., & Martyn, I. G. (2003b). International franchisors due diligence checklist. In I. Alon & D. H. B. Welsh (Eds.), *International franchising in industrialized markets: Western and Northern Europe* (pp. 511–516). Riverwoods, IL: CCH, Inc.

McCosker, C. F. (1996, February). Franchising into Asia: An overview of selected target markets. *Proceedings of the International Society of Franchising, Honolulu, H*I.

Mehta, R., & Kaushik, R. (2015). Growth prospects of retail franchising business in India. *IUP Journal of Entrepreneurship Development, 12*(2), 43–53. Retrieved from https://login.libproxy.uncg.edu/login?url=http://search.proquest.com/docview/1700064833?accountid=14604

Mendelsohn, M. (2003). Comparative review of legal issues in Europe. In I. Alon & D. H. B. Welsh (Eds.), *International franchising in industrialized markets: Western and Northern Europe* (pp. 75–92). Riverwoods, IL: CCH, Inc.

Miles, M. B., & Huberman, M. A. (1994). *Qualitative data analysis* (2nd ed.). Beverly Hills, CA: Sage Publications.

Morran, C. (2013, August 21). *Subway now outnumbers 30 of the 50 largest fast food chains... combined.* Retrieved from http://consumerist.com/2013/08/21/subway-now-outnumbers-30-of-the-50-largest-fast-food-chains-combined/

Nair, S. R. (2001). Franchising opportunities in China from the perspective of a franchisee. In I. Alon & D. H. B. Welsh (Eds.), *International franchising in emerging markets: China, India, and other Asian countries* (pp. 109–121). Riverwoods, IL: CCH, Inc.

Neialkova, A. A. (2001). Bulgaria-economic development and franchising. In D. H. B. Welsh & I. Alon (Eds.), *International franchising in emerging markets: Central and Eastern Europe and Latin America* (pp. 203–214). Riverwoods, IL: CCH, Inc.

Nilssen, B. (2004). *What is franchise?* Retrieved from http://www.franchiseforeningen.no/index.php?p=1_15_Hva-er-franchise

Oches, S. (2011, August). *Top 50 sorted by average sales per unit.* Retrieved from http://www.qsrmagazine.com/reports/top-50-sorted-average-sales-unit

Payne, G., & Drakes, G. (2013). New franchise regulations in Indonesia: Fine line between stimulating the local market and protectionism. *International Journal of Franchising Law, 11*(1), 27–30.

Pasquali, V. (2013, January). *World's GDP growth by region.* Retrieved from http://www.gfmag.com/component/content/article/119-economic-data/12376-economic-dataworlds-gdp-growth-by-regionhtml.html

Paswan, A. K., & Dant, R. P. (1995, February). Franchising in India: An introduction. *Proceedings of the International Society of Franchising, San Juan, Puerto Rico.*

Paswan, A. K., Dant, R. P., & Young, J. A. (2001). The evolution of franchising in India: Prospects and caveats. In I. Alon & D. H. B. Welsh (Eds.), *International franchising in emerging markets: China, India, and other Asian countries* (pp. 131–158). Riverwoods, IL: CCH, Inc.

Paswan, A. K., Young, J. A., & Kantamneni, S. P. (2001). Public opinion about franchising in an emerging market: An exploratory investigation involving Indian consumers. In I. Alon & D. H. B. Welsh (Eds.), *International franchising in emerging markets: China, India, and other Asian countries* (pp. 173–186). Riverwoods, IL: CCH, Inc.

Pavlin, I. (2001). New trends in Slovenian franchising. In D. H. B. Welsh & I. Alon (Eds.), *International franchising in emerging markets: Central and Eastern Europe and Latin America* (pp. 189–202). Riverwoods, IL: CCH, Inc.

Paynter, J. (2002). Franchising in New Zealand: History and current status. In D. H. B. Welsh & I. Alon (Eds.), *International franchising in industrialized markets: North America, the Pacific Rim, and other countries* (pp. 297–312). Riverwoods, IL: CCH, Inc.

Penard, T., Raynaud, E., & Saussier, S. (2003). An overview of franchising in France. In I. Alon & D. H. B. Welsh (Eds.), *International franchising in industrialized markets: Western and Northern Europe* (pp. 189–206). Riverwoods, IL: CCH, Inc.

Pine, R., Zhang, H. Q., & Qi, P. (2001). The challenge and opportunities of franchising in China's hotel industry. In I. Alon & D. H. B. Welsh (Eds.), *International franchising in emerging markets: China, India, and other Asian countries* (pp. 67–81). Riverwoods, IL: CCH, Inc.

Quinn, B. (2003). The internationalization process of a franchise system: An ethnographic study. In I. Alon & D. H. B. Welsh (Eds.), *International franchising in industrialized markets: Western and Northern Europe* (pp. 471–490). Riverwoods, IL: CCH, Inc.

Reynolds, J. (2002). Forward. In D. H. B. Welsh & I. Alon (Eds.), *International franchising in industrialized markets: North America, the Pacific Rim, and other countries* (pp. 9–10). Riverwoods, IL: CCH, Inc.

Reynolds, J. (2013, November). Franchising industry growth holds steady. Technology and franchising. *Franchising World, 45*(11), 46–48.

Rugman, A. M. (2001). The myth of global strategy. *Insights, 2,* 11–14.

Sanghavi, N. (1997, March). Franchising as a tool for SME development in transitional economies: The case of Central European countries. *Proceedings of the International Society of Franchising, Orlando, FL.*

Sanghavi, N. (2001). The use of franchising as a tool for SME development in developing economies—the case of central European countries. In I. Alon & D. H. B. Welsh (Eds.), *International franchising in emerging markets: Central and Eastern Europe and Latin America.* (pp. 171–188). Chicago, IL: CCH, Inc.

Sanghavi, N. (2002a). Retail franchising in Denmark: Strategic overview. In I. Alon & D. H. B. Welsh (Eds.), *International franchising in industrialized markets: Western and Northern Europe* (pp. 111–136). Riverwoods, IL: CCH, Inc.

Sanghavi, N. (2002b). Franchising as a growth strategy in the Japanese retail market. In D. H. B. Welsh & I. Alon (Eds.), *International franchising in industrialized markets: North America, the Pacific Rim, and other countries* (pp. 269–286). Riverwoods, IL: CCH, Inc.

Sauter, M. B. (2011, August 2). The countries with the fastest growing populations. 24/7 Wall St., Fox News.

Sayabaev, K., Nurgaliyeva, Z., Temirova, A., Kasenova, A., Dzhamburbaeva, M., Zhangirova, R., …Zhansagimova, A. (2016). Finance, Franchise and Their Impact on Tourism. *Journal of Internet Banking and Commerce, 21*(3), pp. 1–12. Retrieved from http://search.proquest.com/docview/1877374746?pq-origsite=gscholar.

Schlamp, S. (2003). Women and franchising in Germany. In I. Alon & D. H. B. Welsh (Eds.), *International franchising in industrialized markets: Western and Northern Europe* (pp. 271–278). Riverwoods, IL: CCH, Inc.

Scholtz, G. J. (1996, February). Franchising in South Africa. *Proceedings of the International Society of Franchising, Honolulu, HI.*

Scholtz, G. J. (1997). An overview of South African franchising. *Franchising Research: An International Journal, 2*(4), 145–151.

Sherman, A. (2003). Final reflections: Key trends for European franchisors. In I. Alon & D. H. B. Welsh (Eds.), *International franchising in developed markets: Western and Northern Europe.* Riverwoods, IL: CCH, Inc.

Singh, S. (2003). Understanding Norway for potential franchising. In I. Alon & D. H. B. Welsh (Eds.), *International franchising in industrialized markets: Western and Northern Europe* (pp. 353–372). Riverwoods, IL: CCH, Inc.

Smit & Van Wyk, Inc. (2013). *South Africa franchise statistics.* Retrieved from http://www.franchise-law.co.za/blog/south-africa-franchise-statistics.html

Spencer, C. E. (2010). *The regulation of franchising in the new global economy.* (p. 8). Northampton, MA: Edward Elgar Publishing, Inc.

Stanford, A. O. (2016). Franchising Opportunities and Threats in Singapore. *International Journal of Business, Marketing, and Decision Science, 9*(1), 116–127.

Stanworth, J., & Purdy, D. (2001). Franchising as a source of technology transfer to developing countries. In D. H. B. Welsh & I. Alon (Eds.), *International franchising in emerging markets: Central and Eastern Europe and Latin America* (pp. 87–104). Riverwoods, IL: CCH, Inc.

Stanworth, J., & Purdy, D. (2002). Breaking into the European Union using franchising. In I. Alon & D. H. B. Welsh (Eds.), *International franchising in industrialized markets: Western and Northern Europe* (pp. 55–74). Riverwoods, IL: CCH, Inc.

Starbucks Corporation. (2014). *Starbucks mena.* Retrieved from http://mena.starbucks.com/en/newsroomarticle/sections/about-starbucks/starbucks-mena.html

Subway. (2014). *Subway faqs.* Retrieved from http://www.subway.com/ContactUs/CustServFAQs.aspx

Swartz, L. N. (2001). Franchising successfully circles the globe. In D. H. B. Welsh & I. Alon (Eds.), *International franchising in emerging markets: Central and Eastern Europe and Latin America* (pp. 43–62). Riverwoods, IL: CCH, Inc.

Swerdlow, S., & Bushmarin, N. (1994, February). Does business format management master Marxism in post-coup Russia? Franchise system mentality creeps into the lodging industry. *Proceedings of the International Society of Franchising, Las Vegas, NV.*

Swerdlow, S., Roehl, W. S., & Welsh, D. H. B. (2001). Hospitality franchising in Russia for the 21st century: Issues, strategies, and challenges. In D. H. B. Welsh & I. Alon (Eds.), *International franchising in emerging markets: Central and Eastern Europe and Latin America* (pp. 149–170). Riverwoods, IL: CCH, Inc.

Sydow, J. (2002). Franchise systems as strategic networks: Studying network leadership in the service sector. In D. H. B. Welsh & I. Alon (Eds.), *International franchising in industrialized markets: North America, the Pacific Rim, and other countries* (pp. 185–198). Riverwoods, IL: CCH, Inc.

Teegan, H. (2001). Franchising in Mexico. In D. H. B. Welsh & I. Alon (Eds.), *International franchising in emerging markets: Central and Eastern Europe and Latin America* (pp. 265–292). Riverwoods, IL: CCH, Inc.

Thompson, M., & Merrilees, B. (2001). A modular approach to branding and operations for international franchising systems in emerging markets. In D. H. B. Welsh & I. Alon (Eds.), *International franchising in emerging markets: Central and Eastern Europe and Latin America* (pp. 105–118). Riverwoods, IL: CCH, Inc.

Torikka, J. & Tuunanen, M. (2003). Finnish franchisee training program: An exploratory study. In I. Alon & D. H. B. Welsh (Eds.), *International franchising in industrialized markets: Western and Northern Europe* (pp. 165–188). Riverwoods, IL: CCH, Inc.

Travel China Guide. (2007). *2007 China tourism facts & figures.* Retrieved from http://www.travelchinaguide.com/tourism/2006statistics/fact-figures/

Tuunanen, M. (2003). Compilation of Finnish franchising statistics. In I. Alon & D. H. B. Welsh (Eds.), *International franchising in industrialized markets: Western and Northern Europe* (pp. 137–164). Riverwoods, IL: CCH, Inc.

U.S. Census Bureau. (2010, Sept. 14). *Census Bureau's first release of comprehensive franchise data shows franchises make up more than 10 percent of employer businesses.* Washington, DC: U.S. Government Printing Office. Retrieved from http://www.census.gov/newsroom/releases/archives/economic_census/cb10-141.html

U.S. Census Bureau. (2010 a). *2007 economic census franchise statistics.* Washington, DC: U.S. Government Printing Office.

U.S. Department of Commerce. (2012). *Doing business in Finland: 2012 country commercial guide for U.S. companies.* Retrieved from http://www.buyusainfo.net/docs/x_1581258.pdf

U.S. Department of Commerce. (2013). *Doing business in Kazakhstan: 2013 country commercial guide for U.S. companies.* Retrieved from http://www.buyusainfo.net/docs/x_8568037.pdf

U.S. Department of Commerce. MBDA Web Portal. MBDA Web Portal. Retrieved, from http://www.mbda.gov/

Vianelli, D. (2003). Franchising as a mode of entry for Italian companies in international markets. In I. Alon & D. H. B. Welsh (Eds.), *International franchising in industrialized markets: Western and Northern Europe* (pp. 331–352). Riverwoods, IL: CCH, Inc.

Viducic, L. (2001). The role of franchising in establishing and internationalization of business with special reference to Croatia. In D. H. B. Welsh & I. Alon (Eds.), *International franchising in emerging markets: Central and Eastern Europe and Latin America* (pp. 215–222). Riverwoods, IL: CCH, Inc.

Welsh, D. H. B. (2003). Franchising: A 21st century perspective. In D. H. B. Welsh & I. Alon (Eds.), *International franchising in industrialized markets: North America, the Pacific Rim, and other countries* (pp. 47–64). Riverwoods, IL: CCH, Inc.

Welsh, D. H. B., Adler, M. F., Falbe, C. M., Gardner, R. O., & Rennick, L. A. (2001, February). Multiple uses of the internet in franchising. *Symposium at the International Society of Franchising, Las Vegas, NV.*

Welsh, D. H. B., Raven, P., & Al-Bisher, F. (1996). The case of the elegant shoplifter, Shuwaikh, Kuwait. *Franchising Research: An International Journal, 1*(3), 43–45.

Welsh, D. H. B., & Swerdlow, S. (1991, February). Opportunities and challenges for franchisors in the U.S.S.R.: Preliminary results of a survey of Soviet university students. *Proceedings of the International Society of Franchising, Miami Beach, FL.*

Welsh, D. H. B., & Swerdlow, S. (1993, February). A cross-cultural study of American and Russian hotel employees: A preliminary review and its implications for franchisors. *Proceedings of the International Society of Franchising, San Francisco, CA.*

WhichFranchise Australia. (2014). *Franchising in Australia facts.* Retrieved from http://www.whichfranchise.net.au/index.cfm?event=getArticle&articleId=6

Wright, J. W. (2000). *2001 The New York Times Almanac.* New York, NY: The New York Times.

Yin, Robert K. (1994). *Case study research design and methods* (2nd ed.). Beverly Hills, CA: Sage Publications.

Young, J. A., McIntryre, F. S., & Green, R. D. (2000). The International Society of Franchising: A thirteen-year review. *Proceedings of the International Society of Franchising, San Diego, CA.*

Going International? Alternative Modes of Entry for Entrepreneurial Firms

Nadia Ballard and
Ilan Alon

International Research Consultant
Professor of Strategy and International Marketing,
School of Business & Law, University of Agder, Norway

Key Terms

External factors

Fully owned subsidiary

Indirect and direct exporting

Internal factors

International franchising

International joint venture

International licensing

Management contract

Turnkey operations

Learning Objectives

Upon completion of this chapter, students should be able to:

1. Understand the various modes of entry that are available to small and medium enterprises (SMEs).
2. Understand the factors that motivate the mode of entry decision from the standpoint of the company and the environment in which it operates.
3. Understand the advantages and disadvantages of the different modes of entry.
4. Understand the approaches that an SME can utilize in expanding its business abroad.

Introduction

Entrepreneurs are used to taking high risks for the potential of high returns on their ventures. Entering foreign markets can be both more risky and more rewarding for many entrepreneurial businesses, but with a well thought-out entry strategy and sound execution, most entrepreneurs can minimize the risks and increase their chances for success in the international marketplace.

This chapter examines the various modes of entry that are available to small- or medium-sized enterprises (SMEs). In particular, it discusses the exporting, licensing, franchising, contract manufacturing, turn-key operations, management contracts, international joint ventures (IJVs), and fully owned subsidiaries as they relate to SMEs.

In today's globally connected world, one likely scenario is that the company's entry into foreign markets starts with that first order from abroad as a result of the company's online presence, or a mention of the company's products on social media (see "Facebook wants to help businesses expand internationally"). If a company is taking a full advantage of its Internet presence, it should virtually expect to gain international clients within months.[1]

Whether a firm takes a more deliberate action to grow its international market share after the first few successful exports is up to the entrepreneur and his or her vision for the company. However, business owners today should not think that just because they are well entrenched in their home market, they are immune to the competitive pressures of globalization. It is likely that, even if a business does not pursue international strategy, international competitors, suppliers, buyers, etc. would eventually pursue it. The authors of this chapter are of the opinion that a company that decides to limit itself to a single domestic market is likely to be much less competitive and successful than its internationalized counterparts.

Some of the many reasons for going international include:

- Expand beyond a saturated domestic market
- Find a new source of profits
- Add to your firm's competitive edge
- Diversify and grow your markets to hedge against economic crises
- Follow customers who are going abroad.

The remainder of this chapter is divided into three sections. The first section discusses the factors that motivate the mode of entry decision from the standpoint of the company and the environment in which it operates. The second section analyzes

---

[1] Assuming that the company is conducting an active online marketing campaign with emphasis on search engine optimization, website advertisements and other marketing methods. Also, to be appealing and understandable to international visitors, a website should use (at a minimum) common English language, simple graphics and clear pictures and descriptions of the products/services offered.

the advantages and disadvantages of the different modes of entry. Within this section, several illustrations and SME practices are provided. Finally, the conclusion reflects on approaches that an SME can utilize in expanding its business abroad.

Selling Internationally with Social Media

Facebook wants to help businesses expand internationally

Facebook is trying to help small businesses become global businesses with new tweaks to its advertising platforms.

The company is offering businesses with Facebook pages the chance to easily reach international audiences on the social network and will offer suggestions about which country to take their business to next.

"More than 1 billion people on Facebook are connected to a small business in another country," Sheryl Sandberg, Facebook's chief operating officer, said in a statement to The Post. "As technology brings the world closer, it can also help businesses grow."

Businesses can use the new feature by going to Facebook's Lookalike Audiences tool, which recommended new audiences to business owners in their own countries but will now also offer information on international audiences.

Facebook has also updated its location-targeting tools to allow business owners to serve ads to a worldwide region or trade zone, and then will automatically adjust the campaign to serve ads to the countries that offer the best return.

According to the company, more than 60 percent of U.S. Facebook users are connected to at least one business outside the country. (The same holds true for other countries, the company said: 60 percent in Brazil, 70 percent in Germany, 70 percent in the U.K., 40 percent in India, 75 percent in Australia.) And, the company said, more than a half-billion people outside the United States are connected to U.S. businesses on Facebook.

The benefit will be for small businesses such as Little Passports, a company co-founded by two moms, which makes educational tools to teach kids about world cultures. Amy Norman, the company's co-founder, said the firm initially shipped only to the United States and Canada but wanted to expand after customers reached out to the firm asking them to ship to other countries.

"When we were looking at which international markets we wanted to expand into," Norman said, they looked at everything from the structure of the postal service to the median income. "We needed to validate that, so we looked to Facebook," she said.

Using Facebook's tools, Norman said, the firm was able to quickly test the appeal of its products in several markets without breaking the bank.

"As a small-to-medium-sized business, we have to make sure that every dollar we spend counts," Norman said.

Source: Adapted from Tsukayama, Hayley. (2016) "Facebook wants to help businesses expand internationally," *The Washington Post* [electronic version]. Sep 8, 2016. Retrieved April 28, 2017 from https://www.washingtonpost.com/news/the-switch/wp/2016/09/08/facebook-wants-to-help-businesses-expand-internationally/

Once a decision has been made to go international, a deliberate consideration of the mode of entry should ensue. The decision process is influenced by a number of factors that may often pull the decision-makers in opposite directions. An SME goes through a successive decision-making process that includes answering some of the following questions:

- Can our product be marketed abroad?
- What are the key success factors for our products?
- Is secondary data available for those markets/products?

- What additional data is needed and how can we get it?
- Which of our products have the highest potential abroad?
- Which markets have the greatest potential for our products?
- Do we have excess production capacity?
- What are the characteristics of our target market?
- What are the international capabilities of the firm?

Answering these questions is the first step in a preliminary market analysis for market and mode of entry selection.

To discuss the different forces involved in the entry mode decision process, we categorize them into two major groups: internal and external factors. The *internal factors* have to do with the firm's resources, overall strategy, management mindset, time commitment and, most importantly, types of products or services considered for international markets. For most entrepreneurial firms, the key issues discussed during this initial stage of the decision process revolve around:

- Financial resources—how much can we spend on international market expansion; should we borrow funds or use accumulated financial assets, are the potential rewards of this initiative worth the financial risks, etc.
- Human resources—should we hire new staff or use existing personnel to lead the expansion effort; what would be the compensation for the new position, how would the new management role be defined, where would the position be located, etc.
- Type of product and/or service—which of our products/services should we market internationally, how adaptable are they, what is required to make them ready for the target market, etc.
- Time horizons—how much time can we dedicate to the international expansion effort, are we willing to accommodate longer receivables cycles, etc.
- Risk tolerance—are we prepared to absorb the higher risks inherent in dealing with currency exchange rates, unfamiliar political, legal and market environments, economic cycles, etc.

Recent studies have focused on the accelerated timeframe in which small- and medium-sized firms move from domestic to internationalized operations, leading academics to question the stage model for the internationalization process (see Figure 12.1). In fact, a new breed of "born global" firms—young, small, fast-growing and entrepreneurial in nature—has been defined and new models of internationalization have been developed to explore the nature of these international new ventures. Most of the research confirms that these firms tend to cluster in certain knowledge-based industries and rely strongly on technology and their key personnel's extensive international business networks and skills to prosper in the global marketplace. These findings further underscore the importance of internal evaluation before moving into international business.

In addition to the internal factors, many external factors also need to be considered before a final decision on the mode of entry can be made. Factors that affect the company's choice to enter a foreign market but are independent of management's decisions are called **external factors**. External factors fall under two categories: target country factors and domestic country factors.

Target country factors that should be considered when choosing a mode of entry include:

- Market—its size, competitive environment, marketing infrastructure, etc.
- Production conditions—everything from the cost, quality, and quantity of local materials and labor, to the transportation, communications, energy supply, and other similar economic infrastructure components.
- Environmental conditions—this broad category includes most of the political, economic, geographic, and social factors that make one country more attractive for international commerce than another. Examples include government policies toward foreign trade, the overall rate of foreign investment, the gross national product, the diversification level of the local economy, the country's corruption ratings, and cultural and language barriers.

Some *domestic country factors* also strongly influence the foreign market entry mode. For example, if a company has a large enough domestic market, it can grow to a significant size before it chooses or needs to expand internationally. The choices of market entry methods can differ significantly for small and large companies, depending on their capitalization, production capacity, and marketing resources, among other issues. Conversely, a large domestic market can make some companies disinterested in expanding internationally due to the significant growth opportunities at home, while a small domestic market would spur even small companies to seek international expansion sooner. Other domestic country factors that would spur a company to seek international markets include competitive pressure at home, high domestic production costs, and favorable government policies toward exporting (tax incentives, trade support programs), for example.

Methods of Entry to International Markets

Because most entrepreneurial businesses are small to medium in size, their initial choices for international market entry tend to include low- to moderate-risk strategies, such as exporting, licensing, and franchising. As the companies become bigger and more successful internationally, some may decide to deepen their presence and commitment to particular foreign markets by entering into contract manufacturing, turnkey operations agreements or management contracts and even forming IJVs or investing in fully owned subsidiaries.

Figure 12.1 is a graphic representation of these most common market entry methods, ranked by the increase in risk for the entering firm. Another form of international market entry, the international business alliance, is discussed separately later.

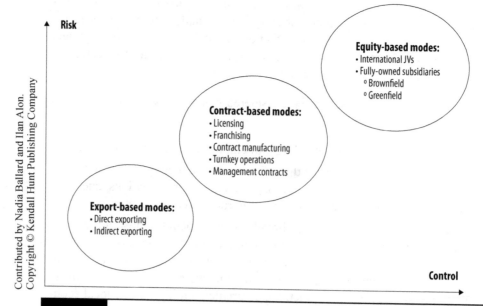

Figure 12.1   Risk and Control Considerations in Choosing Modes of Entry

Exporting

The most common and low-risk method of entering overseas markets, exporting is also the one requiring the least investment in financial, marketing, and human resources, and time. Because of its requirements of low commitment, exporting is the preferred mode of entry of most small and entrepreneurial businesses. It is an especially well-suited method for initial market tests due to the relative ease of pulling out of a market if it turns out to not be profitable (Deresky, 2000, p. 238).

The main difference between exporting and the other entry modes is that exporting is limited to physical products that are produced outside the target country market. Exported products can be sold overseas by intermediaries who specialize in this activity from the home base—*indirect exporting*, or they can be distributed directly through agents and/or distributors in the target country—*direct exporting*. E-commerce, where overseas customers buy goods directly from the company's website, is one recent and important form of direct exporting today (Boumphrey, 2016).

One small electronics firm's experience with direct exporting started after the company decided to actively pursue international markets for its specialized products. The management of the company took a deliberate, analytical approach to selecting its first international target markets, while remaining mindful of the limited resources they could dedicate to the expansion. First, with the help of the US

Department of Commerce, they researched product exports based on commodity numbers taken directly from the export documentation's schedule B.[2] This is an excellent indicator of market export potential because it is directly related to the company's products.

Next, they analyzed the hits on their website to see where most of their visitors are coming from. While this measure can be volatile, over time it can provide a rich source of data on the countries that show most interest in the company's products. Third, management looked at the company's customers and/or competitors to find relevant foreign markets. Since their competitors tend to be other small firms, not publicly traded or known, little information existed on competitors. However, examining the internationalization of the industry as a whole or the internationalization of large multinational companies proved to be helpful. Finding the local buying centers of the multinational companies was the most challenging part of this research. After settling on several potential markets, the company ranked them first by their market potential and next by the ease of entry. The firm evaluated and prioritized the most promising markets before moving on to the decision of the actual mode of entry.

The company decided to use direct exporting as mode of entry due to the specialized nature of its products and the specific industries that held the largest market potential. The next step in the process centered on deciding whether it will be more advantageous to divide their target markets by geographic or industry-specific criteria and, consequently, whether to look for distributors whose network covers a wide geographic area or for distributors who are well established in the specific industries chosen as target markets. The company decided industry-specific knowledge and relationships were more important than geographical coverage of the market. Therefore, the following indicators were used to select the appropriate distributor:

- Does the distributor have established connections in the targeted industries?
- Is the distributor familiar with the type of products manufactured by the company?
- Does the distributor have experience working with American companies?
- What are the distributor's size, current product lineup and revenues?
- Will the distributor allow the company to conduct independent marketing and sales within the country?

The company's search for the right distributor started with a visit to the US Commercial Service's industry specialists located in the target countries. These international trade professionals were instrumental in providing in-depth analysis and contact information for the first stage of the selection process.

---

[2] A Schedule B number is a 10-digit number used in the United States to classify physical goods for export to another country. The Schedule B is based on the international Harmonized System (HS) of 6-digit commodity classification codes.

After several meetings and evaluations of a few potential partners, the company was able to form an agreement with a distributor based on mutual business objectives, interest, and compatibility.

As with all others forms of market entry, an entrepreneur who is considering exporting should do plenty of research and planning before committing to a market or a distributor. Despite the advance of global free trade, some countries remain hostile to imports and impose many barriers on them such as high tariffs, taxes, or currency exchange restrictions. Learning about the importing environment of one's target country market or hiring a country specialist who knows the local government's import requirements for the specific product(s) is essential. Also, a must is researching and hiring a reputable and trusted distributor, whether at home or abroad. Some of the ways to ensure that an exporting partner(s) meets the company's criteria for doing business in the target market is by researching the company's market reach and infrastructure, ethic standards, financials, and track record. References and current client interviews are an excellent way to ensure that an intermediary in the international market(s) maintains and enhances the company's good brand by providing an equivalent levels of service, pricing and ethical behavior. Lastly, to ensure that the importing company's legal rights and privileges are protected, one should review the country's laws and regulations regarding import/export partnerships. The laws and regulations of some countries make it problematic to pull out of a distribution or an agent contract even when that party is not performing its contractual duties (Deresky, 2000, p. 238).

Profile of U.S. SMBs who Export

Small- and medium-sized companies (those employing fewer than 500 workers, including number of employees unknown) comprised 97.7 percent of all identified exporters in a study by the U.S. Census Bureau, Department of Commerce. The study that sought to develop the profile of American importing and exporting companies in 2013–2014. It found that SMBs account for 33.4 percent and 31.2 percent of the known export and import value, respectively. The following findings were also extracted from the report:

- 96.5 percent of manufacturing exporters were small- and medium-sized companies and they contributed 20.0 percent of the sector's $848 billion in exports.

- 99.2 percent of exporting wholesalers were small- and medium-sized companies; they accounted for 60.6 percent of the sector's $329 billion in exports.

- 97.2 percent of other companies with exports were small- and medium-sized companies.

- Among companies that both exported and imported in 2014, small- and medium-sized companies accounted for 94.4 percent of such companies, accounting for 23.7 percent of the known export value and 26.8 percent of the known import value.

- Among 3-digit NAICS for wholesale industries, Merchant Wholesalers, Nondurable Goods (NAICS 424) experienced the largest percent increase in export value by small- and medium-sized companies from 2013 to 2014 at 3.6 percent.

- For 3-digit manufacturing industry NAICS, Beverage and Tobacco Product Manufacturing (NAICS 312) saw the largest percent increase in export value by small- and medium-sized companies at 16.7 percent.

Adapted from US Census Bureau, Department of Commerce. (2016). "A Profile of U.S. Importing and Exporting Companies, 2013–2014" [electronic version]. Apr 5, 2016. Retrieved April 28, 2017 from https://www.census.gov/foreign-trade/Press-Release/edb/2014/edbrel.pdf

Licensing

Another popular method for market entry is through licensing. *International licensing* is the process of transferring the rights to a firm's products to an overseas company for the purpose of producing or selling it there. For a set royalty fee, the *licensor* allows the licensee to use its technology, trademark(s), patent(s) and other intellectual property in order to gain presence in the market(s) covered by the licensee.

Licensing is an attractive mode of entry for many entrepreneurial firms because, like exporting, it involves smaller upfront risks and expenditures. Since most of the costs of developing the licensed products have already been incurred, the royalties received often translate into direct profits for the licensor (Griffin & Pustay, 2003, p. 326). This form of market entry is most appropriate for countries that impose barriers to imports such as high tariffs and profit repatriation restrictions, and for mature products with relatively standardized production (Deresky, 2000, p. 239).

Licensing is not without its drawbacks, however. As with export partners, a firm considering licensing is advised to thoroughly research its potential licensees and their professional standards and to devise detailed legal contracts specifying the agreement's constraints, compensation rates, duration, and other similar issues. Such a cautious approach is important especially for countries where the legal protection for intellectual property is weak or not strongly enforced by the government. All too often, licensing companies have found themselves competing against their very licensees who have copied their know-how and entered the markets with little or no R&D expenses. High-tech firms considering licensing should be especially wary of the dangers of technology expropriation.

Franchising

A form of licensing that eliminates some of the concerns described in the previous section is international franchising. *International franchising* gives more control to the *franchisor* company over the *franchisee* who has licensed the company's trademarks, products and/or services, and production and/or operation processes. Control is exerted through the franchise fee that can be expropriated if contracts are not adhered to, and elaborate contracts that govern the relationship between the franchisor and the franchisee/s. On the flip side, the franchisor is also required to provide more materials, training and other forms of support to the franchisee. A well-functioning franchise provides a win-win arrangement for both parties: the franchisor gets to expand into new markets with little or no risk and investment, and the franchisee gets a proven brand, marketing exposure, established client base, and management expertise to help him or her succeed.

Although franchising in most developed countries of North America and Europe has reached a saturation point, many emerging markets are experiencing phenomenal growth in international franchising. To succeed in developing countries, an entrepreneur who is considering this mode of market entry should consider several important environmental factors such as the level of economic development, the economic growth rate of the country, and its market governance policies before starting to look for potential franchisees there (Welsh & Alon, 2001, pp. 33–34).

While franchising has been the domain of mostly large, multinational corporations (MNCs) such as McDonald's, Dunkin' Donuts, and Holiday Inn, the advent of international franchising is opening unprecedented opportunities to smaller companies which are diligent with their contracts, revenue oversight, and quality control to enter new free markets and compete successfully.

Contract Manufacturing

Contract manufacturing or outsourcing has garnered much attention for its economic and business benefits, as well as for its controversial, but inherent trend to move production jobs across borders. Contract manufacturing's growing popularity is due to the large savings it can produce in the financial and human resources areas of a business.

The arrangement of using cheaper overseas labor for the production of finished goods or parts by following an established production process is called *contract manufacturing* or *outsourcing*. Companies using this mode of entry benefit not only from lowering their production costs but also from an entry to a new market with small amounts of capital and with no ownership hassles. Some of the drawbacks of using outsourcing methods is the loss of control over the manufacturing process and the working conditions in the facilities, which can potentially lead to lower quality of the goods and/or human rights abuses and result in bad publicity and financial damages to the company's brand. Nike, Timberland, and several other high-profile American firms have served as unintentional examples of this undesirable scenario. In recent years, multiple firms from emerging markets such as China and India have emerged to help SMEs lower their costs by sourcing products, manufacturing, and services abroad. Contract manufacturing can enable future competitors who acquire critical skills in manufacturing your product, learn about your market, and are more likely to vertically integrate forward.

Turnkey Operations

Another contractual entry mode to a new market is participation in a turnkey project. *Turnkey operations* typically involve the design, construction, equipment, and, often, the initial personnel training of a large facility by an overseas company which then turns the key to the ready-to-run facility over to the purchaser.

Most often the province of the largest specialized construction and manufacturing companies, turnkey operations projects are usually contracted out by governments for enormous projects such as the building of dams, oil refineries, airports, and energy plants. Nevertheless, opportunities exist for the participation of smaller entrepreneurial firms as subcontractors for turnkey projects (Daniels & Radebaugh, 2001, p. 495).

Because of their extraordinary size and scope, many such projects require the long-term commitment of personnel, financial reserves, supplies, and other resources. Before a small company decides to participate in turnkey operations, it should carefully examine whether it is ready to absorb the long-term currency exchange fluctuations, the extended drain on its resources, and the other elevated political, economic, and financial risks that are likely to come up in such complex undertakings. Some SMEs providing specialized services can sell their service/product through turnkey operations. One such company in Orlando markets airport development services to developing countries' governments using regional joint venture partners for the construction and financing the project through major international banks. There is always a risk that the last payment for the project upon completion will not be paid as the incentives to pay decrease.

Management Contract

A mode of entry into new markets that is most widely used in the hotel and airline industries is management contracting. Under a *management contract*, a company in one country can utilize the expertise, technology, or specialized services of a company from another country to run its business for a set time and fee or percentage of sales. For example, many owners of hotel buildings contract with well-known hotel management firms such as The Ritz-Carlton Hotel Company and LLC to develop and manage their properties.

While the management company is responsible for day-to-day operations, it cannot decide on ownership, financial, strategic, or policies-related issues for the business (Deresky, 2000, p. 240). Such arrangement is suitable for companies that are interested in earning extra revenues abroad without getting entangled in long-term financial or legal obligations in the foreign market.

International Joint Ventures

As part of the larger category of international business alliances (see "International Business Alliances" text box), IJVs have been one of the most popular methods for entering international markets. *Joint ventures*—a form of foreign direct investment (FDI)—are created when two or more companies share the ownership of a third commercial entity and collaborate in the production of its goods or services. IJVs are attractive to businesses because of the relative ease of market entry they offer, their shared risk, shared knowledge and expertise, and the potential for synergy and competitive advantage in the global marketplace (Griffin & Pustay, 2003, pp. 346–348).

IJVs are formed for different reasons, the four main being to continue the expansion of an existing business, to introduce the company's products to new markets, to introduce foreign products to the company's existing markets, and to branch out into new business (Beamish, Morrison, Inkpen, & Rosenzweig, 2003, p. 122). IJVs can also take many different forms (see Figure 12.2):

- Two or more companies from the same country form an alliance to enter another country.
- An overseas company joins a local company to enter its domestic market.
- Firms from two or more countries band together in a JV formed in a third country.
- A foreign private business and a government agree to join forces in a pursuit of mutual interests.
- A foreign private firm enters into a JV with a government-owned firm to enter into a third national market.

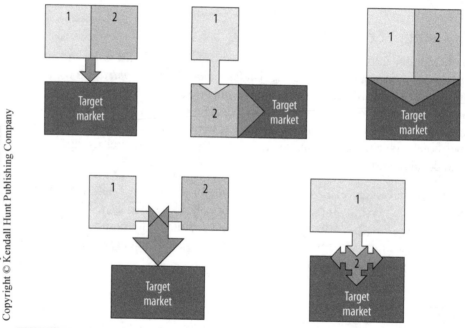

Figure 12.2   International Joint Ventures Arrangements

Much has been written about the factors contributing to the success and (more often) failures of cross-border strategic alliances such as joint ventures. To summarize, the most general issue with such an arrangement is maintaining the delicate balance between the partners' goals and objectives, management requirements, contributions, organizational and national cultures, and the myriad of other factors that make some collaborations successful and others not.

For entrepreneurs, joint ventures are a fitting way of entering into new markets with little or no international business experience, and for entering some specific countries where people tend to value trust as a cultural characteristic and are more open to international collaboration (Daniels & Radebaugh, 2001, p. 496).

Fully Owned Subsidiaries

As the most capital-intensive mode of entry, fully owned subsidiaries are usually considered viable only for large, internationally experienced corporations which can afford the great risks associated with the ownership and operation of a business in a foreign country. Entering a market through a *fully owned subsidiary* involves buying an existing business (also called *brownfield strategy*) or building new facilities (also called *greenfield strategy*) in a new target country. While both of these scenarios allow companies to exercise maximum control over their operations and to decisively enter the target country's markets, they also expose the company to the highest level of political, environmental, legal, and financial risks.

For a comprehensive review of the advantages and disadvantages of all modes of entry discussed in this chapter, please see Table 12.1.

Table 12.1   Advantages and Disadvantages of International Modes of Entry

MODE OF ENTRY	ADVANTAGES	DISADVANTAGES
Exporting	Low risk Easy market entry or exit Gain local market knowledge Bypass FDI restrictions	Tariffs and quotas Transportation costs Possible distributor relationship issues
Licensing	Low risk Fast market access Bypass regulations and tariffs Gain local market knowledge	Less control over market and revenues Intellectual property concerns Potential problems with licensees/future competitors
Franchising	Low financial risk Bypass regulations and tariffs Keep more control Gain local market knowledge	Less control over market and revenues Some loss of control over operations Potential franchisee relationship issues
Contract manufacturing	Low financial risk Save on manufacturing costs Flexibility of short term commitment Emphasis on marketing/sales	Less control over operations Less knowledge about local market Potential damage to brand/finances if human rights issues arise
Management contracts	Insider access to market Emphasis on firm's expertise Low financial risk	Limited profits and market access Potential copyright and intellectual property issues
Turnkey operations	Access to FDI-unfriendly markets No long term operational risks Emphasis on firm's expertise	Some financial risks Potential issues with partners/ infrastructure/ labor / profit repatriation
Joint ventures	Insider access to market High profit potential More control over operations Shared risks Gain knowledge from partner(s)	High investment of resources Potential issues between partners over control/contributions/goals, etc. More management levels Potential intellectual property issues
Fully owned subsidiaries	Full market access/acceptance Full control over operations/profits Bypass tariffs Diversify operations	High financial/resources investment High political and environmental risks Potential profits repatriation issues More management levels

As global communications, travel, and trade have become easier and more wide-spread, many companies have found it possible and even beneficial to use more than one entry mode simultaneously. Such a strategy is most often used for two main reasons: to enter several markets at the same time and to leverage the advantages of one entry mode before transitioning to another.

A medium-size financial services firm based in Florida used such a twofold approach when it decided to expand its offering of Real Estate Investment Trusts (REITs) to international investors. The company used a quantitative approach to determine the most promising markets for entry, followed by a strategic analysis of its investment division against the backdrop of the global real estate environment.

Applying a factor weighting method, that combined quantitative and qualitative factors, provided a general framework for determining the four markets that showed the most promise for further evaluation. Each market was then investigated further to determine its specific domestic REIT environment, its regulatory environment, primary local competitors, tax ramifications, and investment alternatives.

The company ultimately decided to enter its chosen international markets with a two-step plan. The first phase included using the resources of the firm's domestic financial partners who are active in these markets to build a local presence and brand recognition (international alliance). The second step revolved around the building of new distribution agreements with local, established brokers/dealers that could further expand the regional markets for the firm's REITs (direct exporting).

The first option, although limited in scope, allowed the company to leverage its existing relationships and enter international markets using minimal amount of its resources and benefiting from the networks and market knowledge of its partners. The second option, although more expensive, provided a greater coverage and market penetration of the products, while capitalizing on the already existent name recognition and client base. By combining the international alliances and direct exporting modes of entry, this financial services firm was able to enter several markets simultaneously and safely while preserving its resources and gaining market intelligence that proved invaluable for the second, more aggressive step of their international market expansion.

International Business Alliances

International Business Alliances

International alliances are defined as "relatively enduring inter-firm cooperative arrangements, involving flows and linkages that use resources and/or governance structures from autonomous organizations, for the joining accomplishment of individual goals linked to the corporate mission of each sponsoring firm." International strategic alliances are becoming a fast-growing method of foreign market entry. Compared to foreign direct investment, international strategic alliances embody a lower level of financial investment and risk, and allow for the pooling of resources, skills and abilities across multiple firms with the goal of achieving a joint purpose. International strategic alliances however, are not risk-free. The different decision style of the alliance companies, the loose association that exists among the alliance firms, and the sharing of strategic resources, exposes firms to potential failure and an unstable business environment in which one partner may take advantage of another.

Despite the risk factors associated with strategic alliances, this mode of entry into foreign markets has its advantages. For example, strategic alliances have the potential to lower the transaction costs, hedge against strategic uncertainty, acquire needed resources, allow firms to evade international barriers to entry, protect a firm's home market from international competition, broaden a firm's product line, allow a firm to enter new product markets, and enhance resource use efficiency. Tallman argued that firms utilizing strategic alliances could enhance their firm-specific resources (physical assets, intangible property, patents and trademarks, human resources, complementary resources), technical capabilities (R&D, manufacturing, marketing, sales, market knowledge), and managerial competencies (management skills and abilities, value-added activities).

The advantages gained by using international strategic alliances depend on the type of industry and way in which the alliance is structures. For example, some researchers contended that firms in a mature industry are more likely to benefit from strategic alliances, whereas others proposed that technology-based alliances tend to benefit high-tech industries more than traditional industries.

Many different frameworks have been developed for the proper formation and execution of an international business alliance, including conducting SWOT, goal compatibility, and value-added analyses for participating firms, and/or examining their market power, efficiency and competencies. Nevertheless, the most vital issues for a successful international business alliance remain selecting the right partner, developing trust, and developing appropriate contractual framework.

Alon, Ilan. (2003). "International Business Alliances: A Practical Perspective from the Packaging Industry." *Proceedings, Annual Academy of International Business, Southeast Meeting.*

SMEs tend to reflexively rely on nonequity modes of entry (exporting, licensing) because they would rather preserve capital and avoid high risks when moving into international markets. However, recent research suggests (Brouthers & Nakos, 2004) that using transaction cost analysis to select an international mode of entry—a method usually associated with large corporations—can actually improve their chances of selecting the most efficient method for their specific organization. The authors of the study recommend that SMEs evaluate three specific transaction cost criteria:

- *Level of investment required for each asset.* If no particular asset requires a large investment, nonequity modes such as licensing or franchising may be suitable for market entry. If such entry requires a high level of specific-asset investment, equity modes of entry, such as IJVs or fully owned subsidiaries may be more appropriate.

- *Environmental factors of the target country.* A more stable and economically and politically secure country would be more inviting to an equity mode of entry, whereas a country where political or social turmoil and frequent economic crises would be suitable for nonequity modes of entry.

- *Status of internal control systems and processes.* A business that is built on strong internal culture and regulations would be more comfortable upholding them in their new markets by entering through equity modes. On the other hand, a more open and flexible firm may be comfortable with relying on the controls of partners such as exporting agents or licensees.

SME decision-makers can rely on transaction cost theory to make more informed decisions about the most appropriate mode of entry for their company. Decisions made using this method seem to lead to a better performance abroad, according to this limited study.

Whether a firm uses transaction cost analysis or any other accepted method to evaluate their international market strategy, the choice of entry mode should be carefully considered and planned to ensure smoother, more profitable operations abroad.

Discussion Questions

1. Describe some internal factors that need to be considered before deciding on the mode of entry for a company. How does a company's internal makeup affect the speed in which it goes global?

2. Describe some external factors that need to be considered before deciding on the mode of entry for a company. Be sure to include target country factors and domestic country factors in your answer.

3. As with all other forms of market entry, an entrepreneur who is considering exporting should do plenty of research and planning before committing to a market or a distributor. What indicators should be considered in selecting a distributor?

4. How does international franchising differ from contract manufacturing?

5. How do the environmental factors of a target country affect the mode of entry into that particular market?

References

Beamish, P. W., Morrison, A. J., Inkpen, A. C., & Rosenzweig, P. M. (2003). *International management*. New York, NY: McGraw-Hill Irwin.

Boumphrey, S. (2016). How to perfect your market entry strategy. *Euromonitor International* [electronic version]. Retrieved April 28, 2017 from http://blog.euromonitor.com/2016/12/perfect-market-entry-strategy.html.

Brouthers, K. D., & Nakos, G. (2004). SME entry mode choice and performance: A transaction cost perspective. *Entrepreneurship: Theory and Practice, 3*(28) 229–247.

Daniels, J. D., & Radebaugh, L. H. (2001). *International business: Environments and operations* (9th ed.). Upper Saddle River, NJ: Prentice Hall.

Deresky, H. (2000). *International management: Managing across borders and cultures* (3rd ed.). Upper Saddle River, NJ: Prentice Hall.

Griffin, R. W., & Pustay, M. W. (2003). *International business: A managerial perspective* (3rd ed.). Upper Saddle River, NJ: Prentice Hall.

Welsh, D. H. B., & Alon, I. (Eds.). (2001). *International franchising in emerging markets. Central and Eastern Europe and Latin America*. Chicago, IL: CCH Incorporated.

PART THREE

Central and Eastern Europe Entrepreneurship: A Multilevel Risk Analysis

Barbara Weiss

Senior Research Associate, St. Petersburg Institute of International Political Economy, Florida

Key Terms

Risk-taking entrepreneurship

Institutional overhead

Microeconomic business risk

Political risk

Security risk

Entrepreneurial business risk

Mesolevel risk analysis

Learning Objectives

Upon completion of this chapter, students should be able to:

1. Better understand risk-taking capitalism under uncertain conditions

2. Distinguish between viable (market-creating and sustainable economic growth-inducing) entrepreneurship and that which leads to corporatism, corruption and worse collusion, and organized crime

3. Assess entrepreneurial conditions in the Central and Eastern European (CEE) regions

4. Develop a nuanced notion of risk and that many risks represent an opportunity for entrepreneurs to take them

5. Analyze the effect of political, security, and business risks on entrepreneurship

6. Develop the ability to conduct mesolevel, in this case, risk analysis that includes microeconomic business and industry risk and macrolevel, systemic political and security risk analysis

Abstract

The Central and Eastern European (CEE) regions have been thrust into ever greater uncertainty. The effect this has had on entrepreneurship there is devastating. Not only do start-ups and small and medium enterprises (SMEs) have to compete with large incumbent firms that dominate many of the economies in the regions, but they also have to operate, in some places, without facilitating infrastructure, in environments rife with corruption, and worse, rising insecurity both domestic and external. The primary external destabilizing factor is Russia, the world's second largest arms exporter that is promoting military adventurism and even outright aggression, military and otherwise, abroad. At home, the civil liberties of the Russian people are suppressed, and its markets are collusive and isolated from the rest of the world. Rising populism and rising corporatism are the internal sources of political risk in the regions. That being said, most of the 22 CEE (CEE22) countries are among the most internationalized markets in the world, in terms openness to trade and investment. They also have high levels of human capital and high propensities for technology absorption and process innovation. This combination of factors has led to restiveness among the peoples of an increasing number of CEE22 countries that has led to civil protests not seen in a very long time. Entrepreneurship in the CEE region has enormous potential. It only needs to be un-impeded. A healthy competitive market environment would allay the concern of European countries going widely different directions, in terms of their international relations and market economies. However, entrepreneurial initiative challenges market incumbents and the self-interested gatekeepers of political institutions.

Markets require ever broader access in order to sustain competition and broader economic growth.

Entrepreneurship is a source of long-term economic growth and is a key determinant of the international competitiveness that drives much economic policy-making. Entrepreneurship is also an indicator of individual initiative in private sector development. In short, entrepreneurs shape nations (NYSE, 2008).

Households are the ultimate shareholders of the system (Groom et al., 2006, p. 3). They own all resources either directly as workers or as entrepreneurs or indirectly through their ownership of business corporations (McConnell & Brue, 2005, p. 36). Entrepreneurship, therefore, is both an economic phenomenon and a social phenomenon, and capital is comprised of both financial, or monetary capital and valuable capabilities or human capital. Entrepreneurship capital is an important conduit for knowledge, which is the basic ingredient of the innovative process, but the gain in power from techno-economic progress is being increasingly overshadowed by the production of risks (Audretsch, Thurik, Kwaak, & Bosma, 2003; Beck, 1992, p. 13; Dosi, Llerena, & Labini, 2005). Households and consumers are also the ultimate bearers of those risks, having always been the ultimate bearers of financial and other risks (Groome et al., 2006, p. 39).

While the global community has been successful in ending the direst of poverty, many people are not participating in the global market with the prospect of becoming viable partners. Globalization tends to be highly uneven in its consequences (Giddens, 2000, p. 22; Keohane & Nye, 2001, p. 253). It continues to be accompanied by the greater risk of dislocation and financial uncertainty for some workers, families, and communities across the world (G8, June 20, 1999). Frequent financial crises of the magnitude of the crisis of 1997–1999 could lead to popular movements to limit interdependence, and to a reversal of economic globalization (Keohane & Nye 2001, p. 243). The shocks of 2001 risked worsening this long-standing marginalization (*The Economist*, February 2, 2002, p. 66). The rate of financial risk transfer, from the banking and financial sectors to individuals and families, greatly increased the burden of household consumers and ordinary citizens (de Rato, 2007; Groome et al., 2006, p. 39). The long-term effects on market capitalism of the global economic crisis that began in 2008 are unfathomable. Now, we have what appears to be ever greater uncertainty arising from political risks and security risks.

Risk-taking entrepreneurial capitalism is in short supply (J. Flynn, 2008, personal conversation at the Annual Meeting of the National Association of Chain Drug Stores). Entrepreneurialism need not be engendered but unimpeded (Ireland et al., 2008). In some places, entrepreneurial initiative has been long inhibited, even repressed. Policy considerations regarding the desirable risk profile of the household sector, involving important cultural, social, and political issues, are likely to be addressed differently across countries or regions (Groome et al., 2006, p. 39).

The Regional Economy: Central and Eastern Europe (CEE)

Taking up where the conclusion of this chapter in the second edition of the textbook left off, we look again at the state of political and economic participation in Eastern European countries and expanding it to an overview the state of entrepreneurship of 22 Central and Eastern European (CEE22) countries. Map 13.1, CEE, identifies the 22 countries included in this study. They are, for the most part, located from north to south in the eastern part of Europe. Among the CEE22 countries, 12 are European Union (EU) members (Bulgaria, Croatia, Cyprus, Czech Republic, Estonia, Hungary, Latvia, Lithuania, Poland, Romania, Slovakia, and Slovenia), 4 are EU candidates (Albania, Macedonia, Montenegro, and Serbia), or potential EU candidates (2) (Bosnia and Herzegovina, and Kosovo). Russia and the 3 remaining CEE22 are listed as Commonwealth of Independent States (CIS) member states (Belarus, Moldova, and Ukraine).

The focus of the 2014–2015 second edition was on the effect of the global economic crisis on countries in Europe, which were dramatically lower economic growth rates and declining share of the world economy after 2008. After growing at a robust average annual growth rate of over 8% between 2001 and 2008, CEE22 countries, on average, grew at a lower than world average (4.6%) of 2.1% between 2009 and 2016. Only Kosovo, Moldova, and Poland grew at about the world average rate during the 2009–2016 period. CEE22 lackluster economic growth is expected to continue for the foreseeable future. Between 2017 and 2022, the six Balkan countries—Albania, Moldova, Kosovo, Bosnia and Herzegovina, Macedonia, and Serbia—are expected to grow at a faster than world average pace (IMF, April 18, 2017).

Map 13.1   Central and Eastern Europe

Figure 13.1 indicates CEE22 share of the world economy peaked at 7.5% in 2008, declined to the 6.5% in 2000, leveled again in 2015, and is expected to decline to under 6% after 2018 (IMF, April 18, 2017). The CEE22 average unemployment rate declined from almost 14% in 2000 to about 9% in 2008, surged back up to 13% after the global economic crisis, and had slowly declined to 12% by 2014. The lowest level of the unemployment rate coincided with the CEE22's highest GDP (PPP) share in 2008. Where the inverse relationship between economic growth, as indicated by the relative size of a country's GDP in purchasing power parity (PPP) terms, and the unemployment rate is evident until 2008, it appears to dissipate thereafter. What continues is a declining, albeit stubbornly elevated level of unemployment and declining share of world GDP (PPP). Regionally, the CEE22 share of the EU, CIS, and emerging and developing Europe (E&DE) rose to over 25% in 2008 and has held steady at 25% thereafter. This suggests a Europe-wide trend lower economic growth compared to the other places in the world.

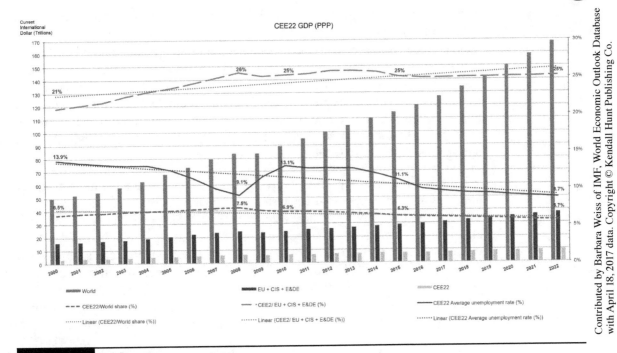

Contributed by Barbara Weiss of IMF, World Economic Outlook Database with April 18, 2017 data. Copyright © Kendall Hunt Publishing Co.

Figure 13.1 Average Unemployment Rate

The trend lines for the CEE22 share of world and regional GDP (PPP) are, respectively, negative and positive. While the CEE22 share of regional GDP (PPP) is rising, its world share is declining, albeit not dramatically so. The employment rate is also declining, a trend that is expected to continue. This lackluster growth—higher unemployment scenario does not bode well for European and CEE entrepreneurial risk-taking, even though these are the very economic maladies it can help to alleviate.

European Entrepreneurship

Micro-, small-, and medium-sized enterprises (SMEs) account for 99% of the European firms. They generate two-thirds of the region's employment and create 58% of business value-added at factor costs to the economy (European Commission [EC], June 28, 2017; EC, November 26, 2013, p. 10; World Economic Forum [WEF], January 17, 2014, p. 8). Promoting entrepreneurship in Europe has been a core EU objective since the Lisbon European Council decided in March 2000 to improve the EU's performance in the areas of employment, economic reform, and social cohesion (EC, September 1, 2013, p. 2). The Small Business Act was introduced in June 2008 to mitigate the effects of the global economic crisis and create EU-wide pro-SME policy momentum (EC, November 26, 2012, p. 8). Improving access to the single market for small businesses and developing entrepreneurship was also an objective of the Europe 2020 strategy (EC, March 3, 2010).

Yet, while European SMEs were an initial buffer, in terms of employment and value-added to the economy at the onset of the crisis, the sector lost 1.5 million jobs between 2008 and 2010 (EC, November 26, 2013, pp. 17, 23). The EC stresses that the decline of SME employment in the United States was even more significant (EC, November 26, 11 2013, pp. 28, 29). Moreover, the sole proprietor (i.e., own-account employer) share of total EU employment declined from 6% in 2000 to 4.8% after 2013. In Central Europe and Baltic countries, it averaged just under 3.5% between 2000 and 2015 (World Bank, April 27, 2017). This indicates that entrepreneurial activity is limited in the region.

What's missing in European entrepreneurship? Some of the most important elements of an "entrepreneurial ecosystem" are market access, human capital, and sources of funding (WEF, January 24, 2014, p. 21). Supportive cultural and societal norms, accountable and effective institutions that are free of bias and outside influence and that effectively formulate and implement policies, and a stable environment are also needed. These factors build on and support the other elements or pillars of an entrepreneurial culture, namely, innovation clusters often with a university at its center, new business support mechanisms such as business incubators, small business programs, angel investors, mentors, and serial entrepreneurs.

According to the Global Entrepreneurship Index (GEI) and the Global Entrepreneurship Monitor (GEM), the CEE22 countries are above average according to such measures as human capital, start-up skills, rates of technology absorption and process (not product) innovation, and internationalization. Concentrated markets (i.e., high barriers to entry), the lack of government support, including entrepreneurship training, and the lack of research and development (R&D) transfer are some of the biggest hindrances to CEE22 entrepreneurship (Global Entrepreneurship Development Institute [GEDI], November 13, 2016; Global Entrepreneurship Research Association [GERA], February 4, 2017). Existing legal and financial barriers that include high interest rates, an unstable currency, and high and variable tax rates, are perceived as insurmountable barriers to many Belarusian SMEs (Mazol, September 7, 2016). The lack of cultural and social norms that encourage personal wealth and income is also a significant entrepreneurship-limiting factor (GERA, February 4, 2017).

Europe still lacks an entrepreneurial culture (WEF, January 24, 2014, p. 16). Where 45% of EU citizens would rather have been self-employed in 2009, only 37% preferred self-employment after 2012 compared to 51% in China and the United States (EC, January 9, 2013, p. 5). European workers place a premium on job security (Woolsey, October 10, 2005). The tendency to favor self-employment in Eastern European countries also declined after 2009 (EC, January 9, 2013). As compared to Americans, only half the number of Europeans have ever thought about starting a business (*Eurobarometer*, 2007, p. 4). In 2016–2017, Europe had the lowest belief in entrepreneurship as a good career (58%) and the lowest media publicity for this activity (55%) (GERA, February 4, 2017, p. 8). Europe in 2016–2017 also continues to have the world's lowest rates of entrepreneurial opportunity and capability perception, as well as the lowest entrepreneurial intentions (12%) (GERA, February 4, 2017, p. 20).

While personal independence and self-fulfillment were cited as reasons for favoring self-employment, a low tolerance for risk and fear of failure are high in Europe. The fear of failure among Europeans is twice as high as among Americans (*Euroba-rometer*, 2007, p. 16). Europe's low tolerance of risk and fear of failure is similar to that of South and Central America (WEF, January 24, 2014, p. 16). In Bulgaria, for example, the fear of failure is high and the intention to start a business is low. While risk acceptance is high in Bosnia and Herzegovina, Estonia, the Czech Republic, and Albania, it is much lower in Slovakia, Moldova, and Montenegro (GERA, February 4, 2017).

Entrepreneurial conditions vary among CEE countries, from generally favorable in Estonia, Slovenia, Lithuania, and Poland to unfavorable in Bosnia and Herzegovina, Albania, Moldova, Bulgaria, and Ukraine. Plans to start a business are very low in Russia due to the perceived lack of entrepreneurial opportunities and capabilities. Perceived opportunities are very high and the fear of failure is very low in Estonia. Entrepreneurial intentions among the CEE22 countries are the highest in Macedonia and Latvia (GERA, February 4, 2017).

The lack of financing is often an insurmountable hurdle for start-up firms. Indeed, market access, in terms of access to investment financing, is generally less than sufficient worldwide (GERA, February 4, 2017, pp. 135–136). Venture capital financing, for example, declined by 56% between 2007 and 2013 (WEF, January 17, 2014, p. 15). Limited sources of investment financing have been a market barrier to European entrepreneurialism (Eurobarometer, 2007; EC, January 9, 2013). Of the 11 CEE countries included in the GEM 2016–2017 report, only Latvia and Hungary have "somewhat sufficient" access to finance (GERA, February 4, 2017). Bank loan financing in Poland, Romania, and Ukraine was among the most ready in the world in 2013–2014 (WB, October 29, 2013; WEF, January 17, 2014, p. 18). Access to financing has been an important enabler of business in Serbia, albeit heavily subsidized by the government (WB, October 29, 2013; EC, November 26, 2013, p. 27). The GEI data also indicates that access to finance is comparatively easy in at least 10 of the CEE22 countries, especially in Estonia, Latvia, Montenegro, Slovenia, and Poland (GEDI, November 13, 2016). Slovenia's overleveraged corporate sector and weak banking sector have led to the central government ownership of the Slovenian banking sector, which rose from 15% in 2007 to over 60% between 2013 and 2015, after which it declined to 50% in 2016 and 45% in 2017 (Novak, June 21, 2017; Združenje bank Slovenije, June 26, 2017).

Microeconomic Business Risk

In order to understand the factors affecting entrepreneurial conditions in the CEE22 countries, we have to distinguish between entrepreneurial risk and overall business risk. Many of the CEE22 countries are "easy" places to "do business" with having an impressive average 39th of 190 countries rank of Ease of Doing Business for 2017 (DB2017), ranging from as high as the 10th easiest place in the world to "do business" in Macedonia (FYR) to 80th and 81st for Ukraine and Bosnia and Herzegovina, respectively. The annual World Bank assessment places five CEE countries—Macedonia (FYR), Estonia, Latvia, Lithuania, Poland—among the top

25 countries in which "doing business" is comparatively easy. The study also places Belarus and Serbia among the "top 10 improvers" in 2017 (WB, October 25, 2016). The ease of international trade (i.e., "trade across borders"), as well as "getting credit" account for their high DB2017 rankings. Indeed, the CEE22 countries, with the exception of Russia and Ukraine, are among the most open countries in the world to international trade, as well as foreign direct investment (FDI) (OECD, March 27, 2017). One reason for this openness, perhaps, is that while the single European market has all but eliminated transaction costs, and that while language and consumer preference differences in smaller national markets remain, an entrepreneurial venture may soon be an international venture as well.

The less than optimal prospects for CEE22 economic growth and the very positive "ease of doing business" indicators in those countries compared to the rest of the world are contradictory. A look at the CEE22 business risk index in Figure 13.2 yields some interesting insights into general business conditions there and may explain this contradiction. Namely, "ease of doing business" and additional favorable indicators, such as low business start-up costs and corporate tax rates are not an incentive to start a business. (Please see the Appendix on pages 304–305 for index data sources and methodology.) The biggest impediments to doing business in the CEE22 countries, according to the DB2017 business regulation indicators, are the time it takes to pay taxes, deal with construction permits, and get electricity, as well as the cost of electricity (WB, October 25, 2016). Additionally, the very low number of new business registered in the CEE22 region and the low number of employers in the workforce suggest concentrated markets dominated by large firms. This allows for the distinction between microeconomic business risk and entrepreneurial business risk.

While indications are that entrepreneurial risk is high in much of the CEE region, the data illustrated in Figure 13.2 suggests that average CEE22 business risk is not very high although not as low as the risk associated with the "ease of doing business" measure. The most favorable indicators are that the corporate tax burden and cost of starting a business are much lower than the world average and that they present only just over a 1-level risk on a 0–7 scale of risk to businesses in the region. The "ease of doing business" measure presents 1.4-level risk in a narrow 0.44-to-2.70 range. The other five variables pose variable levels of business risk. Also, the low (solid line), CEE22 average (gray area), and high (dotted line) levels of business risk vary more widely from 1.55 to 3.80 and an average 2.36-level of business risk. Latvia, followed by Estonia and Hungary has the lowest business risk, and Albania, Ukraine, and Kosovo have the highest business risk. Macedonia and Montenegro have the CEE22 average business risk. The outward spikes in the lowest risk countries are in the areas of logistics infrastructure and new business registrations. The CEE22 countries with the highest business risk are negatively affected by a low business start-up rate, concentrated markets, electrical outages, and bribery.

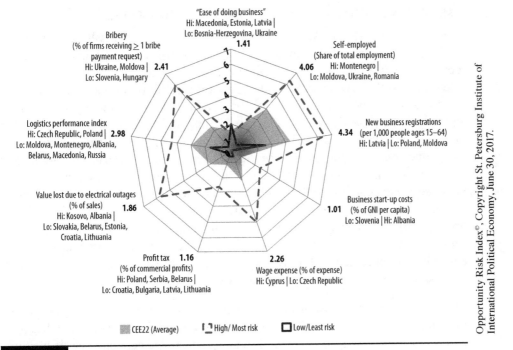

Figure 13.2 Business Risk Index—CEE22

Wage expense is an important business expense, including in the businesses of CEE22 countries. It presents a somewhat 2.36 level of business risk compared to other parts of the world. The range is lower (1.55) in Latvia to an elevated 3.80 risk level in Albania. Bribery risk is also high in Albania and in Kosovo and Bosnia and Herzegovina. The prospect of requests for bribery payments poses more risks to CEE22 businesses, at a 2.41 risk level. The possibility of this is very low in Estonia and high in Moldova, Ukraine, and Russia.

The lack of an adequate logistics infrastructure poses even more risk, at 2.98 risk level, to CEE22 businesses. This situation is especially acute in Montenegro, Moldova, Albania, and Macedonia, as well as in Moldova, Belarus, and Russia. The Czech Republic, Poland, and Hungary have the best logistics infrastructure of the CEE22 countries. In terms of electric utilities infrastructure, while the cost of electricity is high, it is generally reliable. The only exception is Kosovo where the value lost due to electrical outages (as a percent of sales revenue) is among the most in the world. Three other Balkan countries—Albania, Montenegro, and Macedonia—also have to deal with electricity infrastructure risk.

Macrolevel Political Risk and Security Risk

The immediate post-Cold War period saw the CEE22 countries, which were among the former republics of the Soviet Union, re-establish their national sovereignty, rebuild state institutions, and restructure their economies. Everything from the rule of law to the private sector had to be either rebuilt or started from scratch in the countries in the region where the pre-Communist experience was autocratic and feudalistic (*The Economist*, October 23, 2008). The government of a number of these countries has not radically privatized, indeed have renationalized, their economies (Ivanova, 2008, p. 30). In Belarus, for example, Belarusian state-owned (27%) or partially state-owned (23%) enterprises still accounted for half of the value-added to economy (27% and 23%, respectively) in 2014. State-owned enterprises (SOEs) are also the country's largest employers (Dobrinsky et al., 2016, pp. 46, 133). Producer cooperatives and SOEs remain an important part of other European economies, especially in the CEE22. An entrepreneurial culture exists but has emerged with only varying degrees of success due to more deeply entrenched rent-seeking economic interests.

These are some of the reasons for rising political and security risks in recent years, including in some of the CEE22. Uncertainty, both internal and external, has been increasing more generally in the CEE region. The global economic crisis of 2007–2008 and Russia's accelerated military adventurism and outright aggression are external sources of profound uncertainty in the CEE22 regions. Internal uncertainty has long been high in a number of the CEE22 countries and has increased in more of them (Human Rights Watch, January 12, 2017). The political risk variables illustrated in Figure 13.3 provide some indication of the CEE22 political risk factors compared to the rest of the world. The parameters of political risk are state legitimacy, government efficacy and accountability, legal and regulatory systems, political rights and press freedom in civil society, and the level of perceived corruption. (Please see the Appendix on pages 304–305 for index data sources and methodology.) As with CEE22 business risk, political risk averages 2.80 in the CEE22 countries and ranges very widely from 1.10 to 5.42 on a 0-to-7 scale of risk levels relative to all countries in the world. In other words, those CEE22 countries with the highest or most political risk are very risky and those with the lowest or least political risk are not risky at all, except in the areas of corruption, government effectiveness, and voice and accountability, which pose some risk.

Political risks are generally higher than business risks in the CEE22 countries, as the enlarged gray shaded area in Figure 13.3 compared to Figure 13.2 indicates. Political risk is comparatively low in the Baltic countries, especially in Estonia, as well as in Lithuania and Latvia. At the highest level of political risk are their immediate neighbors—Russia, Belarus, and Ukraine to the south, whose political risks range from 4.32 to 5.42. After the Baltic countries, at the lower end of the political risk scale, moving southward in the CEE22 are the Czech Republic, Poland, Slovenia, and Slovakia, which have the similar cumulative levels of political risk that average a 1.65 level on the 0–7 scale. Then come three pairs of country that together have similar cumulative average levels of political risk—Slovakia and Cyprus (1.78), Croatia and Romania (2.37), and Hungary and Bulgaria (2.52).

Moving toward the higher end of CEE22 political risk range are Montenegro, Serbia, Albania, and another pair of countries with similar elevated levels of political risk, Macedonia and Kosovo, at 3.60. At the higher end of the political risk scale in the CEE22 are Bosnia and Herzegovina (3.82) and Moldova (3.98).

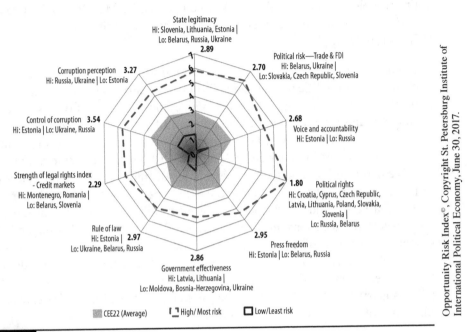

Opportunity Risk Index©, Copyright St. Petersburg Institute of International Political Economy. June 30, 2017.

Figure 13.3   Political Risk Index—CEE22

State legitimacy is high in the three Baltic countries, Slovenia, Lithuania, and Estonia, as well as in Croatia. It is lowest among the CEE22 in Belarus, Russia, and Ukraine, and in Moldova and Bosnia and Herzegovina (Fund for Peace, May 14, 2017). The political risk of state legitimacy in the remaining 13 CEE22 countries is not insignificant, especially in Hungary where the risk level is 3.48. The political risks associated with state legitimacy, namely the rule of law and government effectiveness, are also present in a number of the CEE22 countries. The lack of the rule of law presents the highest political risk. After Ukraine, Belarus, and Russia, the citizens of Kosovo, Moldova, and Albania are not confident in the rule of law in their societies. The rule of law is well established in Estonia, and so is the Estonian government accountability and protection of civil liberties (WB, April 27, 2017). The perceived effectiveness of government policies, as measured by policy quality and implementation, the lack of bias, and the quality of the civil service are low in Moldova, Bosnia and Herzegovina, Ukraine, Belarus, and Kosovo. Among the CEE22, it is highest in Latvia and Lithuania, albeit at a higher average risk level of 1.39 (WB, April 27, 2017).

The market effect of political risk, as indicated by the threat of international trade and FDI disruption and legal infrastructure of credit markets, is evident but not elevated as the other political risks associated with governance aforementioned above. The greatest CEE22 political risks are medium term and are mostly due to exchange rate volatility. Markets are not at all inhibited by the government in Slovakia and they are very little affected by political risk in the Czech Republic and Slovenia. In contrast, political risk is high in Belarus and security risk is high in Ukraine.. The threat of expropriation is high only in Belarus and the threat of political violence is high only in Ukraine (Credendo, May 10, 2017). Credit risk is highest in Belarus and Slovenia due to its banking crisis as already discussed (WB, April 27, 2017).

Freedom House (FH) reported the 11th consecutive year of decline in global freedom, in terms of political rights and civil liberties around the world, at the beginning of 2017 (FH, January 31, 2017). Voice and accountability, an indicator of democracy and the civil liberties of freedom of expression, freedom of association, and a free media, a World Bank governance indicator, is very strong in Estonia and very weak in Belarus, making the CEE22 political risk range for this variable between 0.99 and 6.03. For example, all Internet service providers (ISPs) in Belarus operate through a state-controlled portal (DOS (US), February 2008, p. 3). That being said, civil liberties are protected in all but four of the CEE22 countries. The exceptions, unfortunately, are Russia, Belarus, Bosnia and Herzegovina, and Kosovo. The press in over two-thirds of the CEE22 countries is either "not free" or only "partially free." Even among those CEE countries defined as "free", there were declines in the Czech Republic, Hungary, Poland, and Serbia (FH, January 31, 2017). This leaves only Estonia, Latvia, Lithuania, Slovenia, and Slovakia with press freedom in the CEE22 (FH, April 28, 2017).

Among the political risk factors in the CEE22 political risk index, the widest disparity is in political rights, which ranges from among the most enjoyed in the world in the nine CEE countries listed in Figure 13.3 and the least in the world in Belarus and Russia. Here again are some exceptions and qualifications. Ukraine and Moldova have struggled to build on fragile democratic gains. Highly nationalistic parties rule Hungary and Poland, which, according to FH, raises the possibility that some of the most remarkable transitions from dictatorship to democracy in the 1980s and 1990s will be substantially reversed by elected populist leaders (FH, January 31, 2017). Rising populism is also coupled with rising corporatism in some CEE22 countries. The corporatist leaning of Serbia's current political leadership resembles that of Italy and Thailand where a political leader, in Serbia's case, Aleksandar Vucic, a former information minister, is also an owner of media interests. Andrej Babis, a former finance minister and media billionaire, was also a candidate in the Czech Republic's general election. The October 2017 elections in the Czech Republic will see the rise or defeat of the populist and nationalist ANO party (FH, January 31, 2017).

The "institutional overhead" of corruption weighs most heavily in the CEE22 region. It poses the most political risk in the CEE22 countries. The concurrent rise of corporatism and populism points to the most significant and wide-ranging political risk among the CEE22 countries. Figure 13.3 indicates that corruption is the most significant political risk in the CEE22, especially in Ukraine and Russia. *Global Corruption Barometer* public opinion survey *respondents* ranked the institutions of Russian and Ukrainian societies among the most corrupt in the world. The most corrupt institutions in both countries are the police, public officials, and civil servants, followed closely by the judiciary and legislature (Transparency International [TI], July 9, 2013). Corruption, inefficiency, and political interference in Belarus' judiciary are also prevalent (DOS (US), March 11, 2008).

One of first steps taken by Ukraine's provisional government was to disband the Berkut riot police. The son of ousted Ukrainian President Viktor Yanukovych owned a conglomerate, Management Assets Company (MAKO) that controlled nearly half of the country's coal production and around one-third of its electricity production and distribution. Olexander, the younger Yanukovych, is reported to have amassed a personal fortune of around $500 million since opening a branch in Geneva, Switzerland, in late 2011 (Budzhurova & Zaks, 2014). Having identified corruption and poverty as the main threats to Russia's national security, Russian President Dmitry Medvedev himself became the very face of Russian corruption during widespread anti-corruption demonstrations in 2017 (Cichowlas, 2017; McBride and & Stott, 2008).

Rising economic and political risks has increased uncertainty in the global system, including the CEE22 region. The greatest risks were political and legacy institutional risks, with its knock-on economic growth and civil liberty limiting effects increasing security risks. A security risk index is included in this chapter of the third edition in order to the address these particular risks. The CEE22 security risk index shown in Figure 13.4 includes 10 indicators of the domestic sources and external sources of security risks. (Please see the Appendix on pages 304–305 for index data sources and methodology.)

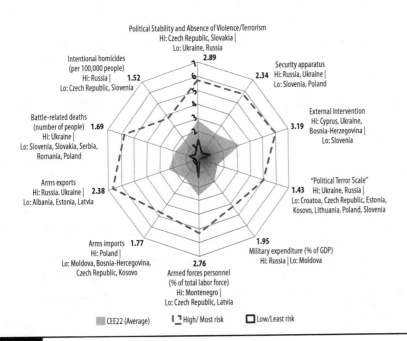

Opportunity Risk Index©, Copyright St. Petersburg Institute of International Political Economy, June 30, 2017.

Figure 13.4   Security Risk Index—CEE22

The security risk index is very high in some CEE22 countries and is also high according to a number of 10 variables shown in Figure 13.4. While the external threat of terrorism and the number of battle-related deaths and internal security risks of the security apparatus, incidence of intentional homicides, and military spending are comparatively low, CEE22 security risk is high for the external threat of external intervention and the internal sources of political instability and violence, the security apparatus, including the size of the armed forces and arms exports. The highest CEE22 security risk is the threat of external intervention followed by the risk of domestic political instability and politically motivated violence.

The level of security varies greatly among the CEE22 countries, with Ukraine and Russia facing the most security risks. The security risks of the 20 of the CEE22 countries do not appear to be as geographically determined as are their political risks. In descending order of security risk are Belarus, Macedonia, Cyprus, Moldova, and Montenegro. Less risky, according to security parameters, are Bosnia and Herzegovina, Bulgaria, and Albania, followed by Serbia and Romania. Then comes Poland, Croatia, Kosovo, and Lithuania. Slovenia followed by Slovakia, Latvia, and the Czech Republic faces the fewest security risks in the CEE22 region.

Mesolevel Entrepreneurial Risk Analysis

Entrepreneurial opportunity risks are at the same time a function of the industry and market determinants of microeconomic business risk, as well as macrolevel political and security risks (St. Petersburg Institute of International Political Economy, June 30, 2017). CEE22 business risk is immediately associated with the long-term effects of the global economic crisis and even longer term limitations imposed by concentrated CEE22 markets. As for entrepreneurial business risk, as indicated by the lack of new business start-ups and markets concentrated with few employers, it presents the highest business risk, on avarege to the CEE22 countries. These variables allow for the crucial distinction between entrepreneurial business risk and microeconomic business risk.

There are multiple causes for elevated CEE22 entrepreneurial business risk. This may be due to the lack of entrepreneurial culture in Europe previously discussed. Security and political conditions, as well as economic and societal conditions, affect entrepreneurship. The orderly transition of political power, government transparency, and unbiased governance—lack of arbitrary interference, bias, corruption, discrimination, undue influence—in the civil justice system and criminal system are indicators of the lack of institutional conditions that are conducive to entrepreneurship (World Justice Project, October 20, 2016). For example, Estonia and Latvia are the countries where SMEs contribute over 70% of GDP. They have the lowest cumulative business and political risks, and among the lowest security risks of the CEE22 countries. Belarus and Russia are the other extreme, with SMEs only contributing 21% of GDP and presents the most risks, especially security and political (GERA, 2017; Mazol, 2016).

The situation in the CEE22 countries, however, is more promising than some other regions in the world. Eurasia in 2016 remained divided between a more democratic-oriented fringe to the West and a core of rigid autocracies in Central Asia (Freedom House, January 31, 2017). The Western CEE22 countries have the lowest political risks, from the Baltic countries, beginning with Estonia and Lithuania in the North to the Czech Republic, Poland, Slovenia, and Slovakia. Political risks are greater in Croatia, Romania, Hungary, Bulgaria, and Montenegro. Further southward in the rest of the Balkan countries, they increase still further. The highest political risks are in Belarus, followed by Russia and Ukraine. Russia accounted for half of the CEE22 GDP (PPP) and was the world's second largest arms exporter after the United States in 2016. Russia's economy is also resource-driven, oligarchic, collusive, and corrupt, and the most isolated in terms of openness to trade and investment due to international sanctions.

The political economy and security implications of pipeline infrastructure have long affected international relations between Russia and countries in the Europe (Prybyla, 1965). Map 13.2 shows the network of natural gas and oil pipelines in the region. The Druzhba (Friendship) oil pipeline, one of the world's largest and longest, began to deliver unrefined oil to Central Europe in 1962. Resource industry and energy security risk became increasingly evident again after 2004 when energy prices began to rise. The northern (Yamal) and southern (Brotherhood) branches of the pipeline transit through Belarus and Poland and Ukraine, respectively, on its way to Central and Western Europe. Indeed, the core political risks in CEE22 countries with the highest political risk—Belarus, Ukraine, and Moldova—are those through which Russian oil and gas pipelines to Europe traverse. Ukraine is the largest transport corridor of Russian gas to Europe (International Energy Agency, March April, 2014).

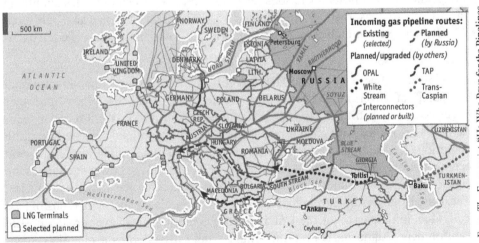

Map 13.2 Primary Russian Oil and Gas Pipelines to Europe

Eighty percent of Russia's natural gas bound for Western Europe flows through four pipelines that traverse Ukraine (Feifer, January 5, 2009). Belarus gets around 400,000 barrels per day (bbl/d) of Druzhba crude oil for its two refineries (*Reuters*, January 8, 2007). The two Nord Stream Pipelines through the Baltic Sea, opened in 2011, sends gas directly from Russia to Germany. Nord Stream and its sister South Stream Pipeline through the Black Sea would let Russia bypass troublesome transit countries, chiefly Ukraine (*The Economist*, July 16, 2009). Serbia is the hub of the South Stream Pipeline (Feifer, January 5, 2009). As its current proposed destination is Romania, the White Stream Pipeline would bring that EEE7 country into the Russia–Europe pipeline network. Another EU-backed pipeline, Nabucco would also traverse Romania on its way to Austria. The 2014–2015 edition of this chapter included this statement: EU-backed White Stream network of pipelines would flow from Tblisi, Georgia, central Ukraine, and the Crimea, making it an international relations "hot potato." What followed at the end of 2014 (some 4–5 months after this textbook manuscript had entered the publication process) was Russia invading Ukraine and annexing Crimea.

Gazprom is Russia's largest firm and largest national oil company (NOC), the 5th largest oil and gas firm, and the world's 40th largest multinational enterprise (MNE) (24th in profits) in 2016 (*Forbes*, May 17, 2017). It is the engine of Russia's foreign policy, especially the flow of energy supplies to Europe from Russia and elsewhere. In mid-2017, Russia's majority (almost 55%) state-owned Gazprom owned almost 200 subsidiaries along the entire oil and gas supply chain, in banking and other services including power generation and transportation, in Russia and throughout Europe and Central Asia (Gazprom, June 27, 2017). Gazprom owns at least 50% of the South Stream pipeline in every country it traverses—Austria, Bulgaria, Greece, Hungary, Serbia, and Slovenia. The Nord Stream pipeline is also 50% Gazprom-owned (Gazprom, June 27, 2017). Gazprom has blocked major foreign investment in its operations (even as it buys European utilities supplying gas directly to consumers) (Feifer, January 5, 2009). The NOC has also cultivated Western energy companies to act as lobbyists for Russian interests (Feifer, January 5, 2009).

Entrepreneurial activity, or the lack thereof, is an indicator of the "institutional overhead" of governmental regulatory frameworks, fiscal discipline, and other governmental capabilities, as well as the pressures of political and broader security risks associated with greater uncertainty. Less than optimal even deteriorating conditions spur entrepreneurial initiative to improve them, albeit in the informal economy. Here, oligarchs and organized crime have filled the power vacuum as the ended Cold War continues to play political and economic roles in these countries. These are examples of entrepreneurship not to be emulated and indications of true individual initiatives to take risk and improve conditions in an ever greater hostile environment. Authoritarian regimes impose not only onerous economic restrictions, but also repress political liberties, expropriate private assets, and increase the state ownership of them. The paternalistic attitudes of long-entrenched leaders and bureaucracies see calls for change from civil society as a threat to stability, an unlawful provocation, even as a betrayal of the state that "houses, feeds, and clothes them."

Conclusion

This installment of the expanded discussion of regional entrepreneurship in 22 CEE countries continues to be based on the notion that entrepreneurial risks increased with global financial crisis that arose from risk-managing capitalism coming at the expense of risk-taking capitalism have destabilized the international system. The consolidation of firms in almost every industry, the resurgence of the state in the wake of market crises, and greater state–firm cooperation, increase barriers to entry, reduce market access, and impede innovation. Moreover, the governments of countries ruled by autocratic and populist regimes are all too often founded on collusive, oligarchic economic interests. If the power of firms and state–firm cooperation becomes so great that it shuts out too many people who want access to markets, markets will continue to fail.

This edition of the CEE chapter re-emphasizes the notion that entrepreneurship, as a measure of economic participation, goes hand-in-hand with political participation and that the lack of civil liberties and high levels of corruption are indicators of the "institutional overhead" that weigh heavily on and dampen the economic dynamism that risk-taking entrepreneurial market capitalism represents. Paternalistic autocrats, corporatist and/or populist leaders many with entrenched interests fear independent action such as entrepreneurial initiative and the impetus that underlies it—self-determination. Growing international and societal uncertainties also present limitations.

The extent to which entrepreneurship is allowed, or is able to flourish, is akin to self-determination. Indeed, entrepreneurship is not only a determinant of competitive market-led economic growth, but it is also an indicator of economic and political participation. The level of entrepreneurship, therefore, is also indicative of a dynamic civil society, self-determination, and the enjoyment of other civil liberties. Conversely, where political participation is restricted and market access limited, entrepreneurship, in its viable form, will also be limited. This edition adds an emphasis on the importance of elevated macrolevel political and security risks as additional destabilizing factors that also affect sustainable growth-generating, market competition-inducing entrepreneurial risk-taking.

While an entrepreneurial ecosystem with as near optimal conditions as possible best supports entrepreneurial capitalism, it is not present in many CEE22 countries. The low number of employers as a share of total employment in the CEE22 economies suggests that relatively large firms predominate and limit competition, in terms of market access, which indicates high entrepreneurial risk. The job security in large public sector employers is an important disincentive for European entrepreneurship, including in the CEE22. Moreover, some of the CEE22 countries are still betwixt and between national sovereignty. Nevertheless, the citizens of these countries are well equipped to take these risks. They are also increasingly impatient with the corruption that affects their daily lives and future prospects.

Efforts to diversify energy supplies from other sources, including renewable energy (RE) suggest pipeline politics may be waning. Because this seems to have coincided with elevated security tensions among suggests other sources of security risks in the CEE22 countries. Indeed, international sanctions coupled with the prospect of less European dependence on Russia's energy exports may even be the cause of stepped up destabilizing actions by Russian interests.

Start-ups and SMEs have to navigate the risks of both competition from bigger firms in their industry and the macrolevels risks of political uncertainty, predatory market behavior by large incumbents, and threats to security. The underlying factors affecting market-creating, legitimate entrepreneurship are political, institutional, and, in extreme cases, security determined. This calls for levels of risk analytical approach to entrepreneurial risk-taking, in order to overcome these impediments, or finding ways to get around them. Mesolevel entrepreneurial risk analysis includes some combination of the macro- and microlevel risks that affect new risk-taking ventures in order to understand how macrolevel systemic risks affect business and other market risks. It differentiates entrepreneurial business risk from microeconomic business risk and identifies location-specific risks of macrolevel, systemic political risks, and security risks.

Discussion Questions

1. What conditions constitute an environment conducive for entrepreneurship?

    a. Is uncertainty, even insecurity always an inhibiting factor?

    b. What makes risk-taking entrepreneurship sustainable, market building, and competition inducing?

2. Describe current political, economic, and market conditions in Central and Eastern Europe (CEE) countries.

    a. How does the geographical location of CEE countries affect entrepreneurship there?

    a. How does this affect the 'state of entrepreneurship' in the region?

3. Rank at least 10 of the CEE22 countries according to their respective levels of business, political, and security risks.

    a. What are the opportunities and risks of entrepreneurship in the region, in each country?

    b. Select one of these countries and determine its particular entrepreneurial risk based on this meso-level analysis.

4. Pick one CEE22 country in which to start a business in a particular industry.

   a. Explain the rationale for selecting the country and the industry. (Be sure to include the implications of the answers to the preceding questions in this discussion to support your argument.)

   b. What markets will this new business serve—domestic, international, or both?

   c. What are the five most important barriers facing this entrepreneurial start-up?

   d. Develop a contingency plan based on worst- and best-case scenarios of changing conditions—country-specific, regional, business conditions including domestic and international competition, security, and political risks.

References

Audretsch, D. B., Thurik, R., Kwaak, T., & Bosma, N. (2003). *SMEs in Europe 2003* (Observatory of European SMEs, No. 7). Luxembourg: European Commission. Retrieved from file:///C:/Users/NJha1/Downloads/smes_observatory_2003_report7_en_1386%20(1).pdf (accessed October 22, 2017).

Beck, U. (1992). *Risk society: Towards a new modernity.* London, Thousand Oaks, and New Delhi: Sage.

Budzhurova, L., & Zaks, D. (February 28, 2014). *Yanukovych emerges as Ukraine leaders warn Russia over Crimea.* Retrieved from http://www.afp.com/en/home/ (accessed February 28, 2014).

Cichowlas, O. (March 28, 2017). The most hated man in Russia. *Foreign policy.* Washington, DC: *Foreign Policy.* Retrieved from http://foreignpolicy.com/2017/03/28/the-most-hated-man-in-russia-dmitry-medvedev-protests-putin/ (accessed May 15, 2017).

Credendo. (May 10, 2017). *Country risks synthesizing chart.* Retrieved from https://www.credendo.com/country_risk (accessed May 10, 2017).

Department of State (DOS) (US). (February 2008). *Background note: Belarus.* Belarus: Bureau of European and Eurasian Affairs. Retrieved from http://www.state.gov/outofdate/bgn/belarus/111465.htm (accessed on June 15, 2009).

Department of State (DOS) (US). (September 20, 2007). *Women entrepreneurs and small business development: A project for Belarus.* International Visitor Leadership Program, Office of International Visitors, Bureau of Educational and Cultural Affairs.

de Rato, R. (March 23, 2007). Responding to shifts in financial risk: The need for leadership. Speech to the Wharton School, University of Pennsylvania. Retrieved from http://www.imf.org/external/np/speeches/2007/032307.htm (June 18, 2007).

Dobrinsky, R., Adarov, A., Bornukova, K., Havlik, P., Hunya, G., Dzmitry, K., & Pindyuk, O. (November 26, 2016). *The Belarus economy: The challenges of stalled reforms* (Research Report No. 143). Austria: The Vienna Institute for International Economic Studies (Wiener Institut für Internationale Wirtschaftsvergleiche). Retrieved from https://wiiw.ac.at/the-belarus-economy-the-challenges-of-stalled-reforms-p-4032.html (accessed on May 11, 2017).

Dosi, G., Llerena, P., & Labini, M. S. (2005). *Science-technology-industry links and the "European Paradox": Some notes on the dynamics of scientific and technological research in Europe* (LEM Paper 2005/02). Pisa: Laboratory of Economics and Management (LEM), Sant'Anna School of Advanced Studies.

European Commission. (June 28, 2017). *Promoting entrepreneurship.* Retrieved from (accessed on June 28, 2017).

European Commission. (9 January 9, 2013). *Entrepreneurship in the EU and beyond* (Flash Barometer 354). Retrieved from http://ec.europa.eu/enterprise/policies/sme/facts-figures-analysis/eurobarometer/index_en.htm (accessed on March 15, 2014).

European Commission. (November 26, 2013). *Annual report on European SMEs 2012/2013: A recovery on the horizon?* Retrieved from http://ec.europa.eu/enterprise/policies/sme/facts-figures-analysis/performance-review/index_en.htm (accessed on March 10, 2014).

European Commission. (March 3, 2010). *Europe 2020: A strategy for smart, sustainable, and inclusive growth.* Retrieved from http://eur-lex.europa.eu/LexUriServ/LexUriServ.do?uri=COM:2010:2020:FIN: EN:PDF (accessed on March 15, 2014).

European Commission. (April 30, 2007). *Entrepreneurship survey of the EU (25 Member States), United States, Iceland and Norway* (Flash Barometer 192). Retrieved from http://ec.europa.eu/public_opinion/flash/fl_192_en.pdf (accessed on May 23, 2008).

Feifer, G. (2009). Gazprom and Russia's foreign policy. *National Public Radio.* Retrieved from http://www.npr.org/templates/story/story.php?storyId=99026745 (accessed on January 6, 2009).

Forbes. (May 24, 2017). Global 2000: The world's biggest public companies. Retrieved from https://www.forbes.com/global2000/#53a9bdda335d (accessed on May 28, 2017).

Freedom House. (April 28, 2017). New report: Freedom of the press 2017—Press freedom's dark horizon. Retrieved from https://freedomhouse.org/article/new-report-freedom-press-2017-press-freedom-s-dark-horizon (accessed on June 3, 2017).

Freedom House. (January 31, 2017). Freedom in the world 2017: Freedom decline continues amid rising populism and autocracy. Retrieved from https://freedomhouse.org/article/freedom-world-2017-freedom-decline-continues-amid-rising-populism-and-autocracy (accessed on February 11, 2017).

The Fund for Peace. (May 14, 2017). Fragile states index—annual report. Retrieved from http://fundforpeace.org/fsi/2017/05/14/fragile-states-index-2017-annual-report/ (June 5, 2017).

Gazprom. (June 27, 2017). Companies with Gazprom's participation and other affiliated entities—by share percent. Retrieved from http://www.gazprom.com/about/subsidiaries/subsidiary/ (June 27, 2017).

Giddens, A. (2000). *Runaway world: How globalization is reshaping our lives.* New York: Routledge.

Global Entrepreneurship Development Institute. (November 13, 2016). Global entrepreneurship index (GEI). Retrieved from https://thegedi.org/global-entrepreneurship-and-development-index/ (May 3, 2017).

Global Entrepreneurship Research Association. (February 4, 2017). Global entrepreneurship monitor. Retrieved from http://gemconsortium.org/report. (accessed on May 3, 2017).

Groome, T., Blancher, N., Haas, F., Kiff, J., Lee, W., Mills, P., Nakagawa, S., … Kim, Y. S. (2006). *The limits of market-based risk transfer and implications for managing systemic risk* (IMF Working Paper No. WP/06/217).

Group of 8. (June 20, 1999). G8 Communiqué Köln. Retrieved from http://www.g8.utoronto.ca/summit/1999koln/finalcom.htm.

Human Rights Watch. (January 12, 2017). World reports 2017—Events of 2016. Retrieved from https://www.hrw.org/news/2017/01/12/world-report-2017-demagogues-threaten-human-rights (March 26, 2017).

International Energy Agency. (March 4, 2014). Facts in brief: Russia, Ukraine, Europe, oil & gas. Retrieved from https://www.iea.org/media/news/20140304UkraineRussiaEuropegasoilfactsheet.pdf (accessed on October 18, 2016).

International Monetary Fund. (April 18, 2017). *World economic outlook.* Retrieved from http://www.imf.org/external/pubs/ft/weo/2017/01/weodata/download.aspx (accessed on April 27, 2017).

Ireland, R. D., Tihanyi, L., & Webb, J. W. (2008). A tale of two politico-economic systems: Implications for entrepreneurship in Central and Eastern Europe. *Entrepreneurship Theory and Practice, 32*(1), 107–130.

Ivanova, Y. V. (2008). Belarus: Entrepreneurial activities in an unfriendly environment. *Journal of East-West Business, 10*(4), 29–54.

Keohane, R. O., & Nye, J. S. (2001). *Power and interdependence: World politics in transition* (3rd ed.). New York, NY: Pearson Professional.

McBride, J., & Stott, M. (June 25, 2008). Poverty and corruption threaten Russia: Medvedev. *Reuters.* Retrieved from http://www.reuters.com/article/2008/06/25/us-russia-medvedev-idUSL248493820080625 (accessed on June 26, 2008).

Mazol, A. (September 7, 2016). Belarus's private sector at a crossroads. *Belarus Digest.* Retrieved from http://belarusdigest.com/story/belaruss-private-sector-crossroads-27222 (accessed on November 3, 2016).

New York Stock Exchange. (2008). China startups: Five entrepreneurs shaping a nation. Second Quarter: 14–21.

Novak, M. (June 21, 2017). Slovenian banks show lower Jan-April profit, lending up. *Reuters*. Retrieved from https://www.reuters.com/article/slovenia-banks-idUSL8N1JI1FG (accessed on June 24, 2017).

Opportunity Risk Index©. (June 30, 2017). St. Petersburg Institute of International Political Economy. Retrieved from https://www.spiipe.org/opportunity-risk-index-ori (accessed on June 30, 2017).

Organization for Economic Cooperation and Development. (March 27, 2017). FDI regulatory restrictiveness index. Retrieved from http://www.oecd.org/investment/fdiindex.htm (accessed on May 3, 2017).

Political Terror Scale. (September 9, 2016). Political terror scale dataset. Retrieved from http://www.politicalterrorscale.org/Data/Download.html (accessed on April 26, 2017).

Prybyla, J. S. (1965). Eastern Europe and Soviet Oil. *The Journal of Industrial Economics, 13*(2)154–167.

Reuters. (January 8, 2007). Factbox—Russia's Druzhba pipeline. Retrieved from http://www.reuters.com/article/uk-belarus-russia-druzhba-idUSL0881252620070108; http://www.reuters.com/article/russia-oil-druzhba-idUSLDE5BR10020091228 (accessed on February 16, 2007).

St. Petersburg Institute of International Political Economy. (June 30, 2017). Business and entrepreneurial risk analysis. Retrieved from https://www.spiipe.org/risk-analysis (accessed on June 30, 2017).

Stockholm International Peace Research Institute. (June 22, 2017). SIPRI arms transfers database. Retrieved from https://www.sipri.org/databases/armstransfers (accessed on June 22, 2017).

The Economist. (February 2, 2002). *Globalization: Is it at risk?* Retrieved from http://www.economist.com/node/965575 (accessed on March 24, 2002).

The Economist. (October 23, 2008). *Eastern Europe: Who's next?* Retrieved from http://www.economist.com/node/12465279 (accessed on February 4, 2009).

The Economist. (July 16, 2009). *He who pays for the pipelines calls the tune.* Retrieved from http://www.economist.com/node/14041672 (accessed on June 22, 2011).

Transparency International. (January 27, 2017). Corruption perception index. Retrieved from https://www.transparency.org/news/feature/corruption_perceptions_index_2016 (accessed on April 12, 2017).

Transparency International. (July 9, 2013). Global corruption barometer. Retrieved from http://www.transparency.org/gcb2013/press (accessed on December 12, 2013).

United Nations. (December 13, 2013). *Concluding observations on the combined fourth to sixth periodic reports of Belarus* (Economic and Social Council Report E/C.12/BLR/CO/4-6). Geneva: Committee on Economic, Social and Cultural Rights. Retrieved from http://tbinternet.ohchr.org/_layouts/treatybodyexternal/Download.aspx?symbolno=E%2fC.12%2fBLR%2fCO%2f4-6&Lang=en (accessed on February 10, 2014).

United Nations. (October 31, 2013). UN expert urges Belarus to guarantee the right to elect and be elected. *UN News Centre*. Retrieved from (accessed on March 30, 2014).

Woolsey, M. (October 10, 2005). Lackluster entrepreneurship in the EU. *Forbes*. Retrieved from http://www.forbes.com/2006/10/09/france-germany-taxes-ent-fin-cx_mw_1010european.html (July 3, 2007).

World Bank. (April 27, 2017). *World development indicators*. Retrieved from http://data.worldbank.org/data-catalog/world-development-indicators (accessed on May 3, 2017).

World Bank. (October 25, 2016). *Doing business 2017: Equal opportunity for all*. Retrieved from http://www.doingbusiness.org/reports/global-reports/doing-business-2017; (accessed on March 22, 2017).

World Bank. (September 23, 2016). *World governance indicators*. Retrieved from http://info.worldbank.org/governance/WGI/#home (accessed on April 18, 2017).

World Economic Forum. (January 24, 2014). *Entrepreneurial ecosystems around the globe and early-stage company growth dynamics*. Retrieved from http://www.weforum.org/reports/entrepreneurial-ecosystems-around-globe-and-early-stage-company-growth-dynamics (accessed on February 23, 2014).

World Economic Forum. (January 17, 2014). *Enhancing Europe's competitiveness: Fostering innovation-driven entrepreneurship in Europe*. Retrieved from http://www.weforum.org/reports/enhancing-europe-s-competitiveness-fostering-innovation-driven-entrepreneurship-europe (accessed on February 23, 2014).

World Justice Project (WJP). (October 20, 2016). *World Justice Project*. Retrieved from https://worldjusticeproject.org/news/2016-wjp-rule-law-index-global-press-release (accessed on May 28, 2017).

Združenje bank Slovenije (ZBS). (June 26, 2017). *Ownership structure of the Slovenian banking sector*. Retrieved from http://www.zbs-giz.si/en/zdruzenje-bank.asp?StructureId=575 (accessed on June 26, 2017).

Appendix

Unless otherwise noted each risk variable is the average of the data score and the rank of each country.

RISK VARIABLE	DATA SOURCE	TIME SERIES		SAMPLE SIZE (N=)	RISK INDEX
"Ease of Doing Business"	World Bank, Doing Business 2017 (DB2017)	25 October 2016	2017	190	Figure 3 Business Risk Index
Employers, total (% of total employment)	World Bank, World Development Indicators (WDI)	27 April 2017	2010–2016 (average)	128	Figure 3 Business Risk Index
New business density (new registrations per 1,000 people ages 15–64)	World Bank, World Development Indicators (WDI)	27 April 2017	2009–2016 (total)	137	Figure 3 Business Risk Index
Cost of business start-up procedures (% of GNI per capita)	World Bank, World Development Indicators (WDI)	27 April 2017	2009–2016 (average)	189	Figure 3 Business Risk Index
Compensation of employees (% of expense)	World Bank, World Development Indicators (WDI)	27 April 2017	2009–2016 (average)	151	Figure 3 Business Risk Index
Profit tax (% of commercial profits) (Range: 10%–30%)	World Bank, World Development Indicators (WDI)	27 April 2017	2013–2016 (average)	177	Figure 3 Business Risk Index
Value lost due to electrical outages (% of sales)	World Bank, World Development Indicators (WDI)	27 April 2017	2009–2016 (average)	135	Figure 3 Business Risk Index
Logistics performance index: Overall (1=low to 5=high)	World Bank, World Development Indicators (WDI)	27 April 2017	2009–2016 (average)	166	Figure 3 Business Risk Index
Bribery incidence (% of firms experiencing at least one bribe payment request)	World Bank, World Development Indicators (WDI)	27 April 2017	2009–2016 (average)	135	Figure 3 Business Risk Index
State Legitimacy (SL)	Fund for Peace, Fragile States Index (FSI)	14 May 2017	2017	178	Figure 4 Political Risk Index
Political risk—Export and Direct Investment	Credendo, County Risks Synthesizing Chart	10 May 2017	2017	248	Figure 4 Political Risk Index
Voice and Accountability	World Bank, World Governance Indicators (WGI)	23 September 2016	2015 (last available)	214	Figure 4 Political Risk Index
Political Rights	Freedom House, Freedom in the World (FIW)	31 January 2017	2016	195	Figure 4 Political Risk Index
Civil Liberties	Freedom House, Freedom in the World (FIW)	31 January 2017	2016	195	Figure 4 Political Risk Index
Press Freedom	Freedom House, Freedom of the Press	28 April 2017	2016	199	Figure 4 Political Risk Index

Appendix (cont.)

Unless otherwise noted each risk variable is the average of the data score and the rank of each country.

RISK VARIABLE	DATA SOURCE		TIME SERIES	SAMPLE SIZE (N=)	RISK INDEX
Government Effectiveness	World Bank, World Governance Indicators (WGI)	23 September 2016	2015 (last available)	214	Figure 4 Political Risk Index
Rule of Law	World Bank, World Governance Indicators (WGI)	23 September 2016	2015 (last available)	214	Figure 4 Political Risk Index
Strength of legal rights index (0=weak to 12=strong)	World Bank, World Development Indicators (WDI)	27 April 2017	2013–2016 (average)	189	Figure 4 Political Risk Index
Control of Corruption	World Bank, World Governance Indicators (WGI)	23 September 2016	2015 (last available)	214	Figure 4 Political Risk Index
Corruption Perception	Transparency International (TI), Corruption Perception Index (CPI)	27 January 2017	2016	176	Figure 4 Political Risk Index
Political Stability and Absence of Violence	World Bank, World Governance Indicators (WGI)	23 September 2016	2015 (last available)	214	Figure 5 Security Risk Index
Security Apparatus	Fund for Peace, Fragile States Index (FSI)	14 May 2017	2017	178	Figure 5 Security Risk Index
External Intervention	Fund for Peace, Fragile States Index (FSI)	14 May 2017	2017	178	Figure 5 Security Risk Index
"Political Terror Scale"	PoliticalTerror.org, Political Terror Scale dataset	9 September 2016	2017	109	Figure 5 Security Risk Index
Military expenditure (% of GDP)	World Bank, World Development Indicators (WDI)	27 April 2017	2010–2016 (total)	156	Figure 5 Security Risk Index
Armed forces personnel (% of total labor force)	World Bank, World Development Indicators (WDI)	27 April 2017	2016	165	Figure 5 Security Risk Index
Arms imports	Stockholm International Peace Research Institute (SIPRI)	22 June 2017	2000–2016 (total)	189	Figure 5 Security Risk Index
Arms exports	Stockholm International Peace Research Institute (SIPRI)	22 June 2017	2000–2016 (total)	119	Figure 5 Security Risk Index
Battle-related deaths (number of people)	World Bank, World Development Indicators (WDI)	27 April 2017	2000–2016 (total)	217	Figure 5 Security Risk Index
Intentional homicides (per 100,000 people)	World Bank, World Development Indicators (WDI)	27 April 2017	2010–2016 (average)	201	Figure 5 Security Risk Index

Entrepreneurship in Emerging Markets

Li Dai and Anatoly Zhuplev

Hilton Center for Business, Loyola Marymount University, Los Angeles, California

Key Terms

Benefit-cost tradeoffs

Bottom of the pyramid

Consumerism

Corruption

Digital divide

Economic growth

First mover advantage

Geographic factors

Global manufacturing

Global marketing

Grassroots support

Hard and soft infrastructure

Informal economy

Institutional trajectories

Institutional voids

Internationalization decision

Microfinancing

Middle class

Private knowledge

Political stability

Pull vs. push strategies

Regional strategies

Sector diversity

Small- and medium-sized enterprises

Social attributes

Step-by-step market approach to foreign market research

Stepping-stone approach

Technological opportunity

Transportation costs

4Ps of marketing

Learning Objectives

Upon completion of this chapter, students should be able to:

1. Understand the opportunities, challenges, and risks of entrepreneurial venturing in emerging markets

2. Comprehend the sociocultural environments of emerging markets and their impact on international entrepreneurship

3. Analyze the political, economic, social, and technological (PEST) aspects of emerging market economies and the implications for foreign entrepreneurs

4. Explore strategic approaches and implications for undertaking entrepreneurial ventures in emerging markets using the 4P marketing framework

5. Assess entry and operational strategies for entrepreneurial venturing in emerging markets

6. Develop knowledge in conducting comparative market research across emerging markets

Introduction

In today's competitive global business environment, developed country firms are increasingly driven to enter emerging markets by both competitive pressures back home and the myriad opportunities in these still-largely untapped markets. From an entrepreneurial standpoint, therefore, emerging market countries offer foreign small- and medium-sized enterprises (SMEs)[1] an alternative platform for both survival and success. Indeed, the emerging markets have become attractive for both global commerce and manufacturing. However, emerging markets and their constituent geographical regions are far from homogeneous, making it difficult to devise entrepreneurial strategies universally applicable to the totality of "emerging markets." In particular, entrepreneurs contemplating their expansion to the emerging markets should take into consideration the strategic opportunities/ benefits, costs, and risks therein.

A shared attribute across these markets is the unbridled rate of development in both tangible progress and value-creating opportunities. While developed countries in the West struggled to recover from the 2008 financial crisis, the traditionally overlooked economies in the emerging markets posted significant growth. As a result of the economic downturn in the Western hemisphere and the internationalization of emerging market firms into developed countries, Western entrepreneurial firms are confronted with unprecedented levels of competition in their home countries. While the developed portions of the world continue to experience slow growth, however, emerging market and developing economies now account for close to 80% of global economic growth and for nearly 85% of the growth in global consumption, in both cases doubling their share from two decades prior.

---

[1] We refer to small- and medium-sized enterprises/firms, entrepreneurial firms, and entrepreneurs interchangeably.

Depending on the industry and attributes such as the size and growth stage of a given Western entrepreneurial firm, emerging market economies that hold fast-growth potential for entrepreneurial activities extend to pockets across the globe. For instance, the emerging markets spanning countries ranging from those in Latin America (such as Mexico, Chile, and Colombia), Eastern Europe (such as Poland and Hungary), to those in Southeast Asia (such as Indonesia, Malaysia, Thailand, Singapore, and Vietnam) comprise to varying extents attractive destinations for entrepreneurial ventures in exporting and/or foreign direct investment.

As a consequence, growth opportunities for Western entrepreneurs are no longer limited to the "old" emerging markets of the BRICS countries (Brazil, Russia, India, China, and South Africa), but rather abound in the hub of dynamism and creativity that characterizes these rising "emerging markets." As a representative case for the "new" emerging markets, six of the world's 10 fastest-growing economies are in Africa. With countries such as Côte d'Ivoire, Ethiopia, Kenya, Morocco, Rwanda, Angola, the Democratic Republic of Congo, Nigeria, and Zambia spearheading the emergence of the continent, Africa is now the second fastest growing region in the world.

In this chapter, we (1) discuss the importance of emerging markets for foreign entrepreneurs, (2) provide a comparison of emerging and established markets in terms of the opportunities, challenges, risks, and market parameters for entrepreneurial firms faced with both necessity and opportunistic drivers, (3) analyze the political, economic, social, and technological (PEST) aspects of emerging market economies for developed country entrepreneurs, (4) distinguish between imperatives for global manufacturing and global marketing in the emerging market context using the price, place, product, and promotion (4P) framework, and (5) present entrepreneurial strategies tailored to emerging market contexts.

Variations in Opportunities, Challenges, and Risks

While an eclectic group of countries on the whole, the emerging markets still share more similarities with one another than with their advanced country counterparts, providing a semblance of generalizability for foreign entrepreneurs. For example, doing business in Russia would be similar to doing business in Brazil than venturing to Western Europe. On the other hand, these emerging markets represent highly challenging business environments, as the World Bank's Doing Business reports and other such guides consistently indicate. We highlight some of the differences between the emerging markets and their developed country counterparts.

In comparison to the opportunities in the emerging markets, the market parameters in established developed country markets present a starkly different picture of market potential for entrepreneurial firms. In terms of market size, growth rate, and purchasing power, the developed countries of the world have reached their carrying capacities. However, the easier access to capital and quality of infrastructure in these countries, and especially for entrepreneurial firms, the quality of life for the main decision makers, make it a challenge to shift focus toward lesser known international domains.

The advent of fast-growing industries such as telecommunications, banking and services, and consumer retail has spawned a growing employed middle class in the emerging markets. Over the next decade, emerging market countries will usher 700 million people into the middle class, with 3 billion, mainly from the developing world, projected to enter the middle class by 2050. With an increasing appetite for consumer lifestyles propagated by the West and the increased purchasing power of the new middle class, the emerging markets present a haven for entrepreneurial firms seeking international opportunities. As a notable case of a "new" emerging market, Kazakhstan is projected to have more households earning at least $50,000 in 2020 than Indonesia, the Philippines, Vietnam, Pakistan and Egypt combined, offering a premium to first movers in the entrepreneurial space. It was also previously estimated that, by 2020, Turkey was due to experience one of the greatest absolute increases in income for $50,000-plus households of any emerging economy (Accenture, 2013). However, the results of the country's 2017 constitutional referendum combined with the effects of the ongoing conflict in bordering nations may hinder the speed of that growth.

In Africa, the emerging middle class represented more than 60% of the continent's overall GDP in 2012, and by some estimates African consumer spending could hit $1.4 trillion by 2020 (World Bank, 2013). In South Africa, the emerging "black middle class" has fueled a shopping boom in imported brands for packaged food, clothing, and electronics, having seen their spending power more than double in the past since the early 2000s. This phenomenon has now spread to the rest of sub-Saharan Africa, with countries such as Nigeria, Kenya, and Cameroon contributing to the fastest-growing middle class in the world. According to the African Development Bank, the number of middle-class Africans, or individuals spending between $2 and $20 a day, is expected to reach 1.1 billion in 2060, or nearly half of the predicted population at that time (Euromonitor International, 2013).

As these statistics indicate, what constitutes "middle-class" in many of these countries may be unimaginable to their counterparts in the advanced economies, with the concept itself fluctuating widely from country to country within the emerging markets. Yet, even as the concept of the middle class will likely remain relative among these countries along their idiosyncratic trajectories of development, the rate of overall expansion for these emerging markets substantially rivals that of developed countries.

Moreover, the large low-income population at the bottom of the pyramid will continue to present a substantial portion of the opportunities for foreign entrepreneurial firms that venture to emerging markets. Although the infrastructure is still weak in many emerging markets, consumers in Africa increasingly have access to air-conditioned supermarkets and shopping centers where in the past open air markets and neighborhood shops stood amidst haggling and spice aromas. The Accra Mall in Ghana and The Palms in Lagos, Nigeria, for example, embody the growing sophistication of the African middle classes.

Indeed, the lack of basic infrastructure provides perhaps as many opportunities as it does problems. Furthermore, the markets spawned by these opportunities have long been saturated in the established markets of the West. For instance, in Africa, a young population with its shifting dietary habits and a trend toward urbanization has prompted growth in food outlets that translate into potential for global entrepreneurs. As another example, the lack of agricultural infrastructure and technology means that many of the inputs for food products must be processed abroad. As such, there are opportunities for foreign SMEs to increase standards as well as cost efficiencies along the value chain, from building factories to roads to transportation systems.

Emerging markets are furthermore characterized by more diverse sectors that offer opportunities to foreign entrepreneurs. Increasingly a kaleidoscope of industries and commercial activity, the emerging markets have come to resemble their more advanced counterparts. A long-time hallmark of an emerging market economy has been the state's dependence on a single industry for its revenues. For example, Slovakia has long been associated with the automotive industry. In other emerging markets, the windfall profits often derived from the exploitation of natural resources fueled "the resource curse."

Yet, the rise in political and social stability in many parts of the emerging world has encouraged the development of new industries. Kazakhstan continues to diversify its economy beyond the oil and gas and mining sectors, which have traditionally served as dominant sources of national revenue (Doing Business in Kazakhstan, 2011b). The Kazakh GDP experienced slowed growth in the face of falling oil prices starting 2014, and to combat this, the country is focused on improving transport infrastructure and strengthening public and market institutions to foster economic diversification and attract investment into the non-oil economy. For a time, it seemed that the improved security situation in Iraq would provide the foundation for robust non-oil growth, and that continued monetary easing in the country would encourage growth in the banking industry, further facilitating projects in infrastructure and reconstruction. However, since the end of 2014, sinking oil prices and the ISIS insurgency, along with political instability, have severely limited the extent of Iraqi economic growth and recovery.

The push toward the diversification of commercial activity in these and other countries reflects a shift in the policy imperatives from reliance on nonrenewable resource extraction toward value creation activities more aligned with entrepreneurial initiatives from abroad.

The growing middle class in emerging market countries has created a retail sector that in many countries surpasses even the natural resources extraction industries traditionally associated with emerging market economies. In contrast to established markets, the growth in modern retailing in emerging markets has been in large part facilitated by an increase in urbanization. Urban communities, especially in Africa, have become a focal point of development, with firms using urban centers as a springboard into the market beyond. The resulting consumerism here and elsewhere is accompanied by real estate developments that have likewise helped to boost spending on furniture and household goods such as electronics.

Despite the presence of attractive market parameters, the emerging markets have yet to become a top destination for global entrepreneurial firms, perhaps because of the elevated costs, risks, as well as political–economic instability posed by these countries. To begin with, emerging market countries are characterized by poor access to land, electricity, logistical support, and opportunities. In other words, both the "hard" and "soft" bases for business activity in the emerging markets are in the infancy stage of development, albeit to varying degrees across countries. Africa especially has been plagued for decades with inadequate electricity supply, cumbersome and expensive transport, political stability and rampant corruption. For entrepreneurial firms with little resources to begin with, the added costs of operating in such conditions may be sufficient to deter their entry into the emerging markets.

In addition, the costs of shipping products pose a potential barrier to entrepreneurial firms that seek to manufacture or sell to the emerging markets. Transportation costs are often determined by a country's geography, which constitutes its "hard" infrastructure. Historically fraught with geographical determinism, emerging market countries that were landlocked became more isolated from international trade and commerce while their coastal counterparts were able to "emerge" from their third-world status. In terms of the costs of doing business, entrepreneurs pay up to 50% more in transportation costs to ship to the median landlocked country than the median coastal nation. In practical terms, these differences can be enormous. For example, shipping a standard container from Baltimore to the Ivory Coast (Cote D'Ivoire) costs about $3,000, while sending the same container to the landlocked Central African Republic costs $13,000.

The geographical impediments to doing business in emerging markets can be further exacerbated by unstable political or commercial relations between neighboring countries. Consider landlocked countries that face the challenge of coordinating infrastructure expenditures with their neighbors. The agricultural potential of the upper Parana River basin in landlocked Paraguay remained dormant until a regional integration agreement (Mercosur) in the 1990s facilitated barge transportation through Brazil and Argentina. Jordan's access to the Mediterranean requires crossing the border of countries such as Israel, Syria, or Lebanon. As another example, Rwanda and Uganda rely on the Kenyan rail system for shipping goods abroad. While economies like Hong Kong, Taiwan, and Singapore have an advantageous geographical position, much of inland Africa, China, and India remains removed from maritime trade.

Not only is it more costly and difficult for foreign entrepreneurs to reach large portions of emerging market countries, all of the "hard" infrastructure problems endemic to these markets may be compounded by "soft" infrastructure failures. As an example, the corruption and cronyism that define many emerging markets often both constrain and enable business activity to a substantial extent. Transparency

International publishes an annual report outlining the position of countries with respect to various indicators that point to their pervasiveness and arbitrariness of corruption. The emerging markets are in addition subject to ubiquity in political violence, crime, and general social disorder to a greater extent than their developed country counterparts, as acts of corruption in the public sector trickle down to the private domain of life.

In addition to downside risks posed by corruption and expropriation of assets, entrepreneurial firms in emerging markets may be limited in the upside growth potential. The "soft" infrastructure related to credit access is likewise deficient in emerging markets, where financial markets are underdeveloped, regulatory and legal frameworks weak, informational asymmetries persistent, and risk management systems not as robust. Nonetheless, given that even the newest of emerging markets lack basic preventative services such as life and property insurance, the proliferation of "microfinancing"—which encompasses a large range of banking and financial services provided to low income and underserved communities— should help to create a more stable supplier and buyer base for foreign entrepreneurial firms.

The labor market in emerging markets constitutes another aspect of the "soft" infrastructure that can affect foreign entrepreneurs. To begin with, unemployed individuals constitute a base of labor for foreign ventures. However, this phenomenon is not uniform across the emerging markets, as workforce dynamics vary drastically depending on the level of firm activity in a country. For example, countries like the Czech Republic are beginning to experience talent shortages based on 15–20 years of success in attracting foreign firms. Furthermore, as individuals in the emerging markets seek various means of survival they can have pronounced effects on the local entrepreneurial scene in these countries, with implications for the competitive and cooperative landscapes therein.

Practically speaking, increasingly globalized and interdependent emerging economies across the world generate business opportunities by *pulling/attracting* companies overseas. By the same token they create competitive challenges and threats by *pushing* companies overseas. Altogether these translate into the push/pull force field dynamics affecting entrepreneurial decision-making. In this competitive and dynamic environment small- and medium-sized companies cannot stand still: they must compete and grow. Otherwise they are likely to be overtaken by competition sooner or later.

A decision on international expansion to emerging markets should begin by analyzing resources available to the company, driving and restraining forces in the international expansion context, including retrospective impacts from the company's preceding development and performance.

Going international: to be or not to be? Does going international fit company's mission, business model, strategic mix and development dynamics? Is this international expansion feasible or sustainable in the short-, medium- and long-term range?

At this stage of international strategic contemplation, a SWOT analysis may play an important analytical role. Is the international expansion compatible with the company mission and key objectives? What resources are available? Does the company have core competencies, expertise, as well as top management commitment and support? What are the constraints? How do these translate into benefits, costs, and risks associated with this international expansion as it relates to the target country, industry, company?

A company's choices may differ significantly, depending on whether international expansion is focused on marketing/selling in emerging markets as opposed to manufacturing overseas. In the case of marketing, some general criteria in country selection may include high and/or fast growing GDP per capita, large and/or fast growing population, high population density, and other factors. The globalEDGE's annual Market Potential Indicator Index can be used as a useful assessment tool for measuring market attractiveness for 26 emerging markets using eight criteria (Market Potential Indicators, 2016—http://globaledge.msu.edu/mpi).

In business terms, the *specific benefits/advantages* of international expansion to emerging economies may include: gaining economies of scale, escaping intensive domestic competition, evading domestic regulations and negative images, gaining low-cost access to mineral resources, components or labor, enhancing global competitiveness and branding, increasing global market share, sales and profits, reducing dependence on existing markets and diversifying product lines globally, extending a life cycle and sales potential of existing products, exploiting corporate technology and know-how, stabilizing seasonal market fluctuations, selling temporary excessive production capacity, overcoming limited seasonal market demand fluctuations, or just gaining information about foreign competition.

Disadvantages associated with international expansion to emerging market countries may include: a need to develop new promotional material, the sacrifice of short-term profits for long-term gains, added costs in shipping, tariffs and other fees, additional operating risks such as political unrest, the need to commit qualified personnel overseas, longer wait times for payments or even defaults, necessary modifications in product, packaging, or labeling, the need for additional financing and export licenses, and the need to overcome trade barriers and other obstacles.

Costs associated with expansion to emerging markets may include start-up expenses and operational costs related to the specific host country and the specific industry and strategic situation of the company. Since 2003, the World Bank has published its annual "Doing Business" survey evaluating the ease and attendant cost of doing business across countries worldwide. The 2017 report covers 190 economies and assesses regulations affecting domestic firms in 11 areas of business regulation, such as starting a business, resolving insolvency, and trading across borders (Doing Business, 2017— http://www.doingbusiness.org/reports).

The third key component of the strategic assessment triad in the international expansion decision, particularly critical for emerging markets, is *risks*. Risks may vary depending on the country, type of industry, stage of the life cycle and other conditions. Major global insurance companies often categorize risks into *political* (short-term, medium-, special-transactions), *commercial*, and *foreign direct investment risks* related to war, expropriation, and government action (https://www.credendo.com/country_risk; Coface, 2014—http://www.coface.com/CofacePortal/COM_en_EN/pages/home/risks_home). Depending on the balance of strategic benefits, costs, and risks, an entrepreneurial firm can select the most attractive emerging market for expansion.

Pest Analysis Of Emerging Market Economies

Political Regime and Stability

The political factors pertinent to Western entrepreneurial efforts in emerging markets mainly center on regime type and level of stability. The lifting of Communist rule, for instance, combined with higher birthrates in Central and Eastern European countries, have fostered a new generation of entrepreneurial-minded individuals motivated by market growth and personal achievement. The emergent middle classes in these regions have created waves of democratization and market liberalization that serve as the basis for both cognitive and material acceptance of foreign products and concepts. As an example, Kazakhstan has emerged as a regional leader in central Asia, due in part to its political stability and the country's status as a democratic state (Doing Business in Kazakhstan, 2011b). Given the exotic nature and largely idiosyncratic regulatory frameworks of the emerging markets, it may be prudent for Western entrepreneurs to treat these politically stable markets as spring boards into other emerging market countries.

Given the political climate of an emerging market country, entrepreneurial firms that venture to totalitarian states will be exposed to varying degrees of difficulty in using the media to establish access to markets. In China, for instance, information is "noise free," or biased, with few people challenging mainstream thinking. In contrast to China's one-party dictatorship and policies of media censorship, India has an open and democratic government, as well as a strong and reliable judiciary system. In India, information flows freely, with more people able to express their point of view and decide which view is better. As the weak link in the viability of emerging market countries as platforms for sales and investments—meaning that much of a foreign entrepreneur's operating environment is contingent on the policies and incentives set in the political realm—the political system of a country deserves thorough analysis.

A feature of the political realm in emerging markets that is not so prominent in the advanced economies is the antagonism among neighboring nations. While countries in Western Europe are effectively eliminating their borders through regional integration, countries in the emerging markets often exacerbate their isolated geographical positions by erecting borders that complicate the movement of goods and the coordination of cross-country infrastructure. Since simply crossing the US–Canadian border is equivalent to adding from 4,000 to 16,000 km worth of transportation costs, the commercial logistics of trading between countries with weak political institutions and a history of cross-border animosity will prove to be infinitely more expensive for foreign entrepreneurs. As such, foreign entrepreneurs not only need to take into account the political stability of a potential host market, but also take stock of the regional stability of the markets that they intend to serve.

Another political dimension by which emerging markets can be evaluated for their attractiveness to foreign entrepreneurs is the level of government support for—or indeed, animosity toward—foreign business interests. To begin with, the emerging markets vary widely in the baseline foreign direct investment inflows each country receives. For instance, many of the Central and Eastern European countries, like emerging markets elsewhere, had regimes which for years protected their home markets by placing ceilings on the level of penetration by foreign firms. There was a minister whose job was to keep AT&T at 10% market share in this region, for example, with many government officials primarily interested in lining their own pockets, a behavior they had learned during the long Soviet occupation.

In some formerly communist countries, in addition, sales and business people developed instincts and methods for protecting their turf. For these locals, the phrase "how are things in Poland" may be interpreted as "so here is Big Brother watching me." Therefore, it is important for SMEs from developed countries to evaluate potential host markets in terms of the openness to foreign business entities, and target those that present neutral or even favorable conditions. Although less developed countries have traditionally been antagonistic to foreign investment, these countries have opened up considerably to varying degrees, both in substantive and in nominal ways. The liberalization of markets in these countries present not only opportunities to large firms from abroad, but also smaller firms that are "pulled" overseas by these firms as either suppliers or partners.

As part of a privatization initiative, for example, the United Arab Emirates now allows both foreign and local investments in the utility sector, although foreign investment is still restricted in oil and gas operations and the petrochemicals sectors. As another example, Chile's laws governing foreign investment are among the most liberal in Latin America, prescribing free-market policies instead of granting incentives, subsidies, or tax abatements. Even in war-torn emerging markets, there is evidence of regulatory liberalization that presents foreign entrepreneurs with opportunities. In the aftermath of Iraq's war in 2012, for example, Al Maabar of the United Arab Emirates launched a US$10 billion mixed use project in Baghdad.

All in all, the proactive management of government relations can be a key driver in entrepreneurial success in emerging markets. Yet, in markets where regime stability is elusive, close relations with the political elite may backfire. When Libya's ruling Gaddafi family was toppled from power as part of the Arab Spring incident in 2011, Turkish firms that had close connections with the family and even bureaucrats in organizations that supported the Gaddafi regime were stripped of their licenses to continue doing business in Libya. In contrast, those firms that hedged their political connections by also appealing to the general public had in effect obtained a social license to continue operating in the country, and were furthermore protected from looting by local insurgents that opposed the old regime.

This illustrates the importance of taking an idiosyncratic approach to viewing and maintaining political relations in the emerging markets, where aligned interests are more critical than what often turn out to be temporary alliances in a shifting political landscape. To counteract the costs and risks faced by foreign entrepreneurs doing business in the emerging markets, it is important to recognize that the opportunities for appealing to stakeholders other than the mainstream political party are not restricted to only large, established firms. In gaining legitimacy as a commercial entity in these countries, smaller entrepreneurial firms that know which stakeholders to side with will be able to reap the benefits of being locally embedded.

Economic Considerations

Economic progress in emerging markets is, to perhaps a greater extent than in advanced economies, inextricably linked to government policies and institutional voids. Institutional voids, a phrase coined by Tarun Khanna in his book *Winning in Emerging Markets*, refers to the absence of intermediaries like market research firms and credit card systems to efficiently connect buyers and sellers. Rather than defining emerging markets by a particular size or growth qualifications, Khanna argued that the primary characteristic of these markets is their lack of developed infrastructures and institutions that enable efficient business operations, factors that are taken for granted in advanced economies. In essence, institutional voids occur whenever these "supporting institutions" do not exist, and foreign firms—especially entrepreneurial ones with constrained resources—will face specific challenges as well as major opportunities.

The ability to protect and monetize investments in the presence of institutional voids is therefore especially salient in emerging market contexts. As a case in point, since emerging from the deep recession of the 1990s, Brazil carried out eight economic stabilization plans, introduced a new currency (the Real), reduced import barriers, and privatized state-owned enterprises in an effort to develop a market economy conducive to economic value creation. The government was furthermore instrumental in promoting strong anti-inflationary measures to curb hyperinflation, reducing rates running at 1,800% in 1989 and 1,500% in 1990 to 6.29% in 2016 (Doing Business in Brazil, 2011a). Entrepreneurial firms face a liability of being small in addition of the liability of being foreign. The resulting lower tolerance of failure makes it important to evaluate the fiscal health of an emerging market country before entering.

Indeed, without a functioning economic system, an emerging market country will not be able to provide the necessary platform for foreign entrepreneurs seeking either global manufacturing or marketing opportunities. The facilitating technologies needed to transport both goods and ideas are contingent on an adequate level of economic growth. As a case in point, India's GDP grew at an average rate of 8.5% for the years 2007–2012, despite the global slowdown. India thus emerged as one of the most attractive destinations for entrepreneurial opportunities with the large English-speaking labor base, diversified natural resources, and strong macroeconomic fundamentals. More significantly, India's robust, transparent and stable financial market has gradually transformed from a highly controlled system to a liberalized one. By seeking to grow in similarly economically viable emerging markets, entrepreneurial firms would be able to raise the necessary capital.

Moreover, borders restrict the flow of capital. Since investment contracts are often enforced at the national level, countries can shelter borrowers who are able but unwilling to repay. This situation introduces "sovereign risk" into financial markets, limiting capital movements and rendering them increasingly fickle in the emerging markets. As such, entrepreneurs that venture to certain emerging markets may need to have secured sources of credit before entering such markets.

As another example of the importance of a well-planned economy for foreign entrepreneurial firms, consider Poland. During the recent global economic downturn, Poland was the only country in Europe to show growth in GDP (Doing Business in Poland, 2011c), due in large part to its successful shift from a centrally planned to market-oriented economic system. Trade liberalization, economic restructuring, privatization, capital inflows, and the gradual adaptation of market-oriented legal and administrative standards and practices have all facilitated Poland's adoption of an attractive investment climate for foreign entrepreneurs and firms alike. The economic and political strength of countries are highly interdependent, such that entrepreneurs that are able to identify stable economies to invest will likely be exposed to less civil strife and political violence, and vice versa.

In addition to market reforms that incentivize market-driven behaviors, policies aimed at increasing value appropriation and modern taxation structures are important to both the motivation of entrepreneurial firms to enter emerging markets and their subsequent survival. In the United Arab Emirates (UAE), for instance, free repatriation of capital or earnings, low import duties, and the existence of free-trade zones constitute attractive incentives to bring in foreign investments. Moreover, the UAE in recent years has signed double tax and investment protection treaties with several countries. However, many emerging market economies still impose costs on foreign firms by requiring a percentage of their profits to be reinvested back in the country. Therefore, it is not so much the extent of opportunities provided by an emerging market, but the amount of actual earnings that a foreign entrepreneur will be able to accrue from its activities overseas that matters.

The various institutional trajectories of countries in the emerging markets moreover contribute to operational complexities. Chile, for example, just like Israel, South Africa, and South Korea, is undergoing a transition from an emerging market to a more mature market. Leveraging learnings in Chile may nonetheless help entrepreneurs to predict the economic future of other markets such as the Middle East, Southeastern Asia, and Africa. Eastern European countries, meanwhile, have their own set of economic challenges, potentially benefiting from the European Union but also at risk of being crowded out.

An important implication is that economies do not function in vacuums but rather are sustained or constrained by their regional circumstances. As such, Western entrepreneurs considering locales such as Ukraine, for example, should seek to understand the historical and ongoing struggles in the region over political economy allegiances to Russia versus the European Union. Only by fully grasping the political and economic ideologies of the emerging market countries they intend to operate in will entrepreneurs be able to make appropriate business-level decisions and avoid costly—and perhaps fatal—mistakes.

Social Factors

The existence of a strong customer base may be one of the most important factors for entrepreneurial firms considering which emerging markets to enter. Consequently, the focal points for market research consist of purchasing power and product fit. For emerging markets, in particular, these elements are highly idiosyncratic to the demographic being targeted, as well as the cultural nuances of the particular subnational region. For instance, certain markets like those in Eastern Europe may offer attractively low wages for resource-constrained entrepreneurial firms, but workers earning 200 to 300 Euros a month may also not be able to afford the products of these foreign firms.

On the other hand, these Eastern European countries share similar cultures that would provide an entrepreneurial firm with multiple platforms for expanding across the continent. Indeed, venturing eastward an entrepreneurial firm would encounter more complex risks akin to those associated with doing business in India or China, making cross-cultural literacy instrumental in the success of firms doing business across emerging markets. As such, entrepreneurs venturing to emerging market countries should consider both the subnational region and the larger continental region associated with a given country so as to be prepared for local particularities and be able to capitalize on its entry into a single country by subsequently entering neighboring markets.

This regional mindset will be especially pertinent to the continent of Africa, where the learning curves and liability of foreignness associated with entering the region for a resource-constrained firm will warrant entering more than one country to recoup costs. Furthermore, relative to other emerging market regions, Africa may exhibit more shared characteristics among its countries. With a large, growing, and youthful population of which 40% is under the age of 30, Africa is a prominent market for product introduction and expansion. Although the attractiveness of this market for global marketing surpasses that for manufacturing, entrepreneurial firms from developed countries seeking either to expand saturated markets back home or to pursue untapped markets abroad will discover both the optimism and perils that preside in Africa.

To begin with, the untapped potential of this emerging market is largely attributable to its social challenges, the most of glaring of which may be its reliance on imports for even basic food needs. While this dependence varies by country, the continent faces an ever increasing challenge in ensuring food security for even essential items such as dairy, meat, sugar, and cereal. The demand for food imports is compounded by a higher population growth rate than any other continent. From 2015 to 2016, the population rose from 1.17 billion to over 1.2 billion, an increase of almost 2.7%. (http://www.prb.org/pdf16/prb-wpds2016-web-2016.pdf). Accordingly, sub-Saharan African countries' food import bill was in excess of $40 billion in 2012 (Food and Agriculture Organisation, 2013).

The rising population and associated rise in food prices are of particular concern to the newest emerging market countries, including those in Africa, where prohibitive prices on such essential rather than discretionary purchases can result in social unrest and political instability. In addition to the macro risks posed by basic deficiencies in food supplies, entrepreneurial firms with only few human resources must make tradeoffs between the abundant opportunities in such markets and the necessary adjustments in lifestyle required to capitalize on such opportunities for each employee. In addition to concerns over room and board, there are additional considerations regarding travel to and from emerging market countries with limited airport infrastructure and flight schedules. All in all, the potential held by the newest emerging markets should be assessed in light of the added hassles of capitalizing on such potential.

One of the many hassles a foreign entrepreneur can expect to encounter in such markets is the often socially condoned informal economy. For instance, an estimated 80% of all enterprises in emerging markets—approximately 280 to 340 million—are informal firms, with the informal sector accounting for around 60% of the labor force in these countries (International Finance Corporation, 2011). Informal firms are defined as all firms that are unregistered with the pertinent office, municipality, or tax authority, or owners and employers of microenterprises that employ few paid workers. Taking nonagricultural sectors as a case in point, the proportion of employment accounted for by the informal economy for countries such as Serbia, Mauritius, Ukraine, and Russia is less than 10%, compared to 75% for countries such as India, Mali, and Bolivia. Since emerging markets vary greatly on the informality dimension, different coping strategies for entrepreneurs may be required depending on the degree of informality present in an economy.

In comparison with foreign SMEs with much knowledge of the workings on the ground, these local businesses may have access to more private knowledge and more importantly, render foreign entities outsiders from the very beginning. These local competitors may be able to gain an advantage with knowledge of tax loopholes and the informal labor market. Referred to as employees without a contract, informal employees are not registered with relevant authorities such as the social security agency or ministry of labor, and are thus not entitled to receive social security benefits. Given the uneven playing field presented by the informal economy, emerging market countries present an added layer of learning costs for entrepreneurial firms seeking opportunities therein.

Technological Environment

Technological progress in many emerging markets is stifled first and foremost due to climate differences that obstruct the transfer of R&D results from advanced economies to emerging markets. As such, technology entrepreneurs seeking to manufacture in these countries should take precaution before investing in facilities. That is, even though innovations such as computers or cellular phones work in many geographical conditions and are therefore easily adopted by emerging market countries, technologies in other sectors often require research that is very location specific. In developing agriculture technology, for instance, plant varieties need to be adapted to the local climate, meaning that R&D geared toward rich, temperate-zone agriculture is of little use in tropical areas.

The technological gap determines both current living standards and future trajectories of growth. For instance, countries like Argentina, Chile, Australia, New Zealand, and South Africa enjoy thriving export sectors in fruit, wine, cereals, oilseeds, and salmon due to the technologies developed for these products in temperate zones in the Northern Hemisphere. In contrast, many tropical countries— with their production of coffee, cocoa, sugar cane, and cassava—are left out of the modern-technology club. Since unproductive agricultural workers can produce little more than what they require for personal subsistence, the most landlocked tropical countries cannot support large urban populations. These emerging markets have rural areas that remain sparsely populated, with small, poor markets, and suffer from high transportation costs. Entrepreneurial firms may thus find these markets to offer various barriers to both upstream and downstream value activities, especially those seeking global marketing opportunities.

In particular, the market potential in many emerging market countries is determined by Eurasia's east–west geographical layout and the north–south layout in Africa and the Americas. Since climate changes little with longitude but quite rapidly with latitude, the Eurasian landmass enjoyed fairly uniform climatic conditions that cultivated that spread of plant and animal varieties throughout the region. In contrast, new varieties developed in the Americas or in Africa could not migrate very far, limiting the technological potential of these regions and stunting market growth in these emerging markets. Entrepreneurs entering such markets need to consider the vicious cycle of technological constraints alongside any opportunities for growth.

Evidently, it is not so much the digital divide that separates the growth of advanced economies and the emerging markets as the geographical constraints on the proliferation of technologies that underlie basic sustenance-related needs. For instance, Latin American countries soon will have more cellular phones than regular telephone lines, allowing for a major expansion in the region's telecommunications system by bypassing the need to install underground cables. In contrast, the dramatic difference between advanced and emerging markets in agricultural and pharmaceutical R&D render the latter countries underdeveloped and less attractive as consumer bases for foreign entrepreneurs.

With the economy in the developed countries succumbing to more financial stress—incomes stagnating, entitlement costs rising, governments facing deficits, and people more value conscious—high-quality products at reasonable prices are in demand. This convergence in the economic preferences of consumers in both the advanced and emerging economies has paved the way for more cross-pollination in commercial technological breakthroughs. In health care, for example, GE produced a computerized tomography (CT) scan machine that is functional without a lot of bells and whistles. It was designed originally for the Chinese market where patients without insurance pay out of pocket for CT scans.

Given increasing demands for simple technologies around the world, the emerging markets provide a ready platform for technological progress in consumer products that entrepreneurial firms from abroad may partake in. In such a context, being creative about empowering local market entrepreneurs allows entrepreneurial firms from abroad to learn from their successes. When Whirlpool decided to establish a separate Central Europe operation in the early/mid-1990s, for example, they found a young entrepreneur in Hungary selling Whirlpool refrigerators out of a pickup truck and made him president of Whirlpool Hungary.

By holding its leaders accountable for absolute profit rather than traditional gross margin metrics and resourcefully leveraging local entrepreneurship, Whirlpool obtained strong absolute profits and a 30% market share. By Western Europe's standards, Whirlpool's operating profit in Hungary may not be high, but emerging markets as such need to be assessed using relative metrics and for their potential as hosts for back office operations and platforms for making developed country technologies ubiquitous.

4P Analysis of Marketing to Emerging Markets

Price

Even as competition between firms is ever prevalent on a global scale, the emerging markets are characterized with an unprecedented level of growth in local business activity among emerging market countries. For instance, with China having displaced the United States as the largest trading partner of both Brazil and India, trade between emerging economies is poised to overtake that between developed economies.

Products and services will accordingly converge at regionally delimited price points as more consumerism and competition gains traction in the emerging markets. At the same time, region-wide price lags behind the emerging markets are accompanied by both domestic and foreign entrepreneurial opportunities. After designing and building the Tata Nano, a vehicle priced at $2,500 to address the needs of the emerging middle class in India, for example, Tata undertook a large number of acquisitions around the world, the most notable being Jaguar and Land Rover. An implication for foreign entrepreneurs is the pressing need to generate more breakthrough innovations with ever decreasing resources.

Another prominent factor in pricing decisions for the emerging markets is the extent to which food expenditure absorbs the disposable income of households. The rise of urbanization in emerging markets has spurred a rise in disposable income. In Africa, for example, Kenya and Algeria showed the largest percentage increases, respectively, at 95% and 73%, between 2007 and 2012. Nigeria and South Africa also experienced dramatic increases, both at nearly 60%. However, poor logistics and institutional voids in many of these emerging markets render food purchases extremely expensive, leading to consumers to be price sensitive with other items.

Entrepreneurs targeting market segments in the emerging markets therefore need to tailor product offerings to the bottom of the pyramid as well as the business buyers that may have more flexibility in dealing with high-price items. As proposed by C. K. Prahalad, doing business at "the bottom of the pyramid" refers to lifting billions of people out of poverty and desperation, averting social decay, political chaos, terrorism, and avoiding environmental meltdown. Serving the world's 4 billion poorest people—or two-thirds of the world's population—will require radical innovations in technology and business models that redefine price–performance relationships for products and services. The focus in these emerging markets, as Prahalad argued, must shift from price to value.

Place

The means by which products and services are provided to consumers in emerging markets are shaped in large part by the physical landscapes that characterize these countries, given their lack of hard roads and transport links. Firms in emerging markets have responded to such infrastructure deficiencies by developing innovative distribution systems that also incorporate consumers into the supply chain. For instance, Peruvian soft-drink manufacturer AJE found success by mobilizing local microentrepreneurs who use their own transportation to reach untapped consumers in remote areas. Especially in remote areas of the world, it seems that local support makes a big difference. As such, it may be prudent for SMEs from developed countries to cultivate trusted relationships before venturing into global manufacturing in the emerging markets.

In response to increased consumer demand for packaged food items, supermarkets have appeared throughout Southern and Eastern Africa, accounting for nearly 40% of the market for packaged food in Kenya, and continue to proliferate beyond middle-class big city markets into smaller towns and poorer townships. However, other types of distribution channels still carry weight on the continent. In Algeria, Morocco, and Cameroon, for example, independent small grocers account for around 60% of all distribution channels, whereas in Nigeria, "other grocery retailers," such as kiosks and outdoor markets make up nearly 50% (Euromonitor International, 2013). In addition, discounters and forecourt retailers have also been gaining share across Africa. In comparison, Central and Eastern European countries are dominated by hypermarkets. Thus, the length and breadth of distribution outlets in the emerging markets vary widely, and entrepreneurial firms from abroad should evaluate the costs and benefits of each type of distributional channel in light of their products.

In addition, creativity in distribution methods may be helpful in navigating the different landscapes in the emerging markets. For example, when P&G entered Romania in 1994, it had to invent a new distribution system for soap in order to serve the small kiosks that dotted the countryside in the absence of hypermarkets. Whirlpool tried a similar program in 1995 in Hungary, setting aside standard operating procedure (and gross margin and data gathering requirements) in order to allow a third tier of entrepreneurs in smaller cities to resell the company's products to build brand awareness and market share. The success of this experiment created new best practices that have since been replicated in several other emerging markets.

Product

Rather than identifying traditional target markets, such as neighboring countries or countries with a common language, firms pursuing growth in emerging markets increasingly look for consumer segments in particular cities or customer segments that may straddle national borders. For example, Procter & Gamble identified the needs of male consumers in areas with scarce water supplies and designed grooming products for this group in multiple markets. Within three months of launch, one shaving product became the best-selling product of its kind in India (Reuters, 2013). The experience of such MNEs underscores the importance of local relevance, which should be even more important to entrepreneurs entering such markets with limited resources.

As another example involving a domestic firm, in China's rural Sichuan province, Haier sells washing machines designed and labeled to wash "clothes, sweet potatoes and peanuts." The constrained budgets of households in the emerging markets present foreign entrepreneurs with opportunities to satisfy multiple needs with fewer products that possess innovative features. For firms with established products, testing the products in specific emerging market countries before manufacturing locally may represent a strategic approach that combines effectiveness with efficiency motives. The ability of foreign brands to penetrate an emerging market economy depends largely on the grasp of local needs, which given the cultural distances between the advanced and emerging economies often require extensive local input.

The level of brand awareness is also uneven throughout the emerging markets, with certain age groups particularly in tune with brands in sectors such as consumer products. Henkel, the laundry and home care company from Germany, started exporting consumer detergents and cosmetics to Eastern Europe in 1984. Rather than build greenfield operations, Henkel developed a staged approach, leveraging joint venture partners with a high market share, production capabilities, and a known brand, and investing in them, improving the recipes, and slowly substituting premium brands. As a manager noted: "we develop the market with a partner and later take over up to 100 percent... you have to start with local brands because washing habits are different from country to country." The need for SMEs to adequately incorporate local preferences and customs makes focus groups and market research especially important before developing products for emerging market countries.

Promotion

The sophistication of the media infrastructure in an emerging market is important to assess, especially for firms that rely on advertising and brand-name recognition. In Brazil, Coca-Cola used social media to better understand consumer preferences and developed a successful local network to supply traditional Coca-Cola products as well as fruit juices tailored to local tastes. In addition, although not as salient of a problem for entrepreneurial firms as established firms, brand counterfeiting affects the emerging markets more than advanced countries. As a result, firms in countries like China and Russia tend to incur higher costs of policing their brands. The costs associated with contractual breaches and potential legal dealings may render foreign entrepreneurial firms disadvantaged compared to both local players and larger foreign competitors.

In addition, it is not new knowledge that the emerging markets generally lag behind advanced economies in terms of technology and reliable data. This is true not only for the least developed countries but also for European countries such as Romania and Bulgaria. However, precisely due to the lack of publicly available information, the value of sophisticated market intelligence is higher by magnitudes for promoting products and services in emerging markets. For example, DHL has leveraged its data from operating in many markets to pursue opportunities in emerging market regions, flying into Czechoslovakia 10 days after the communist government resigned. At this point DHL has developed the ability to confidently enter countries by testing new initiatives based on their experience and gut feel. However, for entrepreneurial firms with fewer resources, it may be less risky to rely on intuition than on a trusted local source.

Finally, promotion efforts in emerging market economies that take into account the availability of market intelligence may result in synergies across business segments. SMEs that invest in analytics capabilities to maximize the value of existing proprietary customer data where market data is scarce will have a distinct advantage over competition both foreign and local. Analysis of projected demand for specific products and services in multiple target locations can help determine which demographics to target and when. Powerful new mobile and social media tools can help improve the collection of reliable local data and insights direct from consumers. For example, Mexican retailer Grupo Elektra used detailed customer data to diversify into financial services and built a large network of bank branches to complement its retail chain. Indeed, the knowledge required of customers may make the promotion function the most specific of the 4Ps for any given emerging market country.

Entrepreneurial Strategies in Emerging Markets

A study of Canadian entrepreneurial firms over the period 1994–2008, conducted by researchers at the Conference Board of Canada, reveals some common denominators of a small group of these exporting firms that almost doubled their sales every year in emerging markets. These SMEs had previous experience in domestic or industrialized markets, constantly innovated to introduce new products to these markets, paid higher wages—signaling higher productivity and higher skilled employees, diversified their risk by exporting to a larger number of markets, had greater access to financing, and were relatively larger in size than their counterparts (closer to 500 employees).

According to the study, SMEs that lacked these attributes could pursue other strategies in order to enter emerging markets. One approach may be to become a supplier to MNEs already active in emerging markets, with the goal of developing capabilities in advanced markets prior to undertaking expansion to emerging market economies. The analysis also shows the downside to entering emerging markets without being fully prepared, revealing a huge gap between the best and worst performing entrepreneurial firms.

Among the SMEs with the weakest performance, sales to emerging markets dropped by 70% annually on average, with these firms making full exits within the year. Evidently, the liabilities of smallness and newness are especially salient in contexts involving high risk and high rewards. Even established multinationals realize a need to employ a stepping-stone approach in entering emerging markets. Skoda, for example, chose to enter markets in Eastern Europe and Asia by building wholly owned local car plants over a long period of time, as importing cars into these emerging markets would have been difficult due to luxury import taxes, local-content requirements, and the need to develop local dealerships and after sales support.

In addition to well-established competition, entrepreneurial firms venturing to emerging markets need to tackle the diversity of growth opportunities and pace of change and do so better than home-grown competitors with in-born advantages. These local players know how to leverage scale advantages with low costs and, in some cases, government support and other established relationships. They face similar operational challenges in their home countries as in neighboring emerging markets, such as dealing with infrastructure deficits and scarce or unreliable data. They increasingly conduct business with their counterparts across borders, gaining insights and experience on how to best serve one another's markets. Their inherent advantage over competitors from mature economies unfamiliar with operating in such conditions increase the latter's liability of foreignness.

Knowledge asymmetry adds to the potential risks faced by foreign firms. Russia, for example, presents incredibly complex regulatory rules and bureaucratic procedures. To take advantage of the potential of this emerging market, it is important to be armed with intimate knowledge of the country, its business practices, and its commercial and tax systems. Taking a cue from multinationals, a viable means for entrepreneurs to enter emerging markets may be to collaborate with local players. For example, Carrefour, the leading French grocery retailer, partnered with African distribution company CFAO to expand its presence in Nigeria, Cote d'Ivoire, and Ghana in 2013. In response to the increasing demand for trendy fashion in Africa, the Spanish clothing retailer Zara entered Kenya in 2013 through a distribution agreement with local retailer Deacons.

Piggybacking on key customers as they expand in emerging markets is an effective approach for entrepreneurial firms from advanced economies. Cargill's agricultural products group was initially pulled into Eastern Europe in the early 1990s by its customers, who needed local ingredients as they started selling consumer product such as candy bars. The company eventually bought another firm in Russia for less than a million dollars, slowly learning how to operate in the country until they felt comfortable. When Russia had its financial crisis in 1998, Cargill decided to stay, which not only helped them to persist in building relationships and knowledge in an important market, but also to capitalize on the greater demand for locally produced food products from the currency devaluation. After expanding on its first acquisition to build plants for producing fats, malt, oils, and pigments, Cargill then entered neighboring countries such as Poland, Romania, and Turkey after conducting a market analysis that focused on factors like population and agricultural base.

Human resources strategy may need to be configured specifically for each emerging market entered. As a result of the presence of firms like DHL and the German stock exchange, bright information technology graduates in places like Prague are not readily available for low wages. For this and other reasons, proactively shaping the dialog with labor is key for foreign SMEs entering emerging markets, where unions are often nonexistent or immature. In addition, it may be important for foreign entrepreneurs to take a regional view of hiring in emerging market contexts. In Slovakia, for instance, where there are only four million people, foreign companies that view people applying for jobs from Hungary, Ukraine, Poland, etc., as part of their potential labor pool are the ones that obtain advantageous access to human capital. This regional paradigm will only strengthen with increasing formal economic integration and informal cultural exchanges facilitated by communication technologies around the world.

As a result of uneven distributions of talent and demand conditions, location strategy is important for entrepreneurial firms in emerging markets. Many countries have designated cities that offer lower tax rates and other investment incentives to attract foreign investors. For instance, Chile has declared as free-trade zones the northern city of Iquique and the southern city of Punta Arenas for the purpose of import duties. In addition, given their immense diversity, the emerging markets render a regional approach less attractive than a "global hub" model for both purchasing and selling decisions. That is, the pockets of knowledge present in even certain emerging markets for *certain* domains makes it more resourceful to view countries as pockets of expertise than embedded in a region, per se. For instance, China is known as a hub for industrial buyers of aluminum, because it has the best processes, the volume, as well as the domain knowledge.

Getting involved in local communities is a valuable locally responsive strategy for doing business in emerging markets. For instance, Cargill became perceived as a local company in Eastern Europe by helping with schools or hospitals. However, as with many other aspects of doing business in the emerging markets, countries vary greatly on the dimension of how much goodwill is generated from appealing to community stakeholders. For instance, in China there is little interest in this area because the Chinese tend to be of the opinion that they know perfectly well what is good for their communities.

In addition, networking with local entrepreneurs may not only provide a chance to give back to the community, but offer foreign entrepreneurs invaluable sources of information and inspiration. The opportunities for engaging local entrepreneurs should grow exponentially as the entrepreneurial profession and lifestyle gain traction in the emerging markets. While people in the emerging markets often resort to borrowing for immediate consumption needs, the findings of a survey conducted by Gallup World Poll revealed that the second highest reason given for saving in sub-Saharan Africa was to start a business.

Depending on the balance of strategic benefits, costs and risks associated with an expansion to emerging markets, as discussed earlier, the expanding company can choose from different entry strategies: exporting (direct or indirect), employing foreign sales representatives and importing distributors, international franchising and licensing, turnkey projects, wholly owned subsidiaries, or international joint ventures.

Some comparative advantages and disadvantages of these entry strategies are summarized in Figure 14.1.

ENTRY MODE	ADVANTAGES	DISADVANTAGES
Exporting	Ability to realize location and experience curve economies	High transport costs Trade barriers Problems with local marketing agents
Turnkey contracts	Ability to earn returns from process technology skills in countries where FDI is restricted	Creating efficient competitors Lack of long-term market presence
Licensing	Low development costs and risks	Lack of control over technology Inability to realize location and experience curve economies Inability to engage in global strategic coordination
Franchising	Low development costs and risks	Lack of control over quality Inability to engage in global strategic coordination
Joint ventures	Access to local partner's knowledge Sharing development costs and risks Politically acceptable	Lack of control over technology Inability to engage in global strategic coordination Inability to realize location and experience economies
Wholly owned subsidiaries	Protection of technology Ability to engage in global strategic coordination Ability to realize location experience economies	High costs and risks

Source: Hill, 2013

Figure 14.1   Entry Strategies in International Expansion: Advantages and Disadvantages

The simplest, although perhaps not so much in absolute as in relative terms, and most common, entry strategy utilized by SMEs is exporting/importing. The US Department of Commerce provides US-based exporters with a wealth of information and support for international trade (http://export.gov/index.asp). In the context of our discussion, a particularly useful analytical tool is the Step-by-Step Approach to Market Research (http://export.gov) summarized below.

Step-by-Step Approach to Foreign Market Research

Step 1. Find Potential Markets

- Obtain *trade statistics* that indicate which countries import your type(s) of products.

- Perform a thorough review of the available *market research reports* in the country(ies) and industries in question to determine market openness, common practices, tariffs and taxes, distribution channels, and other important considerations.

- Identify 5–10 large and fast-growing markets for the firm's product(s). Analyze them over the past 3–5 years for market growth in good and bad times.

- Identify some smaller but fast-emerging markets where there may be fewer competitors.

- Target three to five of the most statistically promising markets for further assessment. Consult with the nearest *US Export Assistance Center*.

Step 2. Assess Targeted Markets

- Examine consumption and production of competitive products, as well as overall demographic and economic trends in the target country.

- Ascertain the sources of competition, including the extent of domestic industry production and the major home countries of firms that the firm would compete against.

- Analyze factors affecting marketing and use of the product in each market, such as end-user sectors, channels of distribution, cultural idiosyncrasies, and business practices.

- Identify any foreign barriers (*tariff or nontariff*) for the product being imported into the country and identify any *US export controls*.

- Identify United States or foreign incentives to promote the export of your product or service.

- Determine whether your product is price competitive after packaging, shipping, marketing, sales commissions, taxes & tariffs, and other associated costs have been accounted for. See *pricing considerations*.

Step 3. Draw Conclusions

If the company is new to exporting, it is probably a good idea to target two or three markets initially. A local *Export Assistance Center* can provide valuable insight into "optimal" market opportunities.

Step 4. Test Demand

There are a number of low-cost on-line and off-line services that can help new exporters gauge foreign market interest and collect overseas inquiries:

- *Catalog Exhibitions*
- *Commercial News USA*
- *Foreign Partner Matching and Trade Lead Services*

Summary

In conclusion, the strategies that generate above-average performance in developed markets may not necessarily work in emerging market contexts, as giants like Carrefour, McDonalds, and others have discovered. New sets of strategic approaches, insights and assumptions are needed, especially for SMEs with limited resources and vicarious knowledge of the international arena. Indeed, oftentimes, even strategies appropriate for well-known emerging market countries such as China and India may not suffice for tackling markets like Myanmar, Vietnam, Russia, South Africa, and Latin America. To succeed in emerging markets, smaller firms and individual entrepreneurs often need to overcome a host of policy barriers, rapidly grasp the nuances of the local markets, and find trusted local partners, all with relatively fewer resources and talent compared with large companies. Given the informal economy that characterizes many of these markets, it will be important for entrepreneurs to engage relevant stakeholders at the grassroots in seeking to create value on their nascent business landscape.

Skill Development Exercise 1

Memo

To: XXX class

From: Instructor

Date: [   ]

Re: Skill development exercise: comparative assessment of the attractiveness, costs, and risks of expansion to emerging markets:

Goal: skill development in global strategic positioning in emerging markets (EM).

You are part of EM Consult, a US-based international consulting firm. XYZ, your client, is a big international conglomerate planning an aggressive international expansion in manufacturing with its business units (divisions) operating in the following industries:

MANUFACTURING		RESEARCH & DEVELOPMENT	DIGITAL
• Aerospace	• Medical devices	• Biotechnology	• Digital entertainment
• Agri-food	• Metal components	• Clinical trials	• Software design
• Automotive	• Pharmaceuticals	• Product testing	**CORPORATE SERVICES**
• Chemicals	• Plastics		• Professional services
• Electronics	• Precision manufacturing		• Support services
• Green energy	• Telecommunications		

EM Consult is asked to make recommendations for XYZ on the best emerging market (country) location worldwide to minimize short-term costs and risks. Meanwhile, in 5–10 years XYZ intends to expand from manufacturing only to marketing its products in the region.

Assignment: estimated completion time—30 min

1. Work individually or in groups of 2.

2. Go to the globalEDGE http://globaledge.msu.edu/knowledge-tools/mpi and look at the table of the latest available Market Potential Indicators for Emerging Markets report.

   - Out of the 26 countries included in the list, select three best (target) emerging markets with the highest overall rating: one from Asia, one from Europe, and one from South/Central America.

3. Go to the 2016 COMPETITIVE ALTERNATIVES report by KPMG at http://www.competitivealternatives.com/. Choose an industry that you like (no need to coordinate your choice with the instructor or other students/ groups in class).

   - Identify best location (country) for a production/manufacturing facility based on the lowest overall cost of operation in your chosen industry from KPMG report.

4. Go to the World Bank's DOING BUSINESS web site: http:// www.doingbusiness.org/. Click on the GET ALL DATA link in the upper right corner. In the *"Choose Economies"* → SHOW ALL → check your three target markets identified in step 1; In the *"Choose Topics"* → check STARTING A BUSINESS, TRADING ACROSS BORDERS, and ENFORCING CONTRACTS; In *"Which Data Years do You Wish to Display?"* → check DOING BUSINESS [THE LATEST REPORT].

   - Click on the "Create report" button on the right-hand side. Contrast and compare the costs of starting a business in the best cost-effective country from the KPMG report with the three emerging target markets from step 2.

5. Go to the Credendo group/ONDD web site at http://www.ducroire.be/ WebONDD/WebSite.nsf/weben/Country+risks?OpenDocument and identify strategic risks of doing business in these three target emerging markets by clicking on these countries in the scroll-down window on the right-hand side.

Report your findings to the class (please be specific) and give a recommendation to XYZ on the best location (country) for expansion.

Skill Development Exercise 2

Memo

To: XXX class

From: Instructor

Date: [   ]

Re: Step-by-Step Approach to Export-Related Market Research

You are acting as an individual EMERGING MARKETS business consultant. XYZ, your US-based client firm, has been briefed about healthy returns in overseas business and is seeking your advice on international business expansion. XYZ asked you to conduct an international marketing feasibility study and develop strategic recommendations for its international expansion.

Your international business feasibility study should map out your client's international expansion and set up a business venture with a view of a medium-term success (a profitable business). Your client limits your choice by one of the emerging markets; no other limitations, constraints, or conditions imposed on your research (it is your task to advice on those issues, if any).

Assignment:

1. Select 1 (one) product or service from business proposals/ads that you like the most (please refer to "COMMERCIAL NEWS USA" at http://www.thinkglobal.us/). There is no need to coordinate your choice with other class members. For verification, please include in your report a one-page electronic copy (picture) of your chosen product.

2. Based on the chosen product/service, conduct a comprehensive market research and find the best market (country) for your client's international business expansion. Use a step-by-step international market research methodology at http://export.gov.

3. Suggest and provide justification a practical entry strategy (exporting, joint venture, licensing/franchise, or a wholly owned subsidiary).

4. Give your assessment of strategic benefits/costs/risks and contingency strategies related to your recommendations.

Report your findings to the class. Be specific in a justification of your recommendations.

References

Accenture (2013). Fast forward to growth: Seizing opportunities in high-growth markets. Retrieved from http://www.accenture.com/us-en/Pages/insight-fast-forward-growth-seizing-opportunities-high-growth-markets.aspx (accessed March 21, 2014)..

Ernst & Young. (2011a). Doing business in Brazil.

Ernst & Young. (2011b). Doing business in Kazakhstan.

Ernst & Young. (2011c). Doing business in Poland.

Euromonitor International. (2013). Business opportunities and challenges in Africa. Retrieved from http://mba.americaeconomia.com/sites/mba.americaeconomia.com/files/business_opportunities_and_challenges_in_africa.pdf (accessed April 1, 2014).

Food and Agriculture Organisation of the United Nations. (2013). The state of food insecurity in the world.

International Finance Corporation. (2013). Closing the credit gap for formal and informal micro, small, and medium enterprises.

Reuters. (2013). How smart businesses are winning in emerging markets. Retrieved from http://blogs.reuters.com/great-debate/2013/02/22/how-smart-businesses-are-winning-in-emerging-markets/ (accessed January 20, 2014).

The World Bank. (2016). Iraq's economic outlook—Spring 2017. Retrieved from http://www.worldbank.org/en/country/iraq/publication/economic-outlook-spring-2016 (accessed April 20, 2017).

The World Bank. Africa Competitiveness Report. (2013).

Latin America

Karla Mendoza-Abarca and
Frank Hoy

Worcester Polytechnic Institute

Key Terms

CAFTA

Family roles

Import substitution

Industrialization

NAFTA

Neoliberalism

Privatization

Property rights

Learning Objectives

Upon completion of this chapter, students should be able to:

1. Understand the environment presented to an entrepreneur interested in Latin America: history, geography, and language; government and legal system; economic structure; culture and religion; educational system; demographics and physical infrastructure; industrial structure; trade agreements and associations; import or export information; and small business practices.

Introduction

Latin America is a region of great diversity, yet with some remarkable consistencies as related to political and economic history and conditions. Although other factors have been at play, it is primarily through politics, cultures, and economics that we can comprehend the environments for entrepreneurship across Latin America.

This is a region that stretches from Mexico, through Central America, to South America and down to the Southern Cone. Many island countries of the Caribbean Basin are also considered part of Latin America due to historic colonization and language dominance.

History, Geography, and Languages[1]

Archeologists peg the first migrations from Asia to the Americas at approximately 35,000 years ago. Tribal groups concentrated in the Pacific Northwest for eons, with initial incursions into South America occurring 25,000 years later. Nomadic tribes began small crop development, eventually evolving into city and regional states in many areas. During the European colonization period, two predominant empires had arisen: the Incas—now Peru and neighboring countries—and the Aztecs—modern-day Mexico.

The indigenous populations throughout were severely depleted following the European conquest beginning in the sixteenth century. War, disease, enslavement, and dislocation had disastrous effects. The early economies resulting from European settlement were labeled hacienda forms of land use. This practice combined Iberian and American Indian systems. Many pre-Columbian Indians were clustered in communal villages loosely governed by absentee aristocratic landlords. The Spaniards overlaid this system through huge royal land grants. They imposed taxes, but were expected to protect the natives and educate them in the Catholic faith.

Conquest and colonization were led by Spain and Portugal, countries speaking Romance languages derived from Latin, hence the term Latin America. A third Romance-language country, France, bequeathed its language to Haiti, French Guiana, and the French West Indies. Despite the decimation of the Indians described above, many tribal groups flourish to this day and use their native languages. At least, 50 distinct language groups are identified in modern-day Mexico alone.

The large landholding systems survived through revolutionary periods as the various colonies in Latin America won their independence from the Europeans. *Criollos*, American-born descendants of Europeans, emerged as the political and economic elite, controlling indigenous populations through the *hacienda* system. Resources for export and domestic use were in the hands of large landowners. Eventually, industrialization began to change the political and economic environments of the continent in the nineteenth century. Yet, the region remains characterized by family capitalism in which elite entrepreneurial families control large businesses or business groups (Dávila, 2012).

---

[1]Unless otherwise indicated, the source of information on Latin America is the *New Encyclopædia Britannica*, 2002.

The map showing the nations of Latin America looks today much similar to what it did in the post-revolutionary period of the 1800s. There is extraordinary variation in the geography of the Americas. The Western Hemisphere from Mexico to Chile contains islands as well as the continental land mass. Beginning with oceans on both sides of the continent, to lowlands, high plains, volcanoes, highlands, and mountain ranges, the region consists of deserts, tropical rain forests, temperate zones, and more. Until recent advances in transportation, communication, and information technology, opportunities for entrepreneurs were defined and often restricted by the geography of the location of their enterprise. Even today, the dominance of the micro-enterprises in the small business sector results in local firms using local resources to satisfy local needs.

Government and Legal Systems

Following colonial exploitation, Latin America splintered into multiple nations, often controlled by political, military, and economic elites. There was a continuation of the suppression and deprivation of the indigenous populations. The earliest constitutions were adopted in the beginning of the nineteenth century and were designed for representative governments. The failures of these initial governments led to greater centralization of political power.

Latin American countries have been characterized by frequent changes in government, although the underlying political structures may have evolved in very different ways. For some, the shape of governance derived from revolution. Examples would be Bolivia, Cuba, and Mexico. Others have been affected by extended periods of military rule. Some of the countries in this category are Argentina, Brazil, and Peru. A third force shaping political development is constitutional democracy, with Chile, Colombia, and Venezuela as examples (Sigmund, 1970).

The global depression of the 1930s began a period of aggressive state involvement in economic systems that continues in many Latin American countries to the present. Political leaders expanded government functions to stabilize and improve their national economies. They also increased the role of the state in addressing social problems. In some countries, this resulted in legislation that subordinated property rights to the social needs of the population.

The twentieth century saw a reduced role of the Church, increased nationalism, experiments with various ideologies, including socialism, communism, and fascism. By the end of the century, some form of democracy prevailed in most countries, with the Communist dictatorship in Cuba as an exception.

Two major factors discouraging entrepreneurs from creating and growing legitimate businesses are (1) the lack of access to capital due to extensive government debt and (2) perceived unfairness of judicial systems. If a prospective business owner questions whether property rights will be protected and whether contracts will be upheld, the risk associated with the venture is magnified. For instance, to enforce a contract through the courts, an entrepreneur can expect to pay around 31% of the claim in attorney, court, and enforcement fees. It may take 749 days on average from the time the case is filed until the enforcement of the ruling (World Bank, 2017). This cumbersome process deters entrepreneurs from even filing a claim.

Despite the political turmoil and weak legal systems in the region, countries such as Argentina, Brazil, and Chile have developed relatively higher quality legal systems and reduced their political hazards. This in turn has encouraged sizable venture capital investments directed toward early- and middle-stage ventures (Khoury, Junkunc, & Mingo, 2010).

Economic Structure

Preceding the Conquest, the Americas were sparsely populated with few cities of any size. Economies were primarily agricultural, with some nomadic tribes and hunter gatherers. Although there were merchants who carried on trade among various peoples and across considerable distances, inter-tribal warfare was endemic and shaped many cultures and economies.

European conquerors introduced feudal economic systems through which they extracted resources for the benefit of the mother countries. Eventually, a merchant class began to emerge to provide a distribution system both for the silver trade[2] and for the produce of the haciendas. Mercantile economies were built on the backs of slave labor, both Indian and African.

It is interesting to observe, in our current era of trade debate, that Spain instituted free trade throughout its possessions in the New World in the latter half of the 1700s. Commercial trade volume increased dramatically at this time, though cause and effect are not clear. Population grew considerably in the region, and industrial growth was expanding the economies of Europe, creating markets for the materials from mines and farms.

It may be noted that the economic growth combined with English control of trade routes to Europe contributed to struggles for independence as the colonies engaged in greater commerce among themselves. The revolutions during the first quarter of the nineteenth century, however, had a devastating effect on the economies of the newly independent nations. Compounding the destruction of lives and property were the foreign debt burdens and lack of infrastructure. All this led to a shortage of capital for business investment. In the latter half of the century, the situation reversed with extensive foreign investment focusing both on technological advances for basic industries and on the export of raw materials. A negative consequence was the evolution of single-product economies in many countries.

According to Dietz and Street (1987), the Great Depression of the 1930s was magnified in Latin America due to its dependence on export and import markets. Countries suffered successions of balance of trade crises. They responded by shifting their political and economic interests from the landed oligarchies toward

---

[2]For the Portuguese, the primary export was brazilwood, closely followed by sugar.

production by incipient capitalists. Governments erected trade barriers as they instituted import substitution industrialization strategies. Figure 15.1 summarizes the stages of economic development for the region.

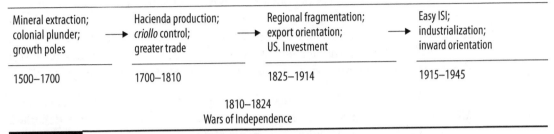

Mineral extraction; colonial plunder; growth poles	→	Hacienda production; *criollo* control; greater trade	→	Regional fragmentation; export orientation; US. Investment	→	Easy ISI; industrialization; inward orientation
1500–1700		1700–1810		1825–1914		1915–1945

1810–1824
Wars of Independence

Figure 15.1 Stages of Latin America's Development, 1500–1945

Source: Dietz and Street, 1987, p. 8.

The regional commission of the United Nations, the Economic Commission for Latin America, and the Caribbean labeled the five decades of the second half of the twentieth century as indicated below (ECLAC, 2003)[3]:

- The 1950s: industrialization through import substitution
- The 1960s: reforms to facilitate industrialization
- The 1970s: reorientation of development "styles" toward social homogeneity and toward diversification as a means of promoting exports
- The 1980s: overcoming the external debt crisis through "adjustment with growth"
- The 1990s: changing production patterns with social equity

The post-World War II years were generally good ones for Latin American economies. By the 1980s, however, what had been described as economic miracles were turning sour. Dietz and James (1990) listed the following as the driving factors in economic development:

1. Science and technology
2. Debt crises
3. Neoliberalism
4. Economic slump

Dietz and James contended that governments and lenders overexpanded in unrealistic expectations of continued growth. They found that countries continued to be overly specialized in product categories, for example, Brazil and Columbia in coffee, Chile in copper, Costa Rica in bananas, and Panama is dependent on the Canal. Academic studies in science and technology led to lower status careers than law and other professions. Thus, science and technology developments were not

[3]In Spanish, the acronym is CEPAL, Comisión Económica para América Latina y el Caribe.

supported from within, and talented individuals were not attracted to those fields. Spikes in oil prices in the 1970s helped some countries and hurt others, but in the longer term hurt all due to borrowing. The economic slump of the 1980s created debt crises, which were exacerbated by the protectionist policies focused on industrial development. Neoliberal policies included credit tightening, which in turn limited capital for prospective entrepreneurs and for business owners. Restricting the development of new businesses generated a feeling of economic frustration among the population, which enabled recurrent periods of populism that gave rise to political and economic crises in the region (Larroulet & Couyoumdjian, 2009).

Many countries engaged in neoliberal approaches to managing their economies. While lifting trade barriers and encouraging foreign investment, some defaulted on loans and others rescheduled repayments. Interest rates were boosted to control inflation. State enterprises were privatized and regulations reduced on industries. Countries entered into free trade agreements. Economic conditions varied significantly among Latin American countries in the 1990s, but there was general growth corresponding to the strengthening of democratic political systems. The first decade of the twenty-first century was characterized by uneven economic growth in the region, which resulted in slow GDP expansion. Countries such as Chile, Panama, and Peru significantly improved their economic activity, while two of the biggest economies, Brazil and Mexico, lagged behind (ECLAC, 2013). During the second decade of the twenty-first century, the region experienced an economic slowdown reaching an average GDP growth rate of only 0.9% in 2014, a significant decrease from the 2.9% growth rate a year earlier. The South America subregion reported the lowest GDP growth rate in the region at 0.6%, while Central America reported the highest rate at 4% (ECLAC, 2016).

In the modern era, "Latin America's history is replete with economic reforms that have failed due to the lack of credibility" (Edwards, 1991, p. 158). Credibility has been lost by the reversals of reforms that have occurred with changes in governments and by the lack of internal consistency of some of the reform strategies. Continuing bottlenecks to economic development include inefficient supply systems for food products, rigidity in government tax and expenditure structures, insufficient internal savings, and the lack of supply of intermediate agricultural and industrial inputs. Some examples are fuels, fertilizers, transportation facilities, and credit availability. Additionally, there are many sections of Latin America that continue to be relatively closed market systems. These are typically geographically isolated areas in which residents communicate in local Indian dialects. The citizenry of these areas often lack education and are impoverished, limiting the interest by other groups in engaging them in trade.

One of the changes in direction of national governments in recent years has been the movement away from national control of industries. Several countries have experimented with privatization, much along the lines of the former Soviet Republics and Soviet satellite countries. For example, in Mexico there were almost 1200 state-owned enterprises in 1982. By 1994, that number had been reduced to just over 200 (Rogozinski, 1999).

With the exception of Cuba, nearly all of Latin America can be described as functioning within capitalist systems. In terms of stages of economic development, most countries are factor-driven economies, with only the biggest economies in the region being efficiency-driven (López-Claros, Altinger, Blanke, Drzeniek, & Mía, 2006). Key facilitators for entrepreneurs tend to be state enterprise privatization, low labor costs, and free trade opportunities. Factors hindering entrepreneurship in current economic environments include lack of capital for starting and growing ventures, low education levels, and dysfunctional political involvement in the private sector (fiscal and monetary policies as well as corruption in some countries). Additionally, the cultural and religious heritages of the region have not been as supportive of risk taking and innovation in the private sector as other parts of the world.

Culture and Religion

As evidenced in the section on history, the culture of the region has been heavily influenced by the countries of the Iberian peninsula. The native populations on islands and coastal areas were culturally assimilated by the conquerors in many cases. Interior and isolated tribes and communities retained more of their beliefs longer, including religious and marital practices. With these groups there has been more of a blending as many languages and traditions were retained.

Catholic priests and missionaries were major influencing factors in imposing European values on the indigenous populace. Representatives of the Church sometimes protected and sometimes abused their charges. They traveled incredible distances enduring incredible hardships, often sacrificing their lives in the years following the conquests. Many of the priests became the historians both of the European colonizers and of the Indians they sought to convert.

Over the centuries, Roman Catholicism waxed and waned in its influence, but by most objective measures would have to be labeled a powerful force across the continent. Historically, the Church played a conservative role and was aligned with social, political and economic elites. In the twentieth century, evangelical Protestant denominations began having a more visible presence. Mainstream Catholicism continued to espouse traditional Church doctrine, but emphasized social advancement, criticizing dictatorial regimes and the failure of capitalism to result in more egalitarian societies.

In many Latin American countries, culture and traditions are succumbing to corruption and violence (De Soto, 2003). Public sector corruption extends from petty bribery of low level officials to indictments of elected officials at the highest levels for misappropriation of public funds and other crimes. Civil insurrections once associated with political ideologies have degenerated to acts of terrorism, often connected with drug trafficking. Drug-related violence has also affected entrepreneurs and their business ventures. The national manufacturing industry chamber[4]

---

[4]In Spanish the acronym is CANACINTRA, Camara Nacional de la Industria de la Transformación

estimated that, in Mexico alone, 10,000 small and medium enterprises were put out of business in 2010. The closings were mostly due to extortions and threats by criminal groups (Miglierini, 2011).

Despite the weakening influence of the Church, abuses in the public sector, and crime and insurgencies, various traditions and values continue to be deeply embedded in population groups in Latin America. Cochran (1960) contended that entrepreneurial activity is more a function of culture than economics. He contrasted three Latin American countries with the United States to make his point. He argued that cultures in Latin America were less supportive of economic development, based on the following distinctions:

1. Family interests supersede profit maximization.
2. Social and personal interests take precedence over business obligations.
3. Nepotism preempts able top management.
4. Managers and workers are less accepting of constructive criticism.

Young (1993) supported Cochran's observations about the role of family as both facilitator and obstacle for entrepreneurship in his study of business owners in Mexico, one of the three countries Cochran examined. An additional obstacle is that status in Latin American countries is more often associated with professional careers than with entrepreneurship. According to GEM, the Latin American and Caribbean region reports the lowest percentage of adults believing entrepreneurs are highly regarded. As such, a substantial share of the entrepreneurial activity in the region is motivated by necessity rather than opportunity (GEM, 2017). Entrepreneurs are perceived as individuals who are unable to otherwise join the workforce. In fact, as employment becomes available, entrepreneurs abandon their necessity-driven ventures in favor of formal employment (Acs & Amorós, 2008).

We see, therefore, that entrepreneurs are both affected by the cultural systems in which they abide and conduct business, and are also able to deviate from those traditions in order to innovate, create and grow their ventures. In Latin America, entrepreneurs appear to have to operate counter to the risk aversion inherent in the religious and cultural mores that dominate the region. Perhaps the most critical obstacle to economic development through entrepreneurship in Latin America is the low level of educational achievement of the general population.

Educational Systems

Few dispute the promise of education in enhancing the quality of life in Latin America, yet the record is dismal by nearly any standard. Although there have been gains in universal access, quality suffers. Segments of the population are excluded from higher education by a primary and secondary school system that encourages repetition and dropping out rather than excellence. Public primary education has been emaciated as dollars are funneled into public university systems. Teachers are poorly trained and managed. (Franko, 2003, p. 374).

According to United Nations' statistics, about one quarter of adults in Latin America and the Caribbean have not completed primary school and about half have not completed secondary schools. Some progress has been made on educational attainment, in 2014 94% of school-aged children were enrolled in primary education. However, the enrollment rate was 76% for upper secondary education (US high school equivalent), and only 44% for post-secondary education. The average illiteracy rate in the region amounts to 7% of the adult population, with some countries having rates in excess of 20% (UNESCO, 2016). Despite recent progress, inequality in education remains an issue inhibiting opportunity and class mobility. As of 2013, 80% of adults in the highest income bracket had completed secondary education, compared to only 34% of adults in the lowest income bracket (ECLAC, 2016). The recent wave of crime and violence has also contributed to low participation in formal schooling, limiting the number of skilled workers and inhibiting economic progress in the region (OECD/ECLAC/CAF, 2016; UNESCO, 2016).

Educational systems in Latin America tend to be centralized under ministries of education. Problems that occur among multiple countries include lack of qualified instructors, high rates of illiteracy, inequality between rural and urban schools, political instability, and inadequate provisions for Indian tribes. Adult education is recognized as a critical need. Many countries experience difficulty in keeping up with population growth and in preparing students for the rapid technology changes that impact industries. Higher educational programs have been characterized by imbalances between the courses of study offered and the economic development needs of the countries.

Expectations have risen along with improvements in communication and transportation. As with developed countries, education is perceived in lesser developed Latin American nations as a requisite for good employment and improved status. Studies have found that educational attainment is strongly related to social upward mobility. Notably, children of entrepreneurs tend to attain higher education levels (Castellani & Lora, 2013).

Education programs for entrepreneurship came later to Latin America than to Europe and the United States. The focus of education to date has been primarily on microenterprises and self-employment. This kind of programs, coupled with a poor emphasis on technology and science education, intensifies the prevalence of necessity-based entrepreneurship and hinders innovation. Latin America also lags behind in other innovation inputs such as R&D spending and number of scientists, and outputs such as number of patents and scientific journal publications (Olavarrieta & Villena, 2013; Gonzalez-Brambila, Jenkis, & Lloret, 2016).

Thus, entrepreneurship in the region is constrained on two fronts. Because entrepreneurs have higher levels of education than the general population, the failure to educate larger segments of population reduces the supply of business owners. Second, an undereducated workforce limits the availability of a qualified labor force for starting and growing enterprises. The latter is compounded by global competitiveness. Other regions of the world are paying lower wages to workers whose skills exceed those of the Latin Americans.

Demographics and Physical Infrastructure

Latin America was one of the fastest growing regions of the world during the twentieth century, with an annual rate in excess of 3% in many years. As a percentage of world population, Latin America nearly doubled from 4.5% in 1900 to 8.6% in 2016 (Population Reference Bureau, 2016). From 1960 to 1980, life expectancy in the region increased by ten years (Hartlyn & Morley, 1986). As of 2016, the estimated life expectancy was 72 years for males and 79 for females (Population Reference Bureau, 2016). The region's population was estimated in 2016 at 637 million (Population Reference Bureau, 2016). Growth rate declined in recent years to under 1.5%.

The twentieth century was also characterized by dramatic rural to urban migrations. It was estimated in 2013 that 80% of the population lived in urban areas (Population Reference Bureau, 2016). From 1950 to 1980, per capita income rose 2.4% per year. Overall, however, the period of import substitution industrialization ended in massive devaluations and a fall in real wages. By 2012, income per capita growth declined to 1.9% for the year (World Bank, 2012). Additionally, the prevalence of uneven income distribution resulted in a significant share of the population being at the base of the pyramid. This population continues to fuel the creation of informal businesses by acting as both entrepreneurs and customers (Vassolo, De Castro, & Gomez-Mejia, 2011). Economists project that the region will resume per capita income growth starting in 2017, though the expected growth rates are modest ranging from two to three percent (OECD/ECLAC/CAF, 2016).

Rapid industrial growth following World War II created huge demands for new and better roads, schools, telephones, water, and the government bureaucracies to oversee these expansions. This in turn led to tax increases. Tax increases in turn have generated increased tax avoidance by individuals and businesses. As a result, governments do not generate sufficient revenues to satisfy infrastructure demands caused by population growth and technological advancement.

Despite this bleak picture, wealth is being created in Latin America, though not evenly across the region. There are growing markets for entrepreneurs to penetrate. Recent economic growth has been largely due to increases in domestic consumption (ECLAC, 2013). Multinational corporations have recognized these opportunities by expanding their marketing efforts in many countries. Locally owned ventures are serving as suppliers and distributors for these foreign investments. Lagging infrastructure, however, handicaps entrepreneurial companies from expanding in the region.

Industrial Structures

As explained previously, the economies of Latin American countries were traditionally reliant on single products. The lack of export diversity resulted in declining productivity in industries that had diminishingly lucrative outputs (Dietz and Street, 1987). Lip service was paid to free markets, but the political systems neither permit free labor organizations nor free press. Until democratization movements took hold, the concentration of property and income were extreme. Transnational corporations held monopoly power in many industries.

A period of import substitution industrialization (ISI) was instigated by many governments beginning in the 1930s in an effort to stimulate the formation of domestic companies and reduce dependence on foreign investment and the implied external control associated with that investment. ISI policies typically involved the imposition of trade barriers and were accompanied by post-war decades of economic growth. Brazil applied this strategy in growing a minicomputer industry and an aeronautics industry. Immediately following World War II, some countries saw their imports increase due to pent up demand and dollar reserves having been accumulated. Local industries flourished, but needed more parts and materials and labor skills than the countries could supply. Attempts to protect local industries extended to suppliers, which had the downside of increasing costs because of inefficiencies.

Alternatively, the military governments of Argentina and Chile chose more open market courses. The policy of the regime in Chile was generally supported by the business community, whereas Argentina achieved less success and greater opposition from within. The Argentine government intervened in the private sector to the extent of dissolving associations of entrepreneurs in the 1970s (Ominami, 1991).

According to Story (1983), stereotypical industrial entrepreneurs in Latin America have been weak and dependent on the national government. As a result, they are much at the mercy of governmental policies, such as when countries reacted to the oil price shock of the 1970s by heavy international borrowing to maintain and expand social programs.

It is difficult if not impossible for individual entrepreneurs to build successful businesses in industries that lack critical mass. Few start-ups can fulfill all the requirements of a supply chain. Government policies that concentrate on one or a small number of industries inhibit creativity and innovation in alternative arenas. Industrial policies to build complete supply chains for particular products actually foster inefficiencies in global competition, ultimately spelling doom for the smaller companies that may exist only to serve a declining industry. Free trade agreements may encourage greater diversity and support entrepreneurial development.

Trade Agreements and Associations

Trade agreements received attention in popular media in the 1990s with the formalization of the European Union and the North American Free Trade Agreement. As explained previously, however, inter and intra-regional trade practices were issues in the Western Hemisphere even during the Spanish colonial period. Some of the more significant trade agreements and associations affecting Latin America in recent years include those enumerated below.

The Latin American Free Trade Association (LAFTA) was formed under the Treaty of Montevideo in 1960. Original members were Argentina, Bolivia, Brazil, Chile, Colombia, Ecuador, Mexico, Paraguay, Peru, Uruguay, and Venezuela. The purpose of LAFTA was to liberalize trade among the members, eventually leading to a Latin American common market. Progress lagged, and in 1980 LAFTA was replaced with the Latin American Integration Association (LAIA), which continued the goal to reduce trade barriers, but with no goal for a common market.

Mercosur is the Common Market of the Southern Cone. It originated with the Asunción Treaty in 1991. Original members were Argentina, Brazil, Paraguay[5] and Uruguay. Venezuela joined as a full member in 2006 and Bolivia was officially adhered in 2015 (Mercosur, 2017). The participating nations agreed to move toward the free movement of goods and services among the members, the establishment of common external tariffs, the coordination of macroeconomic policies, and the harmonization of relevant legislation. Mercosur is the fourth largest economic bloc in the world. It has a bilateral trading agreement with the European Union, its principal trading and investment partner.

The Andean Community, evolved from the Cartagena Agreement, signed in 1969. The Andean Community members are Bolivia, Colombia, Ecuador, and Peru. In 1993, all countries except Peru approved a free trade zone. Peru began phasing into the trade zone in 1997. In 1998, the Andean Community signed a framework agreement with Mercosur to begin efforts to establish a free trade zone. In December 2003, the two blocs reached a trade agreement linking 350 million people in countries with more than $1 trillion in gross national product (Wall Street Journal, 2003). By 2005, Andean Community countries were granted associate membership in Mercosur and vice versa (CAN, 2010).

In 2003, El Salvador, Guatemala, Honduras, Nicaragua, and the United States concluded the Central American Free Trade Agreement (CAFTA), to reduce trade barriers, eliminate tariffs, open markets, and promote investment and economic growth among the signatories (Office of the United States Trade Representative, 2003). In 2006, the agreement was renamed CAFTA-DR and was signed to include Costa Rica and the Dominican Republic (Office of the United States Trade Representative, 2013).

Other trade groups include the Association of Caribbean States (ACS), the Caribbean Community and Common Market (CARICOM), the Central American Common Market (CACM), the North American Free Trade Agreement (NAFTA), and the System of Central American Integration (SICA). Additionally, there are numerous bi-lateral agreements, associate memberships, and other associations among and between nations in Latin America.

Trade agreements and associations present both opportunities and threats to domestic entrepreneurs. The most severe threats are likely to be toward business owners in protected industries that cannot compete effectively in the global marketplace. Opportunities are associated with expanded markets and with exploiting the market inefficiencies in other nations.

---

[5]Paraguay was suspended in June, 2012 due to the impeachment of President Lugo. The country is expected to re-establish full membership by 2014 (Mercopress, 2013)

Import/Export Information

Latin American countries have historically relied on primary sector exports such as agricultural and mining products (Vassolo et al., 2011). This has made the region vulnerable to economic shocks that affect commodities prices worldwide (Brenes, Camacho, Ciravegna, & Pichardo, 2016). Figure 15.2 contains available export information for 26 Latin American countries from 2013 to 2015. The downward trend during this period is partly due to the reduction in the prices of traded goods, particularly commodities and oil. In fact, the remarkable growth in trade that the region experienced from 2009 to 2012 was purely the result of higher prices, indicating that the region's share of world trade has been stagnant for years. Another factor contributing to the trade performance of the region is the declining demand from developing countries. For example, Chinese purchases from Latin American countries fell by 18% in 2015 (Inter-American Development Bank, 2016).

Trade openness[6] of the region increased from 21% in 1980 to 51% in 2010 (ECLAC, 2013). This growth has been driven by increasing degrees of trade openness in Central America and the Caribbean. However, in 2015, trade openness decreased to 44%, mainly due to the large South American economies being the least open to trade (International Monetary Fund, 2017).

The region has also relied heavily on preferential trade agreements as reflected by increased share of exports to partner countries during the first decade of the twenty-first century (Inter-American Development Bank, 2012). In recent years, trade agreements have focused on partners outside the region such as the European Union, Asia, and the Pacific. These efforts are limited by the relative difficulty of engaging in international trade with the region's countries. For example, compared to the most developed countries in the world, importing or exporting in Latin America costs almost double and takes twice as long (World Bank, 2013).

Though the barriers to trade in the region may limit the ability of entrepreneurial firms to expand internationally, it may also create opportunities for entrepreneurs to serve local firms at a lower cost than their import partners. There are also opportunities for entrepreneurs to find other sources for exports that are more competitive and more stable than commodities. For example, the arrival of Intel to Costa Rica marked the improvement of the country's share of high technology exports, which was 40% of all manufacturing exports in 2011 (Olavarrieta & Villena, 2013).

---

[6]Trade openness is expressed as the imports and exports share of GDP

	US$ BILLION			GROWTH RATES (%)			
	2013	2014	2015	2003–2008	2014	2015	ACCUM. JULY 2016
LATIN AMERICA AND THE CARIBBEAN	**1090.3**	**1058.8**	**900.0**	**16.8**	**-2.9**	**-15.0**	**n.a.**
LATIN AMERICA	**1063.9**	**1037.3**	**883.3**	**16.6**	**-2.5**	**-14.8**	**-8.5**
MESOAMERICA	**423.5**	**442.4**	**423.8**	**10.3**	**4.5**	**-4.2**	**-5.2**
Mexico	380.0	396.9	380.6	10.4	4.4	-4.1	-5.7
Central America	**43.5**	**45.5**	**43.2**	**9.6**	**4.6**	**-5.0**	**-1.7**
Costa Rica	8.6	9.2	9.2	10.3	6.8	0.0	6.2
El Salvador	5.5	5.3	5.5	7.6	-4.0	4.0	-4.7
Guatemala	10.0	10.8	10.7	10.9	7.8	-1.2	-5.2
Honduras	3.9	4.1	3.9	13.6	4.7	-3.6	-8.3
Nicaragua	5.2	5.4	4.8	28.7	4.4	-10.8	-1.6
Panama	0.8	0.8	0.7	7.3	-3.2	-14.9	-7.3
Dominican Republic	9.4	9.9	8.4	4.1	5.0	-15.3	-0.2
SOUTH AMERICA	**640.4**	**594.9**	**459.5**	**22.1**	**-7.1**	**-22.8**	**-11.5**
Argentina	76.0	68.4	56.8	18.2	-9.9	-17.0	-3.9
Bolivia	12.3	12.9	8.7	31.7	5.2	-32.3	-25.7
Brazil	242.0	225.1	191.1	21.9	-7.0	-15.1	-5.6
Chile	76.4	74.9	62.2	23.5	-1.9	-16.9	-9.0
Columbia	58.8	54.8	35.7	21.1	-6.8	-34.9	-25.9
Ecuador	24.8	25.7	18.3	24.6	3.6	-28.8	-17.4
Paraguay	9.5	9.6	8.3	18.4	1.9	-13.6	2.4
Peru	42.9	39.5	34.2	26.1	-7.8	-13.4	-3.1
Uruguay	9.1	9.1	7.7	21.3	0.7	-15.8	-10.9
Venezuela	88.8	74.7	36.4	23.7	-15.8	-51.3	-10.9
CARIBBEAN	**26.4**	**21.5**	**16.6**	**24.4**	**-18.3**	**-22.8**	**n.a.**
Bahamas	0.8	0.7	0.5	10.3	-15.1	-29.1	n.a.
Barbados	0.3	0.3	0.3	8.1	6.6	-9.4	n.a.
Belize	0.3	0.3	0.3	9.7	-8.1	-12.9	n.a.
Guyana	1.4	1.2	1.1	7.0	-15.2	-4.8	n.a.
Haiti	0.9	1.0	0.9	12.9	7.0	-5.7	n.a.
Jamaica	1.6	1.4	1.3	16.1	-8.3	-12.6	n.a.
Suriname	2.4	2.1	1.7	29.5	-11.2	-23.0	n.a.
Trinidad and Tobago	18.7	14.5	10.7	29.8	-22.3	-26.6	n.a.

Figure 15.2   Exports in Goods by Country and by Sub-region[7]

[7]Table compiled by the Inter-American Development Bank (2012).

Small Business Practices

All environments present both opportunities and threats. As in other regions of the world, small businesses in Latin America have the advantage of flexibility—flexibility in both decision-making and in production. Also, as in other regions, the imposition of government, that is, adherence to regulation, falls disproportionately on small firms. The Foundation for Development and Integration, located in Cali, Columbia, calculated that government compliance costs in that country resulted in losses of about 23% for small businesses (CIPE, 1993). Alternatively, Abetti and Wheeler (1990), in a study comparing France, Mexico, and the United States, found entrepreneurial success consistently in communities with governments that successfully build infrastructures for technological entrepreneurship.

As the review of cultural influences suggests, family involvement in enterprises permeates the region. "The persistence of family-centeredness is a common feature of (Mexico and) other Latin American countries" (Derossi, 1971, p. 101). Another aspect of culture affecting entrepreneurship is risk avoidance. Albert Lauterbach observed almost forty years ago that "this attitude is a far cry from the Schumpeterian entrepreneur whom some contemporary observers consider the mainstay of economic development in less developed areas today" (p. 210).

Studies have also found that entrepreneurs in Latin America have different demographic characteristics than the general populations of their countries (Lipman, 1965). They are more likely to be higher educated, from wealthier (predominantly middle class backgrounds), and urban.

Franko (1966) cited evidence in support of Schumpeterian economics in Mexico and in Colombia. Reviewing historic economic patterns, he observed specific entrepreneurial breaks with the formation of new industries. For Mexico, disruptions occurred with sugar refining in 1901, textile mills beginning in 1906, and cement plants in 1909. The implication of this analysis is that countries with single industry dominance are still capable of innovating in other industries in which they may develop a competitive advantage.

One study found that important sources of capital and entrepreneurial expertise may come from expatriates (Befus, Mescon, Mescon, & Vozikis, 1988). These venturers typically have family business backgrounds. They are likely to be seeking quality of life and reduced initial investment. In their literature reviews of groups that generate entrepreneurial activity, Shapiro and Sokol (1981) and Lipset (2000) gave examples from Argentina, Brazil, Columbia, Cuba, Mexico, and other countries that indicated migrant populations display a disproportionate degree of entrepreneurial behavior when compared with indigenous groups.

Small firms are discovering that the global economy is real and affecting them directly. For example, special incentives for pharmaceutical manufacturers have brought foreign investment to Puerto Rico with accompanying local sourcing (Orengo Serra, 2003). On the other hand, the expansion of Wal-Mart in Latin

America is impacting smaller firms both positively and negatively. Opportunities are being created for local suppliers, but competitors are finding margins cut drastically (Duggal, 2003).

No discussion of the small business sector would be complete without addressing the economy sometimes labeled informal, extralegal, unauthorized, unlicensed, underground or black market. The informal economy in the region is estimated to be 54.8% of GDP, with some countries such as Honduras, Nicaragua, Guatemala, and Peru reporting shares of over 80% (OECD/ECLAC/CAF, 2016). Some of the factors that contribute to the size of the informal sector are the prevalence of necessity-based entrepreneurship, the high number of procedures required to register a business, the difficulty of obtaining credit, the lack of investor's protection, and the difficulty of paying taxes. For example, a formal business in Latin America is expected to make 29 tax payments per year and spend about 343 hours per year in tax preparation, compared to 11 payments and 163 hours in OECD countries. Furthermore, total average taxes amount to 46% of business profits (World Bank, 2017).

The International Labour Organization reported that about 50% of Latin American jobs belong to the informal economy (ILO, 2013). In Mexico alone, more than 10 million people engaged in unreported business activity, particularly pirated merchandise (Maquila Portal, 2003). In examining failures of capitalism in Latin America, De Soto (2003) recorded estimates that 60–70% of all construction in Brazil is never reported and that 80% of all real estate throughout Latin America is held outside of the law. He compared Latin America with Russia: both had strong underground economies, glaring inequalities, pervasive mafias, political instability, capital flight, and flagrant disregard for the law. De Soto concluded that these conditions limit the ability of national economies to produce and use capital efficiently. In addition, the informal economy also prevents labor unionization, reduces contributions to social security, and results in lower enrollment rates in education (Vuletin, 2008).

Many countries are proactively encouraging small business formation and development as part of their economic development strategies (Mello, 1987). Examples include:

- fostering technological entrepreneurship through the creation of a science park in Brazil (Filho and Rosa, 1993);
- training students to start ventures and business owners to improve their firms' performance at an innovation and entrepreneurship development center in Honduras (Yu-Way and Zuniga, 1987);
- providing equity-free seed capital and temporary visas to early stage entrepreneurs through a start-ups program in Chile (Dube, 2013).
- providing seed funding to entrepreneurs through investments in local startup accelerators in Argentina (Kiwi, 2015)

Quezada and Mello (1987) cautioned, however, that greater trust is needed between the program delivery partners, i.e. government, industry and universities, for these programs to be effective. This comports with Hoeser's (2003) investigation of incubators in Argentina, which he found to be unsuccessful, especially when compared to other countries, such as Brazil.

It would appear that a propensity for entrepreneurship exists throughout Latin America, but that several prerequisites are missing that would otherwise increase the number of start-ups and provide an environment for innovative and high-growth potential ventures. Obvious gaps are education, capital, and technological expertise. Expanding markets, reduced trade barriers, large labor pools, government support programs, and other factors may provide stimuli for small business development in the future.

The Rise of Social Entrepreneurship

In recent years, a growing number of Latin American entrepreneurs have focused on developing solutions to a variety of social problems through their ventures. These social entrepreneurs address societal problems that governments and the private sector have been unable to tackle efficiently. As such, the World Bank considers social entrepreneurship as the third arm of development (Adrienne Arsht Latin America Center, 2015).

The changing trends in socio-economic progress in Latin America have accentuated the prevalence of social problems permeating the region, giving rise to opportunities for social entrepreneurship (González, Husted, & Aigner, 2017). Among those social problems, poverty and economic inequality are the most prominent. During the last two decades, the region experienced remarkable progress in these areas. Poverty rates decreased from 48.4% to 28.2% of the total population between 1990 and 2014, which translates into 60 million people escaping poverty during that period (ECLAC, 2016). Similarly, the region experienced a decrease in inequality with the average Gini coefficient falling at a pace of 0.1 points a year since 2002, reaching .49 points in 2010 (Gasparini, Cruces, & Tornarrolli, 2016). Despite this progress, the Latin American region still exhibits the highest income inequality in the world (Domanski, Howaldt, & Schröder, 2017). After decades of progress across the region, several macroeconomic and social factors stalled socio-economic growth after 2014. By 2015 the region reported the largest increase in poverty rates since the late 1980s, reaching 29.2% or 175 million people (ECLAC, 2016).

Given the pervasive social problems derived from poverty and inequality, it is unsurprising that social entrepreneurship has experienced unprecedented growth in the last decade. According to the Global Entrepreneurship Monitor (GEM) about 4% of the adult population is engaged in activities geared toward starting a social venture (the startup phase) in Latin America and the Caribbean. About 3% of the adult population in the region is currently running a social enterprise (operational phase). In comparison, the combined United States and Australia region, in which social entrepreneurship is at a higher level of maturity, reports 5% of their population in the startup phase and 9% in the operational phase (Bosma, Schøtt, Terjesen, & Kew, 2016). Though the higher rate of entrepreneurs in the operational phase is indicative of higher conversion rates in developed countries, it also reflects the relative newness of social entrepreneurship in Latin America and the Caribbean.

The growth of social entrepreneurship in Latin America is also a result of a variety of initiatives that have originated in both the private and public sectors. A variety of international organizations provide financial support and training to social entrepreneurs in the region. Some notable examples are the World Bank, the Inter-American Development Bank, Ashoka, and the Schwab Foundation (Adrienne Arsht Latin America Center, 2015; González et al., 2017). Though a specific legal designation for social enterprises does not exist in Latin America, countries such as Chile, Colombia, and Mexico are currently in the process of developing new legal forms to identify social enterprises (Buckland, Orejas, & Castizo, 2016). In 2011, the B Corporation certification (Systema B in Spanish) was adopted by a handful of South American countries and rapidly expanded across the region. As of 2015, Systema B had certified more than 230 Latin American enterprises that generated a combined annual revenue of three billion dollars (Sistema B, 2015).

Social entrepreneurship in Latin America is characterized by strong involvement of NGOs and communities (Domanski et al., 2017). Private sector involvement, specifically, through philanthropic donations is rare (Orejas, Buckland, & Castizo, 2016). These factors contribute to a sector that mainly consists of small organizations whose impact is limited to their locales. A survey of Latin American social entrepreneurs found that about 78% of these organizations served less than 1000 beneficiaries in a narrow geographical area, 44% of respondents did not generate any paid employment, and only 10% employed more than 10 professionals (Symmes, Jäger, & Rodriguez, 2016). In a few countries, however, government and private sector involvement has fueled larger and scalable organizations. For example, Colombia and Mexico have proactively encouraged the development of impact investment funds and social entrepreneurs in these countries have received significant government support (Orejas et al., 2016). Other countries such as Brazil, Ecuador, and Peru offer multiple tax exemptions for businesses dedicated to a social purpose (Adrienne Arsht Latin America Center, 2015).

Latin American Social entrepreneurs tend to be highly educated individuals. A survey found that about 77% of respondents, whose average age was 34 years old, were college educated and some had maters' and doctorate degrees (Symmes et al., 2016; Orejast et al., 2016). According to GEM, 72% of Latin American social entrepreneurs invest their own money to start and grow their ventures (Bosma et al., 2016). This is in part due to their ability to invest their own money, and in part to the scarcity of other investment sources. Notably, the majority of social entrepreneurs legally register their enterprises, despite the high levels of informal economic activity in the region (Orejas et al., 2016).

Even though support for social entrepreneurship is growing, a variety of challenges need to be overcome for the sector to become more prevalent in the region. Lack of government involvement, political instability, and high levels of bureaucracy not only prevent the creation of social enterprises but can also thwart the growth and scaling of existing organizations (Domanski et al., 2017; Buckland et al., 2016). The lack of a legal structure for social enterprises acts a barrier for the effective implementation of market-based solutions to social problems because these organizations have to compete head on with their purely commercial counterparts (Buckland et al., 2016). The Atlantic Council (2014) identified other challenges including the need to develop more ecosystems and better infrastructure for startups, the lack of favorable policies regarding impact investment, and the low levels of cultural awareness regarding the benefits of impact investment across the region.

Discussion Questions

1. What are two major factors that discouraged entrepreneurs in Latin America from creating and growing legitimate businesses? Be sure to include the notion of property rights in your answer.

2. Dietz and Dilmus contended that governments and lenders over-expanded in unrealistic expectation of continued growth. In the late 1970s and through the 1980s what kinds of crises were created? What types of policies were they exacerbated by?

References

Abetti, P. A., & Wheeler, P. A. (1990). Planning and building the infrastructure for technological entrepreneurship: Field studies in the USA, France and Mexico. In Neil C. Churchill, William D. Bygrave, John A. Hornaday, Daniel F. Muzyka, Karl H. Vesper, & William E. Wetzel, Jr. (Eds.), *Frontiers of entrepreneurship research*: Proceedings of the Tenth Annual Babson College Entrepreneurship Research Conference. Babson College Babson Park, MA 02157-0310

Acs, Z. J., & Amorós, J. E. (2008). Entrepreneurship and competitiveness dynamics in Latin America. *Small Business Economics, 31*(3), 305–322.

Adrienne Arsht Latin America Center. (2015). *Social entrepreneurship in the Americas.* Spotlight, Atlantic Council. Retrieved from http://www.atlanticcouncil.org/publications/articles/social-entrepreneurship-in-the-americas

Atlantic Council. (2014). *Latin America is ripe for social impact investment.*Retrieved from http://www.atlanticcouncil.org/events/past-events/latin-america-is-ripe-for-social-impact-investment

Befus, D. R., Mescon, T. S., Mescon, D. L., & Vozikis, G. S. (1988). International investment of expatriate entrepreneurs: The case of Honduras. *Journal of Small Business Management, 26*(3), 40–47.

Bosma, N. S., Schøtt, T., Terjesen, S. A., & Kew, P. (2016). *Global entrepreneurship monitor 2015 to 2016: Special report on social entrepreneurship.* Global Entrepreneurship Research Association. Retrieved from www. gemconsortium.org

Buckland, H., Orejas, R., & Castizo, R. (2016). *Study of social entrepreneurship and innovation ecosystems in the Latin American pacific alliance countries* (Technical Note No. IDB-TN-1207). Inter-American Development Bank. Retrieved from https://publications.iadb.org/handle/11319/8055

Brenes, E. R., Camacho, A. R., Ciravegna, L., & Pichardo, C. A. (2016). Strategy and innovation in emerging economies after the end of the commodity boom—Insights from Latin America. *Journal of Business Research, 69*(10), 4363–4367.

CAN. (2010). Comunidad Andina. Retrieved from http://www.comunidadandina.org/Seccion.aspx?id=111&tipo=TE&title=mercosur

Castellani, F., & Lora, E. (2013). Is entrepreneurship a channel of social mobility in Latin America? (Working Paper Series No. 425). Inter-American Development Bank.

Center for International Private Enterprise (CIPE). (1993). Fostering entrepreneurship. *Prosperity papers series.* Retrieved from http://www.cipe.org/publications/education/prosperity/ppl.htm

Cochran, T. C. (1960). Cultural factors in economic growth. *Journal of Economic History, 20*(4), 515–530.

Dávila, C. (2012). The current state of business history in Latin America. *Australian Economic History Review, 53*(2), 109–120.

De Soto, H. (2003). *The mystery of capital: Why capitalism triumphs in the West and fails everywhere else.* Basic Books: New York, NY.

Derossi, F. (1971). *The Mexican entrepreneur.* Paris: Development Centre of the Organization for Economic Co-Operation and Development.

Dietz, J. L., & Dilmus, D. James (Eds.). (1990). *Progress toward development in Latin America: From prebisch to technological autonomy.* Boulder, CO: Lynne Rienner Publishers.

Dietz, J. L., & James, H. Street (Eds.). (1987). *Latin America's economic development: Institutionalist and structuralist perspectives.* Boulder, CO: Lynne Rienner Publishers.

Domanski, D., Howaldt, J., & Schröder, A. (2017). Social innovation in Latin America. *Journal of Human Development and Capabilities.* doi: 10.1080/19452829.2017.1299698

Dube, R. (2013). The creators of growth. *Latin trade,* retrieved on March 11, 2014 from http://latintrade.com/2013/04/the-creators-of-growth

Duggal, V. P. (2003). Small business versus big business—Amigo & mega retailer Wal-Mart. *International Council for Small Business World Conference,* Belfast, Northern Ireland, United Kingdom.

ECLAC. (2003). *Economic Commission for Latin America and the Caribbean.* Retrieved from http://www.eclac.cl

ECLAC. (2013). Economic Survey of Latin America: Three decades of uneven and Unstable Growth. *United Nations Publication.* ISBN: 978-92-1-121833-6

ECLAC. (2016). Social Panorama of Latin America, 2015 (LC/G.2691-P), United Nations Publication: Santiago. ISBN: 978-92-1-058487-6

Sebastián, E. (1991). Structural adjustment reforms and the external debt crisis in Latin America. In *The Latin American development debate: Neostructuralism, neomonetarism, and adjustment processes.* Boulder, CO: Westview Press.

Sergio Perussi, F., & Sylvio Goulart Rosa, J.R. (1993). Planning and building the infrastructure for technological entrepreneurship: The case of São Carlos Science Park, Brasil.

Franko, Lawrence G. (1966). Politics and economics of joint ventures in Latin America. In *Entrepreneurship and industrialization in Latin America: Three essays,* Lawrence G. Franko, Michael Dixon, and Carlos Arturo Marulanda R (Eds). Austin, TX: The University of Texas.

Franko, Patrice M. (2003). *The puzzle of Latin American economic development.* Lanham, England: Rowman & Littlefield Publishers.

Gasparini, L., Cruces, G., & Tornarrolli, L. (2016). Chronicle of a deceleration foretold: Income inequality in Latin America in the 2010s. CEDLAS Working Paper, No. 198, *Center for Distributive, Labor and Social Studies, Universidad Nacional de La Plata (UNLP),* La Plata, Argentina.

GEM. (2017). *Global Entrepreneurship Monitor: Global Report 2016/2017.* Retrieved from http://www.gemconsortium.org/report

González, M. F., Husted, Brian W., & Dennis J. Aigner. (2017). Opportunity discovery and creation in social entrepreneurship: An exploratory study in Mexico. *Journal of Business Research.* doi: 10.1016/j.jbusres.2016.10.032

Gonzalez-Brambila, C., Jenkins, M. & Lloret, A. (2016). Challenges for scholarly business research in Latin America. *Journal of Business Research, 69*(2): 383–387.

Hartlyn, J., & Samuel A. Morley (Eds.). (1986). *Latin American political economy: Financial crisis and political change.* Boulder, CO: Westview Press.

Hoeser, U. (2003). The slow development of the Argentinean incubation sector. International Council for Small Business World Conference, Belfast, Northern Ireland, United Kingdom.

Inter-American Development Bank. (2012). Trade and integration monitor 2012: Trade performance and policies after the crisis. Publication Code: IDB-MG-141

Inter-American Development Bank. (2016). Trade and integration monitor 2016: Downshifting Latin America and the Caribbean in the new normal of global trade. Publication Code: IDB-MG-483

International Monetary Fund. (2017). Cluster report: Trade integration in Latin America and the Caribbean. ISBN: 9781475586015/1934-7685. Retrieved from https://www.imf.org/en/Publications/CR/Issues/2017/03/10/Cluster-Report-Trade-Integration-in-Latin-America-and-the-Caribbean-44735

ILO. (2013). International Labour Organization. Retrieved from http://www.ilo.org

Khoury, T. A., Junkunc, M., & Mingo, S. (2012). Navigating political hazard risks and legal system quality venture capital investments in Latin America. *Journal of Management*. doi: 10.1177/0149206312453737

Kiwi, T. (2015). The 5 top cities in Latin America for startups. London School of Business and Finance. Retrieved from http://www.lsbf.org.uk/blog/news/entrepreneurs-startups/5-top-cities-latin-america-for-startups/81291

Larroulet, C., & Couyoumdjian, J.P. (2009). Entrepreneurship and growth. *The Independent Review: A Journal of Political Economy, 14*(1), 81–100.

Lauterbach, A. (1965). Government and development: Managerial attitudes in Latin America. Journal of Inter-American Studies, 7: 201–225.

Lipman, A. (1965). Social backgrounds of the Bogota entrepreneur. *Journal of Inter-American Studies* (7): 227–235.

Lipset, S. M. (2000). Values and entrepreneurship in the Americas. In *Entrepreneurship: The Social Science View*, Richard Swedberg (Ed.). London: Oxford.

López-Claros, A., Altinger, L., Blanke, J., Drzeniek, M., & Mía, I. (2006). Assessing Latin American competitiveness: Challenges and opportunities. In A. López-Claros (Ed.), The *Latin America competitiveness review 2006*, pp. 3–36. Geneva: World Economic Forum.

Maquila, P. (2003). More than 10 million Mexicans living off black market: Concamin. Weekly Bulletin # 192. http://www.maquilaportal.com

Mello, Alvaro A.A. (1987). Patterns and profiles of Brazilian entrepreneurs: Data from entrepreneurship development programs sponsored by the Empretec Programme—United Nations and Sebrae—Brazilian agency for micro and small business assistance programme.

Mercopress. (2013). Paraguay expects to return to Mercosur in 2014; Chile offers closer links and access to the Pacific. Retrieved on March 10, 2014 from: http://en.mercopress.com/2013/09/18/paraguay-expects-to-return-to-mercosur-in-2014-chile-offers-closer-links-and-access-to-the-pacific

Mercosur. (2017). Países del Mercosur. Retrieved from http://www.mercosur.int/innovaportal/v/7823/1/innova.front/paises-del-mercosur

Miglierini, J. (2011). The price of Mexico's 'drugs war'. *BBC News*. Retrieved on March 11, 2014 from: http://www.bbc.co.uk/news/business-13120598

New Encyclopædia Britannica. (2002). Chicago: Encyclopaedia Britannica, Inc.

OECD/ECLAC/CAF. (2016). Latin American Economic Outlook 2017: Youth, Skills and Entrepreneurship, OECD Publishing, Paris. http://dx.doi.org/10.1787/leo-2017-en

Office of the United States Trade Representative. (2003). U.S. & Central American countries conclude historic free trade agreement. Retrieved from http://www.ustr.gov/releases/2003/12/03-82.pdf

Office of the United States Trade Representative. (2013). Dominican Republic-Central American Free Trade Agreement. Retrieved from http://www.ustr.gov/trade-agreements/free-trade-agreements/cafta-dr-dominican-republic-central-america-fta

Olavarrieta, S., & Villena, M. G. (2013). Innovation and business research in Latin America: An overview. *Journal of Business Research, 67*(4), 489–497

Ominami, C. (1991). Deindustrialization and industrial restructuring in Latin America. In *The Latin American Development Debate*, Patricio Meller (Ed.). Boulder, CO: Westview Press.

Orejas, R., Buckland, H. & Castizo. R. (2016). Study of social entrepreneurship and innovation ecosystems in the Latin American Pacific Alliance countries: regional analysis: Chile, Colombia, Costa Rica, Mexico & Peru. Inter-American Development Bank. Technical Note No. IDB-TN-1148 https://publications.iadb.org/handle/11319/8030

Orengo Serra, K. L. (2003). The pharmaceutical firms and the development of Puerto Rico smes. International Council for Small Business, Belfast, Northern Ireland, United Kingdom.

Population Reference Bureau. (2016). Retrieved from http://www.prb.org/Publications/DataSheets/2016/2016-world-population-data-sheet.aspx

Quezada, F., & Mello, A. (1987). Empirical observations of the new social entrepreneurship in Brazil.

Rogozinski, J. (1999). *High price for change: Privatization in Mexico*. Washington: The Inter-American Development Bank and the Johns Hopkins University Press.

Shapiro, A., & Sokol, L. (1981) . The social dimensions of entrepreneurship. In *Encyclopedia of entrepreneurship*, Calvin A. Kent, Donald L. Sexton and Karl H. Vesper (Eds.). Englewood Cliffs, NJ: Prentice-Hall.

Sigmund, P. E. (Ed.). (1970). *Models of political change in Latin America*. New York: Praeger Publishers.

Sistema, B. (2015). Memoria Histórica: 2011–2015. Retrieved from http://sistemab.org/wp-content/uploads/2017/03/Memoria-SB-2015_FINAL.pdf

Story, D. (1983). Industrial elites in Mexico: Political ideology and influence. *Journal of Inter-American Studies and World Affairs*, 25: 351–376.

Symmes, Felipe, Jäger, U. and & Rodriguez. A. (2016). Moving Latin American Social Entrepreneurs to Scale. *Stanford Social Innovation Review*, Mar 7, 2016. https://ssir.org/articles/entry/moving_latin_american_social_entrepreneurs_to_scale

UNESCO. (2016). Education for people and planet: creating sustainable futures for all. *Global Education Report*. Retrieved from http://en.unesco.org/gem-report/report/2016/education-people-and-planet-creating-sustainable-futures-all/page

Vassolo, R. S., De Castro, J. O., & Gomez-Mejia, L. R. (2011). Managing in Latin America: common issues and a research agenda. *The Academy of Management Perspectives, 25*(4), 22–36.

Wall Street Journal. (2003). South American groups forge free-trade pact. December 17, A20.

World Bank. (2012). Retrieved from http://data.worldbank.org/region/LAC

World Bank. (2013). *Doing business 2014: Understanding smarter regulations for small and medium-size enterprises.* Washington, DC: World Bank Group. DOI: 10.1596/978-0-8213-9615-5. License: Creative Commons Attribution CC BY 3.0

World Bank. (2017). *Doing business 2017: Equal opportunity for all.* Washington, DC: World Bank. DOI: 10.1596/978-1-4648-0948-4. License: Creative Commons Attribution CC BY 3.0 IGO

Young, Earl C. (1993). Major elements in entrepreneurial development in Mexico. *Journal of Small Business Management, 31*(4): 80–85.

Leony, .Y-W., & Zuniga, M. (1987). Innovation and entrepreneurship development center: Honduras. *Journal of Small Business Management,* October, 70–72.

Suggested Readings

De Soto, Hernando. (2003). *The mystery of capital: Why capitalism triumphs in the West and fails everywhere else.* New York: Basic Books

De Soto, Hernando. (2002). *The Other Path. New York: Basic Books*

Gannon, Thomas A. (Ed.). (1968). *Doing business in Latin America.* New York: American Management Association.

China

*Lan-Ying Huang and
Shawn M. Carraher*

National Changhua University of Education, Changhua City, Taiwan,
University of Texas at Dallas, Richardson, Texas

Key Terms

China

Foreign direct investment

Guanxi

Learning Objectives

Upon completion of this chapter, students
should be able to:

1. Understand the culture of China
2. Understand *Guanxi* and its
   importance in doing business in
   China
3. Understand Foreign Direct
   Investment.

Introduction

With nearly one-quarter of the world's population and one of the fastest rates of economic growth, China is perceived as a golden opportunity for success and has become the target for business expansion by many foreign businesses. The record $319 billion inflow in Asia—more than a 300% increase over 1999—was primarily due to an unprecedented boom in Foreign Direct Investment (FDI) in Hong Kong and China. In the current chapter, we shall examine doing businesses in China with a special emphasis on the concept of *guanxi* and its impact on doing business or investing in China.

Guanxi

The Chinese word *guanxi* entails guan and *xi*. The Chinese meaning of "guan" is either "to connect" or "a gate/pass that can be closed" (Yang, 1994). "To connect" is to build a linkage between two independent individuals. The latter explanation meant a "door," and its extended meaning is "to close." Inside the door, you are "one of the group," but outside the door, you are barely recognized. Besides, *guan* can also refer to "doing favor to someone." For example, *guan huai* means "showing care for someone." *Xi* means to tie up and extend into relationships. In addition, it can also refer to maintaining a long-term relationship. *Guanxi* is so prominent in China that it leads scholars to term the arts of establishing and managing *guanxi* as *guanxixue* (relationology) (King, 1991) or the "Chinese gift economy" (Yang, 1994). To sum up, *guanxi* means "doing favors for and maintaining a relationship with someone you recognized."

Many sociologists and anthropologists have attempted to define the nature of *guanxi*. Some qualify it as "particularistic ties" between individuals (Jacobs, 1979) based on trust and affection through which people exchange favors, while others view it as a kind of social networking (King, 1991; Yang, 1994). Chien Chiao, a Chinese anthropologist, defines *guanxi* as "a status in which a person or an organization interacts with another person or organization, and in which they are mutually affected and enjoy mutual gains (Chiao, 1982). Pye defines *guanxi* as "friendship with implications of continued exchange of favors" (Pye, 1982). Scholarly descriptions of *guanxi* include "tight, close-knit networks (Yeung & Tung, 1996)," "interpersonal connections (Xin & Pearce, 1996)," and a "gate or pass" (Yeung & Tung, 1996). Tsui and Farh (1997) remark "the literature shows no consensus in the translation or definition of the term *guanxi*.

Guanxi refers to the concept of drawing on connections or networks in order to secure favors in personal or business relations. It is pivotal at all levels of societal functioning and in all kinds of dealings in the oriental country. *Guanxi* literally binds millions of Chinese firms into a social and business web. No company can go far unless it has extensive *guanxi* (Campbell, 1987). In fact, a new term has arisen in China: *guanxihu*. This term, now applied to specially connected firms, refers to the bond between *guanxi* members that leads them to give highly preferential treatment to other members of their network (Pearce &Robinson, 2000).

Guanxi, renqing (human feelings), and *mianzi* (face) are regarded as key building blocks of the Chinese culture. The three elements are viewed by anthropologists and sociologists as fundamental sociocultural concepts that shape the social behavior and cognitive thinking of the Chinese (King, 1991). *Renqing*, unpaid obligations to the other party as a result of invoking the *guanxi* relationship, is a form of social capital that provides leverage in interpersonal exchanges of favors (Yang, 1994). When the Chinese people weave their networks of *guanxi*, they are also weaving a web of *renqing* obligations that must be repaid in the near future (Hwang, 1987). The person's face (*mianzi*) is also a key component in the dynamics of *guanxi* because one must maintain a certain level of prestige to cultivate and expand a viable network of *guanxi* connections (Yeung & Tung, 1996). *Mianzi* is an intangible form of social currency and personal status. It provides the leverage one needs to successfully expand and manipulate a *guanxi* network.

Characteristics of *Guanxi*

Guanxi is the word that describes the pervasive network of personal or business relations. It refers to a relationship between two people or organizations maintaining implicit mutual obligations and understanding the Chinese attitudes toward long-term social and business relationships. Its roots are deeply embedded in Chinese culture (Luo & Chen, 1996). The following describes the different facets of the characteristics of *guanxi*.

First, *guanxi* is ego-centric. Chiao suggests that *guanxi* is "ego-centric" (Chiao 1996). King indicated that *guanxi* building is "an ego-centered social engineering of relation building." As observed by King, *guanxi* relations in China are "a form of interpersonal relationship which is predominantly based on particularistic criteria" (King, 1991).

Second, *guanxi* is transferable. *Guanxi* network refers to transactions between two persons A and C, who are linked by their mutual relationship with a person B who acts as a facilitator. That is if A has *guanxi* with B and B is a friend of C, then B can introduce A to C or vice versa. Otherwise, the relationship between A and C is impossible.

Third, *guanxi* is reciprocal. *Guanxi* connotes an unspoken commitment of parties involved in the relations. They are supposed to share their resources and are obliged to help one another in an unlimited manner. Specifically, it concludes the notion of a continuing reciprocal relationship over an indefinite period of time. Anyone who refuses to return favors will be condemned as untrustworthy and will lose his face in all connected networks (Alston, 1989). The idea of enjoying the prestige of not losing face (*mianzi*) and at the same time saving other people's face is a key component in the dynamics of *guanxi* (Redding & Ng, 1982). In a *guanxi* network relationship, both parties are required to commit to one another by an invisible and unwritten code of reciprocity and equity.

Fourth, *guanxi* is highly personalized. *Guanxi* network hinges upon personal connection among particular individuals. If one attempts to build a good network with another organization, one must first develop fine *guanxi* with key managers in the organization (Luo & Chen, 1997). That is, *guanxi* between organizations is first established by and continues to build upon personal relationship; when the key individuals are gone, so goes the *guanxi* in the organization as well.

Fifth, *guanxi* is instrumental. Chiao proposes that the construction of *guanxi* is mainly to fulfill utilitarian objectives (Chiao, 1982). That is, the objective of networking in *guanxi* is to have mutual gains. This instrumental nature of *guanxi* is confirmed by King (1991) and Yang (1994). Yang indicated: "*guanxixue* is using people." *Guanxi* relations are built primarily on self-interest.

Finally, *guanxi* is dynamic. Chiao suggests that *guanxi* relations have to be alive and useful (Chiao 1982). In other words, *guanxi* is a long-term nurturing process that requires enormous patience and time. Accordingly, relationships have a longevity dimension in the Chinese culture.

The Difference from Western Networking

Traditional Chinese marketing through *guanxi* (personal relationship) is similar to "relationship marketing" in the West. Ambler et al. (1999) compared relationships and *guanxi* (connections) in China with relationship marketing as it has emerged in the West. The term *guanxi* goes beyond Western ideas of networking or business favoritism (Weidenbaum & Hughes, 1996). Favor exchanges that take place amongst members of the *guanxi* network are not solely commercial, but also social, with the involvement of *renqing* exchange and *mianzi* giving. The feature of favor exchanges often causes *guanxi* to be often named as "social capital." In contrast, networking in the West is a term virtually associated with commercial-based relations. In addition, Western networking emphasizes organizational commitment in the assessment of partner firm's effort to develop the relationship, whereas *guanxi* emphasizes on personal relationship creation and development. Only when the personal relationship is devoted to and used by the organization for whatever purposes, *guanxi* plays a role at the organizational level (Luo, 1997). More specifically, in China, transactions often follow successful *guanxi*, while in the West a relationship follows successful transactions.

Cultivating and Maintaining the Prominence of *Guanxi* in China Markets

Linkage, a broad definition of family ties, is the core of social networks or ethnic ties in Chinese culture. Chinese networks stretch from the core of close family members to distant relatives to those who are connected to someone in one's family as peripherals, such as classmates, people from the same region, and friends. In other words, family is the most fundamental unit of the Chinese society. Individuals are embedded networks of family ties and family-derived social relationships. People prefer to organize different forms of linkage in terms of commonness on some particularistic ties.

Guanxi, often translated as social connections or relationships with implications of a continual exchange of favors, plays an integral role in Chinese life and business. Its existence is a central concept for understanding Chinese networking strategies in economy and society. Chinese social connections can be built in two ways: group identification and altercasting. Group identification is a process by which commonality is cultivated among individuals. In a sense, the commonality is a base upon which *guanxi* connections are built, and it is termed as the "*guanxi* base" (Jacobs, 1979). In the literature, *guanxi* base is often formed through either an ascribed *guanxi* base founded on innate attributes among individuals or an achieved *guanxi* base built by shared experience. An ascribed *guanxi* base is often formed through kinship and locality. Kinship ties, members of a person's immediate and extended families, are supposed to be the most significant. Its significance is confirmed by Chu and Ju (1993) in which a higher percentage of respondents would offer help to a relative rather than to a friend (70.9% versus 64.3%, respectively). Locality *guanxi* base is formed through people who come from the same towns. Achieved *guanxi* bases are established through the shared experience among individuals, such as coworkers, classmates, sworn brothers, teacher-student relations, and many others (Chiao, 1982). Among these, coworkers and classmates have relatively more influence in *guanxi* building (Chiao, 1982).

Guanxi can also be established between strangers as long as there are intermediaries trusted by both sides. Altercasting is a term used for describing the establishment of *guanxi* between individuals who have no commonality (Hwang, 1987). The technique is commonly known in China as "*la guanxi*" (pulling social relationships). One effective way of accomplishing the linkage between two unrelated individuals is through an intermediary who is familiar to both parties.

A *guanxi* base alone is insufficient to establish strong *guanxi*. Alston (1989) noted, "*guanxi* ties have to be continuously reinforced." Two of the most frequently used tactics to enhance *guanxi* in Chinese society are presenting a gift to and holding a banquet for the other party (Hwang, 1987). In a social exchange, according to Yang (1994), when a gift has been received or a request for a favor has been granted, there is a symbolic breaking down of the boundaries between persons, thereby developing an unpaid obligation or liabilities that must be repaid at some point since *guanxi* is reciprocal. This unpaid obligation or *renqing* is the first step in a series of exchanges. When the recipient repays the gift by giving out another gift, or the petitioner returns the favor by giving help in other ways, the indebtedness in the *guanxi*-based relation is cleared.

Another important dimension of *guanxi* is the degree of closeness, which is determined by *ganqing*, or affection. The experience of sharing and interaction through living, working, or studying together is a prerequisite in building up *ganqing*. *Ganqing* is a key determinant of the quality of *guanxi*. In addition, trust is essential to long-term *guanxi* maintenance. It exists only among in-group members who are supposed to fulfill the obligation of responding to the requests of other members in the same network. If individuals abide by the rules of the social interaction and fulfill the obligation, they are considered as reliable and trustworthy and are entitled to the benefits of *guanxi*.

Since China started economic reform and opened the door to the world in 1979, *guanxi* has acquired even more practical importance for the Chinese in both social and business settings (Chen, 1994). The survey of Hong Kong Chinese executives regarding the importance of *guanxi* relationships by Davies et al. (1995) found that business exceutives believed that once good *guanxi* had been established, a number of benefits would follow. Under a weak legal system in China, *guanxi* networks can be used as substitutes for institutional support such as obtaining scarce resources, mitigating various forms of governmental interference, and protecting property rights (Xing & Pearce, 1996). It compensates for systematic inefficiency and institutional weaknesses. In other words, *guanxi* connection is a very useful means of dealing with the Chinese bureaucratic maze because it balances the awkward Chinese bureaucracy by giving individuals a way to circumvent rules through the activation of personal relations. The formal bureaucratic rules often inhibit business dealings, while *guanxi* facilitates them (Alston, 1989). Hence, *guanxi* improves efficiency, saves time, and eases the procurement of necessary production resources (e.g., government approvals, utilities, and local suppliers of labor and materials) (Davies et al., 1995). Developing, expanding, and maintaining one's *guanxi* network have become a form of social investment (Wall, 1990).

On the other hand, a *guanxi* network is imperative for foreign firms that lack marketing experience, distinctive competencies, and distribution channels to cultivate *guanxi* networks to compensate for their deficiencies, to access and expand their local markets, and eventually to be able to compete (Tao, 1988). Given the benefit of obtaining information on government policies, market trends, and business opportunities, *guanxi* networks help firms to reduce uncertainty (Davies et al. 1995). Both Western investors and overseas Chinese firms strive to establish close connections with China government/partners in order to gain an edge over competitors. Therefore, as China continues to attract investors because of its economic perspective, *guanxi* utilization has become increasingly pervasive and has been deemed to have certain implications for international executives active in this economy.

To summarize, in the absence of adequate legal protection, foreign investors rely on *guanxi* to safeguard their property rights and contracts and to seek solutions to investment disputes. Moreover, those who have strong connections in China actually take advantage of the weak legal system to obtain extra lucrative business opportunities for their own benefit. Foreign companies investing in China with varied sizes, sectors, and location, all find informal transnational networks essential to protecting their interests. However, due to the heavy reliance on personal connections, *guanxi* has its limitations as a business strategy, especially in the long run.

While *guanxi* network is an effective alternative to foreign investors in China to obtain protection and benefits under the government bureaucracy, it is important to be aware of the limits of *guanxi* network. First, *guanxi* is not equally effective across areas, and it cannot solve all the problems of a legal system. For example, large FDI projects involve many participants at many levels in China. The role of *guanxi* has been greatly exaggerated. It is impossible for any firm to build all the connections with all the actors since there is always the risk that other people many gang up and become more powerful.

In addition, because *guanxi* is so personalized, the participation of key people is constantly required. Therefore, maintaining *guanxi* connection can be very expensive and time-consuming. The networks hinge on personal connections. But given the lack of political institutionalization in China, the fate of individuals is hard to predict. If the key individuals change positions or lose power, FDI projects based on *guanxi* with them may suffer setbacks or be doomed altogether. Many business consultants realize this dilemma and build good relationships with as many officials in China as possible. But that is easier said than done. The *guanxi* evolution model presented below (Figure 16.1) illustrates the cultivation, maintenance, and benefits of *guanxi*-based relationship. In short, *guanxi* involves cultivating personal relationships through the exchange of favors and gifts for the purpose of obtaining goods and services, developing networks of mutual dependence, and creating a sense of obligation and indebtedness (Yang, 1994).

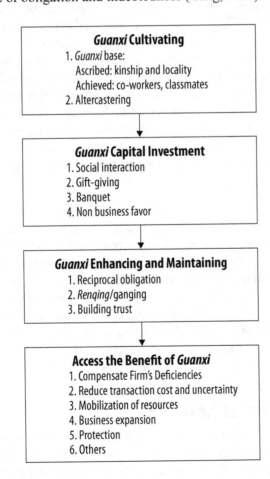

Figure 16.1   *Guanxi* Evolution Model

Guanxi as Social Capital

Social networks are sets of recurrent associations between groups of people linked by occupational, familial, cultural, or affective ties (Portes, 1995). Many scholars have proposed that business and social networks can improve the allocation of resources and promote the trade in the international market (Rauch & Casella, 1998). Weidenbaum and Hughes (1996) use the term "bamboo networks" to describe the role of social networks in Chinese society. Through these networks, trade and investment information is passed along, business introductions are made, and deals are done often on handshakes. Business transactions are often done through personal contacts and recommendations.

The development trend of ethnic economies has generated intense interest among sociologists and economists because it intersects the subjects of interest of economics and sociology (Portes, 1995). They try to explain this phenomenon or influence of social networks and ethnic ties from the perspective of social capital. Social capital refers to the capacity of individuals to command scarce resources by virtue of their membership in networks or broader social structures (Portes, 1995). That is, the resources themselves are not social capital; the concept refers to the individual's ability to mobilize them on demand. Resources acquired through social capital often carry the expectation of reciprocity at some point in the future. Pierre (1986) asserts that entrepreneurs try to build up and invest "social network capital" aimed at generating economic capital. These social resources can then be transformed into firm level resources in the form of access to decision makers and their professional networks, intelligence about market opportunities, licenses, monopolies, rents, etc. Social capital and associated norms can increase productivity by reducing the costs of doing business as well as facilitating coordination and cooperation.

Portes (1995) criticizes the drawback of social capital by saying that communities, groups, or networks that are isolated, parochial, or working at cross-purposes to society's collective interests can actually hinder economic and social development. However, in the case of doing business with mainland China, social capital could be the most crucial competitive advantage of some of the foreign investors. While many Western investors treat social capital as their insurmountable obstacle to investing in Mainland China, some overseas Chinese investors have turned these problems to their advantage through informal channels such as personal contact and family connections. Hodder observed that informal connections have played a large role in transactions among overseas Chinese businesses (Hodder, 1996).

Guanxi and Business Networks

FDI theory does not account for the role and influence of social relationships in business transactions (Granovetter, 1985). Alternatively, network perspective research draws on the theories of social exchange and resource dependency and focuses on firm behavior in the context of interorganizational and interpersonal relationships (Axelsson & Easton, 1992), arguing that organizational boundaries incorporate both business (formal) and social (informal) relationships (Johanson & Mattsson, 1985). According to Johanson and Mattsson (1995), business networks are concerned with relationships among organizations and individuals, while *guanxi* networks govern interactions and transactions in particular between individuals. However, organizations do not have *guanxi*; it is the employees of the organization who have *guanxi*. In practice, most Chinese cultivate intricate and pervasive personal ties, *guanxi*, which govern their attitudes toward not only social but also business relationships (Tsui & Farth, 1997). Hence, the Chinese *guanxi* network is more than merely a symbolic implication of individual and organizational ties. Most scholars agree that the social capital embodied in managerial ties and networks matters (Granovetter, 1985). Building managerial ties centers on networking, which can be defined as both an individual's attempt to mobilize personal contacts in order to profit from entrepreneurial opportunities (Granovetter, 1985), and a firm's efforts to cooperate with others in order to obtain and sustain a competitive advantage (Powell, 1990). Hamilton (1991) and others assert that business networks provide Asian firms with a wide range of competitive advantages in the form of social (relationship) capital based on interlocking connections (*guanxi*) to local or regional business partners, high-ranking officials and local power elites, government entities and so forth to get things done. Many researchers support the network perspective in the form of formal and informal relationships (relationships involving clients, competitors, colleagues, government, friends, and so forth) to the success in entering new international markets (Ford, 1984). Coviello and Kristina (1991) and Coviello and Munro (1995) suggest these network relationships influence initial market selection and also mode of entry. Bjorkman and Kock (1997) conclude that key actors and their social networks and bonds with important international partners have significant impact on internationalization of service firms. Fontes and Coombs (1997) found that firms established relationships with other organizations to complement their activities or compensate for deficiencies. Zafarullah, Ali, and Young (1998) found that the engineering-consulting firms' networks go beyond ethnic ties, relatives, and friends to include more diverse and formal connections.

It is widely recognized that *guanxi* is a key and practically significant business determinant influencing firm performance because the lifeblood of the Chinese economy and business conduct is *guanxi* network. *Guanxi* has a direct impact on the market expansion and sales growth of Chinese firms by affecting resource-sharing and social, economic, and political contexts in inter-firm transactions. In a qualitative study by Ai (1994), it was discovered that Canadian companies that had developed good connections with Chinese local parties achieved higher levels of business performance than firms that had not. Neil and Ai (1999) found that awareness of and experience with the changing Chinese business environment, *guanxi* relationships, and informal interaction patterns for obtaining information seemed to represent key success factors for Canadian companies in China. Abramson and Ai (1994) found that establishing *guanxi* relationships in China based on shared goals and trust were very important to the success of the companies. Xin and Pearce (1996) found that private company executives made more extensive use of *guanxi*, and maintained deeper business connections as a way of reducing environmental uncertainty than did the more institutionally state-owned company executives. Wank (1996) prioritizes various forms of *guanxi* on the basis that the more personal and the longer it precedes the current business relationship, the stronger it is. Luo and Chen (1996) explore the impact of *guanxi* on the performance of firms operating in China from the strategic management perspective. Their findings suggest that *guanxi*-based factors have a significant favorable influence on firm's profitability, asset efficiency, and market growth. This influence appears significant for both local Chinese and foreign ventures. Luo (1997) examined the relationship between *guanxi*-based business variables and the financial performance of foreign-invested enterprises (FIE) operating in China. He found that *guanxi* has a significant and positive effect on FIE's accounting and market performance. More recently, Ambler, Styles, and Wang (1999) have established that channel relationships and prior *guanxi* have a positive impact on the performance of interprovincial export ventures within China. Peng and Luo (2000) demonstrate that firm managers' micro interpersonal ties with top executives at other firms and with government officials help improve macro organizational performance. Their findings show that managerial ties were necessary but insufficient for good performance. A number of traditional strategy variables also drive performance. Ewing, Caruana, and Wong's (2000) study empirically links *guanxi* to performance. It would appear as if long-term success is still strongly influenced by personal connections and relationships resulting from *guanxi*. They agree with Kotler and his colleagues (1996), who maintain that marketers practicing *guanxi* must honor their obligations, be good and loyal friends, and true coregionals. Park and Luo (2001) found that *guanxi* utilization is likely to have a positive effect on sales growth but no effect on profit growth. Their results indicate that *guanxi* networks have a substantial impact on market expansion efforts, but less impact on accounting returns.

In sum, a firm can enhance its accounting and market performance by benefiting from the *guanxi* network it has established. In essence, this network constitutes a firm's core competency and distinctive competitive advantage that can lead to high performance for the firm.

Who Needs *Guanxi* Most?

Yeung and Tung (1996) suggested that *guanxi* was needed by four main types of companies: (1) firms that focus mainly on the China market; (2) less-experienced executives who are more dependent on *guanxi* to break the ice; (3) small and medium-sized firms that tend to rely more on *guanxi* to obtain favorable arrangements and resources; and (4) firms in tertiary sectors that need to rely more on *guanxi*.

Because firms with different organizational dynamics vary in their capabilities to scan information, control uncertainty, and benefit from exchange favors, they have different levels of need and capacity to build and sustain *guanxi* network connections. In general, firms that lack organization capabilities tend to have increased need for *guanxi* cultivation. Additionally, in a transition economy with increasing competition and decreasing government protection, firms may need to invest even more in *guanxi* development to be able to continue to offer and exchange favors with their competitive forces and government authorities.

Xin and Pearce (1996) observed that private company executives made more extensive use of *guanxi*, and maintained deeper business connections as a way of reducing environmental uncertainty than did the state-owned company executives. As Xin and Pearce (1996) found in China, smaller firms typically need to rapidly establish ties with other organizations. However, Park and Luo (2001) proposed that the weak support for organizational factors as antecedents to *guanxi* utilization but found that there appear to be no differences between organizations with strong and weak organizational capabilities in terms of their attempts to develop *guanxi* networks. For example, they indicate that companies in China need to network actively with the business community and government authorities both to overcome the liability of newness or to ensure the survival and growth of older firms (Park & Luo, 2001). Firms in China develop and maintain good connections with government authorities regardless of their resources.

Investing in China

China's "open door" policy has captured enormous attention in the past 20 years. One result of China's opening to the world is the inflow of FDI from developed countries, newly industrialized countries (NICs), and some developing countries, because China's opening to the world has provided many opportunities to many, and has exerted noticeable impact on the world. The presence of FDI in China, which is mainly from the NICs and the West, creates a unique area of study within the domain of international production. What is so special about China is that it has been a planned economy. Hence, doing business in China is more complex than in the other countries. In China, *guanxi* is an important resource for individuals and firms to induce cooperation and govern relationships efficiently. *Guanxi* networks might be viewed as significant factors for firms investing in China.

When it comes to international trade and investment it is important to remember that China has been involved in worldwide trading for over 4000 years. For instance, recent DNA testing has found that Egyptian pharaohs had consumed cocoa beans and coca leaves both of which come from South and Central America. Attempts to explain these findings proved fruitless when seeking to find Egyptian exploration of the Americas. However, it was then found that Chinese traders had traveled as far north as California and were also active traders with pre-Incan people groups in South America. Some of the objects traded would then travel along the Silk Road to Egypt and later to Rome. As new methods and modes of research such as DNA testing and tracking make their way into Global Entrepreneurship and International Business research, it is expected that research shall find far more involvement of Chinese traders as pioneers in exploration and trade.

FDI in the global economy has increased dramatically since the early 1980s. FDI flows to China, at $81.1 billion in the first 10 months of 2008, grew at a rate of 35.1% (China Post, 2008). China, with Hong Kong, is the single largest FDI recipient in

Asia. It is noteworthy that the portfolio of FDI in China has been broadening over the past 20 years. In its effort to become a member of World Trade Organization (WTO), China is considering adopting a number of new policy measures relating to FDI. In the last couple of years, while FDI has continued to grow, it has slowed down to a growth rate of between 5% and 10%.

China presently constitutes the largest FDI absorption territory, and one of the major sources of outward FDI in the world since its open-door policy began in 1979. Many foreign investors are eager to gain a foothold in this populous market. However, doing business in China is complicated and can be particularly difficult. Foreign investors can be confused and irritated by the long negotiation process, government hierarchy, and the distinctive practices that they meet in China (Davies, 1989). Instead, foreign investors depend on personal connections (*guanxi*) with regional authorities, bureaucracies, and individuals in China to safeguard and enhance their business interests. Therefore, in addition to the advantages firms possess, both Western and overseas Chinese firms strive to establish close connections, *guanxi*, with Chinese government/partners in order to gain an edge over competitors.

Guanxi as an Advantage in China Market

As mentioned previously, *guanxi* is an important resource for individuals and firms in China to induce cooperation and govern relationships efficiently. *Guanxi-wang* is the network of these continuing relationships used to secure favors in personal and organizational relations (Yang, 1994). The underlying premise is that Chinese firms utilize *guanxi* to manage organizational interdependence and to mitigate institutional disadvantages, structural weaknesses, and other environmental threats (Park & Luo, 2001). With *guanxi*, one is an "insider": negotiations proceed smoothly, and much can be accomplished. Without it, one is an "outsider" with little chance of success. As China continues to attract investors because of its economic perspective, *guanxi* utilization has become increasingly pervasive and has been deemed to have certain implications for international executives active in this economy. In Chinese culture, *guanxi*, or connections, have historically been critical to facilitating business (Tsang, 1998). Nowadays, the art of *guanxi* is essential for obtaining scarce resources as well as dealing with the bureaucratic maze in China. In the business arena, there is a well-accepted "motto" among non-Chinese investors in China: "Whom you know counts more than what you know." It is not only the products that make the deal, but the relationship" (De Keijzer, 1992). Chinese firms develop *guanxi* as a strategic mechanism to overcome competitive and resource disadvantages by cooperating and exchanging favors with competitive forces and government authorities. These informal social networks are developed through natural relationships such as family, marriage, schooling, and work (Wank, 1996). Overseas Chinese businesses—particularly those from Hong Kong and Taiwan—have contributed greatly to the improvement of China's economy in general. Many believe that the overseas Chinese have an inherent advantage over Western investors because of their shared culture, ethnics, and language. Although managers all over the world devote a considerable amount of time and energy in cultivating interpersonal ties (Mintzberg 1973), Chinese managers perhaps "rely more heavily on the cultivation of personal relationships to cope with the exigencies of their situation." (Child, 1994). *Guanxi* as an important asset for overseas Chinese businesses in competing with Western rivals in China.

Foreign Investments in China

Ever since China engaged in economic reforms and adopted an open door policy, their society constituted the largest foreign direct investment (FDI) absorption territory. According to UNCTAD (2008), China is the single largest FDI recipient in the developing world. In 2007, FDI in China reached a record high US$ 83.5 billion. These foreign funds flowed into China from different source countries and were distributed in highly unequal amounts to different regions across the country. Since 2008, while FDI in many parts of the world has declined, it has continued its increase in China. In 2013, FDI grew to US$ 117.6 billion according to China's Ministry of Commerce. In 2017 it should top US$ 160 billion.

Prior to the period of the open door policy, political conflicts and power struggles often hindered China's economic development. China has experienced several stages in its efforts to attract foreign direct investment. In 1979–1985, China invited FDI for the purpose of export expansion; however, the policy had many limitations for foreign investors intending to sell products to the local market. In 1986–1989, China broadened investment opportunities by allowing more manufactured products to enter its domestic market. In the last decade, in an attempt to absorb more investment from Taiwan and other large multinational companies from the developed countries, China improved its investment environment and allowed foreign investors to enter financial and service sectors. Special Economic Zones (SEZs) in two southeastern provinces, Guangdong and Fujian, offered special incentives and infrastructural advantages, and also attracted many mature export-oriented firms.

Current Chinese foreign investment policy encourages export-oriented foreign enterprises and high technology enterprises. Chinese authorities usually emphasize the desirability of attracting FDI that brings in high technology, increases exports, and develops infrastructure. In general, during the past two decades, FDI has been the dominant economic element and has generated special and significant effects on the growth of national income and export performance in the SEZs.

While China's market and its rapid economic growth rate are very attractive to multinational corporations, the present economic retrenchment and other constraints inherent in its legal framework create many uncertainties for foreign investors. Indeed, the booming economy offers foreign investors many attractive business opportunities to access the vast Chinese market and exploit its potentialities. However, China is a country where information exchange through official channels is limited, and the legal system and various intergovernmental mechanisms do not provide adequate protection of foreign property and contracts. Foreign investors may face additional difficulties if they are unfamiliar with China's unique business environment. Moreover, language and cultural barriers, and omnipresent and burdensome Chinese bureaucracy also present additional difficulties to foreign (especially Western) investors. A most striking feature of Chinese business environment and one likely to confuse newcomers is the importance of personal connections (*guanxi*) with regional authorities, bureaucracies, and individuals in conducting business operations.

While many Western firms—especially small to medium-sized entrepreneurial organizations—balk at seemingly insurmountable obstacles, some overseas Chinese firms have managed to get around them and turned these problems to their advantage through informal channels such as personal contact and family connections. Through these networks, trade and investment information is passed along, business introductions are made, and deals are done often on handshakes. Gao investigates whether overseas ethnic Chinese play a positive role in FDI in China and how important this role is quantitatively (Gao, 2000). Ethnicity, common language, and many other factors may have contributed to the large FDI flow from Hong Kong and Taiwan into China. It is natural for businesses in these two regions to turn to a neighbor such as mainland China that offers both unlimited supply of cheap labor and a potentially large market. Geographic proximity, labor costs, and market potential can all play a role in the large inflows of FDI in China from Hong Kong and Taiwan. When seeking to do business in China, it is important to remember the importance of *guanxi* and seek to be patient when working through the mazes of the government bureaucracy.

Summary

With 1.3 billion people, China has nearly one-fourth of the world's population and continues to be an economic giant that is continuing to grow while much of the rest of the world continues to contract. At the core of the Chinese business world is the importance of *guanxi*, a multidimensional construct dealing with social interactions and relationships. Foreign Direct Investment has continued to increase in China, and while expected to slow down during times of recession, it is expected to continue to increase as happened in the downturn of 1999–2000.

Discussion Questions

1. Define *renqing* (human feelings) and *mianzi* (face) and how they play a part in *guanxi*.

2. Explain what is meant by the *guanxi* being reciprocal. What unspoken rules are implied between parties?

3. Describe group identification and altercasting as ways to build *guanxi*.

4. Describe Chinese economic development prior to its period of "open door" policy.

5. Other than geographical proximity, why would countries like Hong Kong and Taiwan invest heavily in China?

References

Abramson, N. R., & Ai, J. X. (1999). Canadian companies doing business in China: Key success factors. *Management International Review, 39*(1), 7–35.

Ai, J. (1994). Canadian companies doing business in China: Key success factors. Unpublished MBA thesis. Simon Fraser University.

Alston, J. P. (1989, March-April). Wa, *gianxi*, and inhwa: Managerial principles in Japan, China, and Korea. *Business Horizons*, 26–31.

Ambler, T., Styles, C., & Wang, X. (1999). The effect of channel relationships and *guanxi* on the performance of inter-province export ventures in the People's Republic of China. *International Journal of Research in Marketing, 16*(1), 75–87.

Axelsson, B., & Easton, G. (1992). *Industrial networks: A new view of reality*. London: Routledge.

Burt, R. (1997). The contingent value of social capital. *Administrative Science Quarterly, 42*, 339–365

Bjorkman, I., & Kock, S. (1997). Inward international activities in service firms—illustrated by three firms from the tourism industry. *International Journal of Service Industries Management, 8*, 362–376.

Campbell, N. (1987, July). Experiences of Western companies in China. *Euro-Asia Business Review*, 35–38.

Chen, M. (1994, Summer). *Guanxi* and the Chinese art of network building. *New Asia Review*, 40–43.

Chiao, C. (1982). *Guanxi*: A preliminary conceptualization. In K.S. Yang & Wen, C. I. (Eds.), *The socialization of social and behavioral science research in China*. Taipei: Academia Sinica: 345–360.

Child, J. (1994). *Management in China during the age of reform*. Cambridge University Press: Cambridge, England, 150.

China Post (2008, Nov. 13). China says foreign direct investment up 35.1 percent.

Chu, G. C., & Ju, Y. (1993). *The great wall in ruins*. Albany: State University of New York Press.

Coviello, N. E., & Kristina, M. (1999). Internationalization of service SMEs: an integrated perspective from the engineering consulting sector. *Journal of International Marketing, 7(4)*, 42–66.

Coviello, N., & Munro, H. (1995). Growing the entrepreneurial firm: Networking for international market development. *European Journal of Marketing, 29 (7)*, 49–61.

Davies, H. (1995). *China business: Context and issues*. Longman Asia Ltd.: Hong Kong.

Davies, H., Leung, T. K., Luk, S.T., & Wong, Y. (1995). The benefits of *"guanxi." Industrial Marketing Management, 24(3)*, 207–214.

De Keijzer, A. J. (1992). *China: Business strategies for the 90s.* Berkeley, CA, Pacific View Press.

Ewing, M., Caruana, A., & Wong, H. (2000). Some consequences of guanxi: A Sino-Singaporean perspective. *Journal of International Consumer Marketing, 12 (4)*, 75–89.

Fontes, M., & Coombs, R. (1997). The coincidence of technology and market objectives in the internationalization of new technology-based firms. *International Small Business Journal, 15(4)*, 14–35.

Ford, D. (1984). Buyer seller relationships in international industrial markets, 13, 101–112.

Gao, Ting. (2000). Ethnic Chinese networks and international investment evidence from inward FDI in China. September Unpublished paper

Granovetter, M. (1985). Economic action and social structure: The problem of embeddedness. *American Journal of Sociology, 91*, 481–510.

Hamilton, G. (1991). *Business networks and economic development in East and Southeast Asia.* Hong Kong: Centre of Asian Studies, University of Hong Kong.

Hodder, R. (1996). *Far Eastern Economic Review, Hong Kong; 159 (5), 28.*

Hwang, E. R. (1987). Face and favor: The Chinese power game. *American Journal of Sociology, 92*, 35–41.

Jacobs, B. J. (1979). A preliminary model of particularistic ties in Chinese political alliances: Kan-Ching and Huan-His in a rural Taiwanese Township. *China Quarterly, 78*: 237–273.

Johanson, J., & Mattsson, L. (1985). Marketing investments and market investments in industrial networks. *International Journal of Research in Marketing, 2(3)*, 185–195.

King, A. (1991). *Guanxi* and network building: a sociological interpretation. *Daedalus 120(2): 63.*

Kotler, P., Ang, S. W., Leong, S. M., & Tan, C. T. (1996). *Marketing management: an Asian perspective.* Singapore: Prentice-Hall Pergamon, Oxford.

Luo, Y. (1997). *Guanxi* and International joint venture performance in China: An empirical inquiry. *Management International Review, 37*, 20–39.

Luo, Y. (1997). Pioneering in China: Risks and benefits. *Long Range Planning, 30*, 768–776.

Luo, Y., & Chen, M. (1997). Does *guanxi* influence firm performance. *Asia Pacific Journal of Management*, 14–16.

Luo, Y., & Chen M. (1996). Managerial implications of *guanxi*-based business strategies. *Journal of International Management, 2(4)*, 293–316.

Mintzberg, H. (1973). *The nature of managerial work.* New York: Harper & Row.

Neil, R. A., & Ai, X. J. (1999). Canadian companies doing business in China: Key success factors. *Management International Review, 39,* 7–35.

Park, S. H., & Luo, Y. (2001), *Guanxi* and organizational dynamics: Organizational networking in Chinese firms. *Strategic Management Journal, 22,* 455–477.

Pearce, J., & R. Robinson, Jr. (2000, January-February). Cultivating *guanxi* as a foreign investor strategy. *Business Horizons,* 31–38.

Peng, M. W., & Luo, Y. (2000). Managerial ties and firm performance in a transition economy: The nature of a micro-macro link. *Academy of Management Journal, 43,* 486–501.

Pierre, B. (1986). The forms of capital. In J. G. Richardson (Ed.), *Handbook of theory and research for the sociology of education.* New York, Greenwood Press, 241–258.

Portes, A. (1995). Economic Sociology and the Sociology of Immigration: A Conceptual Overview. In Portes, A. (Ed.), *The Economic Sociology of Immigration.* New York, NY: Russell Sage Foundation, 1–41.

Powell, W. W. (1990). Neither market nor hierarchy: Network forms of organizational. In B. M. Staw and L. L. Cummings (Eds.), *Research in organizational behavior, Vol, 12.* Greenwich, CT: JAI Press, 295–336.

Punnett, B. J., & Yu, P. (1990). Attitudes toward doing business with the PRC. *International Studies of Management and Organization, 20,* 149–160.

Pye, L. W. (1982). *Chinese commercial negotiating style.* Cambridge: Oelgesclager, Gunn & Hain Publishers Inc.

Rauch, J., & Casella, A. (1998). *Overcoming informational barriers to international resource allocation: Prices and group ties.* NBER Working Paper No. 6628.

Redding, S.G., & Ng, M. (1982). The role of face in the organizational perceptions of Chinese managers. *Organizational Studies, 3,* 204–209.

Tao, J. (1988). Cooperative joint ventures in China. *International Financial Law Review, 7(10),* 34–36.

Tsang, W. K. (1998). Can *guanxi* be a source of sustained competitive advantage for doing business in China? *Academy of Management Executive, 12(2),* 64–73

Tsui, A. S., & Farh, J. L. (1997). Where *guanxi* matters: Relational demography in the Chinese context. *Work and Occupations, 24,* 56–79.

UNCTAD World Investment Report 2008.

Wall, J. A. (1990). Managers in the People's Republic of China. *Academy of Management Executive, 4,* 19–32.

Wank, D. (1996). The institutional process of market clientelism: *Guanxi* and private business in a South China city. *The China Quarterly, 147,* 820–838.

Weidenbaum, M., & Hughes, S. (1996). *The Bamboo Networks*. Martin Kessler Books, the Free Press: New York.

Xin, K., & J. L. Pearce. (1996). *Guanxi*: connections as substitutes for formal institutional support. *Academy of Management Journal 39(6)*, 1641–1658.

Yang, M. (1994). *Gifts, favors, and banquets: The art of social relationships in China*. New York: Cornell University Press, 49.

Yeung, Y., & Tung, R. L. (1996). Achieving business success in Confucian societies: The importance of *guanxi* (connections). *Organizational Dynamics, 25(2)*, 54–65.

Zafarullah, M., Ali, M., & Young, S. (1998). The internationalization of the small firm in developing countries: Exploratory research from Pakistan. *Journal of Global Marketing, 11(3)*, 21–40.

Direct Selling Worldwide: The Mary Kay Cosmetics Story

Dianne H. B. Welsh

University of North Carolina Greensboro

Key Terms

Cosmetics

Direct selling

International direct selling

Learning Objectives

Upon completion of this chapter, students should be able to:

1. Understand the history of Mary Kay, Inc. and how Mary Kay Ash's basic guideposts on the human spirit and her belief in the abilities of women in particular have made the company a worldwide success

2. Understand the strategy behind their expansion around the globe

3. Understand the beliefs, norms, values, and culture that has made Mary Kay, Inc. one of the strongest direct selling companies in history

The authors would like to thank Robin Diamond, Direct Selling Educational Foundation (DSEF), the employees of Mary Kay, Inc., and Joan Gillman, the University of Wisconsin, for their assistance. A previous version of this case was presented at the International Council for Small Business (ICSB) Conference in Washington, DC, in June, 2005.

Abstract

This case involves the story of one entrepreneur, Mary Kay Ash, and how she took her cosmetics company, Mary Kay, Inc. to international prominence. Her basic guideposts on the human spirit and her belief in the abilities of women have made the company's successes worldwide almost revolutionary. The case encompasses the history of the company, the strategy behind their expansion around the globe, and the beliefs, norms, values, and culture that has made Mary Kay, Inc. one of the strongest direct selling companies in history.

Introduction

Mary Kay, Inc. had achieved prominence as a US cosmetics company and direct seller, but the company had not even reached its 10th year when international opportunities knocked on its Dallas door. It was 1971 when a couple of Australian entrepreneurs—so impressed by what they had seen and read about the company—persisted to get Mary Kay's first international outpost in this faraway land "Down Under." And so, it came to be that Mary Kay was in Australia before it was anywhere else outside the United States. The company now has a presence in more than 35 international markets on five continents and the focus for expansion is clearly on those places where the opportunity will be most appealing for entrepreneurial women.

What has transpired throughout the world is the creation of an interpersonal business model that seems to translate into a language and economic opportunity that women understand. Mary Kay's history illustrates how an American company can expertly tailor its marketing plan to emphasize specific market strengths. In regions where women are even more under-employed than they were in the United States in the mid-60s, Mary Kay can be the great equalizer, the quintessential entrepreneurial opportunity that has the potential to bring an entire family up from poverty or dire straits. Even in countries where infrastructures are far inferior to those of the United States, the company has experienced the great loyalty of women who—once they are exposed to the company philosophy and possibilities—will go to great lengths to make it work for their lives—in their market. According to President and CEO David Holl, it is in developing an independent sales force and a corporate staff that understand the importance of Mary Kay's culture that the company's global development plan has the greatest chance for success. When the culture is understood, and acted upon, Mary Kay has seen success. Where it is not understood, or embraced, the company has seen difficulty.

The same year that Mary Kay opened in Australia was coincidentally also the year that the company took another measure that would have far-reaching effects on the culture and the company's success.

In 1971, the company named the first two Mary Kay Independent National Sales Directors—establishing an extremely prophetic leadership role that would come to be viewed as one of the smartest succession plans in the business world. It was, pure and simple, a strategic move—instigated by Mary Kay Ash herself—that has fostered female entrepreneurs like few others. It has been generally accepted that no one would ever replace the dynamic and charismatic company Founder, but the Founder had embarked——in establishing this position—upon a program where she could encourage her leaders, and succeeding generations, to create new leaders. The prospect of achieving this pinnacle has greatly enhanced the appeal of the organization worldwide to entrepreneurial women aspiring for leadership.

Texas entrepreneur Mary Kay Ash had founded her company on her life savings of $5,000 in a small Dallas office center after vowing to create a company where women were provided opportunities long denied them in the workplace. She always said that she never imagined her cosmetics company would make it much outside Dallas city limits, let alone to nearly every time zone in the world. What the illustrious company Founder did realize was that—just like in the America of the 1960s—the carving out of opportunity reverberates extremely well throughout every culture and language. "We discovered that all women want the same thing," Mary Kay Ash once said. "They want a better life for themselves, their families and their countries. And they are willing to work for that."

Perhaps it is that common thread—paired with Mary Kay's 1963 founding belief that she wanted to create opportunities for women—that has contributed most to the company's fame as well as its growth as a company whose mission is to "enrich women's lives."

Corporate employees of Mary Kay, including the Founder's own grandson, attest that seeing this mission to fruition in the United States is exhilarating. However, it is in the witnessing of this phenomenon outside the United States that they come to understand the strength, stability, and long-term possibilities of the Company's mission. After a more than 50-year run, the potential for Mary Kay remains large.

The Americas

By 1976, when the Company's stock was first listed on the New York Stock Exchange, it had already opened three US distribution centers in the South and on the East and West Coasts when a major opportunity arose. That opportunity was Canada, where in 1978, Mary Kay Ash answered repeated requests from its neighbor to the North. Canadians love to relate the cosmetic icon's first visit to their country. It was amid a deadly winter storm that the petite dynamo came, sans boots, to meet and rally the Canadian independent sales force. Despite radio safety warnings to stay at home because of difficulty traveling, Canadian women came out to meet and greet Mary Kay in a hotel ballroom. It was said to be so cold that there was ice forming inside the ballroom windows, yet Mary Kay's magnetism warmed the crowd. They definitely warmed to her message. That began a lifelong mutual admiration between the Texan and her Canadian operation. One executive who traveled with Mary Kay Ash on several subsequent visits said, "She was the consummate hands-on leader and that made a real impression with the women of Canada." Mary Kay never hesitated to get out from behind her desk and get up close and personal to disseminate her caring leadership style.

A Reader's Digest article, "Mary Kay's Sweet Smell of Success," appeared in late 1978, and just one year later the Company and its Founder were profiled on television's "60 Minutes." This latter 1970s media attention would—coincidentally—set the stage for a continued bright future for the company, both domestically and globally.

Mary Kay expanded to Argentina in 1980. In 1986—shortly after the company was returned to private ownership—its first European operation, Mary Kay Germany, was established. Expansion to Asia didn't begin in earnest until the 1990s.

Argentina and Mexico offer two great examples in the South American region that validate and provide insight into how closely the Company's global success is aligned to its culture. Both countries have weathered economic crises that—rather than rocking them—only solidified Mary Kay's position in those markets. Argentina joined the team in 1980 but it wasn't until 2001 that its staying power was proved. There was an economic crisis that year that saw a blistering 300% devaluation as well as a financial collapse. According to Mary Kay Latin America President, Jose Smeke, even amidst these dire straits, "Our sales force count nearly doubled from 12,000 Independent Beauty Consultants to 20,000. There was a 28% sales increase in local currency." Why? How? Smeke says Mary Kay Argentina knew what to do in 2001 during this economic crisis because one of its most successful sister subsidiaries, Mary Kay Mexico—founded in 1988—had survived and thrived through a similar economic crisis in 1994. In Mexico that year, there was a currency devaluation of more than 150% in one day, 20% unemployment rate, political uncertainty, and price increases of up to 60%.

"We faced daunting obstacles, but we had a commitment to our independent sales force and their families, and so we took some risks for them," says Smeke, who believes the appreciation and support of Mary Kay, Inc. to Mary Kay Mexico at that time (and to Argentina seven years later) provided the trust and confidence that would see sales increase by 80% by the end of 1995, as well as a 35% increase in Independent Consultant count. "We had," Smeke recalls, "a sales force in very high spirits. Their accomplishments proved that during a crisis a direct selling company can be a very good option for women who need to help support their families." In Mexico and elsewhere in the Mary Kay world, one key most certainly makes a huge difference. "We always said to these small business owners, 'you are in business *for* yourself, but not *alone*," explains one corporate veteran.

The Company's fortunes are closely tied to the performance of its independent sales force. Mary Kay Mexico had opened in 1988 when the US parent company was 25 years old. In, Mexico, Mary Kay has already celebrated its 20th anniversary with an independent sales force of more than 250,000. In Mexico and elsewhere in the region, there are dramatic and life-changing stories of triumph over illiteracy, poverty, and even war. Who are the women of this sales force? Throughout the world, their backgrounds and lifestyles are as varied as they are in the United States. Their stories portray the Mary Kay mission to enrich women's lives poignantly. When Mary Kay Mexico published a call for stories to celebrate its

15th anniversary in 2003, hundreds of stories poured in. The best of those stories were published in *Reader's Digest Mexico*. Among them were numerous stories, like that of the fruit store merchant who had worked long hours with little to show for it. Without a car, but with the mentoring of her Independent National Sales Director, she decided to devote as much time to her Mary Kay business as she had to her fruit stand. Now, she is a successful Mary Kay Independent Sales Director in Mexico, planting many more fruitful seeds for growth than her produce stand ever would or could have provided.

Even husbands of sales force members, on occasion, will testify to the life-changing potential that this opportunity offers their wives and families. One of the things they always express appreciation for is Mary Kay's emphasis on family and balance, which resonates particularly well in these cultures. The Company is also proud of the 12 shelters it has helped fund across Mexico for women and children who are victims of domestic violence.

Mary Kay Ash saw the huge potential to change women's lives in Mexico very early on. Not only did she enroll in Spanish classes, she often spoke to Spanish-speaking leaders in their native tongue. Even though in Mexico she was known to have ordered "a grandfather" once in a restaurant when she wanted a glass of milk, Mary Kay's love for the language and the culture was always a source of great pride to her Spanish-speaking "daughters" as she called them. The first Independent National Sales Director in the United States of Spanish decent was an immigrant who had been airlifted from Cuba to the United States with parental consent in 1961 to prevent her indoctrination into communism. By 1975, she was enamored with the idea that she could earn a pink Cadillac like the one she had seen in the Mary Kay literature. By 1977, she had her first of many pink Cadillacs, and in 1991 was named a Mary Kay Independent National Sales Director.

Mary Kay Brazil celebrated its 10th anniversary in 2008 with impressive increases in growth as well as sales. The seeds of entrepreneurship also flourish today in Brazil, where an American woman of Brazilian descent decided to take her knowledge and skills as a Mary Kay Independent Sales Director and start over in the land of her forebears. With 18 years of Mary Kay business experience in the United States, she knew the huge potential Brazil would have for this company and its mission to enrich women's lives. She took a giant leap of faith, returning to Brazil to begin a new Mary Kay chapter in her life. It paid off. Only four years after starting over, she became Brazil's first Independent National Sales Director in August 2003—just five years following Mary Kay's opening in Brazil.

Mary Kay's General Manager in Brazil says that this woman's successful journey represents a true milestone. "Other women have started to see everything that's possible. She is, they reasoned, 'just like me' and so they came to understand how they could do the same."

Europe

The company had celebrated its 30th anniversary and had crossed the threshold as a billion-dollar business at retail by the time Mary Kay Russia opened in 1993. By 2008, this market continued to grow in sales and profitability with a remarkable compounded annual sales growth rate of over 35%. Not only has it become a pillar of strength, but it is also clearly among the best places on the globe to see the power of success potential that results from entrepreneurs with a penchant for hard work. Looking at Russia and the surrounding nations, it's apparent that the principles, career path, and the products of this Dallas Company have made the transition into an international opportunity that transcends generations, language, and culture. Today, there are more than 498,000 Independent Beauty Consultants in Russia and nearly 100 women in Russia have ascended to the most prestigious sales force position of Independent National Sales Director. Mary Kay Russia also symbolizes that it is possible to transcend weather and wartime.

The story of one Independent National Sales Director from a region in the Far East of Russia illustrates how enterprising women can overcome economic woes and a severe climate. For this woman, building her business often necessitated month-long waits for products to arrive because inclement weather prohibited air travel to and from the area. She built it anyway. Another woman was so intent to get her products to her market that she would routinely fly in the cargo hold of an airplane to make the nine-hour trek to the distribution center.

Another Independent National Sales Director hails from Chechnya, a region torn by war since the time of the czars, through the Soviet period, and even today. This former music teacher left Chechnya for Moscow to discover the only work she could find was cleaning floors. Her Mary Kay business brought a radical lifestyle change—affording her the luxury of owning her first car in the mid-1990s and the financial ability to unite her family, long separated by poverty and unrest at home. Mary Kay was also an important phenomenon during the second phase of "perestroika"—the end of the USSR and the start of privatization and reform.

The president of Mary Kay's Europe Region, Tara Eustace, resides in Russia where she says she has seen Mary Kay contribute to a better way of life; a change of thinking and many positive influences. She recalls how Mary Kay Ash was overjoyed and proud to bring the Mary Kay opportunity to the former Eastern Bloc countries. Many in the Mary Kay world fondly recall the Founder's visit to Germany shortly after the fall of the Berlin Wall. Germany had come on board in 1986 but shortly after reunification of East and West Germany, a newly free East German Independent Beauty Consultant just couldn't contain her enthusiasm when she walked across the stage to shake the hand of Mary Kay Ash. She grabbed the microphone and proclaimed, "First we get freedom, and then we get Mary Kay!"

Eustace says Europe has followed the Mary Kay model very closely. Russia, especially, has adapted to the lack of infrastructure (post, delivery, poor phone lines, emerging bank infrastructure, lack of personal check, or credit card systems) by developing a Customer Service operation center where placement and payment for orders as well as education can take place. Some of the largest recognition meetings for Mary Kay Russia have been held at the Kremlin, which at one time was one of the few venues large enough.

Eustace believes that oftentimes the most effective way to deal with a less than positive impression of the direct selling model is by careful attention to teaching and focusing on quality rather than quantity. "A great Mary Kay staff," she concludes, "helps the new market attract and teach those very first vital Independent Beauty Consultants. Together they will build the opportunity in their country."

Eustace recalls hearing the poignant story of a woman from Odessa who is an Independent National Sales Director in the Ukraine. The home she lived in had no plumbing and no water. Today, the woman recounts one hot summer day when she and her young son were dust-covered from hitchhiking along the motorway. "I was angry at myself and my miserable life," she writes, "when suddenly in the row of dusty cars, I see a white, clean Mercedes. That Mercedes became my dream." Today the woman drives a pink Mercedes courtesy of Mary Kay. She and her family vacation at the best international seaside resorts; her son studies at the most prestigious school and attends the finest sports club. "And owing to Mary Kay, I managed to make my dreams real," she says.

The entire Europe region is filled with stories of dreams come true and lives changed. Mary Kay Europe covers 13 time zones, and occupies 11 main offices and warehouses in the region. Its independent sales force numbers more than 832,000.

Asia Pacific

If the prospect of a recognition and rally meeting of a US-based capitalist company taking place at the Kremlin isn't enough of a contrast, imagine then that kind of a rally taking place in China. It is in this ancient land that Mary Kay has seen wonderful success. The National Bureau of Statistics of China (NBS) reports that retail sales of cosmetics of enterprises reached 162.5 billion yuan, up by 13.3% in 2013. (Fung Business Intelligence Center, 2014). Per a 2016 Morgan Stanley Research report (https://www.morganstanley.com/ideas/china-beauty-market-consumer-boom), China was set to become the world's largest beauty market that year. It is also recognized by the business community. *Fortune China* named Mary Kay one of the top 10 companies to work for in China for three years running. Not only is the marketing plan successful, Mary Kay manufactures its products at its facility in Hangzhou, and was the first cosmetics company that China granted a quality control and guarantee system certificate in 1998, just three short years after Mary Kay opened for business in China. Perhaps even more significant is the impact that the venerable culture of this American company has had on the historic land and its people. K.K. Chua, president of Mary Kay Asia, says he knew from the beginning that Mary Kay principles would transfer well into Chinese culture. "Confucius taught if you want others to treat you well, you must first treat others the same." As we examine the various components of what constitutes the Mary Kay culture, it is closely aligned with the Asian culture.

The region has not been an easy one to excel in. Mary Kay China faced daunting obstacles including a government ban on direct selling shortly after it opened. During the six months of the ban, more than 4,000 Mary Kay Independent Sales Force says Chua, "refused to go away." By the time Mary Kay was back in business, these faithful sales force members were ready to carry China to its current status as the company's largest subsidiary.

In addition to many inspiring stories, Chua points out that Mary Kay has made its way in China by following yet another of the founding principles. The belief in giving back to the communities has taken root in re-investing part of its profits into the lives of the country's women. There is a microcredit fund for female workers, schools in mountain regions where female children have been too poor to attend school, scholarships for female students at two prominent universities, and youth projects emphasizing skills training. The most telling of the impact of Mary Kay Ash on a culture so far removed from her own is the small rose garden outside a maternity hospital in Shanghai. It commemorates Mary Kay's life and philosophy and this Mary Kay garden honors the fact that this American woman's legacy is firmly established in China.

Equally heartwarming is a painting that hangs in the Mary Kay Museum at the world headquarters in Dallas. The Chinese street scene was painted by a renowned Chinese artist as a thank you to Mary Kay Ash. The artist paid tribute to this American businesswoman who had provided her a first chance at developing her personality. In the tribute letter, she poured out the heartwarming story of never having spoken until her teens. Although recognized as an artist she was extremely uncomfortable around people until her own Mary Kay network gave her the confidence among people that had eluded her for her entire adult life.

Another strong testament comes from the woman who ranks among the top Independent National Sales Directors in international operations. In China, she was one of the 15 pioneers in the Mary Kay Independent Sales Force—one whose fierce determination to excel at her Mary Kay business could not be dampened. By her late 20s, she had attained the prestigious Independent National Sales Director position and in her mid-30s, ascended to first place among international Independent National Sales Directors. A medical doctor and National Sales Director told of never having worn makeup before she was 30 years old. Her mother believed only "bad girls" wore cosmetics. She came to know the company through its products and eventually left the medical profession to pursue a Mary Kay business. She says today, "In my mind, Mary Kay is a footstone. On this base, women's dreams could come true: beautiful appearance, harmonious family, bright life."

Another National Sales Director in China today has difficulty believing how her life has changed since she first began her Mary Kay business. She fondly recalls how she would regale her skin care class participants by telling them about the Texas-based legend and those infamous pink cars of the Mary Kay world. She went on to qualify, in 2000, for the first pink car in China. Having gone from being a jobless, homeless, and poverty stricken divorced mother to becoming an international success story is indeed a powerful journey. It is a journey that breathes belief into other women aspiring for their own brand of Mary Kay success. It is a confidence-inspiring journey that Mary Kay's history has proven others will emulate.

The Asia Pacific region, Mary Kay's largest outside the United States, encompasses nearly half the world's population, making it instrumental in the Company's long range growth vision. Today, Mary Kay operates in 10 countries throughout Asia Pacific with more than 1,153,000 Independent Beauty Consultants.

Conclusion

It is the culture and principles of Mary Kay that shape the heart of the Company, no matter its location worldwide. Mary Kay is intent upon continuing its success and in fact achieved six years early an internal corporate challenge that by the Company's 50th anniversary in 2013—international sales as well as the international independent sales force would exceed that of the United States. By 2004, the international business sales projection was expected to exceed what the entire United States did in the year 2001.

With its vision to enrich women's lives, the Company has gone to extra lengths to make the heart of the Company the focus of international education and development. While the lucrative nature of the Mary Kay marketing plan and the staying power of a recognized brand would seemingly be sufficient, that's not enough. It's not enough, Holl says, that a woman can earn potentially at 100 times the average per capita income of her country. This success works so much better and lasts longer when it is applied according to Mary Kay's founding principles. In 1963 when Mary Kay Ash stressed her Golden Rule style of doing business, it was a foreign concept to even a US-based company. Today, that style is so celebrated that a recent newsletter took the time to spell out how the Golden Rule translates into all the major cultures and faiths of the world, and Mary Kay has adapted Golden Rule Customer Service as one of its most important platforms. There is always the emphasis on what Mary Kay saw as, "belief in the beautiful potential of women" that also drives Mary Kay's global success. Once the sales force understands the Mary Kay culture, adapting business systems to the customs and mores of each new country becomes a much simpler process. But it is never simple.

Mary Kay's International staff will talk of a starter kit designed for the tastes of Western women who drive their cars everywhere and how its size wreaked havoc on women in Asia who typically walk and take bicycles or buses everywhere. They will allude to how much more "global" the color palette and formulas of Mary Kay brands are today as they routinely conduct product focus groups on a multitude of skin tones and in nine languages. Even a recent new Independent Sales Director education session in Dallas featured fully one-tenth of the attendees needing translation into languages such as Polish, French, Cantonese, and Spanish. But more important than the language is the common and shared experience all women relate to. That will, in summary, make the difference for this American company. When accepting the posthumous academic award given Mary Kay

Ash as "Greatest Female Entrepreneur in American History," her grandson and company executive Ryan Rogers said, "Mary Kay tapped into one of the greatest under-used natural resources this nation had to offer—the hearts and minds of its women." It is much the same today throughout the more than 35 markets where Mary Kay has a presence, and in those parts of the world that women have even fewer opportunities.

Direct selling is one of the only forms of retailing that can adapt to virtually any conditions or circumstances and Mary Kay is a great example of this. Entrepreneurs and capitalists alike have come to see that when direct selling operates by the highest of standards, it can make amazing strides in contributing toward solid world economies. Mary Kay, Inc. believes so strongly in the business principles established by Mary Kay Ash that in 2008 it released an updated version of the Founder's 1984 best seller, her only book about the business, now titled, *The Mary Kay Way: Timeless Principles from America's Greatest Woman Entrepreneur* (Wiley), Mary Kay, Inc. follows the ethical standards set by the Direct Selling Association (DSA), and was instrumental in seeing the document to fruition in the 1970s and strengthening it in the 1990s and again in 2007 when two of its top corporate officers chaired the DSA. The DSA is the industry trade organization comprised of 150 direct selling member companies worldwide and has been an advocate of ethical business practices and consumer services. The DSA Code of Ethics has served the industry well, an industry now comprised of some 15 million independent sales people.

The culture of Mary Kay, Inc. reflects today the caring attitude its founder, Mary Kay Ash, established at the outset. David Holl, President and Chief Executive Officer believes that, "A fiscally sound company can also be a nurturing and caring company. We have a larger goal than selling a product. I have seen firsthand the stories of self-esteem and personal growth that abound throughout the Mary Kay world. I know nothing would please our Founder more." Holl continues, "We have experienced in more than four decades that the businesses that succeed the most in Mary Kay are those built and based on the number of lives touched. Having someone in your market break a belief barrier is extremely important. Having them succeed by following Mary Kay principles is even more important."

Discussion Questions

1. What are the characteristics of the entrepreneur in this case and how did they affect the organization?

2. Are the characteristics of female entrepreneurs different from those of male entrepreneurs? Which ones do you think are different for women v. men?
   What have been the research findings in this area?

3. What is social entrepreneurship? How is it tied to the founding principles of the organization? Give an example from the case of social entrepreneurship in action.

GLOSSARY

A

absolute advantage – a condition in which one economic unit (person, business or country) is more efficient, that is, requires a smaller total input of economic resources, than does another economic unit.

achievement vs. ascription – achievement-oriented type in negotiations tends to have characteristics similar to those associated with high individualism, masculinity, and short-term orientation. Ascription cultures are likely to be associated with the characteristics of collectivism, femininity, and long-term orientation.

ATLAS (Automated Trade Locator Assistance System) – assists the entrepreneur considering exporting by identifying the largest potential markets for their products and/or services using a variety of criteria (including sales and dollar volume).

B

banker's acceptance – a short-term promissory note drawn by a company to pay for goods on which a bank guarantees payment at maturity. Usually used in international trade.

big data – large data sets that can be mined or analyzed to identify patterns, trends, or behavior

bill of exchange – an unconditional order issued by a person or business which directs the recipient to pay a fixed sum of money to a third party at a future date.

body language – surrounding events and circumstances, facial expression, and other unintended and informal communication aspects beyond the message itself.

born global entrepreneurs – early adopters of internationalization; they apply knowledge-based resources to sell output in multiple countries from at or near their founding.

C

CAFTA (Central American Free Trade Agreement) – a trade agreement linking 350 million people in countries with more than $1 trillion in gross national product, in order to reduce trade barriers, eliminate tariffs, open markets, and promote investment and economic growth among the signatories.

communication – involves initiating, transmitting, and sharing meaning by messages through media such as words, behavior, or material artifacts. Business communication is grounded in human behavior-based interactions that tend to be more loosely correlated with each other. That implies higher uncertainty and dissonance in various aspects of business communications compared to the fields of engineering and technology.

comparative advantage – a condition in which one economic unit (person, business or country) has the ability to produce some particular good or service at a lower opportunity cost than other economic units can.

comparative entrepreneurship – the study of how entrepreneurial practice differs across nations, and investigates the similarities and differences between international entrepreneurs base on their country of origin.

competency – underlying characteristics of an individual that help predict success at a task or on the job. Also referred to as the knowledge, skills and abilities (KSA's) that individuals possess, as well as personal traits that help them succeed in their endeavors.

contagion – is a phenomenon in which small shocks which initially affect one country will spread to other countries. Contagion can refer to the spread of either economic booms or economic crises throughout a geographic region. The phenomenon has become more prominent as the global economy has grown and economies within certain geographic regions have become more correlated with one another.

contingency theory – a theoretical perspective which concludes that the most profitable firms are likely to be those that "fit" with their environments. An entrepreneurial strategy is more likely to be successful when it is consistent with the organization's mission, competitive environment, and resources.

content versus context in communication – cross-cultural variations in the balance between content and context in communication across national cultures. Low-context/high content cultures assume that individuals know little about what they are being told, and therefore must be given a lot of background information. High-context/low content cultures assume the individuals are knowledgeable about the subject and have to be given little background information. High content/low context cultures stress a straightforward exchange. On the contrary, high context/low content cultures communication emphasizes shared experience and established personal relations that make certain things well understood without them needing to be stated explicitly—people can "read between the lines" and understand the "body language."

contract manufacturing – the arrangement of using cheaper overseas labor for the production of finished goods or parts by following an established production process.

cosmetics – They (also known as *makeup* or *make-up*) are "intended to be applied to the human body for cleansing, beautifying, promoting attractiveness, or altering the appearance without affecting the body's structure or functions." (US Food and Drug Administration)

country risk premium – an increment in interest rates that would have to be paid for loans and investment projects in a particular country compared to some standard.

crisis management – the process of planning for and implementing the response to a wide range of negative events that could severely affect an organization.

critical reading – reading a text to understand its core concepts and why those concepts matter

critical thinking – evaluating a text or situation in order to form a judgment

cross-cultural communication – an entrepreneur from Culture A may initiate his/her international business venture by sending ideas, inquiries, intentions, proposals, descriptions, samples, etc. to an individual from Culture B.

cross-cultural dimensions – power distance, individualism, masculinity, uncertainty avoidance, long-term orientation, universalism, neutrality, specificity, achievement orientation, time orientation, view of environment.

cultural awareness – comparing individual cultures to other cultures to not only learn about similarities and differences, but also about whom they are in comparison to others; and to gain specific knowledge about working and living in other countries and how to manage cultural differences.

culture – the collective programming of the mind that distinguishes the members of one human group from another, also viewed as a system of ideas and norms that are shared among a group of people and that when taken together constitute a design for living. It includes a society's norms, beliefs, and values.

culture shock – a sense of disorientation or distress that may result when individual is experiencing an unfamiliar way of life due to immigration or a visit to a different country or an immersion in a different sociocultural environment. Typical reasons, symptoms, or problems include language barriers, information overload, generation gap, technological barriers, skill gap, homesickness, boredom, and others.

currency board – a form of pegged exchange rate in which management of both the exchange rate and the money supply are taken away from the central bank and placed with a special agency (board) with instructions to back every unit of circulating domestic currency with a specified amount of foreign (anchor) currency.

D

demand side perspective – the rates or the context in which entrepreneurship occurs. It deals with sources of opportunities and the entrepreneurial roles that need to be filled in an economy.

derived demand – the demand for a good, service or resource that depends on the demand for the product that it helps to produce or acquire.

direct communication – preference for explicit one or two-way communication, primarily in words, including identification, diagnosis, and management of conflict.

direct exporting – products distributed directly through agents and/or distributors in the target country.

direct selling – It is the marketing and *selling* of products directly to consumers away from a fixed retail location (*en.wikipedia.org/wiki/Direct_selling*)

dollarization – a monetary strategy in which a country abandons its own currency and adopts the US dollar as its official monetary unit.

E

e-commerce – helps businesses compete in an increasingly demanding marketplace with a wide scope of domestic and international exposure by improving operations, decreasing costs, increasing sales, and facilitating communication with customers, partners, and employees.

economic factors – indicators such as physical and financial infrastructures, access to capital, gross national product, balance of payment and balance of trade situation, debt and servicing costs, inflation rate, interest rate, exchange rate, and exchange rate stability influencing entrepreneurship in an economy.

economic participation – among the central tenets of market capitalism defined as freedom to pursue individual well-being (i.e., freedom of enterprise), private ownership of resources including property rights, market access, low barriers to entry, and competitive markets.

economies of (global) scope – when a firm produces more it increases production levels, thereby fostering standardization and economies of scale. The company may also enjoy greater efficiencies in marketing and distribution.

ELAN (Export Legal Assistance Network) – connects the entrepreneur with experienced international trade attorneys to address issues such as contracts, agreements between parities involved in the various aspects of exporting, and payment resolution matter.

electronic database – a database that can be accessed by computers.

emerging markets – while there is no consensus definition for the term "emerging markets" Czinkota and Ronkainen (1997) identified three characteristics associated with an emerging economy: Level of Economic Development, Economic Growth, and Market Governance.

entrepreneurial capacity – the ability of entrepreneurs to respond to new opportunities.

entrepreneurial capitalism – risk taking entrepreneurial spirit in which an individual or company seeks the potential for economic growth and development and profit.

entrepreneurial culture – when opportunities are declined within the strategic vision of a corporation, many bright minds either become an extension or leave the organization to build their own organization of leadership and vision.

entrepreneurial opportunity environment – the in-country conditions that create opportunities for entrepreneurs.

entrepreneurial support organizations – resources the entrepreneur may call upon to assist him or her in the entire export process, particularly in the analysis of foreign markets. These resources help the entrepreneur better identify a foreign market and determine whether or not it will be a viable market for the entrepreneur.

ethnic culture – distinctive ethnic groups populating a nation.

ethnocentric firm – firms that are home-country oriented.

ethnocentric versus polycentric staffing culture – ethnocentric culture in staffing takes place when headquarters send employees from the home or parent country to the host country and places them in top managerial positions there. Polycentric culture in overseas staffing relies on hiring and promoting local talent.

expatriate assignment – students work in organizations as expatriates and after that experience, use their learning to turn to entrepreneurship later in their lives as a means to self-development and economic progress.

export costs – licenses, fees, insurance, overseas shipping, customs agents, bills of lading, and a large investment of entrepreneur's time.

export management company – an organization that assists in the export of the product/service of the business that is seeking to export its items to an international market.

export trading company – a trade intermediary that purchases the product or service from the entrepreneur's business and then proceeds to transport and sell the item in an international market(s).

exporting – the process of selling goods or services to a buyer in another country.

export marketing mix – the four "P"s of marketing from the point of view of the exporter: product, price, promotion, and place (or channel of distribution).

exporting mindset – an assessment of the enterprise and of the entrepreneur to determine the export readiness and what skills/abilities of the firm and the entrepreneur could benefit from training/assistance from an export specialist. It is a planned activity with a recognized commitment of the resources of the entrepreneur and his or her firm.

external factors – factors that affect a company's choice to enter a foreign market but are independent of management's decisions.

F

factor endowment – the amount of land, labor, capital and entrepreneurship that a country possesses and can exploit for production.

factoring – the sale of accounts receivable to another firm, which takes responsibility for collections.

family roles – strong family influences on the mission and values of business enterprises. Family goals may override those of the company even for relatively large firms.

financials – financial data which reports a company's performance including profit and loss, cash flow forecast, balance sheet, break-even analysis, assumptions and comments.

financing options – the U.S. small business has three loan packages for entrepreneurs participating in exporting seeking financial and technical assistance: SBA Export*Express*, The Export Working Capital Loan, and the International Trade Loan.

foreign direct investment – foreign funds flowing directly into a country's economy, bringing in high technology, increased exports, and develops infrastructure and has significant effect on the growth of national income and export performance in the Special Economic Zones (SEZs).

forex – the foreign exchange market, the world's highest volume and most liquid market where international currencies are priced in terms of one another Import market selection: The process of identifying a foreign country for the purpose of exporting a product to one or more buyers in that country.

formal communication – places high emphasis on following protocol and social order.

franchising – a form of licensing that eliminates some of the concerns associated with technology, trademarks, patents and other intellectual property by giving more control to the franchisor company over the franchisee who has licensed the company's trademarks, products and/or services and production and/or operation processes.

freight forwarder – an organization that will transport the items of the exporting organization to the international destination.

fully-owned subsidiaries – involves buying an existing business or building new facilities in a new target country. Allows companies to exercise maximum control over their operations and to decisively enter the target country's markets, they also expose the country to the highest level of political, environmental, legal and financial risk.

G

GATT (General Agreement on Tariffs and Trade) – expanding over 110 nations and over several decades, this cooperative agreement between several countries assists in relaxing quota and import license requirements, introducing fairer customs evaluation methods, and establishing a common mechanism to resolve trade disputes.

GEM global entrepreneurship monitor – systematic approach to comparing entrepreneurship across nations by measuring differences in the level of entrepreneurial activity among countries, uncovering factors determining the levels of entrepreneurial activity, and by identifying policies that may enhance the level of entrepreneurial activity.

geocentric enterprise – firms that are world oriented and do not reflect any cultural superiority.

Global entrepreneurial leader – discovery-oriented individual who can operate in a highly uncertain environment where he or she continually repositions the organization to capture new opportunities.

global market integration – when countries increase the flexibility of their economies through structural reforms and speed up their economies through their own integration into the global economy.

global mindset – While many scholars and practitioners offer different definitions for the term "global mindset," the core competencies include:

- a broad world view;
- knowledge about global business;
- cultural awareness and sensitivity;
- adaptability to different cultures;
- an ability to influence others from diverse cultures; and a
- cosmopolitan outlook.

global perspective – business leaders with the following skills:

1. knowledge about many cultures;
2. willingness to learn from people from many cultures;
3. ability to live in many foreign cultures;
4. ability to interact with others from different cultures on a daily basis;
5. ability to interact with foreign colleagues as equals.

guanxi – the chinese meaning of "Guan" is either "to connect" or "a gate/pass that can be closed." To connect is to build a linkage between two independent individuals. The latter explanation meant a "door" and its extended meaning is "to close." Inside the door, you are "one of the group," but outside the door, you are barely recognized. "Xi" means to tie up and extend into relationships. To sum up, guanxi means "doing favors for and maintaining a relationship with someone you recognized." Particular ties between individuals based on trust and affection through which people exchange favors, social networking. "A status in which a person or an organization interacts with another person or organization, and in which they are mutually affected and enjoy mutual gains."

H

high content/low context communication – high content stresses straight forward exchange of facts in communication. Information is given primarily in words, and the meaning is expressed explicitly, often in writing: the entrepreneur says what is meant and means what is said. High content cultures tend to emphasize an intended content put in a structured, straightforward format.

high context/low content communication – shared experience and established personal relations make certain things well understood without them needing to be stated explicitly (people can read between the lines and understand each other's "body language." Rules for speaking, keeping silence, and behaving are implicit in the context.

hofstede study – reduced the world's vast cultural variety to six universal dimensions allowing for international comparisons in managerial patterns: power distance, individualism, masculinity, uncertainty avoidance, pragmatic, and indulgence.

human security – security viewed as emerging from the conditions of daily life—assurance of civil liberties, food, shelter, employment, health, public safety, freedom from fear—rather than flowing downward from a country's foreign relations and military strength.

I

import industrialization strategies – shifting Latin America's political and economic interests from landed oligarchies toward production by incipient capitalists.

import market selection – the process of identifying a foreign country for the purpose of exporting a product to one or more buyers in that country.

incoterms – a common set of rules and terms used to describe terms of trade associated with international trade. The objective of Incoterms is to mitigate the confusion over the control and insurance products at the various stages of the shipping process.

indirect communication – preference for implicit communication and conflict avoidance; expressive (emotive) and personal communication style with high degree of subjectivity, stress on relationships.

indirect exporting – exported products sold overseas by intermediaries who specialize in entry modes activity from the home base.

individual vs. collectivism – individualism leads to reliance on self and focus on individual achievement; the extent to which individuals or closely knit social structures such as the extended family (collectivism) are the basis for social systems.

indulgence – in societies high in indulgence individuals' value free gratification of basic and natural human drives related to enjoying life and having fun.

industrial organization – a branch of microeconomics, which emphasizes the influence of the industry environment upon a firm. A firm must adapt to influences in its industry to survive and prosper; its financial performance is primarily determined by the success of the industry in which it competes.

industrial policy – government policy aimed at influencing which industries in the economy are able (and encouraged) to expand and thrive. Tax breaks, subsidies, research support and other inducements are afforded the targeted industry with the intent of developing competitive advantage.

industrialized markets – industrialized countries are developed countries with a high GDP per capita.

informal communication – stress on dispensing with ceremony and rigid protocol.

institutional factors – laws, policies, and regulations that promote and support entrepreneurial development.

institutional overhead – to the burden inefficient, unaccountable, subpar regulatory frameworks of a country's political and economic policy institutions place on the private sector. In extreme cases, these institutions are corrupt, government actors are predatory, and civil society is oppressed.

intellectual capital – reflects an individuals' current knowledge of the global environment and their ability to adapt and navigate cultural complexities. The three elements of intellectual capital include global business savvy, a cosmopolitan outlook and the ability to work in an environment with more cognitive complexity.

intelligent career model – DeFillippi and Arthur's model of education which focuses on developing students' individual competencies so that they may identify and act upon entrepreneurial opportunities. In business they advocate a learning-centered approach that reflects the shifts from employees' assumed long term commitment to a firm, in which competencies were built according to organizational needs to a model of occupational excellence, wherein employees seek to continually upgrade skills valuable to the global marketplace.

internal factors – a firm's resources, overall strategy, management mindset, time commitment and, very importantly, types of products or services considered for international markets. Key issues include: Financial Resources, Human Resources and types of products/services.

international direct selling – It is direct selling on an international or worldwide basis or to a specific country (Welsh, 2014).

international entrepreneurship – the discovery and evaluation of opportunities and the organization of resources to exploit opportunities across national borders to create fundamentally new goods and services.

international franchising – franchising which allows firms to achieve the expanded reach and efficiencies associated with internationalization more rapidly and effectively than firms could have on their own. The system of franchising used around the world sells over one trillion dollars worth of goods and services.

international joint ventures – a method for entering international markets when two or more companies share ownership of a third commercial entity and collaborate in the production of its goods and services.

international licensing – the process of transferring the rights to a firm's products to an overseas company for the purpose of producing or selling it there.

international management – a system or process of management taking place in international environment that commonly involves cross-border transactions and operations or diverse cross-cultural environment in the organization. International management varies across general function of planning, organizing, influencing (organizational motivating, leading, communicating), and controlling.

international negotiations – business parties learn about the venture itself, the surrounding business environment, and of utmost importance, building trust while trying to strategically protect themselves.

internationalization – the transformation of a domestic entrepreneur into one who does business in more than one country. A business response to globalization that occurs when a domestic firm begins to sell or operate across national borders.

internationalized – when a firm moves from being a domestic firm to providing goods or services overseas.

intrapreneurial culture – formulated strategies with a positive outlook towards global expansion for many multinational corporations.

K

knowing competencies – reflects a person's values and motivation and relates to a person's identity and the fit between this identity and choices made relative to tasks, projects, organizations and countries, in addition it refers to the skills and knowledge needed for performance on the job, and the person's level of expertise.

L

law of one price – the principle that if two or more countries produce an identical good, the price of that good should be the same no matter which country produces it.

Leontief's paradox – the finding of Wassily Leontief (1954) that US imports embodied a higher ratio of capital to labor than us exports. This finding conflicted with what would have been predicted by the Heckscher-Ohlin theory.

level of economic development – measured in terms of GDP (Gross Domestic Product) per capita.

economic growth – usually measured in terms of the country's GDP growth rate.

market governance – the extent of free market government control of key resources, stability of the market system, and the regulatory environment.

liberalization – the decreased role of government in the economy, such as the privatization of government owned industries.

M

management contract – a company in one country can utilize the expertise, technology, or specialized services of a company from another country to run its business for a set time and fee or percentage of sales.

market sustainability – the optimal level of government policy that fosters long-term economic growth as illustrated by the Market Sustainability Curve.

marketing – the blueprint or description of products and services offered that keeps a company building upward toward customer satisfaction and business success. It involves tailoring product, price, packaging, position, and presentation based on industry analysis, competitive analysis, and customer analysis.

masculinity vs. femininity – the extent to which assertiveness and independence from others is valued. High masculinity leads to high sex-role differentiation, ambition, and material goods.

mercantilism – an economic philosophy of the sixteenth and seventeenth centuries that international trade should serve primarily to increase a country's financial wealth, especially of gold and foreign currency. Exports were viewed as desirable and something to be encouraged, and imports as generally undesirable.

N

NAFTA (North American Free Trade Agreement) – a trilateral trade block consisting of Canada, Mexico and the United States. NAFTA seeks to strengthen cooperation, expand trade, and promote development among the three nations.

national culture – comprised of different subcultures existing in a nation along the lines of its ethnic groups, regions, industries, firms, social/interest groups, business firms, and individuals.

necessity entrepreneurs – entrepreneurs who create ventures for self-employment to make up for the lack of other job opportunities in their environment.

negotiation – a discussion between two or more people or parties, intended to reach understanding, resolve differences, or gain advantage in outcome of discussion, to produce an agreement upon courses of action, to bargain for individual or collective advantage, to facilitate outcomes satisfactory to people/parties involved in a negotiation.

neoliberalism – an economic philosophy blending concerns for social justice with an emphasis on economic growth.

neutral vs. emotional – interactions are based on objectivity and neutrality, or they are based on emotional bonds.

nonverbal communication – involves sending and receiving wordless (mostly visual) cues in interaction between people. Nonverbal communications encompasses numerous nonverbal signals such as use of voice, touch, distance, physical appearance, body language (including body postures, gestures, facial expressions, and eye movements), the use of time, eye contact etc. It also includes intended and unintended voice-related signals and actions like voice tone, volume, speaking style, rhythm, intonation, stress, accent, and others.

O

OPIC (Overseas Private Investment Corporations) – a U.S. governmental development agency that works to encourage economic growth and development in emerging markets principally by issuing insurance programs designed to mitigate the risk a business may encounter in international trade especially as related to political instability and market reforms.

opportunity entrepreneurs – entrepreneurs who form new ventures because they see the opportunity for potential rewards.

opportunity environment – the in-country conditions that create opportunities for entrepreneurs.

organizational culture – external vs. internal, task vs. focus, conformity vs. individuality, safety vs. risk, ad-hoc vs. planned, industry-based specifics, company size, community impact and other.

outsourcing – contracting out a firm's non-core, non-revenue-producing activities to other organizations primarily (but not always) to reduce costs. When implemented properly, outsourcing can cut costs, improve performance, and refocus the core business.

P

planning – the act that makes all subsequent action go well.

political participation – civil society of a state enjoying the right to elect public officials (i.e., representative democracy) and their public opinion affecting governance.

political stability – the lack of external and internal conflicts in a country.

polycentric firm – firms that are host country oriented.

Porter's Diamond – the diagrammatic shape (and theory) that Michael E. Porter uses as the basis for a framework to illustrate the determinants of national competitive advantage.

power distance – the extent to which people accept unequal distribution of power. In higher power distance cultures, there is a wider gap between powerful and the powerless.

pragmatism – in societies with a pragmatic orientation, it is common for individuals to believe that it is impossible to understand fully the complexity of life and that that individuals should seek to lead a virtuous life. Thriftiness and perseverance in achieving results are highly valued.

privatization – the process of transferring a government function to private enterprise.

proactive efforts in exporting – a concerted effort to search, identify, and explore foreign market(s).

Project GLOBE – led by Robert House, this longitudinal study, involved over 150 researchers and drew on the input of 17,000 managers across 62 countries working in different industries. Project GLOBE identified a list of 22 leadership traits that are universally perceived as positive, a list of 8 leadership traits that are universally perceived as negative and a list of 34 leadership traits that are culturally contingent (meaning these traits work in some cultures, but not in others).

property rights – the exclusive and legal right to own, enjoy and dispose of real property and to keep income earned from that property.

protectionism – helps nations utilize legal barriers, exchange barriers, and psychological barriers to restrain entry of unwanted goods. It is established to make global markets conscious of their worldwide shortage on raw materials and natural resources.

psychological capital – enables an individual to have the enthusiasm, energy and self-confidence to work in a more complex global environment. The specific elements include a passion for diversity, a quest for adventure, and self-assurance.

R

reactive efforts in exporting – when a firm responds to product inquiries from foreign consumers and has not employed or actively searched for (new) foreign markets or demand for the entrepreneur's goods.

resource-based view – the perspective that an organization's resources are the primary drivers of firm performance. These resources include all of a firm's tangible and intangible assets, such as capital, equipment, employees, knowledge, and information.

risk – a complex and interactive phenomenon that involves both (bio) physical attributes and social dimensions. It is symptomatic of a lack of knowledge about the course of future events. Human beings have invented the concept of risk to help them to understand and cope with the dangers and uncertainties of life.

risk analysis – illuminates risk in its full complexity, and is sensitive to the social settings in which risk occurs, and also recognizes that social interactions may either amplify or attenuate the signals to society about the risk.

risk management – managing existing risk (i.e., risk that has already been undertaken) to yield a rate of return; usually a portfolio of financial assets.

risk taking – measures taken to reduce future uncertainty; the essence of entrepreneurial capitalism.

S

SBDC – (Small Business Development Centers), **SBI** (Small Business Institute), **SCORE** (Service Corps of Retired Executives).

self-reference criterion – when a company or manager believes that the leadership styles and organizational culture that work in their home country should work elsewhere, however, organizational values and norms must be tailored to fit the unique culture of each country in which the organization operates.

service learning projects – a form of experiential learning in which students, often working in teams, use their business skills to benefit the community.

social capital – refers to an individuals' ability to behave in a manner that will help build trusting relationships with people from diverse cultures. The specific elements include intercultural empathy, interpersonal impact, and diplomacy.

strategic control – consists of determining the extent to which the organization's strategies are successful in attaining its goals and objectives.

supply side perspective – the individual traits, attributes, and characteristics of entrepreneurs in relation to entrepreneurship.

T

technological effect – a key factor to help moving products from the manufacturer to the end-user, providing local inventory, technical product support, sales, and service. The global competition challenge for entrepreneurs requires them to adapt with broad skills and an incredible ability to learn at faster paces than in previous decades of the technology workforce.

trade intermediaries – a third party to conduct the distribution and sale of the entrepreneur's product/service in an international market.

trade liberalization – policies that reduce government interventions into trade, such as the removal of tariffs or other trade barriers.

turnkey operations – involves the design, construction, equipment, and, often the initial personnel training of a large facility by an overseas company which then turns the key to the ready-to-run facility over to the purchaser.

U

uncertainty avoidance – the extent to which the culture tolerates ambiguity and uncertainty. High uncertainty avoidance leads to low tolerance for uncertainty and to a search for absolute truth and predictability.

universal leadership attributes – a list of 22 leadership traits that are universally perceived as positive.

universalism vs. particularism – universalistic cultures develop rules that apply to all relationships and situations. Particularistic cultures focus on the uniqueness of each situation.

Uppsala Model – named after the Swedish University where researchers Johansen and Vahlne developed a process of theory internationalization. In their model, business progress through a series of discrete steps as a company evolves from a domestic to an international firm.

USAID (U.S. Agency for International Development) – the federal agency that focuses on the delivery of the U.S. Foreign Economic Assistance Program.

W

WTO (World Trade Organization) – an international body designed to supervise and liberalize global trade. Launched in 1995, it has over 150 nation members representing an estimated 95% of world trade. WTO agreements attempt to forge common ground in trading requirements across nations.

INDEX